Thomas A. Head

Campaigns and Battles of the Sixteenth Regiment, Tennessee Volunteers...

Thomas A. Head

Campaigns and Battles of the Sixteenth Regiment, Tennessee Volunteers...

ISBN/EAN: 9783744681001

Printed in Europe, USA, Canada, Australia, Japan

Cover: Foto ©ninafisch / pixelio.de

More available books at **www.hansebooks.com**

CAMPAIGNS AND BATTLES

OF THE

Sixteenth Regiment,

TENNESSEE VOLUNTEERS,

IN THE WAR BETWEEN THE STATES,

WITH INCIDENTAL SKETCHES OF

The Part Performed by other Tennessee Troops in the same War.

1861-1865.

By THOMAS A. HEAD.

NASHVILLE, TENN.:
CUMBERLAND PRESBYTERIAN PUBLISHING HOUSE.
1885.

Entered, according to act of Congress, in the year 1884, by

THOMAS A. HEAD,

in the office of the Librarian of Congress, at Washington, D. C.

DEDICATION.

To the Memory of our Fallen Comrades of the Lost Cause,

To their Families and Descendants,

To the Survivors of the unfortunate struggle from each Army,

And to all who may appreciate Fidelity to Principle and Devotion to Duty,

This Volume is Respectfully Inscribed by

The Author.

Contents.

CHAPTER I.

Organization of the Regiment and stay at Camp Trousdale—Transfer to Virginia—Huntersville—Cheat Mountain Campaign—Sewell Mountain—Winter in North-western Virginia.

CHAPTER II.

Transfer to South Carolina—Battle of Coosaw River—Soldier Life on the Coast of South Carolina—Campaigns in Mississippi—Siege of Corinth—Retreat to Tupelo—Reorganization at Corinth—Transfer of the Army to Chattanooga—Kentucky Campaign—Battle of Perryville—Return of the Army to Tennessee.

CHAPTER III.

Battle of Murfreesboro—Retreat of Confederates to Tullahoma and Shelbyville—Subsequent Retreat to Chattanooga.

CHAPTER IV.

Battle of Chickamauga—Investment of Chattanooga by the Confederates—Siege of Chattanooga—Battle of Missionary Ridge—Retreat of Confederates to Dalton.

CHAPTER V.

Georgia Campaign—Battles of Resaca, Adairsville, and Peach Tree Creek—Battles around Atlanta—Fall of Atlanta and Invasion of Tennessee by Confederates.

CHAPTER VI.

Battle of Franklin—Siege of Nashville—Confederate Repulse at Nashville and the Retreat into North Carolina—Surrender of Confederates under Johnston—Reunion of Sixteenth Tennessee Regiment at McMinnville, Tenn.

CHAPTER VII.

Muster Rolls of the Sixteenth Tennessee Regiment, giving names of every man in the Regiment, by Companies—List of Killed and Wounded, and Died of disease, by Companies.

CHAPTER VIII.

Sketches of other Tennessee Regiments—Eighth Tennessee, with Rolls—Fifth Tennessee—Carnes's Battery—Seventeenth Tennessee—Fiftieth Tennessee—Forty-ninth Tennessee—Seventh Tennessee—Eleventh Tennessee—Seventh Kentucky—Wright's Brigade—Thirty-third Tennessee.

CHAPTER IX.

Sketches of Officers: Captain D. C. Spurlock—Captain J. M. Parks—Colonel Joel A. Battle—Colonel John H. Savage—Captain L. N. Savage—General F. K. Zollicoffer—Major-general B. F. Cheatham—

General William A. Quarles—Colonel C. A. Sugg—Colonel W. F. Young—Brigadier-general William McComb—General Robert Hatton—Major-general W. B. Bate—General J. B. Hood—Major-general P. R. Cleburne—Bishop C. T. Quintard—Rev. Joseph Cross, D.D.

CHAPTER X.

Official Reports: Colonel D. M. Donnell—Colonel John H. Anderson—Colonel John G. Hall—Captain B. Randals—Brigadier-general Wright.

CHAPTER XI.

Forrest's Cavalry.

CHAPTER XII.

Miscellaneous Sketches—Prison Life, etc.

ILLUSTRATIONS.

FRONTISPIECE.

	PAGE.
Brigadier-general F. K. Zollicoffer,	21
General R. E. Lee,	35
Colonel John H. Savage,	49
Captain William G. Etter,	55
Wright S. Hackett,	141
Lieutenant-colonel Thomas B. Murray,	163
Captain D. C. Spurlock,	172
Major Jo. H. Goodbar,	177
Captain J. M. Parks,	184
Colonel William L. Moore,	204
Colonel Ben. J. Hill,	227
Captain W. W. Carnes,	237
Battle of Perryville,	240
Colonel Joel A. Battle,	272
Captain L. N. Savage,	289
Major-general B. F. Cheatham,	313
Major-general P. R. Cleburne,	367
N. B. Stubblefield,	371
Colonel D. M. Donnell,	389
Major H. H. Dillard,	393
General M. J. Wright,	417

PREFACE.

IN compliance with a promise made by the author to his comrades in arms, during the late war, this volume has been written, and is now offered to the public. Many of the events narrated are matters of personal knowledge and personal observation. Every available record has been brought to bear, by which to test the accuracy and authenticity of the narrative. It has been a work of great labor, and each line of its pages has been subjected to every test of authenticity, regardless of labor and cost. The work can be relied upon as correct in every sense. There is no romance upon any of its pages. It has no attempt at eulogy upon the one hand, or disparagement upon the other. It is merely a plain and simple narrative of facts as they occurred.

If an occasional error is found, the indulgence of the reader is invoked, from the mere fact that we are human, and by no means proof against mistakes. If such should be found it will be the result of oversight—by no means intentional—and will be promptly corrected in subsequent editions.

In preparing these pages, the author has been actuated by no selfish motives. It is but justice to the memory of our fallen comrades that a just and correct record be made of their heroic deeds—that their names be preserved in the record of their gallant works. They were brave men and true patriots. They were honest in their convictions of right, and true to their plighted faith. Upon their record is no stain of treason. Their names are to be defended and handed down unsullied to all future generations. The same is equally applicable to their surviving comrades, not only of Tennessee, but of the whole South. They never made the conflict. They were prompt at their country's call to come forward and offer their all in her defense. Descendants of Revolutionary sires who had been baptized at the fountain of liberty—in fire and in blood—their first lessons had been a true and faithful allegiance to their State; that valor was virtue, and a knowledge of war was wisdom. That they were brave men and true to their plighted faith has never been questioned, even by their enemies.

The author extends his grateful acknowledgments to the good people of McMinnville and Warren county, who, with scarcely an exception, have so kindly extended to him every assistance and every indulgence within their power, in the work of preparing these pages. To Lewis Peach, of Fayetteville, John D. Tolley, of Lynchburg, J. M. Morgan, of Gainesboro, and many others, the author is indebted for kind assistance so freely and cheerfully rendered.

This work has been completed and published under many trying difficulties. The people have been liberal in subscribing to the work, and this edition goes to the public with a subscription list of seven hundred copies. The price of this volume is reasonable, and it is hoped that no one will depend upon borrowing from his neighbor, but all may go at once and buy a copy.

The illustrations are from photographs taken

during the war, and engraved mostly by the Crosscup & West Engraving Company, of Philadelphia.

The muster rolls and casualty reports are principally from the memory of survivors, while some are from official records. The Confederate archives being meager, it was impossible to get a full record from that source. For favors in this line, the author is indebted to General Wright, of the War Records office at Washington.

It is hoped that the work may receive a careful perusal at the hands of the public.

T. A. H.

Nashville, 1885.

INTRODUCTION.

FEW indeed appreciate the difficulties that beset the pathway of him who attempts a record of human events, after an interval of a quarter of a century. Such a record necessarily falls under the observation of living witnesses, and is, therefore, the more assailed by critics. Few indeed there are who would write their own history with that impartiality that others might bestow upon it.

Writing extensively the history of the exploits of living parties who are living witnesses of the circumstances of which we write, great care has been taken to submit each item to the severest tests of accuracy and authenticity before giving it a permanent place upon the pages of this book. In some instances the account may not be as full as it might have been if such parties had been preparing the record themselves. In other instances the account may contain more than may be agreeable to others. Knowing these facts the writer has exercised the greatest care and caution, lest injustice might be done in some way. Actuated by this feeling, no account has been given of the misdeeds of any person. That some parties in each regiment acted in an unsoldierly manner cannot be denied. We will attempt no detailed account of the overenthusiasm of some men who insisted on a terrible persecution of their neighbors for opinion's sake merely. That many good citizens and neighbors suffered from this source in the days when excitement ran highest, and "men had lost their reason," cannot be denied. Time adjusted these things. Peace came at last, "with healing on her wings," and man became reconciled to his neighbor. Neither will any record be made of the same class who beset the poor man with promises to see that his family was cared for if he would go to the war. The poor man, in many instances, left his wife and little ones and joined the Southern army under these pledges. We will not record how faithfully these pledges were kept by the parties who made them. The soldier's family received assistance from these parties by paying the most extortionate prices. Neither will any record be made of that class of fireside patriots who insisted that one Southern man could whip ten Yankees, and insisted upon imprisonment or death to those who did not come out and avow their allegiance to the Confederacy. When the "Yankees" did come in these patriots, in many instances, went forth to meet them, and became at once as intensely loyal to the Yankees as they had previously been to the Rebels. Neither will any record be made of the Southern soldier who deserted his standard and resorted to the occupation of pillaging and murdering his neighbors. As these were few in number, and in many instances paid for their treachery with their lives, we pass over their record in silence.

That a prosperous people were estranged and divided into factions by conflicting interests was of itself a calamity. That these factions absorbed the Northern States on the one side and the Southern States on the other, each with a powerful army, was deplorable. These issues were purely sectional, and turned upon exigencies for which the Constitution had made no provision. The one side believed that the general government conferred rights upon a State. The other asserted that each State was independent, and had been so acknowledged by treaty with Great Britain at the close of the Revolution. This party embraced many of the original thirteen Colonies. They believed that the States went into the Union possessed of all the rights of independent States. They claimed that they entered the confederation for the sake of mutual protection—that it was not the province of the general government to *confer* rights upon a State, but to *protect* a State in its original rights. The Southern States claimed that the institution of slavery was a right of which they were possessed when they entered the original confederation, and the government was bound to protect them in this right. As the anti-slavery party began to strengthen in the North, the Southern States began to be fearful of their interests in this institution. They began to urge a system of legislation in the national Congress with the view of throwing additional protection around it. As these measures were opposed by Northern members, the subject of slavery began to be agitated. Upon the election of Mr. Lincoln to the presidency, the Southern States became dissatisfied, on the ground that he was pledged to a policy detrimental to their interests, and, claiming their rights to withdraw from the Union, passed ordinances of secession, and established a Southern Confederacy. The general government denied them their claimed rights. A four-years war was the result. Tennessee cast her destinies with the South. The best men of each section came forward and enlisted in the armies of their choice. In chronicling the deeds of the Confederate soldiers of Tennessee, we mean no invidious distinctions. Each Southern State marshaled an army of heroes, as did the States of the North, and while we honor the names of the Confederate survivors, and reverence the sacred memory of the dead, we accord due honor and praise to the gallantry and patriotism of the Northern soldiers. All were brothers, bound together by the strongest congenial ties. Conflicting interests had estranged them as time moved onward. Divided, as they finally were, on sectional issues for which the framers of the Constitution had failed to make provision, they each maintained their position with that steadiness and determination that has not a parallel in ancient or modern wars. They fought each other with a desperation, showing that they were each made of good material, and that,

> When Greek meets Greek
> Then comes the tug of war.

The war ceased; they were brothers again. Identical in interest the victor and vanquished ceased to be enemies. They beat their swords into plowshares, their spears into pruning hooks, and learned war no more. In friendship they conversed over their campaigns and battles, and instead of enemies they treated each other as brothers. Actuated by this impulse, a respect and honor for the Federal soldier, this work is written, in which the deeds of the Tennessee troops in the Confederate army are truly and faithfully portrayed. First among which we mention the history of the Sixteenth Regiment Tennessee Volunteers, to which the writer belonged.

THE SIXTEENTH REGIMENT

TENNESSEE VOLUNTEERS.

CHAPTER I.

THIS regiment was composed of volunteer companies from the counties of Warren, White, DeKalb, Coffee, Van Buren, Putnam, and Grundy. Warren county furnished four companies; White county, one company; White and DeKalb, one company; DeKalb, one company; Coffee and Grundy, one company; Van Buren, one company; Putnam, one company.

These companies were officered as follows:

1. CAPTAIN MURRAY'S COMPANY.
(Warren County.)

Thomas B. Murray..................................*Captain.*
A. P. Smartt......................................*First Lieutenant.*
James Hill.......................................*Second Lieutenant.*
Thomas York......................................*Third Lieutenant.*

2. CAPTAIN DONNELL'S COMPANY.
(Warren County.)

D. M. Donnell....................................*Captain.*
Wright S. Hackett................................*First Lieutenant.*
E. C. Read.......................................*Second Lieutenant.*
J. M. Castleman..................................*Third Lieutenant.*

3. CAPTAIN COFFEE'S COMPANY.
(Warren County.)

P. H. Coffee	Captain.
George Marchbanks	First Lieutenant.
W. W. Mooney	Second Lieutenant.
J. G. Rains	Third Lieutenant.

4. CAPTAIN MEADOWS' COMPANY.
(Warren County.)

L. H. Meadows	Captain.
H. L. Simms	First Lieutenant.
W. G. Etter	Second Lieutenant.
B. J. Solomon	Third Lieutenant.

5. CAPTAIN BROWN'S COMPANY.
(White County.)

D. T. Brown	Captain.
S. B. McMillan	First Lieutenant.
James Revis	Second Lieutenant.
W. D. Turlington	Third Lieutenant.

6. CAPTAIN SHIELDS' COMPANY.
(White and DeKalb Counties.)

P. C. Shields	Captain.
A. T. Fisher	First Lieutenant.
W. L. Woods	Second Lieutenant.
James R. Fisher	Third Lieutenant.

7. CAPTAIN BREWER'S COMPANY.
(Coffee and Grundy Counties.)

Calvin C. Brewer	Captain.
S. G. Crocker	First Lieutenant.
G. W. Turner	Second Lieutenant.
J. E. Bashaw	Third Lieutenant.

8. CAPTAIN YORK'S COMPANY.
(Van Buren County.)

Harmon York	Captain.
Green B. Johnson	First Lieutenant.

M. B. Wood...Second Lieutenant.
A. T. Seitz..Third Lieutenant.

9. CAPTAIN SAVAGE'S COMPANY.
(DeKalb County.)

L. N. Savage ....Captain.
Iraby C. Stone..First Lieutenant.
John K. Bain..Second Lieutenant.
R. B. Anderson ....Third Lieutenant.

10. CAPTAIN DILLARD'S COMPANY.
(Putnam County.)

H. H. Dillard...Captain.
W. K. Sadler...First Lieutenant.
Holland Denton ....Second Lieutenant.
R. A. Young..Third Lieutenant.

The Grundy county company was not complete in numbers, and the greater portion of its men attached themselves to Captain Brewer's company, while the principal portion of the others entered Captain Meadows' company, and a few joined the other companies of the regiment. The commander of the company, Captain Hannah, afterward entered Colonel Hill's regiment, at the head of a company, where he distinguished himself as a good soldier and a gentleman. Captain Hannah fell at the battle of Shiloh, in the thickest of the fight.

The companies were rendezvoused at Estill Springs, near Tullahoma, where most of the companies were mustered into the State service for twelve months. Captain Donnell's company was mustered into the service at the State Capital, and some of the other companies at the camp of organization near Nashville.

On the 24th of May, 1861, the companies left their camp of rendezvous at Estill Springs, and proceeded to Camp Trousdale, on the Louisville and Nashville Railroad, in Sumner county, near the Kentucky line.

At this place they were organized into a regiment about the first of June, 1861. John H. Savage was unanimously chosen colonel of the regiment, which was designated and known as the Sixteenth Regiment of Tennessee Volunteers. The officers received their commissions from the Governor of the State, and the field and staff-officers of the regiment at the time of its organization were as follows:

    JOHN H. SAVAGE, Colonel;
    THOMAS B. MURRAY, Lieutenant-colonel;
    JOSEPH H. GOODBAR, Major;
    GEORGE MARCHBANKS, Adjutant;
    JOHN T. READ, Surgeon;
    CHARLES K. MAUZY, Assistant Surgeon;
    GILBERT R. CAMPBELL, Quarter-master;
    JAMES GLASSCOCK, Commissary;
    J. W. POINDEXTER, Chaplain.

Shortly after organizing, Drs. James B. Ritchey and Thomas Black were assigned to duty in the Medical Department. A. J. Brown was assigned to duty in the Subsistence Department of the army, with the rank of major, and was afterward permanently assigned to duty in the Pay Department of the brigade.

The regiment went into camp of instruction at Camp Trousdale, where were encamped the Seventh Regiment Tennessee Volunteers, Colonel Robert Hatton; the Eighth Regiment Tennessee Volunteers, Colonel Alf. S. Fulton; the Sixteenth Regiment Tennessee Volunteers, Colonel John H. Savage; the Seventeenth Regiment Tennessee Volunteers, Colonel Taz. W. Newman; the Eighteenth Regiment Tennessee Volunteers, Colonel J. B. Palmer; and the Twentieth Regiment Tennessee Volunteers, Colonel Joel A. Battle.

The regiments above-named were commanded by F. K. Zollicoffer, who had been commissioned as brigadier-general in the State service, and placed in command of all the troops collected at Camp Trousdale.

The Sixteenth Regiment was composed principally of young and middle-aged men, of robust health and strong constitutions. The regiment remained at Camp

Trousdale near eight weeks, and performed the usual routine of drill and guard duty. So sudden a change in the manner and habits of life told on the health of the men to some extent, and quite a number were taken sick, but were soon convalescent. With the exception of the casualties resulting from measles, there were few deaths and very little fatal sickness in the regiment during its stay at Camp Trousdale.

The regiment was ordered to East Tennessee about the 21st of July, 1861. The men were jubilant at the prospect of entering into active service. The great battle of Manassas was fought about this time, and the enthusiasm of the boys was boundless. They all wanted to move to the front. Colonel Savage was warmly devoted to his regiment and proud of it. The feeling was reciprocated in full by his men. They all felt the most abiding confidence in his ability, his integrity, and his patriotism, and were ready and eager to follow him, where danger was thickest, to the performance of any duty that their country asked at their hands.

Colonel Savage, the commander of the Sixteenth Regiment Tennessee Volunteers, had seen much hard service, and had a large experience in the former wars, in which he figured prominently in the defense of his country. He had been commissioned three times, in as many different wars, in the service of the United States government. His first service was in General Gaines's call to maintain the neutrality of the Texas frontier when Santa Anna and Houston were engaged in war; his second service was in the Seminole war, and his third service was in the war between the United States and Mexico. In this war he was major of the Fourteenth Infantry, and rendered valuable service to his country in the memorable campaigns and battles in which the United States army was engaged. He was severely wounded while leading his column in an assault upon the Mexican position at Molino del Rey, after which he was promoted to the rank of lieutenant-colonel of the Eleventh Regular Infantry, composed of troops from Pennsylvania, New York, and Virginia. In this war he was in the same brigade and held equal rank with Joseph E. Johnston, who, at the time, was lieutenant-colonel of Voltigeurs.

At the close of the Mexican war Colonel Savage returned to his home and engaged in the practice of law. He was subsequently elected to Congress from the Fourth Congressional District, and represented his people in the Congress of the United States for a period of eight years. When the war broke out between the States he espoused the cause of the South. At the head of his regiment, made up from his congressional district, and of the families of his constituency, he led his men to deeds of noble daring and thrilling achievement.

On the morning of July 21st the tents were struck, and the baggage placed upon the train in the midst of a drenching rain. The men were cheerful and happy at the thought of going to Virginia. The news of the great battle of Manassas was received about this time, and the enthusiasm of the men was at its highest point. The regiment took the train about eight o'clock, and proceeded through Nashville to Chattanooga, and at the latter point remained a few hours awaiting transportation. From Chattanooga they proceeded to Haynesville, East Tennessee, where they went into camp to await further orders.

Brigadier-general S. R. Anderson had been placed in command of all the troops forwarded to East Tennessee. Brigadier-general D. S. Donelson had been assigned to duty in this department, and placed in command of three Tennessee regiments. These regiments were the first forwarded to Virginia, and were commanded by Colonels Hatton, Maney, and Forbes. Savage's and Fulton's regiments were at first placed in

Anderson's brigade and ordered to Western Virginia. These orders were subsequently changed, as will be afterward shown.

Receiving orders at Haynesville from the War Department to proceed immediately to the scene of action, on the 27th of July the regiment took the train and proceeded to Bristol, where it arrived on the 28th, and departed on the following night for Lynchburg. Arriving at Lynchburg on the 29th, the regiment was encamped near the city, and remained in its encampment till August 1st, when it was ordered to Staunton, by the way of Charlottesville, where they arrived about ten o'clock on the morning of August 3d.

The following correspondence shows the disposal that was made of the Tennessee troops at this time:

RICHMOND, July 27, 1861.

General S. R. Anderson, Lynchburg, Va.:—The three Tennessee regiments first advanced will be under the command of General Donelson. The other two regiments under your command you will order to Bristol, where fuller orders will reach you. L. P. WALKER, *Secretary of War.*

LYNCHBURG, July 28, 1861.

Hon. L. P. Walker:—There have been ordered to Lynchburg five regiments, three of whom have been forwarded to, and are now at, Staunton, commanded by Colonel Hatton, Colonel Maney, and Colonel Forbes. These are the three first advanced. The other two are commanded by Colonel Fulton and Colonel Savage. Part of Fulton's command has already reached Lynchburg, and the remainder, with Savage's regiment, will probably reach here to-day or to-night. At Haynesville and Bristol, East Tennessee, there are three regiments, commanded by Colonel Battle, Colonel Newman, and Colonel Rains. Ordered there from Middle Tennessee. Your order yesterday evening was to forward the two additional regiments expected here to Staunton. Under your telegram to-day I have to ask whether I shall order these regiments (Fulton's and Savage's) to remain here, go to

Staunton, or to return to Bristol? I proceed to Bristol this evening. Answer to my acting aid, Colonel Smith, at this point.

S. R. ANDERSON, *Brigadier-general.*

RICHMOND, July 25, 1861, 5:30 P.M.

General S. R. Anderson, Lynchburg, Va.:—The President directs that you proceed immediately to Scott and Lee counties, Va., and seize and punish a party of invaders said to be committing depradations at Estillville and in that region. Make use for this purpose of the two Tennessee regiments at Bristol, and any other troops, volunteer or militia, whose services you may find available. Supply yourself with ammunition, powder, and lead. Celerity and caution are necessary.

S. COOPER, *Adjutant and Inspector-general.*

LYNCHBURG, July 26, 1861.

Hon. L. P. Walker:—Your dispatch received. I have ordered two regiments from Bristol. There is still one more at Bristol. Shall I order that? Shall I remain here? Give me instructions as to my course.

S. R. ANDERSON, *Brigadier-general.*

RICHMOND, July 27, 1861.

General S. R. Anderson, Lynchburg, Va.:—Order the regiment to Lynchburg, and thence to Staunton. You will receive orders controlling your personal movements.

L. P. WALKER.

The people of Charlottesville extended every courtesy and hospitality to the soldiers, and the boys enjoyed their stay of a few hours in the city by visiting the University of Virginia, and seeing the sights of the place in general, till the evening of the 3d, when they took the cars for Staunton, then to Millboro, and arrived at that place about three o'clock on the morning of the 4th. The regiment remained at Millboro till the evening of the next day, arranging baggage and other equipments preparatory to an overland march to Huntersville, about thirty-five miles distant. On the evening of August 5th they took up the line of march, and encamped at a pleasant place a few miles from Millboro the first night. On the following day the march was resumed, and at night the regiment encamped at the celebrated Warm Springs of Virginia. The men partook bountifully of the comforts of the Bath House, and, after a good night's rest, took up their line of march on the morning of the 7th, passed Bath Alum Springs, arrived at Gatewood in the evening, and encamped for the night; proceeding onward at six o'clock on the morning of the 8th, and arriving at Huntersville in the evening.

. The weather was exceedingly warm, and this had been the regiment's first experience in marching. The men were possessed of a large amount of individual baggage, which they wished to carry, as the means of transportation were limited. In addition to their arms and accouterments, many were loaded down with a large quantity of other baggage which they did not wish to lose, and in carrying so great burdens the men were greatly fatigued by this their first marching, and many fell behind before reaching Huntersville; coming on as fast as they could conveniently do so, after resting and recuperating a little on the way.

Some of our men fell sick on the way from Camp Trousdale to Huntersville, but the greater portion of them speedily recovered and rejoined the regiment at Huntersville. On this trip our highly esteemed major, Jo. H. Goodbar, was taken sick at Morristown, and died on the 10th of December, 1861. Major Goodbar was an excellent officer and a most estimable gentleman. His stay with the regiment had been a brief one, yet the officers and men under his command had learned to love him, and they deplored his loss as that of a brother.

The sick of the regiment were left at Millboro under the care of Dr. Thomas Black, then a young physician. As the number of sick increased on the march to Huntersville they were all collected at Bath Alum Springs, where a regular hospital was established under Dr. Black's charge. His labors were incessant until he received assistance from the Medical Department. The sick of the brigade were being collected here, and the hospital had over a hundred patients.*

The regiment arriving at Huntersville on the evening of August 8th was encamped in a field in a narrow valley on the bank of a little stream. The rains had set in and seemed to be almost incessant. The ground on which the regiment encamped was marshy and damp, and the men, weary of the long and arduous march just completed, began to fall sick, and many of them died. The weather became damp and cold, and it rained continually.

The three Tennessee regiments at first assigned to

---

* Dr. Black's labors here at first were so constant that he scarcely had time to sleep. One night he lay down, and by the time he was fully asleep he was called upon to go to a man who had eaten too many huckleberries and was about to die of colic. The man was a detail, and had been on a ramble through the day. The doctor gave his directions before he was awake, and ordered the man to have a dose of *tobacco and sugar*. The order was obeyed promptly and without question. The tobacco was cut fine from a navy plug to the amount of a table-spoonful, and mixed with a similar amount of sugar. This was dissolved in about a gill of water and taken to the man, who said it was a hard dose, but he would take it if the doctor said so, and drank it down. For the next fifteen minutes the heaving and vomiting of that man was a fixed fact. He was then easy. In the morning he was well, and congratulated the doctor on his peculiar remedy. The doctor, till then, knew nothing of the matter.

General Donelson's brigade were now placed under General Anderson. The two regiments at first assigned to Anderson were now placed under Donelson, and constituted his brigade.

The Sixteenth Tennessee Regiment, together with the Eighth Tennessee, was organized into a brigade, and placed under the command of Brigadier-general D. S. Donelson. The troops at Huntersville at this time were the Eighth and Sixteenth Tennessee Regiments; a Georgia regiment, under Colonel Bromly; the Forty-eighth Virginia Regiment; a cavalry battalion, and a battery of artillery. The brigade was placed in Loring's division; which at this time was encamped at Valley Mountain, organizing an expedition against the Federal stronghold at Cheat Mountain. Generals Floyd and Wise were in front of Rosecrans, on the Charleston road, near the Gauley river, in the Kanawha valley. The troops at Huntersville were held in readiness, not to repel any contemplated attack on that post, which was at least fifty miles inside of General Lee's lines, but to be as a kind of reserve force to be sent out to the assistance of General Lee, at Cheat Mountain, or to Generals Wise and Floyd, on the Gauley river, as the occasion might require. Meanwhile, the Sixteenth Tennessee Regiment, with its brigade, remained at Huntersville till early in September. The weather being very damp and cold, and the location of the encampment being exceedingly unfavorable to good health, many of the men died of malarial and typhoid fevers. The large and fearful daily increase of the sick-list in the regiment caused the commander to seek some method of ameliorating the condition of his men. Accordingly, Colonel Savage applied to General Donelson for authority to remove his encampment to a better position, on high and dry ground, and, as an inducement, presented the report of the surgeon of the regiment showing the rapid increase of sickness in his regiment in its present encampment.

On the 23d day of August the tents were struck and, the regiment was removed to a hill-side about three-quarters of a mile distant, where the men were more comfortable. The Eighth Tennessee Regiment, seeing the wisdom of Colonel Savage's course, changed its encampment also; and in a few days General Donelson moved his head-quarters to the hill-side, near the head-quarters of the Sixteenth Regiment. The wisdom of the move thus inaugurated was self-evident. The sickness of the regiment rapidly abated, and the men remained at their hill-side encampment until the 6th day of September, when they were ordered to Valley Mountain, together with all the troops of General Donelson's brigade.

The sick and convalescent of the regiment were left at Huntersville with Dr. C. K. Mauzy, and on the morning of September 6th, the regiment was in line and on the march to report to General Loring, at Valley Mountain. The march on the 6th was pleasant, though it lay along a narrow and fertile valley, bounded on the right and left by lofty and almost perpendicular mountains, the valley merely in the shape of a trough, and the mud was deep and disagreeable. On the evening of the 6th the regiment encamped in a tributary valley, at a place known as Camp Edra. Here the men received fresh beef of the very best quality, but had no salt. Rich, fat, and juicy, the men ate it with their bread, and on the morning of the 7th the column moved onward and arrived in the evening at Big Spring. At eight o'clock on the morning of September 8th, the regiment took up its line of march through a fertile region of country. Having left the tents and heavy baggage at this place, the men proceeded over very muddy roads through the day and arrived at Valley Mountain in the evening, at the head-quarters of General Loring.

The commissary wagons arrived at a late hour of the night, and the men were ordered to prepare five days' rations and be ready to march at daylight of the following morning. On account of the scarcity of commissary stores in that quarter, resulting from limited transportation and bad roads, the men were not encumbered with heavy rations, their five days' supply being scarcely sufficient to do them two full days, yet it was the best that could be done under the circumstances; and the soldiers, with their rations in their haversacks, with forty rounds of ammunition in their cartridge-boxes, and their surplus baggage left with the trains, appeared in line on the morning of the 10th on the summit of Valley Mountain.

At this place Donelson's brigade was joined by the Second Tennessee Brigade, under Brigadier-general S. R. Anderson. This brigade was composed of the First Tennessee Regiment, under Colonel George Maney; the Fourth Tennesseee Regiment, Colonel Forbes; and the Seventh Tennessee Regiment, Colonel Robert Hatton. The five Tennessee regiments were thus brought together on the morning of the 10th, in the face of a defiant and exultant foe. The men were cheerful and buoyant, and were eager for the conflict, when they could test their prowess on the enemy's stronghold at Cheat Mountain.

The morning was bright and beautiful, and the view from the summit of the mountain presented the grandest scenery that the eye could possibly behold. The peaks of the neighboring mountains were radiant with the golden sunshine of the morning, and the huge, craggy rocks of their brows shone forth and sparkled in the distance as magnificent temples on the borders of a populous city. The valley was wrapped in a dense fog, which extended to a certain uniform height, presenting to the view of the beholder the appearance of a vast lake or sea, out of which the different hill-tops emerged at ir-regular intervals as islands. The scenery was delightful to behold, and across this apparent sea of hills and valleys was posted the enemy whom it was our business to dislodge; and the preliminaries to the work, inaugurated on this delightful and memorable morning, involved difficulties and dangers almost without a parallel in history.

General Loring rode along the lines upon a fine white horse, and, instead of his uniform, he was clothed in citizen's garb. He wore a heavy velvet frock coat, and as the men beheld an empty sleeve they learned that he had lost an arm in one of the battles of the Mexican war. With great modesty and little display he rode along the lines and made the necessary disposal of his troops.

This was the first time the commander had been seen by many of his men, and his appearance inspired the fullest confidence in his ability. The men stood in readiness to perform the work before them, and were awaiting the orders of their commander. The work in hand was an arduous one, and required men of the greatest amount of endurance, daring, and nerve to execute it.

The Federals were posted several thousand strong, and strongly fortified, at a position on the Huttonville pike, near the terminus of a mountain ridge that separates Tygert's Valley from a small cove, down which flows a small creek, known as Beckey's Run. A small stream comes down Tygert's Valley, known as Conley's Run, the word "run" being the Virginia term for "creek."

It was the object of General Lee to place a part of Loring's division, with such other troops at his command as were available, in front of the Federal position on the Huttonville pike, and to gain the rear of the position with Donelson's brigade, by way of Tygert's Valley, along Conley's Run to a certain point a few miles from the Federal stronghold, thence across the ridge into the cove, and thence down the cove, along Beckey's Run, to a point opposite the Federals across the ridge; then to ascend the ridge and come down upon the Federal position from the rear. General Jackson was to take position in front of the Federal position on Cheat Mountain, with Anderson's brigade to co-operate with him on the flank and rear. The plan of the campaign thus marked out, each commanding officer proceeded to its execution.

Before leaving Valley Mountain the following orders from the commander-in-chief were read to the troops in line:

General Order No. —.

Head-quarters of the Forces,
Valley Mountain, W. Va.,
September 9, 1861.

The forward movement, announced to the Army of the Northwest in Special Order No. 28, from its head-quarters of this date, gives the general commanding the opportunity of exhorting the troops to keep steadily in view the great principles for which they contend, and to manifest to the world their determination to maintain them. The eyes of the country are upon you. The safety of your homes and the lives of all you hold dear depend upon your exertions. Let each man resolve to be victorious, and that the right of self-government, liberty, and peace shall in him find a defender. The progress of this army must be forward.

R. E. LEE, *General Commanding*.

Donelson's brigade was now separated from Anderson's, and proceeded to penetrate the Federal rear, which involved a winding march of about thirty miles across a series of mountain gulfs, apparently untraversable. The mountains were steep, the valleys narrow, and there was no road—not even a path.

General Donelson was ordered to keep within supporting distance of Loring's column, and had found a guide to the expedition who was thoroughly acquainted with the country. The name of the guide was Butcher, and as he wore the title of "Doctor," it is presumed that he was a physician. He appeared to be a clever gentleman, about forty-five years of age, full of nerve and energy, and with a vast amount of solid and reliable pluck. He was warmly devoted to the cause, and rendered valuable services to the expedition.

Proceeding a few miles from Valley Mountain, the brigade came to the top of a deep mountain gorge at the edge of an old field. Just beyond the field the brink was approached, and looking beyond, lofty heights could be seen across the gorge, with here and there a field and a mountain cottage. A few tents could be seen far off in the distance, but we knew not whether they were the encampments of friend or foe. Beyond and below us was the apparently impassable abyss, the descent of which must be accomplished, and followed by the ascent of the heights immediately following. The field-officers led their horses diagonally with the mountain side to a certain distance, and, turning to the right or left, proceeded at right angles to that direction, thus alternating along a route in a general direction of a straight line, but having the variations and meanderings of a worm-fence. Thus the horses were passed across two deep gulfs. The artillery could not be used, as the route was absolutely impracticable to its transportation. The men passed over the route letting themselves down by the branches of trees and pulling themselves up as occasion might require. In this manner the march proceeded through the day, and having crossed two gulfs, entered a dim road at an old field at the top of the mountain, and camped in line of battle by the roadside in the edge of a skirt of woods.

At daylight on the morning of the 11th the column moved cautiously along till about nine o'clock, when it came to a branch at the head of the cove, and proceeded down the branch until about ten o'clock, when, from the fresh tracks in the road, it was indicated that a column of troops had just preceded us, and it was ascertained further that a Federal column had marched down just ahead of ours, and another was expected along in the afternoon to re-enforce the Federal position down the valley. Our brigade had advanced faster than was intended, and was near six miles farther down the valley than was expected. We were out of supporting distance of General Loring's column, and were in a critical position, the enemy in front and rear, and the mountains on either side.

General Lee had ordered the different commanders to see that each man in their respective commands tack a piece of white cloth or paper on the front of his hat and keep it on during the whole expedition. This order was given on the morning of our departure from Valley Mountain, and its object was to distinguish his men from the enemy, as the war had not been going on a great while, and neither government had yet adopted a regular uniform for its troops. The clothing of the men and the regimentals of the officers of the opposing armies were so near alike that it was difficult to distinguish the one from the other,

GENERAL ROBERT E. LEE.

except by their location. At this particular juncture it was very important that some badge of distinction be adopted, especially by that portion of the army that was to operate in the enemy's rear. This badge of white cloth prevented Anderson's brigade from attacking Donelson's at one time on the march, and also had the effect to puzzle the Yankees. When a prisoner was captured his first question was, "What is that white cloth for?"

Having traveled more rapidly than the other part of the army, on the morning of September 11 General Donelson found himself at the outposts of the enemy, at the head of Tygert's Valley. Learning the position of the pickets, he had a consultation with Colonel Savage, whom he always consulted promptly on critical occasions, and the pickets having been surprised and captured without alarming their confederates, Colonel Savage, with Captain Bryant's company of the Eighth Tennessee, and Captain L. N. Savage's company of the Sixteenth Tennessee, accompanied by the guide, proceeded as an advance-guard down the valley, and soon came upon the second stand of pickets, who attempted to escape, when they were fired upon, and two of their number fell. The others, three in number, were made prisoners, and from them the position of the main picket force was ascertained, which consisted of a full company of infantry, posted a short distance down the valley, at an old house where a road came into the valley across the ridge from Becky's Run. The house was by the side of this road at the foot of the ridge, behind an angle of woods that projected into the valley, and completely concealed them from our view, and as completely concealed our approach.

The advanced pickets and a few stragglers about the main stand having been successfully captured without giving any alarm to the main picket force, Colonel Savage, with his two companies, dashed upon the position furiously, and charging ahead of his force, he rushed into their very midst, and before they were scarcely aware of his presence, he had placed himself between them and their command and cut off their retreat. Having gained this point so suddenly, he demanded the surrender of the whole force. This took the Yankees by surprise, and a few attempted to make their escape, while a few attempted to fire on him from the window of the house. Colonel Savage halted those attempting to escape, and, driving them back into the yard, flourished his pistol in their faces and told them that if they did not surrender instantly, he "would have the last d——d one of them shot in less than five minutes!" At this instant the advance-guard appeared, and, filing on each side of the house, assumed a position confirming the threat, and the whole company surrendered to Colonel Savage on the spot, without the escape of a single man to give the alarm to the encampment below.

This was a daring deed on the part of Colonel Savage, and might be considered by some as reckless, but it was an achievement of much importance to the success of the expedition. Its feasibility and importance were quickly comprehended by Colonel Savage on the very eve of its consummation. This point was an important one, for it guarded the main approach to the Federal position on their left flank, and also the only available approach to Becky's Run in their rear, by way of the road that came down Tygert's Valley at the old house. The importance of this point being understood by the Federal commander, he had placed a heavy picket force here to protect his flank and rear. Colonel Savage, taking in the situation at a glance, saw the importance of making a prompt and speedy capture of this point, without allowing any one to escape to give the alarm, as the Federals could have brought out a heavy force in a few minutes. By thus capturing the position, the column could gain its position on Becky's Run before the Federals could realize the situation. The resolve was quickly made and as quickly pushed to a successful consummation. The prisoners, fifty-six in number, having yielded to the daring and prowess of one gallant officer,* were promptly

---

*The Nashville *Union and American*, under date of December 5, 1861, printed the following account of this transaction, as given by its correspondent from the Army of North-western Virginia, Dr. J. W. Gray:

General Donelson took up his line of march down Conley's Run, and over the mountain to Stewart's Run; took down its waters, and, before proceeding far, one of the guides gave intelligence that the enemy's pickets were stationed at the Matthew's House, a little distance below. This seemed to call back many years of our brave old general's life. He at once had his advance-guard thrown into position, and directed Colonel Fulton, with the guide "Butcher," to proceed on the slope of the hill to the left of the house, with a view to preclude escape; and, as this party proceeded, placed himself at a point from which he had a full view of the house, and then as they came down the hill, and, seeing that they were coming down right, gave the command, "Charge!" He advanced upon the house and witnessed the capture of four pickets by Colonel Fulton and the guide, Dr. Butcher. Here the General placed Colonel Savage, with Captain Savage's company of the Sixteenth and Captain Bryant's company of the Eighth Regiment, as an advance guard. Captain Bryant was in command, being the oldest captain.

Advancing about half a mile they suddenly came upon six other pickets, four of whom surrendered. The other two, endeavoring to escape down the creek (as Tennesseans call a Virginia "run"), were shot mortally. Thirteen were captured without one being left to alarm their comrades in advance of the "rebel's" approach. The two companies, led by the faithful guide, "Butcher," and Colonel Savage, saw another Yankee in the road, gun in hand, looking steadily upon them, and, by the time he discovered for certain that they were not his friends who

secured, and, after allowing each one to retain his baggage and personal outfit, their arms and munitions were duly appropriated. A detail was made to guard the prisoners, and their arms were distributed among the troops for transportation.

were approaching, they had him in pistol range commanding him to surrender. He was much confused, but durst not run. Just at this moment two others were seen to rush into a little brush guard-house below and seize their guns, and, upon reappearing, fled in the direction of a woody hill-side, but before reaching it were overtaken and soon "quicking it" back to the advance-guard, which was hard by, rather than be dispatched in a more summary manner.

About two hundred and fifty yards above a place known as the Simmon's House three others—the captain of a company, a lieutenant, and a private—were seen angling. Colonel Savage and Dr. Butcher rode suddenly up, and, by the flourish of a pistol, caused them to wade the run and surrender. The roar and ripple of the stream prevented them from hearing any thing that had transpired above them. One of these, a fussy Dutchman, was frightened so near out of his wits that in answer to an imperative demand, told them that the whole company was at the house just below, the view to which was fortunately obstructed by a cluster of trees. Colonel Savage ordered the men to "double-quick," and upon turning the grove he, still accompanied by Dr. Butcher, both mounted, posted off at full speed to charge the house in front. The Yankees discovering them began to bustle and stir in all manner of confusion, but the undaunted Savage, with his navy repeater drawn and presented, dashed fearlessly upon them, and, in tones and looks of terror, exclaimed: "Down with your arms, or you die!" "I'll blow out the first man's brains that attempts to fire!" When he had fully gained the opposite side of the house he discovered several running, but with a command that made the cowardly blood shiver about their arteries he halted them and marched them back to the house. Some of the Yankees ran into the house, and, presenting their guns through the window, were in the act of shooting, when Colonel Savage,

The brigade came up at a double-quick, and the alarm having been exaggerated, the men had been hurried up more rapidly than the occasion demanded. Accordingly, to facilitate their advance, many of the troops threw down their knapsacks and blankets, and

---

knowing that his life depended upon some devilish act of daring, fearlessly rode up to the window and rising in his stirrups said, "Fire if you dare, and every man of you dies!"

Captain Bryant's and Captain Savage's men were rapidly approaching. Not a gun was fired. All laid down their arms and were prisoners of war. Two others were now discovered on the hill-side at a long distance attempting to make their escape, but the invincible "Butcher" leveled his Sharpe's rifle upon them and one fell. The guide (Wood), it is supposed, mortally wounded the other, though there were several shots made at him. The Yankee officers delivered up their swords and small arms. The swords were very handsome, and are now worn, one by Colonel Savage, one by Dr. Butcher, and the other by General Donelson's aid, Major James G. Martin. Among their guns were found several Enfield rifles. Of these trophies General Donelson possesses one, Colonel A. S. Fulton one, and Colonel Savage the other.

The bold deed above alluded to was all accomplished in a few minutes, giving the Yankees no time to determine upon any common action. They doubtless could have shot Colonel Savage and Dr. Butcher, and many, if not all of them, could have made their escape, for the woods were near by, and most of our men, Captain Bryant and Captain Savage excepted, some distance off, though coming up with all their speed. But the Yankees were surprised, and seemed to be utterly confounded. Thus it will be seen that we had killed, wounded, and taken prisoners sixty-two inclusive, and this expedition has scarcely a parallel in history, for, while but little blood was spilt and not a large number captured, there is yet something remarkable in the circumstance of having fired guns and taken in succession each set of pickets, all posted so near each other, without the first alarming the second, and the second the third, and so on, until our enterprise had been thwarted.

the brigade was hurried forward into line of battle across the valley. By the time this was accomplished it was ascertained that the trouble was over and the Yankees captured. The prisoners were placed in line at the rear, and the column proceeded up the ridge from the scene of action by way of the road formerly mentioned. At the top of the hill a large bundle of Yankee dispatches were discovered in a pile of leaves in the path. These dispatches were to the commander of the picket force, complaining of the carelessness of a lieutenant, and cautioning him of the danger of surprise. With this information, and some other confidential matter in which some patriotic jealousy and official spleen were manifest, some valuable information was gained in reference to the position and strength of the enemy. The Yankee courier was unable to deliver the package to the commander of the pickets, and see-

---

The *Savannah Republican* contained the following account of this daring adventure shortly after its occurrence, as given by a correspondent from the Army of North-western Virginia, under date of September 21, 1861:

A BOLD CAPTURE.—After marching about three miles from Tygart's river Colonel Savage, of the Sixteenth Tennessee Regiment, desiring to make a reconnoissance, sallied off from his regiment at least a quarter of a mile, and while alone he suddenly and unexpectedly came up to where a company of Yankees were stationed. Both he and they were considerably surprised, but the gallant Colonel, changing not a color in his countenance, in a bold and defiant manner, standing erect in his stirrups, looking in his rear, and then quickly facing the pickets, exclaimed in a stentorian voice, "You damned rascals, if you don't ground arms and surrender immediately, my men shall surround you and shoot you to pieces in a minute!" They did surrender, and he made them prisoners without the firing of a gun. The company consisted of three commissioned, four non-commissioned officers, and sixty privates.

ing his own escape cut off, he dropped the bundle and covered it hastily with leaves. Becoming uncovered as the men passed over it, it was discovered by the writer and handed to Captain Dillard, who made such disposal of it as he thought proper.

It was now raining, and in the afternoon. The column moved cautiously along the ridge, and came to a valley on the upper waters of Becky's Run. Proceeding down the run we arrived about sundown at an old house where a log heap was burning. This was evidently a picket stand, but the pickets, aware of our approach, had withdrawn, and the Federal commander found himself approached by an enemy from every direction.

We were now in the rear of the Federal position. We were occupying the west base of the ridge, they were fortified at the east base, and the ridge terminated on our immediate right. General Donelson ascended the ridge about dark, and moved up carefully to the top, then over the ridge under cover of the night, till Fulton's regiment was within a few hundred yards of the enemy's camp-fires. Savage's regiment stopped at the top of the hill. The path was narrow over which the troops moved, and the undergrowth so thick that the men could scarcely pass through it. The night was very dark, and the rain incessant. About nine o'clock in the night Colonel Savage suggested to General Donelson the propriety of bringing Fulton's regiment to the top of the ridge and encamping. It was accomplished with great difficulty, and the men slept all night on their arms. Every commander had now gained the position assigned him, and the attack was to open on the morning of the 12th. The plan had worked admirably thus far. General Loring was in front of the Federal position on the Huttonville pike, and was to attack in front. General Jackson was in position in front of Cheat Mountain. General Donelson had gained the rear of the position confronted by Loring, and General Anderson had gained a corresponding position to support and co-operate with General Jackson.

The troops lay upon their arms during the night, and the rain was continual. Morning dawned, and the men were put in shape for battle. It had rained continually throughout the night, and, having flint-lock muskets, which had been loaded the evening before, the loads had become wet, and the first thing the men did in the morning was to extract the charges from their guns and put them in good order. They had all kept their powder dry, and having rubbed up their guns and examined their flints they awaited the signal for attack. Hours passed and no signal was given. It was eight o'clock before the cause of delay was made known. General H. R. Jackson was to open the attack on Cheat Mountain pass with Colonel Rust's brigade, and the other commanders were to follow in the atttack upon the positions in their respective fronts. The men were becoming anxious, and were realizing that if any thing had happened to frustrate the plan of operations our situation was critical indeed.

General Loring had gained his position in front of the Federals on the Huttonville pike as before mentioned. The pike ran along the base of the ridge in front of the Federal works, and the Valley River ran parallel with the pike near by. General Loring had to cross the river before he could attack this position. The rains the previous night had swollen the river, and he was unable to cross.

General Jackson occupied the first summit of Cheat Mountain, while the Federals were fortified between the first and second summits at a point known as Cheat Mountain pass. Colonel Albert Rust, of the Third Arkansas, was ordered by Jackson to attack the pass on the morning of September 12, but finding by reconnoissance on the evening of the 11th that he was unable to carry the position, General Jackson ordered him back to camp, and the attempt was abandoned. Colonel Rust was a gallant commander, of sterling qualities, and stood high in the estimation of his superior officers. As his assault was to be the signal for a general assault on all the positions, and the failure of the expedition turned upon his movements (though through no fault of his), the following report of his movements, and the cause of the failure of the expedition, are given in the correspondence between him and General Loring.

ORDERS FROM GENERAL JACKSON TO COLONEL RUST.

Dear Colonel:—Return with your command into camp. So soon as you arrive address a letter to General Loring, explaining the failure and the reasons for it. Show this to Captain Neal, quarter-master, and let him at once furnish an express ready to take your letter by the near route. If possible, get the postmaster, Mr. Abagast, to go, and go rapidly and at once. Say in your letter that I am in possession of the first summit of Cheat Mountain, and am in hopes of something going on in Tygart's Valley, and shall retain command of it until I receive orders from headquarters. It may bring on an engagement, but I am prepared, and shall whip them if they come.

Very truly, · H. R. JACKSON.

P. S.—I cannot write here. Inclose this scrawl in your letter. You had better return yourself at once to camp, leaving your command to follow. We had several skirmishes yesterday, and killed several of the enemy.

COLONEL RUST'S REPORT TO GENERAL LORING.

CAMP BARTOW, September 13, 1861.

General:—The expedition against Cheat Mountain failed. My command consisted of between fifteen hundred and sixteen hundred men. Got there at the appointed time, notwithstanding the rain. I seized a number of their pickets and scouts. Learned from them that the enemy was between four thousand and five thousand strong, and they reported them to be strongly fortified. Upon reconnoissance their representations were fully corroborated. A fort or block-house on the point or elbow of the road, intrenchments on the south, and outside of the intrenchments, and all around up to the road, heavy and impassable abatis, if the enemy were not behind them. Colonel Barton, my lieutenant-colonel, and all the field officers, declared it would be madness to make an attack. We learned from the prisoners that they were aware of your movements, and had telegraphed for reinforcements, and I heard three pieces of artillery pass down the road toward your encampment while we were seeking to make an assault upon them. I took the assistant commissary, and for one regiment I found upon his person a requisition for nine hundred and thirty rations, also a letter indicating that they had very little subsistence.

I brought only one prisoner back with me. The cowardice of the guard (not Arkansans) permitted the others to escape. Spies had evidently communicated our movements to the enemy. The fort was completed, as reported by the prisoners (examined separately), and another in process of construction. We got near enough to see the enemy in the trenches beyond the abatis. The most of my command behaved admirably; some I would prefer to be without upon any expedition.

General Jackson requests me to say that he is in possession of the first summit of Cheat Mountain, and hopes you are doing something in Tygart's Valley, and will retain command of it until he receives orders from your quarters. My own opinion is that there is nothing to be gained by occupying the mountain. It will take a heavy force to take the pass, and at a heavy loss. I knew the enemy had four times my force, but for the abatis we would have made the assault. We could not get to them to make it. The General says in his note to me that his occupying Cheat

Mountain may bring on an engagement, but he is prepared and will whip them if they come. I see from his postscript that he requests his note to me to be inclosed to you.

I can only say that all human power could do toward success in my expedition failed of success. The taking of the pickets seemed like a providential interposition. I took the first one myself, being at the head of the column when I got to the road.

In great haste, very respectfully your obedient servant,

A. RUST, *Colonel.*

GENERAL LORING, *Commanding.*

The expedition had proved a failure after every command of Lee's army had gained its position, and a general retreat was ordered.

While General Lee was reconnoitering the Federal position at Cheat Mountain pass on the 11th, Colonel Washington, his chief of engineers, while examining a position with the view of planting a battery, ran into an ambuscade, and being fired upon by a whole platoon of Federal infantry, fell, pierced by many bullets, and died instantly. Colonel Washington was an able and gallant officer, and a near relative of the Father of his Country.

The whole expedition having failed, General Lee resolved to withdraw his forces a short distance. Having given orders to the other commanders he proceeded personally to the position occupied by Donelson's Brigade, and came up to the top of the ridge, accompanied by an orderly. It was the first time the Tennessee troops had seen him. As soon as General Lee arrived at the top of the mountain he ordered General Donelson to withdraw his brigade into the valley, with his left in front. The rear-guard now became the front guard, and *vice versa.* A general stir was going on in the whole country below us. The enemy was approaching our position, and had a heavy force near the top of the mountain on the ground occupied by Fulton's regiment the evening before. We were also being approached by a Yankee column by way of Becky's Run. Each column was closing in upon us under cover of a dense undergrowth, which was so thick it was almost impossible to see any thing before us. We were in a complete thicket of brush and tall weeds, and our brigade was in a narrow path that crossed the ridge. A detail was made from the Sixteenth Tennessee Regiment, under Captain H. H. Dillard, to move in advance of the column, and it had scarcely reached the foot of the hill when it was fired upon by the Federal advance-guard, and the fire was returned. At this juncture of the proceedings the Federals threw their column into line of battle, and began to advance up the hill. Their advance-guard fronted the advance-guard of the Sixteenth Regiment, but their main line diverged from Donelson's line at an angle of about fifty degrees. The brigade proceeded down the hill rapidly, and in a few minutes the left of the Sixteenth became engaged. The Federals had not learned our position, and fired a volley at the Sixteenth, but the bullets hit in the tree-tops. Some of the boys seemed amused at such wild shooting, and shouted to the Yankees at the top of their voices that they were shooting into the tree-tops.

A moving fight now began, though no line of battle was formed. The men, as they did in Tygart's Valley the day before, began to throw down their knapsacks and blankets, and to divest themselves of all incumbrances. The Federals at one point were within a few steps of us, but were firing at random, the smoke of the guns and the report being the only means of distinguishing their true position. Colonel Savage ordered a charge. With his shrill and commanding voice he gave the command, "Charge the damned rascals, and pack them off on your bayonets!" The order was no sooner given than executed with a will. The men

COLONEL JOHN H. SAVAGE.

raised the old rebel yell that echoed along the valley for miles. The Yankees retreated in hot haste through the field at the foot of the hill, with the old Sixteenth at their heels. The Eighth came on as fast as the nature of the position would allow.

The Yankees retreated to the run about the middle of the valley, about three hundred yards distant. The run being very narrow, and having dirt banks, was swollen by the night rains and the banks were soft and slippery. In attempting to jump the run many would light on the brink of the opposite bank and slip down into the water to their armpits, and were thus made prisoners.

As soon as the Yankees passed Becky's Run they fell back upon their main line, and the fight was over. The Federal loss was eight or ten killed, and about eighteen prisoners. The Confederate loss was one man killed, private Alpha Martin, of Captain Meadows' company, and one or two slightly wounded. Mr. Martin was a gallant soldier, and a splendid fellow. His comrades all respected and loved him, and his loss was deeply regretted. He was the first man of the Sixteenth Tennessee who fell upon the field of battle. This was the first time the regiment was ever under fire, and the men acted bravely.

The skirmish was a small affair compared with other engagements. It did not exceed ten minutes' duration, though a hasty retreat was all that prevented a general engagement, with the odds all against us.

The brigade was withdrawn up Becky's Run, and the whole Yankee force had come out from the works to the top of the ridge where we were stationed but a few minutes before. The men were unable to recover their baggage, which they dropped in the first of the charge, as the enemy was now on the ground from our rear. The Federals, mentioning this circumstance, exaggerated the defeat of General Lee's campaign, and gave it the appearance of a rout. The Confederates threw down their baggage in the charge, and not in the retreat.

The brigade proceeded up the valley for a while and, turning to the right, marched about eight miles to the top of a high mountain, whose sides and base were covered with meadows and fields. This was the possession of a wealthy farmer and stock-raiser. Here the men were supplied with beef of the best quality, but without bread or salt. As the men were hungry as well as weary, they broiled their beef upon the coals and ate it. The brigade rested here during the night, and till the afternoon of the following day, when they marched to a spring on the bench of the mountain, and on the day following took position in Tygart's Valley, near the very point where the pickets had been captured on the 11th. A heavy guard was placed around the brigade to prevent surprise, and a detail was sent on horseback to the wagon train to get bread for the men.

The attempt upon Cheat Mountain having failed, General Lee resolved to renew the expedition, and, on the 14th of September, issued the following order to his troops:

General Order } HEAD-QUARTERS, VALLEY RIVER, VA., }
No. —.   }   September 14, 1861. }

The forced reconnoissance of the enemy's position, both at Cheat Mountain pass and on Valley River, having been completed, and the character of the natural approaches and the nature of the artificial defenses exposed, the Army of the Northwest will resume its former position, and at such time and in such manner as General Loring shall direct, and continue its preparations for further operations. The commanding general experienced much gratification at the cheerfulness and alacrity displayed by the troops in this arduous operation. The promptitude with which they surmounted every difficulty, driving in and capturing the enemy's pickets on the fronts examined, and exhibiting that readiness for attack, gives assurance of victory when opportunity offers. R. E. LEE, *General Commanding.*

In accordance with this order, the troops were all placed in readiness for a renewal of the campaign, but subsequent developments changed the purpose of the commander-in-chief, and he resolved to withdraw the whole force nearer to his base of supplies.

Accordingly, on the 15th, the column set out on a general retreat, and the Sixteenth Tennessee was assigned to the responsible duty of bringing up the rear. On the evening of the 16th the brigade arrived at Big Spring. On the 17th flour and bacon were issued to the men, and they enjoyed the luxury of cooking and eating in a more civilized manner. The brigade remained at Big Spring during the 19th and 20th of September, and the men, resting from their severe campaign, enjoyed themselves as best they could. Some of the boys of the Sixteenth went out foraging, and returned with chickens, vegetables, and other luxuries, purchased from the natives after much persuading, and paying fabulous prices in Confederate money. One peculiar luxury at this point and date was the blackberry. It was now the 20th day of September, and these berries were just beginning to ripen in the old fields and fence-corners about Big Spring, on this portion of the mountains of North-western Virginia. The briers were thick and prolific, and the boys interviewed them liberally with their camp-kettles, bringing in large quantities of fresh berries, which were made into dumplings and cobblers. Though destitute of much of the high flavoring and fancy qualities of more experienced cookery, they were highly agreeable to the palate, and were enjoyed by the men who had before this learned, by repeated experience, that a good appetite is not a severe critic on cookery.

On the 22d of September the Sixteenth Regiment, together with its brigade, left Big Spring and marched to Elk Mountain, seventeen miles distant. The weather was very cold, and many of the men had worn out their shoes and were barefooted. The regiment encamped at the foot of Elk Mountain, and on the morning of the 23d shoes were given to the most destitute, and the column moved to Greenbrier Bridge. The morning was cold and a large frost was on the ground. Remaining all day and all night at Greenbrier Bridge, the march was resumed on the evening of the 25th. The command had received orders to proceed to Sewell Mountain to the relief of Generals Wise and Floyd, who were being pressed by Rosecrans, and were forced to fall back on Meadow Bluff. The regiment marched thirteen miles, and on the morning of the 26th resumed its march through a thrifty and prosperous country, and made seventeen miles, arriving in the evening in a woods pasture where they camped for the night. A cold rain set in about night, and continued the greater part of the night. The regiment was without tents or shelter of any kind, and many of the men groped their way in the darkness to the barns and outhouses of the neighborhood and sheltered till morning. In the morning it was very cold and still raining. Spirits were issued to the companies, and the march was resumed about seven o'clock. The rain continued all day, and after passing through Frankford and Lewisburg the regiment arrived at its camping place late in the evening of the 27th. Colonel Savage marched his regiment into a lot where there was a large barn with long sheds on its sides and end. The owner of the premises told Colonel Savage to put his men under the shelters, and to use his rails to make fires by which to dry themselves. The men were marched under the sheds where, drenched, cold, and weary, they deposited their luggage and built fires along in front. Here they dried themselves and cooked their suppers. After supper they laid down and enjoyed the comforts of a good shelter by good fires. On the morning of September 28, they drew and cooked a day's rations, and marched to Meadow Bluff in the evening. On the evening of the 29th the regiment arrived at Sewell Mountain, within plain sight and hearing of the enemy.

General Lee drew up his forces on Little Sewell, while Rosecrans, with his army and the army of General Cox, were encamped on Big Sewell, with just a small valley between them. The Charleston road ran through the encampment of each army, and the two opposing commanders, with their respective commands, stood comparatively inactive and looked at each other until October 6, when the Federal forces struck their tents and fell back in the direction of Charleston. General Lee sent out a reconnoitering force to see where they had gone, but finding nothing of interest or consequence the party returned to Little Sewell.

Winter was rapidly approaching. The roads were bad, and the Federals were far from their base of supplies. These circumstances caused the Federal commander to fall back to a point nearer his supplies. General Lee remained at Little Sewell and awaited developments. The Federals showed no disposition to come out and renew hostilities, and with each army the campaign was practically over for the winter.

The Sixteenth was moved to the foot of Little Sewell, where it drilled morning and evening. The weather was becoming quite cold, and having a limited amount of clothing, and that badly worn out, the men suffered severely and began to fall sick rapidly. The sick were sent to Lewisburg and the White Sulphur Springs, and the regiment remained at the foot of Little Sewell until the 20th day of October, when the men all received two months' pay; and on the morning of the 21st marched back to Meadow Bluff, a distance of thirteen miles. On the 22d the march was resumed to Lewisburg, seventeen miles distant, and continued on the 23d and 24th to Mill Point, thirty-three miles from Lewisburg. On the 25th the regiment arrived at Greenbrier bridge, which was guarded by a detachment of the Greenbrier militia. These men wore a kind of overcoat with a large cape attached. The boys of the Sixteenth Tennessee at this place received coats of this kind, which they called "militias," a name by which this particular kind of garment was familliarly known during the remainder of the war.

At noon on the 27th the regiment took up its line of march, and camped that evening within one mile of Huntersville, where it remained until November 11, when it took up its line of march and traveled twelve miles in the direction of Lewisburg, having been ordered to that point with the least possible delay. Arriving at Lewisburg on the 14th, the regiment encamped near that place. Winter had now set in in earnest. Snow fell on the 17th and 18th, and the weather was severely cold. On the 19th a supply of clothing arrived for the regiment from the folks at home. There was a bountiful supply of clothing of every kind—coats, shoes, hats, bed-clothing, and all the bodily comforts that the good people at home could devise were received at this time. Letters from fathers, mothers, brothers, sisters, wives, sweethearts, and friends were also received. The Sixteenth now enjoyed itself by its big log fires, dressed up in its new clothes, with nothing to do but to rest and delight in the timely bounty of its friends and relatives at home.

CAPTAIN W. G. ETTER.

Every man was made comfortable. Among the many knick-nacs received at this time from the home folk, was a magnificent and highly appreciated donation from James Hill, Esq., and Hon. H. L. W. Hill, consisting of several hundred bottles of splendid apple brandy, which the boys in their worn-out and wearied condition enjoyed to the fullest, and treasured with the warmest feelings the names and memory of the kind donors.

It was now November 20th, and the regiment had marched over much ground and endured many hardships. The regiment remained in camp near Lewisburg until November 28th, when orders were received to be ready to march on the following morning. The 29th and 30th days of November being very inclement on account of so much rain and mud, the order was suspended. On the 1st day of December the regiment marched eight miles. On the 2d it passed Salt Sulphur Springs, and encamped at night at the Red Sulphur Springs. Proceeding onward on the 4th, passed through Petertown on the 5th, crossing New River in ferryboats, arrived at Dublin depot on the 8th, where orders were received to proceed immediately to Charleston, S. C.

Drawing four days' rations, and taking the cars on the 11th, proceeded by way of Petersburg and Wilmington to Charleston, and from Charleston to Pocotaligo. General Lee had been put in charge of the coast defenses, with head-quarters at Charleston. The Eighth and Sixteenth Tennessee regiments, and the Sixtieth Virginia accompanied General Lee, and, arriving at Pocotaligo about 11 o'clock on the 19th, went into camp near the station.

With the exception of a little demonstration on the part of the enemy at Port Royal ferry, on the 1st of January, there was comparative quiet all along the coast from Charleston to Savannah during the winter. The sick that had been left in Virginia were rapidly recovering, and while many rejoined their commands in

South Carolina, many others were left to sleep their last sleep beneath the Virginia soil.

At Pocotaligo the boys did nothing but drill and do picket duty along the coast to prevent surprises and communication between the Yankees and the negroes. Vegetables and fish being plentiful, and the climate delightful, the men grew healthy and happy, and almost forgot that the war was going on.

On the 24th of January, 1862, orders were received to hold an election for major on the 25th, which resulted in the election of H. H. Faulkner, major of the Sixteenth Tennessee, to fill the vacancy occasioned by the death of Major Goodbar. Shortly afterward the regiment was removed to Grahamville, where it remained in quiet until April 7th, when it was ordered to Corinth, Miss., to reinforce Beauregard.

Campaigns and Battles

OF THE

SIXTEENTH TENNESSEE REGIMENT.

CHAPTER II.

CAMPAIGNS IN SOUTH CAROLINA.

AS soon as the Tennessee troops arrived at Charleston the following order was issued from General Lee's head-quarters:

General Order No. —.   HEAD-QUARTERS OF THE FORCES, CHARLESTON, S. C., December 18, 1861.

General D. S. Donelson, Commanding Third Brigade Tennessee Volunteers—General:—The general commanding desires that you should proceed with your brigade to Coosawhatchie, S. C., as soon as the quarter-master of this place (Major H. Lee) can furnish you with the necessary transportation. Directions have already been given to him to that effect.

Very respectfully,   T. A. WASHINGTON,
Assistant Adjutant-general.

On the evening of the 18th, the troops took the cars on the Charleston and Savannah Railroad. The Eighth Tennessee and Colonel Starke's Virginia regiment were encamped near the bridge over the Salkchatchie, and the Sixteenth Tennessee Regiment encamped at Old Pocotaligo, about six miles east of Coosawhatchie, and two miles south of Pocotaligo station. The Federals were threatening the interior from Port Royal ferry, also from Mackey's point, Page's point, and Cunningham's bluff. From each of those different landings the roads went to the interior and came together near Pocotaligo. It was necessary to place the main force at this point as a reserve to be used against any demonstration of the enemy from either of these points. The enemy was in possession of Beaufort Island, and could land at any of the above landings at any time. This part of the coast defenses was embraced in the Fourth Military District, and was under the command of Major-general John C. Pemberton. General Donelson's brigade was assigned to General Pemberton's command by virtue of the following order from General Lee:

General Order HEAD-QUARTERS, COOSAWHATCHIE, S. C.,
No. —. December 23, 1861.

Brigadier-general D. S. Donelson, commanding Tennessee Brigade, and Colonel W. E. Starke, commanding Sixtieth Regiment Virginia Volunteers, will report their commands to Brigadier-general Pemberton for duty in the Fourth Military District of South Carolina. By order of General Lee.

T. A. WASHINGTON, *Assistant Adjutant-general.*

As Port Royal ferry seemed to be the most threatened, a fortification was thrown up at that point, where there was an old fort of 1812, and a battery was planted. The troops stationed at this point were Colonel Dunnovant's Twelfth Regiment of South Carolina Volunteers, the Fourteenth South Carolina Regiment, Colonel James Jones, Colonel Martin's regiment of cavalry, and a battery of Virginia artillery under Captain Leak. Colonel Jones being the senior officer was in command of the forces in that quarter.

On the morning of January 1, 1862, the Federal gunboats appeared at Port Royal ferry, near the mouth of the Coosaw river, and commenced shelling the Confederate works at a furious rate. The Federal fleet consisted of five gun-boats sent out by Admiral Dupont, and placed under command of Captain Rodgers, of the United States Navy. The land force consisted of Stephen's brigade and the Forty-seventh and Forty-eighth New York Regiments of General Viele's brigade. The troops were landed under cover of a tremendous bombardment. The Federal gun-boats threw thirteen-inch shells into the Confederate lines with remarkable precision, and the Confederates suffered principally from this source. One shell exploded in the ranks of a South Carolina regiment and killed seven men and wounded six more. The cannonading was kept up some time before the Federals landed their troops. The object of the Federals was to destroy the Confederate works at Port Royal ferry, and to collect the stock from the neighboring plantations.

The Federal force that landed consisted of about three thousand troops and a twelve-pound howitzer, under the command of Lieutenant Upshur. The South Carolina troops under Colonel Jones had every thing in readiness to receive them when they landed. A brisk engagement ensued. The Confederates held their ground bravely till two o'clock, when General Pemberton ordered General Donelson to hasten with his command to the relief of Colonel Jones. The Eighth, being nearest, arrived on the ground about four o'clock. The Sixteenth, being farthest, was put in motion within fifteen minutes after the order was received, and hurried forward. Ammunition was given to the men when in the act of starting, and the column moved on at a double-quick. It was near ten miles to Port Royal ferry. The Sixteenth Regiment arrived at Gardner's

Corner about dark, where the wounded were being brought from the field. The groans and shrieks of the suffering men were distressing. The wounds had been inflicted principally with shells, and the men were mangled in a terrible manner.

The Confederates had fallen back, and having established their lines near Gardner's Corner, remained there during the night. Colonel Savage had placed his regiment in line in front of Gardner's Corner, in the edge of a cotton-field, at right angles to the Port Royal road.

Everybody expected the enemy to advance in the morning. Donelson's brigade of Tennessee troops and General Maxey Gregg's brigade of South Carolina troops had now arrived, and every thing was in readiness for a general engagement, with some show for the Confederates, as they had reinforced and withdrawn beyond range of the Federal gun-boats.

On the morning of January 2, the men were in line awaiting the attack, but no enemy appeared. General Pemberton ordered Colonel Savage to make a reconnoissance with his regiment and ascertain, if possible, the true position and strength of the enemy, and report to him the result. It was intended to give the enemy battle if he was found, and every arrangement was made accordingly.. On the evening of the 2d, Colonel Savage, having placed a portion of his regiment on either side of the causeway, and with a detachment of picked men in front, he advanced cautiously with the advance-guard, the regiment following.

It was the general impression that the enemy was in our immediate front, and General Donelson and Major Waddy, of General Pemberton's staff, were each of that opinion, and wanted to report accordingly to General Pemberton. Colonel Savage insisted on a more careful and extensive reconnoissance before reporting, and his counsel prevailed. It was found that the South Carolina troops had been deceived by appearances. It was late in the evening, and objects in the distance had been mistaken for Yankees. Colonel Savage pressed the reconnoissance carefully till he arrived within a short distance of the old fort. Privates G. L. Freeman and Isaac Mercer went on in advance of the detachment to the river and found no enemy. The Confederates withdrew about four miles to a point where the Mackey's point road intersected with the Port Royal road and formed line of battle.

On the morning of the 3d it was found that the enemy had returned to their shipping, and the fleet had departed in the direction of Page's point. The Confederates remained here three or four days in line of battle, but seeing no appearance of a contemplated attack from the Federals each command was ordered to its original encampment.

The battle of Coosaw river, or Port Royal ferry, was the only engagement on the Carolina coast during the winter after January 1. The Federal loss was fifteen in killed, wounded, and missing. The Confederate loss was thirty-two, of whom nine men were killed and twenty-three wounded.

Matters were quiet all along the coast during the rest of the winter. The Sixteenth Tennessee enjoyed the delightful climate of South Carolina in every way. Supplies were plentiful, and the boys found that their task was easy. The regiment was divided into detachments much of its time, and placed on guard at different points of the coast near Pocotaligo.

Early in March the regiment was sent to Grahamville, S. C., where it was quartered in snug cabins and fared sumptuously. While here a number of the boys re-enlisted and formed a cavalry company by authority of General Pemberton. Captain P. H. McBride was placed in command of the company, and the members were allowed a furlough to go home and prepare their equipments. The regiment remained at Grahamville till after the great battle of Shiloh had been fought, when they were sent to Corinth by order of General Lee, who had now been made commander-in-chief of all the armies of the Confederacy.

The army of General Johnson had been forced to withdraw from Kentucky and the greater part of Tennessee after the Confederate reverses at Fort Donelson. The fall of Forts Donelson and Henry was an unfortunate blow upon the Confederacy, and practically broke the backbone of its main defenses. The great Mississippi valley was the main dependence she had for supplies of every kind, and this defeat placed the main river system of the valley in the hands of the Federals. The western army had fallen back to Corinth, and the Federals thus came into possession of the great States of Tennessee and Kentucky, and the greater portion of Missouri.

General Johnston's lines now covered the Memphis and Charleston Railroad from the Tennessee river to Memphis, and the defenses at Island Number Ten covered Memphis from the approaches of the Federal gun-boats. General Johnston resolved to put his army in shape for a decisive battle on the south side of the Tennessee river. General Grant was in command of the Federal forces at Savannah, on the Tennessee river, and Buell was in command of the forces about Nashville. Johnston determined to hurl his whole army upon Grant and defeat him before Buell could come to his support. By the first of April his plans were fully matured and every thing in readiness for the campaign. The roads being in bad condition he was unable to advance his army as rapidly as his plans contemplated. It was his intention to strike Grant on April 5, but the movement was hindered on account of bad roads, and the enemy used the delay to advantage. Buell was ordered to Grant's support in anticipation of Johnston's intentions. Grant was not expecting Johnston to attack him so soon, and before he was aware of the matured plans and prompt executive ability of the Confederate leader, Johnston was upon him on the morning of April 6, 1862. The Confederates took possession of the Federal encampment, and drove the enemy before them for some distance. By this time Grant had time to realize the situation, and his line was formed for battle with the intention of a stubborn resistance. The Confederates pressed onward, and struck Grant's second line at Shiloh church, and the battle became desperate. The Federals finally yielded this line, and the Confederates pressed on to victory. The fight lasted throughout the day, and the Federals had been driven back at every point.

Late in the evening the Federals took another stand, and Johnston ordered another charge, after massing his force at that point of the enemy's line which he considered the key to the position. The gallant Confederate chieftain led the charge in person. The lines of the enemy were broken, and the Confederates had gained a decisive victory. The Federals were driven to the river bank, and to have pressed them farther would have resulted in their capture. This was the result contemplated by General Johnston, but he did not live to execute it. He fell, mortally wounded, while leading the charge that procured the victory, and at the very moment of its consummation. The men were discouraged and dejected when they learned that their leader had fallen. General Beauregard now assumed command. Night closed its mantle over the scene, and the fighting ceased.

During the night Buell's army came up and formed a junction with Grant's forces, and in the morning the Federals came out in the aggressive. The Confederates were now on the defensive, and were confronted by an enemy of fresh troops and their superior in point of numbers. The battle of the 7th was over much of the same ground of the 6th, but with its fortunes reversed. The Confederates gradually gave back, from position to position, as the Federals had done on the day previous. In the afternoon of the 7th, Beauregard withdrew his entire force from the field in good order, and retreated back to Corinth. The losses on both sides had been very great.

General Beauregard saw the tremendous force that was being arrayed against him, and found, after his arrival at Corinth, that with his army of thirty-five thousand he was wholly unable to cope with the concentrated hosts of the enemy, and realized that unless he was promptly reinforced he would be compelled to yield the great Mississippi Valley to the enemy, which would be practically surrendering the cause. He accordingly asked the Confederate authorities to reinforce him from Pemberton's army, of South Carolina, and Van Dorn's and Price's armies, of the Trans-Mississippi Department. He sent the following telegram to Richmond in cipher, which appeared in the Northern papers verbatim on the following morning. The mystery was explained when the Richmond authorities ascertained that this dispatch had also been sent, in common language, by our army correspondent, by way of Huntsville, where it was taken off the wires by a spy.

CORINTH, MISS., April 9, 1862.

General S. Cooper, Richmond, Va.:—All present probabilities are that whenever the enemy moves on this position he will do so with an overwhelming force of not less than eighty thousand men. We now number only about thirty-five thousand effectives. Van Dorn may possibly join us in a few days with about fifteen thousand more. Can we not be reinforced from Pemberton's army? If defeated here we lose the Mississippi Valley, and probably our cause, whereas we could afford to lose Charleston and Savannah for the purpose of defeating Buell's army, which would not only insure us the valley of the Mississippi, but our independence. G. T. BEAUREGARD.

Upon the reception of General Beauregard's dispatch General Lee sent the following to General Pemberton:

RICHMOND, VA., April 10, 1862.

Major-general Pemberton:—Beauregard is pressed for troops. Send him, if possible, Donelson's brigade of two regiments. If Mississippi Valley is lost the Atlantic States will be ruined.

Very respectfully, R. E. LEE.

To this General Pemberton replied as follows:

POCOTALIGO, S. C., April 10, 1862, 6:30 P.M.

General R. E. Lee, Richmond, Va.:—Your telegram just received. I consider it an order. Donelson's brigade—two Tennessee regiments, aggregating fifteen hundred and seventy-two—will move to Corinth as soon as transportation can be got ready. J. C. PEMBERTON, *Major-general Commanding.*

General Pemberton sent the following order to General Ripley:

SAVANNAH, GA., April 13, 1862.

General R. S. Ripley:—Order the troops to take the most direct and practicable route to Corinth. Let the commander telegraph to General Beauregard in advance for his instructions.

J. C. PEMBERTON, *Major-general.*

General Beauregard telegraphed for the troops to be sent by way of Chattanooga, and they were hurried on as fast as possible by way of Charleston, Augusta, and Atlanta. The Federals had taken possession of Huntsville about the time that the troops were getting to Chattanooga on their way to Corinth, and they were forced to go back by way of Mobile, and did not arrive at Corinth until April 23, 1862.

CAMPAIGN IN MISSISSIPPI.

When the Tennessee troops arrived at Corinth they found every thing presenting the true aspect of war in its fullest sense. The whole country about the place was one vast encampment of troops. The wounded from the great battle had been sent to the interior towns and villages along the railroad, while the convalescent were with their commands in camp. The boys of the Sixteenth Regiment went to see friends and acquaintances belonging to the Fifth and other Tennessee regiments, and mingled among their old comrades and acquaintances generally for a few days after their arrival at Corinth. The Eighth and Sixteenth Tennessee Regiments remained a part of Donelson's brigade, which was assigned to Cheatham's division, and became a part of the first army corps under command of Lieutenant-general Polk.

The army of General Halleck now numbered about one hundred thousand men, not including the fleet in the Mississippi river. The army of General Beauregard, including the river defenses, was now near the equal of the enemy in the field in point of numbers, but the inferior in point of equipments.

By May 1, Beauregard had been reinforced by Van Dorn's forces from Missouri and four regiments from Pemberton's army. His forces now numbered as follows:

Polk's corps, 17,185; Bragg's corps, 23,100; Hardee's corps, 15,937; cavalry and artillery, 13,318; Army of the West, 34,035; Villepigue's division, 4,173; reserve, 7,121. Total, 114,869.

This number included the sick and wounded in the hospital, and the absent for any cause. By the transfer of some of the troops, and by deaths, this estimate was reduced by May 15, 1862, to 110,845 total present and absent. The large number of sick and wounded at the different hospitals reduced this number to an aggregate of 74,279 present, including sick and wounded in camp, the different details for sappers and miners, infirmary corps, and other purposes. The aggregate was reduced in this manner to an effective total of 51,218 guns ready for action on May 15, viz.: Army of the Mississippi, 35,705; Army of the West, 12,801; Western Department, 2,612. Effective total, 51,218.

With this force Beauregard felt prepared to give battle to Halleck, who was advancing on the Purdy road. A line of breastworks were thrown up a few miles in front of Corinth, and the troops were employed daily in strengthening the defenses and covering the front of their works with abatis of fallen trees. Van Dorn occupied the right wing of Beauregard's lines, near the Farmington road. Hardee's corps occupied the center, and Polk's corps was on the left wing. Every thing was put in readiness and waiting for the attack, which seemed imminent. General Price seemed to grow impatient for the attack, and moving out his division one morning struck the enemy's left wing and swung it round on their main line and then retired to his original position. The old hero of so many hard-fought battles kept up a row with Halleck's left wing pretty regularly. The principal fighting about Corinth was on the right wing of Beauregard's lines, while the enemy seemed to be seeking an advantage with a view to striking the Confederate rear and taking possession of Chewalla, a point on the Memphis and Charleston Railroad, a few miles south of Corinth. As the Federals moved on Corinth and established their lines, they threw up fortifications at each line.

The battle being daily and almost hourly expected, and General Beauregard having arranged his lines and fortified his position, had every thing in readiness for the conflict, and issued the following address to his men:

HEAD-QUARTERS OF THE FORCES,
CORINTH, Miss., May 2, 1862.

Soldiers of Shiloh and Elkhorn:—We are about to meet once more in the shock of battle the invaders of our soil, the despoilers of our homes, the disturbers of our family ties. Face to face, hand to hand, we are to decide whether we are to be freemen or the vile slaves of those who are free only in name, and who but yesterday were vanquished, although in largely superior numbers in their own encampments, on the ever-memorable field of Shiloh.

Let the impending battle decide our fate, and add one more illustrious page to the history of our revolution—one to which our children will point with noble pride, saying, "Our fathers were at the battle of Corinth!"

I congratulate you on your timely junction—your mingled banners! For the first time in this war we shall meet our foe in strength that should give us victory. Soldiers, can the result be doubted? Shall we not drive back into the Tennessee the presumptuous mercenaries collected for our subjugation? One more manly effort, and trusting in God and the justness of our cause, we shall recover more than we have lately lost. Let the sound of our victorious guns be re-echoed by those of the Army of Virginia on the historic battle-field of Yorktown.

G. T. BEAUREGARD, *General Commanding.*

General Bragg issued the following address to the soldiers of his command, the Second Corps of the Army of the Mississippi:

HEAD-QUARTERS SECOND CORPS,
ARMY OF THE MISSISSIPPI,
CORINTH, MISS., May 3, 1862.

Soldiers:—You are again about to encounter the mercenary invader who pollutes the sacred soil of our beloved country. Severely punished by you, and driven from his chosen position, with the loss of his artillery and his honor, at Shiloh, when double your numbers, he now approaches cautiously and timidly, unwilling to advance, unable to retreat. Could his rank and file enjoy a freeman's right, not one would remain within our limits, but are goaded on by a tyrant's lash—by desperate leaders whose only safety lies in success. Such a foe ought never to conquer freemen battling on their own soil. You will encounter him in your chosen position, strong by nature and improved by art; away from his main support and reliance—gun-boats and heavy batteries—and for the first time in this war, with nearly equal numbers.

The slight reverses we have met on the sea-board have worked us good as well as evil. The brave troops so long retained there have hastened to swell your numbers, while the gallant Van Dorn and invincible Price are now in your midst, with numbers almost equaling the "Army of Shiloh." We have, then, but to strike and destroy, and as the enemy's whole resources are concentrated here, we shall not only redeem Tennessee, Kentucky, and Missouri at one blow, but open the portals of the whole North-west. BRAXTON BRAGG,

General Commanding Second Corps.

The enemy continued to advance slowly and cautiously, fortifying every line of his advancement. General Beauregard, finding that Halleck would not bring on an engagement by attacking the Confederates in their chosen position, finally resolved to move out of his works and advance on the Federal lines, having waited for his attack in vain for several days. Every thing was in readiness for the movement by May 20, when the following order was issued by General Beauregard:

General Orders No. —. } HEAD-QUARTERS WESTERN DEPARTMENT, CORINTH, May 20, 1862.

In the event of a battle, the following regulations will be strictly observed by all medical officers of this department, with the view of affording the greatest comfort to the sick and wounded of the army:

1. All the wounded not requiring surgical operations will be carried to their respective encampments, whence such cases as will bear removal will be subsequently distributed among the various hospitals in the interior under the superintendence of the medical inspectors.

2. Such of the wounded as will not bear transportation will be sent to the hospital at this point, on the order of the division surgeon.

3. Cases requiring immediate surgical operation will be treated as far as possible on the field, and all such will be sent immediately to the hospital at this place.

By command of General Beauregard.

GEO. W. BRENT, *Acting Chief of Staff.*

General Bragg issued the following order to his corps:

HEAD-QUARTERS ARMY OF THE MISSISSIPPI, CORINTH, MISS., May 20, 1862.

As soon as the movement against the enemy takes place, Colonel D. W. Adams, First Regiment Louisiana Infantry, will assume command of that portion of the army left to guard the trenches. By command of General Bragg.

GEO. G. GARNER, *Assistant Adjutant-general.*

The men were ordered to prepare three days' cooked rations for their haversacks, and the wagons were to carry two days' supply of uncooked rations. Forty rounds of ammunition was given for each gun, and the ordinance supplies were to be kept at a convenient distance for additional supply if needed. Every thing was in readiness on the 20th for a general movement on the 21st.

On account of the rains on the morning of the 21st, the movement was suspended for twenty-four hours. The rain ceasing and the weather clearing up in the morning, the whole army was put in shape for a movement on the following day. Colonel Savage made a stirring, patriotic speech to his regiment on the evening of the 21st, and by seven o'clock on the morning of the 22d the whole army was in line. General Donelson addressed his brigade in line by regiments. He told in eloquent tones of the bright escutcheon of Tennessee fame on so many hard fought battle-fields in this and previous wars, where the Tennessee troops had acted their part so nobly, and that in the arduous task before them to be performed this day, when the enemy was to be attacked in superior numbers and in a position of his own choosing, he had the fullest confidence in the valor of the Tennessee troops, and he knew that they would, by their noble achievements, add new luster to the lofty name that their State so justly and proudly bore. The enemy must be driven back. His heavy batteries must be charged and his guns taken. They were fighting for their homes and all they held dear, which they would wrest from the hand of the invader, but it was a work that would involve much sacrifice and the loss of many lives. The Tennessee troops would do their part well, and "strike where danger was thickest." This stirring address was delivered to the regiment in double column by the General, who rode along the front line as he spoke. The men responded with loud and prolonged cheers, and in a few minutes the whole column was moving to the front.

As before stated, Polk's corps occupied the left of Beauregard's lines, and the enemy was making his principal demonstrations on the right and center, in front of Van Dorn's, Bragg's, and Hardee's corps. It was near six miles from Polk's position to the point of the enemy's line where he was expected to strike. Polk, Hardee, and Bragg gained their positions promptly and waited for Van Dorn to come up, when a signal would be given for a general attack.

Beauregard's army was about fifty thousand effective men, and the enemy was about eighty thousand. The opposing armies were looking at each other, both ready for the awful work of death. On account of the topography of the country, Van Dorn was delayed in bringing up his command, and meeting with unforeseen obstacles, he consulted Generals Price and Hardee in reference to the difficulties before him, and at noon dispatched to Beauregard as follows:

> HEAD-QUARTERS ARMY OF THE WEST,
> May 22, 1862.
>
> *General:*—It pains me to say that I have, after consultation with Generals Hardee and Price, determined to return to my intrenchments. I have found unexpected obstacles, topographical and otherwise, and I have been delayed until this hour (12 M.), and yet not in position. It is too late to begin a general engagement, and I cannot wait to hear from you to get orders. I have, therefore, determined to act myself and return. I will explain more fully when I see you. EARL VAN DORN.

When General Beauregard received this dispatch he indorsed it with his approval and returned it to General Van Dorn. He then gave orders to the corps commanders to withdraw their commands to their intrenchments, and before sundown the whole army was in its original encampment along the trenches. Not a gun had been fired, and every thing was quiet.

The Confederates resumed their position in the fortifications before Corinth, and prepared for repelling an attack by strengthening their works and felling the timber in their front. The Federals crept on slowly and fortified every line of their advancement. Daily the line of Federal intrenchments drew nearer the place until the 27th, when they had their batteries planted and their lines fortified within cannon shot of Beauregard's lines. For miles to the Federal rear the country was one series of parallel intrenchments.

The enemy had gathered principally on the east of the railroad, and every thing gave evidence that he did not meditate an attack upon Corinth, but a regular bombardment and siege. General Beauregard's communications were severely threatened on the right, where the enemy seemed determined to extend his fortified lines, and thus cut off supplies by railroad. To counteract these demonstrations, General Price, of Van Dorn's army, kept Halleck's left wing busy. There was no difficulty in getting up a fight in front of Price's division. If the enemy came around too presumptuously he was sure of a warm reception, for Price always accepted any thing in the way of a challenge. In the different sorties on the right the enemy was driven back in the first stages of the siege, and on one occasion Price took possession of the enemy's telegraph office and telegraphed his compliments to the President of the United States.

By May 25 the forces of the enemy had thickened on the right and had gained so strong a foothold that Van Dorn was unable to dislodge him. His lines of intrenchments drew nearer and nearer. The Confederates were now completely on the defensive, with every resource taxed to the utmost. The lines of the enemy had been re-enforced, and the fall of Corinth seemed only a question of time. The commander in chief took in the situation at a glance. One of three things must be promptly done: the Confederates must attack the enemy, or be attacked by him, or evacuate the place. This was the nature of the situation as viewed by the corps commanders of the army, and as the first two propositions involved serious difficulties, the latter expedient was suggested by General Hardee, and the various reasons explained in the following communication to General Beauregard:

CORINTH, MISS., May 25, 1862.

General G. T. Beauregard, Commanding, etc.:—The situation at Corinth requires that we should attack the enemy at once, await his attack, or evacuate the place.

Assuming that we have 50,000 men and the enemy nearly twice that number, protected by intrenchments, I am clearly of opinion that no attack should be made. Our forces are inferior, and the battle of Shiloh proves, with only the advantage of position, it was hazardous to contend against his superior strength; and to attack him in his intrenchments now would probably inflict on us and the Confederacy a fatal blow. Neither the numbers nor the instruction of our troops renders them equal to the task.

I think we can successfully repel any attack on our camp by the enemy, but it is manifest no attack is meditated. It will be approached gradually, and will be shelled and bombarded, without equal means to respond. This will compel us to make sorties against his intrenched positions, under most adverse circumstances, or to evacuate the place. The latter seems to me inevitable. If so, the only remaining question is whether the place should be evacuated before, after, or during the defense. After fire is opened, or the place is actively shelled or bombarded, or during such an attack, it will be difficult to evacuate the place in good order. With a large body of men imperfectly disciplined any idle rumor may spread a panic, and inextricable confusion may follow, so that the retreat may become a rout. The same objections would apply to any partial or feeble defense of the place, and an attempt to evacuate it in the meantime. If the defense be not determined or the battle decisive, no useful result would follow, but it would afford an opportunity to our enemies to magnify the facts—give them a pretext to claim a victory, and to discourage our friends at home and abroad, and diminish, if not destroy, all claims of foreign intervention.

Under these circumstances, I think the evacuation, if it be determined upon, should be made before the enemy opens fire, and not coupled with a sortie against the enemy in his intrenchments or partial battle. It should be done promptly, if done at all. Even now the enemy can shell our camp. It should be done in good order, so as not to discourage our friends or give a pretext for the triumph of our enemies.

With the forces at our disposition, with a vast territory behind us, with a patriotic and devoted people to support us, the enemy, as he moved southward, away from rivers and railroads, would find insurmountable obstacles in moving columns so heavy that we cannot strike them, and over a country where his mechanical superiority will not avail him.

If we resolve to evacuate, every hour of delay only serves to augment our difficulties. The enemy every day grows stronger on our flanks, and menaces more and more our communications. If he effects his designs, we must fight at every disadvantage or retreat disastrously. History and the country will judge us, not by the movement, but by its consequences.

W. J. HARDEE, *Major-general.*

To which General Beauregard replied as follows:

CORINTH, MISS., May 26, 1862.

Major-general W. J. Hardee—Dear General:—I fully concur in the views contained in your letter of the 25th inst., received last night, and I have already commenced giving orders to my chiefs of staff departments for its execution. But every thing that is done must be done under the plea of the intention to take the offensive at the opportune moment. Every commandant of corps must get every thing ready to move at a moment's notice and must see to the proper condition of the roads and bridges his corps is to travel upon.

Thanking you for your kind wishes, I remain yours truly,

G. T. BEAUREGARD.

On the evening of May 27, Donelson's brigade was placed on picket in front of the breastworks on the left of General Hardee's line. On the morning of the 28th the Federals began to press the Confederate outpost very severely, and all indications were favorable to a general engagement all along the line. This was the first vigorous demonstration of the Federals on the Confederate left wing. The right and center had been pressed for the last three days. The enemy massed heavy columns in the immediate front of the Confederate skirmish lines, and placed their artillery in position. When this was accomplished they commenced shelling the woods with a view to ascertaining the position of the reserve lines of the Confederates and the location of their batteries. The firing along the skirmish line was kept up with vigor, and the Federal batteries kept up a general cannonade all day. The Confederate artillery kept silent, though placed in a position to be most effective in the event of an attack from the Federals. The Federal batteries had learned the position of the Confederate lines, and sent showers of grape-shot through the woods. The men lay close upon the ground, and the enemy's missiles passed over them without inflicting any injury. The skirmishing continued throughout the day. The Sixteenth Tennessee Regiment lost three men on May 28. Stephen Tate, of Captain Womack's company, was killed on the skirmish line in the morning. Sergeant John Grissom and private William Creely, both of Captain Randal's company, were killed by a charge of grape-shot from a Federal battery.

The skirmishing on the right and center was lively all through the day. Hardee's corps was engaged in hot skirmish fighting all along the line. General Cleburn was desirous of gaining an elevated position in his immediate front known as Shelton Hill. This position, if once gained and protected by artillery, would add greatly to the strength of the Confederate lines. General Cleburn ordered his men to move upon this point, which lay in the immediate front of the Fifth Tennessee Regiment. The way seemed open to the top of the elevation, and the right and left were flanked by underbrush. Colonel B. J. Hill ordered a charge, and the gallant old Fifth raised the old rebel yell that could be heard for miles over the din and shock of battle. Colonel Hill led the charge, and his men followed with that dauntless valor that had ever characterized the gallant old Fifth and its daring leader. The regiment was repulsed with a fearful loss in killed and wounded. It was practically an ambuscade. The Federals occupied the hill, and their right and left lines diverged inwardly in the shape of a V, and were concealed by a plum hedge. The Fifth Tennessee charged into the opening, and were subjected to a withering cross-fire of musketry and artillery on its right, left, and front. This was the principal event of the 28th in Hardee's front. For this daring exploit at Shelton Hill, Colonel Hill and his regiment were complimented by General Beauregard in general orders read to the troops of the whole army. On the evening of the 28th, the skirmish lines were relieved by fresh troops, and the army retired to the trenches. The Federals fortified, on the night of the 28th, the ground they had gained during the day.

It was the intention of General Beauregard to abandon the trenches on the night of the 28th, and withdraw his army from Corinth on the 29th. General Bragg was placed in charge of the removal of stores from Corinth, and the work progressed so slowly that he suggested to General Beauregard that the place be held another day, in order to enable him to remove more of the military stores. General Bragg about this time became commander in chief, and assumed command of the army after the evacuation of Corinth.

The following correspondence explains the different movements of the army at this time:

CORINTH, MISS., May 28, 1862, 2:30 P.M.

General:—The prospect at the railroad is not encouraging. Things move very slowly—a want of management with the cars as well as the sick. The medical department is now doing better, but I really do not think it possible to get off to-night, without abandoning arms, ammunition, baggage, etc., which we cannot afford to lose. My baggage is gone, but I am prepared to bivouac for one day in order to save what we can.

The force crossing toward Chewalla has retired again. The firing is between Van Dorn's battery and the enemy, who are trying to force Hardee back on the lower Farmington road.

Yours truly,   BRAXTON BRAGG.

[Confidential.]   CORINTH, MISS., May 28, 1862.

General:—Considering that we have still so much yet to be removed from this place, I have decided that the retrograde movement shall not take place until the 30th instead of the 29th. You will issue all necessary orders to that effect to the forces under your command. It would be advisable to stop at once the ammunition and provision trains at convenient points to this place.

Respectfully your obedient servant,

       G. T. BEAUREGARD, *General Commanding.*

General BRAXTON BRAGG, Commanding Army of Mississippi, Corinth, Miss.

The troops bivouaced about the trenches all day on

the 29th. Every thing was quiet all along the line. Occasionally the sound of a cannon and a little picket firing was heard. Generally a dull, foreboding silence rested over the scene. Every thing movable was being sent to the rear. General Bragg was at the depot superintending the removal in person. During the day he sent the following dispatch to General Beauregard:

RAILROAD DEPOT, May 29, 1862, 11:30 A.M.

General Beauregard—My Dear General:—I have found it necessary to take charge here personally. Col. O. B. is working with me. It will be impossible to save all. Army, ammunition, and the sick, I fear, will be all we can do, but hospital things and provisions will be saved, if possible. I find trunks enough here to load all trains for a day. They are being piled for burning, and great is the consternation. My guard have to be loaded to prevent plundering, but all is going on well. If we had trains all could be well by 12 o'clock to-night, but there is great want of cars. Nothing in our power will be left undone. It is the first time I have played chief quarter-master, but it is no difficult task.

Yours truly, BRAXTON BRAGG.

Every thing was ready for the movement by eight o'clock on the night of the 29th. The camp-fires were kindled. The cooking vessels that could not be removed were broken up by the light of the blazing camp-fires. In fact, the Confederates replenished their camp-fires by such combustible material of their camp equipage as they found inconvenient to remove. The main army was withdrawn in the direction of Guntown. Colonel Savage was ordered to take his regiment to Smith's Bridge, over the Tuscumbia river, and cover the retreat of the army by holding the bridge while the army retired to Baldwin. The regiment arrived at the bridge about four o'clock on the morning of May 30, and, after putting out pickets to guard the approaches, cut down trees and completely blockaded the road for some distance through the swamp from the river bank to the north and destroyed the bridge. Placing pickets along the river the regiment retired a short distance and bivouaced. Colonel Savage then reported to General Polk as follows:

SMITH'S BRIDGE, TUSCUMBIA, May 30, 1862.

Colonel W. B. Richmond, Aid-de-camp:—Your note of this date has been received, and, in reply, I request you to inform Major-general Polk that my regiment reached this point about daylight. The work of cutting the timber and destroying the bridge commenced immediately and was completed about 8 o'clock. The regiment is posted near the bridge, with pickets on the river to detect an advance by this road. I will move back a few hundred yards (keeping pickets on the river), to a point where a road leads to the right in a north-western direction.

I do not think the enemy can force a passage easily, or get in my rear, without moving from a point on the railroad near Chewalla. I directed Captain Saffaran to obstruct the upper crossing, but did not visit that point. I will send cavalry there when it arrives. This route is obscure, but with labor the enemy could have passed the ford with cavalry or infantry.

Forage and subsistence must be drawn from the train on your route, as none can be obtained here, unless I should kill a beef from the pastures and get forage from the plantations near, which I shall do if the regular supply fails.

I am, Colonel, very respectfully,   JOHN H. SAVAGE,
Colonel Sixteenth Regiment Tennessee Volunteers.

The Sixteenth Tennessee remained at Smith's Bridge during May 30 and 31 and the first day of June. The enemy made no active demonstration on its front, but seemed to strike in the direction of Baldwin. During the stay of three days at Smith's Bridge the regiment was isolated from the rest of the army, and held an important position. Being out of the convenient reach of the supply train the regiment subsisted from the locality. Beef was procured in the neighborhood, and the people on a neighboring plantation supplied the men with corn-bread. On the evening of June 2 he withdrew to Baldwin, and on the evening of June 3 Colonel Savage sent in the following report to Major Williamson, of General Polk's staff:

Head-quarters Sixteenth Regiment
Tennessee Volunteers,
Donelson's Brigade, June 3, 1862.

Major George Williamson, Assistant Adjutant-general—Major:—In accordance with the order of Major-general Polk, my regiment (conducted by Captain Rucker) destroyed Smith's Bridge at daylight on Friday morning. The timber was cut by Captain Saffaran's party and the road effectually blockaded. Captain Yerger, with his company of cavalry, reported and scouted up and down the river for several miles. No artillery reported, and I was satisfied to be without it.

On Saturday a citizen scout reported two hundred Yankee cavalry picketed about a mile from the bridge on the road which I came; and that the horses were very poor and the men looking badly. He informed them of my force at the bridge. I sent him to find a road to their rear, which he promised, but did not return, and I hear nothing more of the enemy in that direction.

On Saturday evening I was informed by a citizen that up to that time no enemy had appeared at Chewalla, or near there.

On Sunday, about 10 o'clock P.M., I received a note from Colonel Hunt stating that the enemy were rebuilding the bridge at Danville, and that he and Colonel Deas had agreed to march at 4 o'clock, to prevent being cut off, asking my co-operation, to which I consented.

My regiment marched at 5 o'clock, leaving Captain Yerger's company to remain until dark. I fell in with Colonel Clanton's regiment of cavalry near Kossuth, who continued in the rear throughout the march. Colonels Hunt and Deas were not overtaken till after midnight.

Information of the enemy on our left was received from citizens and scouts, and about one mile beyond Blackland a body of two thousand of the enemy's cavalry were reported as marching on that point. A consultation was had between Colonels Hunt,

Deas, Adams, Slemons, Clanton, and myself, when it was determined to march forward and fight whatever force might appear. We saw nothing of the enemy, but I am sure he had active scouts on our left, and a considerable force four or five miles from Blackland.

It is thirty miles or more to Smith's Bridge the route I came. I reached General Bragg's camp about 4 o'clock yesterday evening. The men being exhausted, we encamped and came on this morning. I had a rear-guard with the strictest orders, yet seven men are missing, and as they are strong men (with one exception), it is feared that they have fallen out of ranks until the regiment passed, and afterward took the wrong road. About eighty axes were left upon the road by Captain Saffaran's party. I brought forward twelve, threw twelve into the yard of Albert Jones, near Kossuth, and deposited the others with a planter named Spencer, near Smith's Bridge.

My men captured a man near Smith's Bridge, believing him to be a Yankee. He denied having been in either service. When we came to General Bragg's camp he admitted that he belonged to the First Louisiana Regiment. I have him yet in charge, and should be glad to get rid of him.

I am, Major, very respectfully, JOHN H. SAVAGE,
 Colonel Sixteenth Regiment Tennessee Volunteers.

The Confederates continued the retreat from Baldwin to Saltillo, and thence to Tupelo, where they arrived June 10, and encamped on a range of ridges about three miles west of the depot. The men were worn out with fatigue after so long a march, but they soon recuperated. Clearing off the timber for their encampment, they pitched their tents and enjoyed the benefits of rest and quiet. Finding that good water could be obtained by digging a short distance, the men commenced sinking wells, and in a day or so good wells could be found over the encampment, by which the men were supplied bountifully with good water. Supplies were plentiful, for the resources of the Confederacy were not so severely taxed as at subsequent periods. The men here began to have their first experience in high prices. The troops were supplied with clothing. Every thing was plentiful, and the men were all in good spirits.

General Bragg was now in command of the whole army. The greatest care was now devoted to the drilling and disciplining of the troops, and the army remained here until the latter part of July, when it started on its celebrated campaign into Kentucky.

REORGANIZATION.

We will now return to the reorganization of the Sixteenth Tennessee Regiment, and of the whole army, which took place at Corinth during the earlier part of May. The greater portion of the Confederate troops enlisted for twelve months, and while at Corinth their time expired. The enemy had this circumstance in view, and had organized tremendous armies in front of Richmond and Corinth, and seemed to be leisurely awaiting the discharge of the twelve-month troops of the Confederacy, whose term would expire the latter part of April or early in May, 1862. The Confederate authorities had considered this circumstance carefully, and saw, if they disbanded the regiments as their time expired, that the cause of the Confederacy would be hopelessly lost. A general conscription was promptly decided upon, as recommended to the Confederate Congress in a special message from the President, and a general conscript act was passed by that body about the middle of April, 1862. By the terms of this act, all soldiers between the ages of eighteen and forty-five were to be retained in the service to the close of the war. Such soldiers as were over forty-five or under eighteen years of age were to be discharged, and a bounty was offered to all such for re-enlistment. The commissioned officers had the privilege of resigning, and to all who were not included in the catalogue of exemption, a certain time was given them to choose the branch of service they were to enter.

The same provision that applied to soldiers applied also to civilians, and enrolling officers were to be appointed in each civil district to enforce these provisions. To the civilians, the exemption included all civil officers, physicians, ministers of the gospel, millers, shoe-makers, blacksmiths, all government employes, and school-teachers in actual employment as such. This placed an armed force in every neighborhood. These enrolling officers and their men gathered up the people and sent them to the army, and the ranks were recruited in this manner.

Many saw the approach of the conscript officer and enlisted. Such men made good soldiers. Of the conscript force, the majority went under protest. Of this number there were few effective soldiers. Some fought well in the different battles, and many deserted at the first opportunity and persistently avoided all participation in the war. To look after this class required the services of efficient soldiers, and with this class of recruits the rolls were enlarged and the Confederate ranks nominally strengthened, but practically weakened.

The conscript act had reference, first, to the army, and required the reorganization of all the forces, by virtue of the following order:

General Order) HEAD-QUARTERS WESTERN DEPARTMENT,)
No. 39. }   CORINTH, MISS., May 6, 1862. }

I. In pursuance of the provisions of an act of the Confederate Congress, entitled "An Act to further provide for the public defense," all regiments, battalions, squadrons, and companies of twelve-month volunteers of this army, will proceed to organize by electing their proper company and field officers. This election the several brigade commanders will cause to be held within their respective brigades at 12 meridian on the 8th inst., except in regiments, or battalions, on picket or outpost service, which will hold elections as soon as relieved.

II. The form of election and certifying these elections will conform, as far as practicable, with the laws of the State from which the men, or a major part thereof, may come; and in all cases where the field officers are elected by the company officers, the latter shall be first chosen.

III. All certificates of election will be forwarded through these head-quarters to the Adjutant-general's office at Richmond. Officers thus elected, upon receiving a copy of the certificate of their election, will immediately enter upon duty; and such as are not re-elected will be relieved from duty and their names forwarded by brigade commanders, through these head-quarters, to the War Department.

IV. In the elections herein directed no person who is to be discharged from the service under the provisions of this act will be allowed to take part.

V. In case any regiment, battalion, or company shall have been already duly reorganized, and elections held in accordance with the provisions of this act, new elections will not be required.

VI. The commanding general regards it of the utmost importance at this juncture that only intelligent and capable officers should be elected by the men; none others are worthy to lead them; none others can do so creditably or safely. Therefore he will not recommend any one for commission by the President without said officer shall have been reported duly qualified by a board of three officers for the examination of all elected under this order.

VII. These boards will require all officers to be of good physical and mental ability and of fair moral character. All field officers must be able to maneuver or drill a battalion in the "School of the Battalion," and be found acquainted with the "Articles of War," and the "Army Regulations" touching their duties, especially in the camp, on the march, and on outpost service, as prescribed from these head-quarters. And all company officers must be able to drill a company in the "School of the Company" and "Soldier," and be acquainted with the duties of a company officer and officer of the guard, as prescribed in the Army Regulations.

VIII. Boards for the examination of field officers will be appointed by corps or division commanders, and for company officers, by brigade commanders.

By command of General Beauregard.

THOMAS JORDAN, *Assistant Adjutant-general.*

The conscript act and the order to reorganize under its provisions caused some dissatisfaction among the troops. The men of the Sixteenth Tennessee Regiment had made arrangement to enter the cavalry service at the expiration of their twelve months, and had bought their equipments at Mobile. They murmured at the thought of being placed at the mercy of arbitrary power that would assume such absolute control of their liberties. They soon came to realize that the conscript law was an act of desperation, and unless it was enforced the Confederacy would be forced to surrender the cause. It was soon ascertained that the majority of the commissioned officers intended to remain with their men, and they (the men) then became reconciled to the situation, and proceeded to reorganize the regiment.

The following officers were elected at the reorganization:

FIELD AND STAFF.

John H. Savage, Colonel;
D. M. Donnell, Lieutenant-colonel;
P. H. Coffee, Major;
John R. Paine, Adjutant;
Thomas W. Leak, Surgeon;
Charles K. Mauzy, Assistant Surgeon;
Frank Marchbanks, Quarter-master;
James Brown, Commissary.

In the absence of a regular regimental chaplain, the religious services were conducted by the Rev. M. B. De Witt, Chaplain of the Eighth Tennessee Regiment.

The following company officers were elected:

COMPANY A.
L. N. Savage .... Captain.
R. B. Anderson .... First Lieutenant.
G. L. Talley .... Second Lieutenant.
W. C. Potter .... Third Lieutenant.

COMPANY B.
J. H. L. Duncan .... Captain.
E. W. Walker .... First Lieutenant.
John K. Ensey .... Second Lieutenant.
W. H. Fisher .... Third Lieutenant.

COMPANY C.
D. C. Spurlock .... Captain.
E. C. Read .... First Lieutenant.
Cicero Spurlock .... Second Lieutenant.
J. L. Thompson .... Third Lieutenant.

COMPANY D.
J. G. Lamberth .... Captain.
William White .... First Lieutenant.
F. M. York .... Second Lieutenant.
H. L. Brown .... Third Lieutenant.

COMPANY E.

J. J. Womack	Captain.
J. K. P. Webb	First Lieutenant.
B. P. Green	Second Lieutenant.
Jesse Walling	Third Lieutenant.

COMPANY F.

John B. Vance	Captain.
W. W. Baldwin	First Lieutenant.
D. G. Pointer	Second Lieutenant.
W. W. Wallace	Third Lieutenant.

COMPANY G.

A. T. Fisher	Captain.
W. L. Woods	First Lieutenant.
A. Fisk	Second Lieutenant.
James R. Fisher	Third Lieutenant.

COMPANY H.

James M. Parks	Captain.
W. G. Etter	First Lieutenant.
H. L. Hayes	Second Lieutenant.
John Akeman	Third Lieutenant.

COMPANY I.

Ben Randals	Captain.
James Worthington	First Lieutenant.
S. D. Mitchell	Second Lieutenant.
Denny Cummings	Third Lieutenant.

COMPANY K.

D. T. Brown	Captain.
W. D. Turlington	First Lieutenant.
J. Ed. Rotan	Second Lieutenant.
Wm. Lowry.	Third Lieutenant.

This constituted the reorganization of the Sixteenth Tennessee Regiment, which was effected at Corinth, May 8, 1862. These officers led the men of the Sixteenth Tennessee during the siege of Corinth and on the memorable retreat to Tupelo. Some changes were subsequently made where vacancies were filled by promotions, which will be duly noted in another part of this work.

The army remained at Tupelo during the months of June and July. Memphis had fallen into the hands of the Federals. A similar fate had attended New Orleans. The Federal gun-boats had approached Baton Rouge from below, and were threatening Vicksburg from above. The Federal army had dispersed to other points, and the Western Department of Bragg's army had returned to the Trans-Mississippi Department.

General Bragg had placed his army in shape for an aggressive movement into Kentucky. The object of this movement was threefold. First, it would cause the Federal army to evacuate Tennessee; second, it would enable him to recruit his army in Tennessee and Kentucky; and third, it would enable him to gather supplies of such articles as were becoming scarce in the Confederacy. The whole army having been thoroughly reorganized and equipped for the campaign, General Bragg sent his wagon trains to Chattanooga early in July, and on the 21st of the month he began to send his troops to that point on the cars. On July 22, the Sixteenth Tennessee Regiment took the cars at Tupelo and proceeded to Mobile, thence by way of Montgomery and Atlanta, and arrived at Chattanooga on the 27th. The whole army was being gathered at Chattanooga as fast as the railroads could transport the troops. General Bragg encamped his army to the east of Chattanooga, at the western base of Missionary Ridge, and remained in this encampment for a few weeks. Many of the Tennessee troops were approaching their homes, and were met at Chattanooga by relatives and friends, who brought them supplies of different kinds from home.

On August 17, Bragg commenced his forward movement from Chattanooga. Crossing the Tennessee river at this point, he moved forward a few miles and encamped for a few days at a place known to the army as Stringer's. Proceeding northward from this point, he moved leisurely with his army till August 30, when he camped for two days at the foot of Walden's Ridge. At this place a detail of fifteen men was made from the Sixteenth Tennessee Regiment to recruit the battery. Volunteers came forward to fill the detail, and those men were permanently assigned to duty in the artillery.

Captain Randals' company of the Sixteenth was detailed to guard the wagon trains across Walden's Ridge and Cumberland Mountain, and proceeded in advance of the army. The army following the trains, passed through Pikeville September 1, crossed Cumberland Mountain, and encamped for a few days at the mouth of Cane Creek, on the west base of the Cumberland Mountain.

While encamped here, the families of the soldiers from Van Buren and White counties met them at this place with refreshments, and the boys enjoyed the occasion to the fullest. It was a great pleasure to meet with relatives and friends; besides, they were supplied bountifully with every thing that was good to eat. The boys who lived near by were granted a brief leave of absence to visit their homes, and to many the return to their camp was their permanent parting from their families and homes. Many of those men fell in the battle of Perryville shortly afterward.

On the morning of the 5th, the regiment arrived at

Sparta and encamped. At this point there was a general reunion of the White county boys of the regiment and their families and friends. On the 6th. the regiment left Sparta and proceeded to Gainesboro. The army moved on rapidly now. The men thought before this that they were moving on Nashville. It was now learned that Louisville was the objective point. The Federals in Tennessee were commanded by General Buell, who seemed completely deceived as to the intention of the Confederates. He had completely lost sight of Bragg after he crossed the Tennessee river. The Northern press seemed to know nothing of his whereabouts till he appeared with his army at Sparta. His plans now being understood by the Federals, they began to withdraw from Tennessee, and bore in the direction of Louisville.

It was Bragg's intention to strike the Louisville and Nashville Railroad north of Green river before Buell could arrive. To accomplish this his army crossed the Cumberland river near Gainesboro, and pressed onward by way of Tompkinsville and Glasgow, Ky., to Mumfordville, on the Louisville and Nashville Railroad. This point was garrisoned with 4,500 men under Colonel Wilder. Bragg invested the place on the night of September 16, and on the morning of the 17th the garrison surrendered. Bragg then moved up the railroad to Bacon Creek, where he learned that Buell was at Cave City, and he returned to Mumfordville with the intention of giving him battle. Bragg returned to Mumfordville on the morning of the 18th, and placed his army in shape for action. He spent the day in line, but Buell failed to appear.

The wounded were at Mumfordville, the result of a battle on the 15th. General Bragg had sent Chalmers's brigade from Glasgow to Mumfordville for the purpose of ascertaining the nature of the defenses and the strength of the enemy's forces. General Chalmers hastened to the point and drew up his brigade before the works. He was supported by a detachment of cavalry and two pieces of artillery. He was directed to make a feint movement in order to ascertain their strength. Either misconstruing the order or underestimating the enemy's strength and overestimating his own, he assaulted the Federal fort and his brigade was cut to pieces. The fort was almost impregnable to assault, and was defended by numbers superior to Chalmers's force. The result was that Chalmers's brigade was at once repulsed, with a loss of four hundred men. The wounded were being cared for at Mumfordville when Bragg returned, after its capture, to give battle to Buell.

After spending the day at Mumfordville, it was ascertained that Buell had determined to avoid battle at Mumfordville and to hasten on to Louisville. Accordingly, he set out on the evening of September 18 with his whole army, and Bragg moved at the same time to Bacon Creek. During the night of the 18th and throughout the day on the 19th, the two opposing armies seemed to be running a race. They moved side by side, with scarcely a dozen miles intervening. In this manner the march was kept up till September 20. Bragg had moved along the Louisville and Nashville Railroad, and Buell moved on the dirt road running parallel, and from ten to fifteen miles to the west of the railroad. By this time it was learned that Buell had gained some advantage in distance, and when Bragg learned that Buell would be the first to Louisville, he abandoned his intentions on the city from his present route.

He now left the railroad and proceeded to Bardstown, where he arrived about September 25. The army was encamped near Bardstown for several days. On October 4, Buell came out from Louisville with his whole army, and moved on Bardstown. Bragg moved out on the morning of the 5th, and passing Fredericksburg and Springfield, encamped for the -night, and proceeded on the 6th by way of Perryville to Danville, where his army was encamped for the night. On the morning of the 7th, the Confederates resumed their march and arrived at Harrodsburg about 3 o'clock in the afternoon. Encamping near the place, the men prepared their rations and had every thing ready to march by 8 o'clock in the evening. Buell had appeared before Perryville, and the determination was established by General Bragg to give him battle at that point. It was twelve miles from Harrodsburg to Perryville.

Bragg's army was put in motion on the night of the 7th, and returned to Perryville about midnight. Hardee's corps was placed in front of Perryville, and Polk's corps was placed upon an elevation behind the town, and held as a reserve. Early on the morning of the 8th the enemy engaged the skirmish lines in Hardee's front. The skirmishing increased as the day advanced, and merged into a regular artillery duel. The Federals had superior numbers. Bragg's army consisted of Polk's and Hardee's corps. Buell's army was forced to operate under great disadvantages. The country roundabout was destitute of water. Being a high limestone region, and a severe drouth prevailing at the time, the creeks and branches were all dry. Bragg's army had exhausted the supply of water during its retreat, and Buell following immediately after him found it very difficult to obtain water for his men. This was the situation at Perryville on the morning of October 8, 1862. The Chaplin Creek runs through the center of the town. At this time there was no water in the channel of this creek about the town. Two miles below Perryville there was a depression in the channel of the creek. This depression was about two hundred yards long, the width of the entire channel, and filled with water to the depth of from two to four feet. When Buell became aware of the existence of this pool of water and a spring near by, he resolved to shift the scene of operations to this point. Sending a couple of infantry regiments in this direction, he continued to engage Hardee's skirmish lines and bore in the direction of the spring. In the afternoon he commenced moving his whole army to the left. Polk was ordered to counteract this movement. Some Texas cavalry charged the advance-guard of two regiments about the time of their arrival at the spring and drove them back. Polk's corps was hurried to the right. Hastening down the Chaplin at a double-quick, it was formed in line of battle near the spring before mentioned. The enemy's advance having been checked by the Texas cavalry, formed a line of battle in double column about eight hundred yards from the top of the bluff, on the west bank of the Chaplin and on the east side of a hill. Polk's corps appeared before the bluff. Ascending the bluff in line of battle, by brigades, the top was gained with difficulty. Donelson's brigade was the first to gain the top of the heights. The enemy was posted in their front, in double column, eight hundred yards distant. The men were given a moment to rest at the top of the bluff, and the word "Forward" was given. The men obeyed with a yell. For six hundred yards the ground was irregular, and having stone fences running in different directions, the men scaled them without difficulty. At this point there was a slight trough-like depression in the ground, running parallel with the enemy's lines. As the Sixteenth Tennessee approached the lowest point of this depression the enemy opened a murderous fire upon them with musketry and artillery from right, left, and front. The ranks of the Sixteenth Regiment were mowed down at a fearful rate, and the Fifteenth Regiment also suffered severely. The ranks closed up and the brigade pressed onward in the charge. Colonel Savage was with his men directing their movements as calmly as if it had been a regimental drill.

As the Fifteenth and Sixteenth Tennessee Regiments moved up the hill and came nearer to the enemy, the fight grew more and more desperate. Heavy charges of grape and canister were hurled into their ranks from the front and on the flanks. Stewart's brigade now came up and formed on the left of Donelson's brigade, by which support the Fifteenth Tennessee was partially relieved of the severe cross-fire upon its left wing. Buell was still bearing to his left, and a heavy force was now massed in front, and on the right of the Sixteenth Tennessee Regiment. The enemy bending his line around the right flank of the Sixteenth Tennessee Regiment near an old log cabin, an enfilading fire of musketry and artillery was poured into its ranks; yet the regiment held its ground for half an hour, when Maney's brigade came up and formed on its right. General Maney charged this flanking party of the enemy, and swung it around on its main line, forming an angle in the shape of the letter V. This opened the way for artillery, which was hurried to the scene, and planted at the point of the angle. The battle on the right now raged with fury, and the slaughter was terrible. The enemy finally yielded this line and fell back to a lane at the top of the hill, about three hundred yards distant. In this lane he reformed his lines and planted his batteries. The Confederates were prompt to appropriate every inch of ground which they gained from the enemy, and were quickly pouring destructive volleys into his ranks along the lane. The enemy contested this ground stubbornly. The Confederates pressed the assault with vigor. The enemy, after losing several of his guns and many valuable officers, including two brigadier-generals,* yielded this line about sundown, and the battle ended for the day. The enemy retired to a timbered region about three miles from their first line of the evening. The Confederates held the field at night, and had gained a decided victory.

The losses on both sides had been heavy, and the battle, for the number of men and the length of time engaged, was the severest of the war. The Sixteenth Tennessee lost over two hundred men. The Eighth Tennessee suffered severely, as did also the Fifteenth Tennessee, of Donelson's, and the First Tennessee, of Maney's brigades. The Sixteenth Tennessee engaged the Thirty-third Ohio, and subsequently the Seventh Ohio, which was commanded by Colonel Oscar F. Moore.

Colonel Savage received two wounds early in the fight, and had his horse shot under him, but he remained on the field till the issue was decided. Late in the evening he became exhausted from loss of blood. Dr. Charles K. Mauzy, Surgeon of the Six-

---

* Webster and Terrell.

teenth Tennessee Regiment, dressed his wound, and Dr. Cross, the brigade chaplain, procured quarters for him in a farm-house, and attended him through the night. The Federal general, Jackson, was killed by Savage's men. A Federal colonel was brought in a prisoner, and severely wounded. This man proved to be Colonel Oscar F. Moore, said to be of the Seventh Ohio, and was personally acquainted with Colonel Savage in the United States Congress. He told Colonel Savage that his regiment had suffered severely, and had lost near half its number. Colonel Savage told the Federal officer the same of his own regiment. The two regiments had engaged each other through the day. Both had suffered greatly, and the commander of each regiment was wounded, and one a prisoner. Colonel Savage assured Colonel Moore that he should have the best attention that it was in his power to bestow, and ordered the surgeons and attendants to bestow upon Colonel Moore the same attention they would bestow upon one of their own men. General Jackson and Colonel Savage had known each other in public life.

The wounded were cared for as well as the circumstances would allow. All who could travel were sent to Harrodsburg. Those not able to bear transportation were taken to the farm-houses of the neighborhood, where hospitals were established.

General Bragg withdrew his army early in the morning and returned to Harrodsburg. From Harrodsburg he retreated to Camp Dick Robertson, and thence to Knoxville. The wounded were left in the field hospitals and fell into the hands of the enemy. The dead were left on the field unburied. The enemy buried their own dead, but left the Confederate dead, which lay upon the field for four days. They were then partially buried by the people of Perryville and vicinity. The ground was very hard and they were just merely covered up, and remained thus for six or eight weeks, when they were gathered up by the good people of the place and decently buried in one common grave-yard. Those who died of wounds were buried in the cemeteries at Harrodsburg and Perryville. The people of Perryville afforded every assistance in their power to the suffering of either army. As the Confederate wounded recovered they were paroled and sent to Vicksburg for exchange.

CHAPTER III.

BATTLE OF MURFREESBORO.

General Bragg's army now returned to Middle Tennessee. The troops were transported on the cars to Chattanooga, from which place they marched to Bridgeport and thence to Tullahoma. The railroad bridge was rebuilt at Bridgeport, and General Bragg was then able to bring supplies by railroad.

After the retreat from Kentucky, target practice was instituted with a view to ascertaining who were the picked marksmen of the army. J. D. Phillips, of Company A, Sixteenth Tennessee, won the prize, which was a Whitworth rifle, of accurate range at three thousand yards. These guns were charged to the men at $1,500 each, and were used for sharp-shooting purposes.

The Confederates now advanced in the direction of Nashville and encamped near Murfreesboro. Many of the Tennessee troops received furloughs and visited their homes. Being now in their own country, many of the soldiers received the benefits of supplies from home. The Confederate encampment was visited daily by the relatives and friends of the soldiers, and during the month of December the army recuperated, and was now in readiness for further operations upon the enemy.

The Federals were around Nashville under command of General Rosecrans, who was being re-enforced, and was preparing for an aggressive movement upon the Confederates about Murfreesboro. The Confederate outposts extended to Lavergne, and the cavalry made frequent reconnoisance in front to Antioch, on the railroad, and to Dogtown, on Mill Creek. Rosecrans moved out from Nashville during the latter part of December. As his lines advanced, his outposts were engaged by the Confederate cavalry and infantry, who gradually fell back in the direction of Murfreesboro. On December 30, 1862, the Confederate lines were established in front of Murfreesboro, and Rosecrans had placed his army in battle array a few miles to the Confederate front. A general skirmishing and cannonading was kept up all day during December 30, during which time each army was maneuvering its forces with a view to obtaining the advantage of position. Hardee's corps occupied the left wing of Bragg's army and Polk's corps occupied the right wing. Cheatham's division was on the right of Polk's corps; Donelson's brigade was on the right of the division, and the Sixteenth Tennessee Regiment was on the right of the brigade, and with two companies of the regiment extending across the railroad. The Sixteenth Tennessee was on the extreme right of the Confederate lines during the first day's battle. Breckinridge's division was placed behind Stone's river, on Cheatham's right, as a reserve, and was not engaged on that part of the line during the first day's fight. General Bragg made a general attack on the Federal lines on the morning of December 31, and the battle continued through the day, with heavy losses on both sides, but no definite advantage to either at the close of the day.

The Federals bore to their left during the first day's fight, and seemed determined to turn the Confederate right wing. This made the battle desperate in Cheatham's front, and especially on the extreme right on the railroad track. This part of the field was held by Savage's regiment, and was considered by the commanding general to be the key to the position. The regiment held its ground at this point for three hours against fearful odds, until it was relieved by General Adams's brigade.

On the morning of January 1, Rosecrans had succeeded in massing a heavy force upon an elevation on the Confederate right wing. Breckinridge was ordered to attack this point on the Federal lines, which he did on the morning of January 1, but was repulsed with heavy loss. The position was a very strong one, and Breckinridge's forces were inferior to the Federals in point of numbers.

It was now ascertained that Rosecrans had gained a decided advantage over the Confederates in the way of position, and having been re-enforced to numbers by far the superior of the Confederates, Bragg saw at once his inability to hold his position, and a retreat was ordered. The Confederates withdrew to Shelbyville and Tullahoma.

The battle of Murfreesboro had been a severe and desperate conflict. The Tennessee troops fought with desperation, because they felt that they were fighting for their homes. The Sixteenth Tennessee Regiment lost two hundred and five men in killed, wounded, and missing. The regiment held the most critical position on the field, and the manner in which it defended its position, and performed the responsible and arduous duty assigned it, is more fully described in the official report of General Donelson, a few extracts from which we give below:

> The brigade was composed of the following regiments and battery, viz.: The Sixteenth Regiment Tennessee Volunteers, Colonel John H. Savage; the Thirty-eighth Regiment Tennessee Volunteers, Colonel John C. Carter; the Fifty-first Regiment Tennessee Volunteers, Colonel John Chester; the Eighth Regiment Tennessee Volunteers, Colonel W. L. Moore; the Eighty-fourth Regiment Tennessee Volunteers, Colonel S. S. Stanton; and Captain Carnes's battery. The Eighty-fourth Regiment, being a new and very small regiment, was assigned to my command on the morning of the 29th of December, 1862, only two days before the battle.
>
> In obedience to orders, the tents were struck and the wagons packed and sent to the rear Sunday night, December 27. At daylight Monday morning the brigade was moved to and assumed its line of battle, which was second and supporting to the first line of battle—two companies of Colonel Savage's, the right regiment, extending across the railroad, and Colonel Carter's, the left regiment, across the Wilkerson pike, its left resting on the right of Stewart's brigade. This line of battle, with General Chalmers's brigade in front, which mine was to support, was formed on the brow of the hill, about three hundred yards in a south-east direction from the white house, known as Mrs. Jones's. That position was retained under an occasional shelling, with but few casualties, until dark Tuesday evening, when, in obedience to orders from Lieutenant-general Polk, the brigade was moved forward to the front line to relieve General Chalmers's brigade, which had already held that position for three days and nights. . . . . The brigade had occupied the front line behind Chalmers's breastworks but a few minutes when General Chalmers having received a severe wound, his brigade was broken, and the greater portion of it fell back in disorder and confusion. Under orders from Lieutenant-general Polk, I immediately advanced my brigade to its support, and, indeed, to its relief, under a shower of shot and shell of almost every description. During this advance my horse was shot under me, from which, and another wound received at the Cowan House, he died during the day. In ad-

vancing upon and attacking the enemy under such a fire, my brigade found it impossible to preserve its alignment, because of the walls of the burnt house, known as Cowan's, and the yard and garden fence and picketing left standing around and about it; in consequence of which Savage's regiment, with three companies of Chester's regiment, went to the right of the Cowan. House, and advanced upon the enemy until they were checked by three batteries of the enemy, with a heavy infantry support, on the hill to the right of the railroad; while the other two regiments—Carter's and Moore's—with seven companies of Chester's regiment, went to the left of that house through a most destructive cross-fire, both of artillery and small arms, driving the enemy and sweeping every thing before them, until they arrived at the open field beyond the cedar brake in a north-west direction from the Cowan House. .... Colonel Savage's regiment held, in my judgment, the most critical position of that part of the field—unable to advance and determined not to retire. Having received a message from Lieutenant-general Polk that I should in a short time be re-enforced and properly supported, I ordered Colonel Savage to hold his position at all hazards, and I felt it my duty to remain with that part of the brigade holding so important and hazardous a position as that occupied by him. Colonel Savage, finding the line he had to defend entirely too long for the number of men under his command, and that there was danger of his being flanked, either to the right or left, as the one or the other wing presented the weaker front, finally threw out the greater part of his command as skirmishers, as well to deceive the enemy as to our strength in his rear as to protect his long line, and held his position with characteristic coolness and most commendable tenacity for over three hours. At the expiration of that time, Jackson's brigade came up to my support; but instead of going to the right of the Cowan House and to the support of Colonel Savage, it went to the left of the house, and over the ground which the two left regiments and seven companies of my brigade had gone over. After Jackson's, General Adams's brigade came up to the support of Colonel Savage, when the latter withdrawing his regiment to make way for it, it attacked the enemy with spirit for a short time, but it was soon driven back in disorder and confusion, Colonel Savage's regiment retreating with it. . . . . .

The field officers, Colonels Savage, Carter, Chester, Anderson, and Major Cotter, all distinguished themselves by the coolness and courage displayed upon the field, and greatly contributed to the success achieved by their respective commands, by the skill with which they managed and maneuvered them. . . . . . .

. We have to mourn the loss of many gallant officers and brave men, who fell in the faithful discharge of their duty on the field of battle. Captain L. N. Savage, acting lieutenant-colonel, and Captain Womack, acting major of the Sixteenth Regiment, were severely, if not mortally, wounded, and Captain Spurlock, of the same regiment, an excellent officer and most estimable gentleman, was killed. . . . . . The long list of casualties shows how closely the field was contested, and how bravely the regiment held its important position on the most critical part of the battle-field.

REPORT OF COLONEL JOHN H. SAVAGE.

JANUARY 8, 1863.

SIR:—The following report of the conduct of the Sixteenth Tennessee Regiment at the battle before Murfreesboro, December 31, 1862, is respectfully submitted:

When the advance was ordered, my regiment being the right of Cheatham's division, I was ordered by General Donelson (through his aid, Captain Bradford) to move along the railroad, put two companies to its right and eight on its left, taking the guide to the right. The advance was made under a heavy cannonade, and the line of battle and direction maintained, although serious obstructions impeded the march. The eight companies to the left advanced between the railroad and the turnpike, in front of the Cowan House, without the slightest protection, engaging a battery and the enemy's infantry in the woods, at a distance of less than one hundred and fifty yards. The companies to the right advanced through a stalk-field to the edge of a cotton patch. Here the enemy opened a heavy fire at short range, from a line extending to the right as far as I could see. This killed Captain Spurlock, who fell while leading his men in the most gallant manner.

At this moment it seemed to me that I was without the expected support on my left, and that the line had divided and gone off in that direction. My men shot the horses and gunners of the battery in front, but I could not advance without being outflanked and captured by the enemy on my right. I, therefore, ordered them to halt and fire. In a few moments my acting lieutenant-colonel, L. N. Savage, fell by my side supposed mortally wounded, and my acting major, Captain J. J. Womack, had his right arm badly broken.

There were batteries to the right and left of the railroad which literally swept the ground. The men maintained the fight against superior numbers with great spirit and obstinacy. The left companies being very near and without any protection, sustained a heavy loss. Thirty men were left dead upon the spot where they halted, dressed in perfect line of battle. It was, on the day following, a sad spectacle, speaking more eloquently for the discipline and courage of the men than any words I could employ.

Here the Thirty-ninth North Carolina came up in my rear, and I ordered it into line of battle on my right, but before it got into position the lieutenant-colonel was shot down and was carried from the field. Under the command of Captain ———, it continued under my command and did good service until driven from this position, after which I lost sight of it.

Seeing a heavy force of the enemy crossing a field to my right and rear, I ordered the line to fall back to the river, and formed two lines to the front and right. To cover this space the men were deployed as skirmishers. I also ordered formed a portion of Blythe's Mississippi regiment that had collected near the railroad, and was joined by Lieutenants J. J. Williamson and T. W. McMurry, Fifty-first Regiment, with three companies, who continued with me and did good service. This force checked and drove back the enemy advancing up the river, and a column that attempted to cut off my whole party along the railroad.

Lieutenant R. B. Anderson, of the Sixteenth, a valuable officer, while directing the skirmishers, was dangerously wounded and carried under the river bank by privates Thompson and Adcock, all of whom were captured by the enemy in his subsequent advance.

When Adams's brigade advanced I drew back my little force to let it move to the front, which it did in gallant style, but only for a short distance, when it broke and fled in confusion. Most of the men I had been controlling moved with it.

I collected the men of the Sixteenth and Fifty-first and moved to the front, *en echelon*, of Chalmers's position, and remained during the heavy cannonade on the enemy. While here two of my men were killed by a shell.

I afterward moved, in connection with Colonel Stanton, near the burnt gin-house, and halting the regiment, went on foot to my first line of battle. About dark I sent a party after the body of Captain Spurlock, which captured a Yankee captain from his lines.

I claim for my command great gallantry in action; that it engaged and held in check superior forces of the enemy, who were attempting to turn our right forces, that afterward drove Adams's and Preston's brigades.

My flag-bearer, Sergeant Maberry, was disabled early in the charge. The flag was afterward borne by private Womack, who was also wounded. The flag-staff was broken and hit with balls in three places—the flag literally shot to pieces. The fragments were brought to me at midnight.

I carried about 400 officers and men into action. The killed amounted to 36—the killed, wounded, and missing to 205, a list of which is forwarded. My men did not strip or rob the dead.

The conduct of my recruits was most honorable. Many of them fell in the front rank beside the veteran soldier of the Sixteenth. It is difficult to make distinction where all act well. While others deserve nobly, I feel that I ought not to fail to notice the courage and good conduct of private Hackett, whom I placed in command of the company after the fall of Captain Spurlock.

I am, Major, very respectfully,   JOHN H. SAVAGE,
    Colonel Commanding Sixteenth Tennessee Regiment.
Major J. G. MARTIN, *A. A. G.*

The following is a complete list of the killed and wounded of the Sixteenth Regiment Tennessee Volunteers in the engagement before Murfreesboro, as shown by the report of Thomas B. Porter, Acting Adjutant of the regiment at the time of, and during, the battle, December 31, 1862:

FIELD AND STAFF.

Dangerously Wounded—Captain L. N. Savage, Acting Lieutenant-colonel; Captain J. J. Womack, Acting Major.

COMPANY A.

Killed—Sergeant J. H. Warren; Privates E. League, F. G. Kersey, Lee Patterson. *Wounded*—First Lieutenant R. B. Anderson, Corporals John A. Moore, R. M. Martin; Privates W. A. Hallum, John Mason, dangerous; S. Anderson, M. T. Dozier, J. A. Briggs, Isaac Cantrell, Peter Cantrell, A. J. Kersey, T. Parsley, slight. *Missing*—Second Lieutenant G. W. Witt, Sergeant J. R. Thompson; Privates W. E. Adcock, John Cantrell, L. D. Cantrell, T. M. Hooper, T. J. Harper, E. Lockhart.

COMPANY B.

Wounded—F. M. Church, T. H. Douglas, mortally; James Fuller, W. B. Campbell, L. P. Campbell, severe; W. C. King, slight.

COMPANY C.

Killed—Captain D. C. Spurlock. *Wounded*—Privates B. D. Bybee, mortally; T. M. Brown, J. K. P. Martin, severely; S. H. Alexander, R. H. Henderson, D. W. King, M. D. Smith, J. J. Hensley, J. W. Smith, James Hobbs, R. W. Morrow, slight.

COMPANY D.

Killed—Privates M. S. Edwards, S. Gribble, A. P. Gribble, A. J. Gribble, W. Perry, James Rowland, W. F. Smith. *Wounded*—Walter Cope, J. P. Douglas, J. J. Higginbotham, Thomas Hutson, J. S. McGee, Richmond McGregor, J. K. P. Nichols, B. M. Rowland, Lycurgus Smith, J. J. Templeton, W. J. Ware, T. F. West, severe; Second Lieutenant J. P. A. Hennessee, Brevet Second Lieutenant F. M. York, Sergeant T. F. Martin; Privates W. B. Christian, S. C. Gribble, J. A. Gribble, A. Higginbotham, J. D. Lusk, John McGregor, R. G. Martin, W. M. Moulder, W. T. Perry, John Quick, G. W. Somers, J. B. Smith, J. Templeton, slight. *Missing*—J. F. Moulder, W. H. Edwards.

COMPANY E.

Killed—Sergeant Michael Mauzy; Privates David Bonner, Elias Womack. *Wounded*—Private A. Douglas, Corporal Vanhooser, Corporal James Kirby, mortal; First Lieutenant Jesse

Walling, Color Sergeant W. T. Mabry; Private G. N. Clark, severe; Sergeants J. B. Womack, A. M. Mason; Privates Luke Purser, John Purser, Isaiah Moffitt, G. M. Wallace, A. J. Vanhooser, J. S. Womack, John Green, Randolph Laurence, William Laurence, Lawson Cantrell, slight.

COMPANY F.

Killed—Sergeant Jacob Choate, Corporal John Laycock; Privates James Murray, John Brown, James Noe, John Choate, Joseph Y. Ballard. *Wounded*—First Lieutenant W. W. Wallace, Fifth Sergeant John H. Nichols; Private J. Y. Carroll, severe; First Sergeant T. C. Bledsoe, Corporal C. A. Ballard; Privates James Pleasant, William Webb, John Haggard, R. F. Owens, J. F. Owens, W. N. Caruthers, James Mathis, slight.

COMPANY G.

Killed—Corporal Ben Huchins; Privates J. P. Cantrell, R. P. Moore. *Wounded*—John Fisher, T. L. Hodges, mortal; P. B. Franks, W. Hasty, J. B. Moore, severe; Second Lieutenant A. Fisk, Brevet Second Lieutenant James Fisher, Corporal John Meggerson, Corporal A. Perry; Privates John Atnip, T. A. Cotton, M. D. Fisher, E. M. Greenfield, A. Huchins, R. B. Love, James Hasty, J. M. Pollard, John Stricklin, T. Wiggins, J. W. Wright, A. J. Youngblood. *Missing*—J. L. Britton.

COMPANY H.

Killed—Corporal J. R. Jones; Privates John Estes, H. Pennington, Frank Smith, William Tallent. *Wounded*—First Sergeant John Hughes; Privates T. J. Davis, James Jones, severe; Captain J. M. Parks; Privates John Brown, J. N. Clendennon, Jo Fern, M. Hayes, Aaron Hughes, A. J. Jordan, Ed Parsley, W. A. Russell, W. S. Bullen, slight. *Missing*—John Davis.

COMPANY I.

Killed—Privates Henderson Rhodes, Peter Baker, Marion Priest. *Wounded*—J. C. Moore, Isham Hollansworth, W. J. Underwood, mortal; Sergeants N. B. Hambrick, S. R. York; Privates Thomas Rawlings, Sam Porter, William T. Worthington, severe; Sergeant Sam Worthington, W. R. Paine; Privates S. L. Fleming, C. W. Mooneyham, Sol Porter, G. W. Stype, J. M. Thomasson, Joshua Worley, Shelby Walling, slight.

COMPANY K.

Killed—Elisha Martin, Marshall Capps. *Wounded*—Josh Worldley, John Castile, T. J. Templeton, mortal; Second Lieutenant William Lowry; Privates A. D. Nash, Sylvester Humphreys, James Carland, severe; Sergeants W. G. Simms, J. W. Wilson, D. L. Hensley; Corporals S. M. Snodgrass, Ben Lack; Privates Boyle Pasly, John Bathurs, Gardner Green, Elbert Capps. *Missing*—William Hodges, J. W. White.

Recapitulation—Killed, 36; wounded, 155; missing, 14—total, 205. The regiment mustered 360 men for duty at the beginning of the action.

After the battle of Murfreesboro General Bragg withdrew his army to Tullahoma, and Cheatham's division was ordered to Shelbyville, where it did nothing during the remainder of the winter and spring, except build fortifications. Affairs in both armies remained quiet till June following.

During the following spring General Donelson was promoted to the rank of major-general and assigned to duty in East Tennessee. Colonel Savage was considered the senior colonel of the brigade, and of unquestioned ability, and his men thought he was the one to be promoted. They were surprised to see one whom they thought to be a junior in rank and age placed over him in the command of the brigade. This was an unlooked-for indignity, which Colonel Savage resented severely, and accordingly sent in his resignation, which was accepted in due time, and he accordingly bid adieu to his regiment in the following address:

> HEAD-QUARTERS SIXTEENTH REGIMENT
> TENNESSEE VOLUNTEERS,
> March 6, 1863.

Soldiers of the Sixteenth—My Friends and Companions in Arms:—Nothing but a sense of duty could have forced me to the step which I have taken. When the government selected a junior to command me, it thereby decided that I had not done well in the command of my regiment. Not tired of the war or less devoted to the cause, but it is improper that I should continue in a service where equality is denied me. It is true I did not ask the government for promotion, neither did I ask for the commanders they gave me. In the occurrence which forces me to retire may be seen the hand of a distinguished politician, who stands almost as high in public favor as Andrew Johnson once did, and whose evil offices toward me are as old as my races with Pickett and Stokes.

If selfishness or ambition controlled my conduct, I should at the beginning of the war have asked to have been made a general; but believing one good regiment worth many brigadiers, devotion to the cause, and gratitude to my old friends, induced me to take their children under my charge to protect their lives and honor, and to teach them to be soldiers.

As a regiment, I am proud of you; your friends at home are, and your State has cause so to be. If not the first, your deeds upon the field proclaim you the equal of any regiment in the service. In Virginia and South Carolina you were never off duty, and none dare say that any have done better. In the skirmishes around Corinth, you proved yourselves better soldiers and marksmen than the enemy; and when the retreat commenced, you remained three days upon the Tuscumbia, within six miles of Corinth, confronted by the enemy, and became the rear of the column, an honor that you have passed in silence, while it has been claimed in publications for several commands, brigadiers, and colonels.

On the bloody field of Perryville, far in advance of others, you began the attack on the part of Cheatham's division, which, followed up by the resistless courage of our brothers of this, Stewart's, and Maney's brigades, forever dispelled the cloud of slander and detraction that had darkened the fair fame of the soldiery of our State. The good people south of you never doubted the courage of Tennesseans, and henceforth cowards and miscreants will not dare assail them.

At Murfreesboro, you were the extreme right of our line of attack, and engaged the enemy's line of battle near the center, while your brigade marched to the left. Thus isolated and without protection, at a cost of more than half your numbers, you held in check for three hours the enemy's left wing, and it is believed, but for misfortune not your own, you would have maintained your ground to the last.

I mingle my tears with yours for the heroic dead, our brothers in arms, who sleep upon the fields of Perryville and Murfreesboro. We never can forget them, and they deserve to be remembered by the country.

If in my absence slander shall assail me, let no man believe that I can cease to care for your welfare or the rights of the Southern people. Character is worth more than money. Continue in the pathway of honor and duty, and if hereafter you shall meet the foe, emulate the deeds of former days, that your friends at home may still be proud of you.

My resignation having been accepted, I relinquish my command to the senior officer present, and bid you farewell, hoping that the Great Spirit may guide and protect you through the perils of the future. JOHN H. SAVAGE,
Colonel Sixteenth Tennessee.

The resignation of Colonel Savage having been accepted, the command of the regiment devolved upon Lieutenant-colonel D. M. Donnell, who now became colonel of the regiment by promotion. Captain D. T. Brown, of Company K, was lieutenant-colonel, and Major P. H. Coffee, having resigned on account of ill health, Captain H. H. Dillard, of Company F, became major of the regiment. Colonel Donnell was captain of Company C at the beginning of the war, and became lieutenant-colonel of the regiment at its reorganization at Corinth. In private life he was a teacher by profession, and at the beginning of the war was President of Cumberland Female College, at McMinnville, Tenn. As a soldier, he had no previous military record; as an officer, he was a strict and rigid disciplinarian, and as a gentleman, he was kind and generous. He was warmly and conscientiously devoted to the cause he had vowed to defend, and to the various duties his office imposed. He was zealously devoted to the comfort, the welfare, and efficiency of his men, and was thoroughly alive to their interests in every respect. The promotion gave satisfaction to the men of the regiment, who would have elected him to the position had opportunity offered. They had great confidence in the ability and integrity of Colonel Donnell, who now became Colonel Savage's successor, and they accorded to the new commander the same respect and obedience that had been so faithfully accorded to his illustrious predecessor.

The principal portion of Bragg's army was now at Tullahoma, though Cheatham's division and the greater portion of Polk's corps were at Shelbyville. The army devoted its time to drilling and fortifying in front of the Federal approaches. During the latter part of March the whole Confederate army was concentrated at Tullahoma, and remained till the first of May, when they returned to Shelbyville. About June 20, the Federals began their forward movement, and the Confederates retired to Tullahoma and took position behind the fortifications in front of the place. General Bragg expected at first that Rosecrans would attack him here, but he subsequently learned that it was the intention of the Federal general to flank the position, and accordingly the Confederates withdrew on the night of July 1.

On the morning of July 2, the old Sixteenth passed by their original camp of rendezvous at Camp Harris, near Estill Springs. Two years had elapsed since their departure from the place at the beginning of the war. The place looked natural to the boys, but the changes in the ranks of the companies had been so great! How many had been left behind on the battlefields of Perryville and Murfreesboro! How many had died of disease! The casualties of these two years had been great indeed, and the men looked sad as they passed by their first camping-ground.

The Confederates continued their retreat across the Tennessee river, and arrived at Chattanooga early in July. During this retreat Vicksburg had fallen into the hands of the enemy, by which the whole Mississippi river was now open to the enemy from its source to the Gulf. Other points had fallen into the enemy's hands. The Confederate soldiers began to grow dejected at the loss of so many strongholds, especially when they realized that a place once in the hands of the Federals was permanently lost. It seemed that Confederate history at this time was fast becoming a catalogue of reverses, and the Confederate soldier was growing weary of the many and prominent additions that were being constantly made to the list.

Beset with these feelings, the Confederates upon their arrival at Chattanooga encamped upon the same ground which they occupied the year before on the eve of their campaign into Kentucky. The men, discouraged by so many reverses, had begun to desert the Confederate ranks, and General Bragg had been punishing the evil with the severest penalties known to the Army Regulations. Quite a number of soldiers had been court-martialed and shot while the army was at Tullahoma and Shelbyville. These victims were principally from the Gulf States, though a few were from the border States. When the army arrived at Chattanooga there were quite a number under sentence and awaiting the day set for their execution.

General Bragg rested his army at Chattanooga during the months of July and August, during which time he strengthened the fortifications about the place. As important military movements were expected in the near future, the Confederate leader issued orders to liberate all who had charges preferred against them, except those under sentence of death, and recommended Executive clemency in their behalf. The Confederate authorities heeded his recommendation in general, and the sentence of death was revoked in many instances on the very eve of the hour set for the execution of the sentence, and the culprits were restored to their respective companies. Among the beneficiaries of this Executive clemency was private Hugh Whitehead, of Company F—a resident of Putnam county—the only culprit that was ever known from the ranks of the Sixteenth Tennessee Regiment. This man was partially demented and seemed to be utterly ignorant of the consequences of desertion.

General Bragg remained at Chattanooga and the Federals perfected their plans of operations. Longstreet's corps, consisting of Hood's and Hill's divisions, had been ordered to Bragg from Lee's army, but had not yet arrived.

CHAPTER IV.

BATTLES OF CHICKAMAUGA AND MISSIONARY RIDGE.

On September 6, the advance of Rosecrans's army appeared before Chattanooga and commenced shelling the town. The people were at church at the time and the Federals threw their shells in the vicinity of the church-house, to the great consternation of the worshipers and the citizens in general. The Federals placed a picket line along the north bank of the Tennessee about Chattanooga, which opened fire upon the lower part of town, about the ferry, and wounded the ferryman in his boat on the morning of September 6. General Bragg placed a picket line along the south bank in front, and above, Chattanooga, to the mouth of Chickamauga Creek. On the night of September 7, the writer had the misfortune to fall down the embankment, a distance of fifty feet, while operating upon this picket line. By good luck there was a raft of pine logs anchored to the bank of the river, which circumstance prevented him from receiving a good ducking, as well as a severe fall. Falling upon the rudder of the raft, it swung round and landed him upon the raft in safety and dry shod. The darkness of the night being intense, this accidental and improvised trapeze performance was not beheld by the Federals, who occupied the opposite bank of the river. The embankment, which was an angle of sixty degrees, was quickly ascended by pulling up by the canes and brush. In a few minutes the top was gained and nobody hurt.

The Federals kept up the bombardment of Chattanooga. General Bragg now resolved to withdraw from Chattanooga, and after drawing the Federals to the mountains of North Georgia, his plan was to turn upon them and defeat them. The sequel will show how well his plans were matured, and how far they were successful.

With Longstreet's corps added to Bragg's forces, he now had an army about equal to the army of Rosecrans, and the Confederates were well acquainted with the country. This gave the Confederates great hope of success. On September 8, Bragg withdrew his army from Chattanooga and retreated to Lee and Gordon's Mill, on the upper waters of Chickamauga Creek. Here he spent September 9. A column of the enemy having moved down McLemore's Cove, Bragg moved from Lee and Gordon's Mill to Lafayette, Ga., on the 10th, and on the 12th retured in the direction of Rock Spring Church. On the night of September 12, the army was on the march, and stopped in the road for a while. Being late in the night and the men very tired, they lay down along the roadside and were soon asleep. A caison of the battery getting out of order through the day, it had been stopped to be repaired, and was now hurrying up to rejoin the battery. In its hurry it missed the road and came clattering through the bushes where the boys of the Sixteenth Regiment were sleeping. The drivers were hurrying and yelling at their horses, and the noise and clatter being so violent and sudden, the men of the regiment began to arouse from their slumbers, and rushed pell-mell into the road, over the fences, and a general stampede was the consequence. Those who slept soundest were run over by the general rabble. Order was quickly restored as soon as the men became awake, and the march was resumed. The regiment arrived at Rock Spring Church on the 13th.

The Confederates maneuvered from one position to another during the 14th, 15th, 16th, 17th, and 18th of September. On the evening of the 18th, General Bragg's order was read to his troops announcing that he would engage the enemy on the following day. On the morning of the 19th, the army was drawn up and the order of battle established. Forrest had taken position on the right, Walker's division formed on Forrest's left, Cheatham's division formed on the left of Walker, each division swinging round from column into line by brigades. In this manner the engagement extended to the left. The battle opened about 2 o'clock in the afternoon of Saturday, September 19, 1863. Wright's brigade was on the left of the division, and the Sixteenth Regiment was on the left of the brigade, near Carnes's battery. General Wright misconstrued the order that announced the position of a front line of Confederates, with caution not to fire into it. With this understanding the brigade swung into line, with the battery on its left. The battery rushed right into the Federal lines, and, losing all its horses and half its men, was silenced. The brigade also rushed immediately into the line of the enemy, and received a broadside from his front line before the true situation of affairs was understood. A brisk and spirited engagement ensued. The ground was covered with an undergrowth of pines and brushwood. To the left was a slight valley, which was covered with a heavy timber growth, east of which were the hills of the north bank of Chickamauga Creek. This valley made a curve and discharged its waters into the creek. Longstreet appeared at the top of this hill about 2 o'clock in the evening, having marched from the railroad during the day. Hood's division, of Longstreet's corps, formed on Cheatham's left, and opened a tremendous assault upon the enemy's lines, which made them waver at first and finally give way. This caused the Federal lines to swing round at this place to some extent, and Carnes's battery was soon recovered. The engagement still extended to the left during the evening of the 19th, and before night, was general all along the line.

On Sunday morning, September 20, the battle was resumed by demonstrations at different points of the line. Rosecrans was seeking the most vulnerable point on Bragg's lines, while Bragg was maneuvering his forces for the same purpose on Rosecrans's lines. The forenoon was thus spent in maneuvering by each army, with experimental assaults from each side at different parts of the field. Bragg finally succeeded in finding the point on Rosecrans's line which he resolved to carry, and massed his troops accordingly. The point had been fortified by the Federals during the night, and being considered strong, Rosecrans had drawn off many of his troops from it to maneuver at other points, till this point was comparatively weakened in numbers. As soon as Rosecrans had penetrated Bragg's designs on this point, he began to strengthen the position by throwing other troops upon it. This position of the Federal lines was V shaped, with its point to the Confederates. Bragg struck this position, and his first assault failed. Rosecrans was now rushing every available man to the support of this, the key to his whole position, and which must not be given up. The Confederate general had proven himself the superior in the art of maneuvering.

In the second assault Breckinridge struck the right wing of the Federal stronghold and the line was broken. The exulting and victorious Confederates rushed over the fortifications. This part of the Federal lines not only yielded the position, but its wings were now driven in, and in one confused mass the flower of Rosecrans's army, thus jumbled together, threw down their arms and retreated pell-mell in the direction of Chattanooga, eighteen miles distant. The Confederates had gained a decisive victory and were masters of the field. The Federals had not only been defeated, but had been driven from the field in a confusion that partook of all the features of a rout. The backbone of the Federal line had been broken. Rosecrans's army had been cut in two, its center routed, its wings exposed, and the coolness and skill of Thomas alone saved its remnant from capture. Rosecrans retreated in disorder to Chattanooga on the night of the 20th, and the victorious Confederates followed on the 21st, and took possession of Missionary Ridge and Lookout Mountain. On the morning of September 22, General Bragg moved his army to the suburbs of Chattanooga, and Rosecrans was hemmed in the place, with his communications cut off, both by river and railroad. The two armies thus confronted each other for two months.

The battle of Chickamauga had been a severe and desperate one, and the losses had been severe on both sides. In this battle Brigadier-general Preston Smith was killed, also Brigadier-general Helm, of Kentucky, was killed, and General Hood lost a leg in the engagement of Sunday morning. The brigade not participating in the action of September 20, the losses of the Sixteenth Regiment were not so severe as in previous battles. Captain James M. Parks, of Company H, was killed in the engagement on Saturday evening. Captain Parks was an excellent officer, a good soldier, a gentleman, and a Christian. He was beloved by his comrades and all who knew him, and his loss was deeply mourned by his comrades in arms, his relatives, and friends. All who knew him respected and honored him as a gentleman of unimpeachable integrity and sterling merit. Private William Hodges, of Company F, was killed in Sunday's fight, and private Gardner Green, of Company K, lost a leg.

After the Confederates had besieged the Federals in Chattanooga, matters remained quiet in both armies till November following, when Rosecrans was superseded by Sherman, who raised the siege, and Bragg retreated to Dalton, where he spent the remainder of the winter.

The Confederate lines now extended around Chattanooga from the mouth of Chickamauga Creek above, to Moccasin Point below, the town. Rosecrans was completely besieged, and devoted himself to fortifying his lines, as an attack upon the town by the Confederates was expected any hour. The Confederate pickets were within a few hundred yards of the enemy's outposts. Matters remained thus from day to day.

General Polk was relieved of his command shortly after the battle of Chickamauga, and Lieutenant-general D. H. Hill was placed in command of Polk's corps. This change was caused by some misunderstanding between General Polk and the commander in chief on the morning of Sunday's battle at Chickamauga. General Hill made a good corps commander. General Polk was assigned to duty in Mississippi.

On October 23, Wright's brigade was sent to Charleston, East Tennessee, by way of Tyner Station. The object of this move was to rebuild the railroad bridge over the Hiwassee river, and to guard the line of communication between Chattanooga and Knoxville. Longstreet was detached from Bragg's army at Chattanooga and sent to Knoxville. Burnside was besieged at Knoxville. Affairs remained inactive and monotonous during the month of October and the greater portion of November.

The Confederates were encourged by the victory at Chickamauga. Every effort was brought to bear by the Confederate authorities, to strengthen the army and to encourage the troops. Jeff. Davis visited the army and made a speech to the soldiers on the night of October 11. It was thought by some that there was a remote prospect of foreign intervention at this particular juncture. The Federal authorities were not idle. Re-enforcements were forwarded to Chattanooga.

On November 23, the Federals began to press the Confederate pickets and to marshal a powerful army in the Confederate front. Wright's brigade was returned to Missionary Ridge on the 24th, and arrived on the right wing of the Confederate lines on the morning of November 25, near the mouth of Chickamauga Creek. The brigade came on the cars and the brigade wagon-train was sent through without an escort. On the 24th, the wagon-train was captured by the enemy and destroyed. When the brigade arrived at the north end of Missionary Ridge on the morning of November 25, it was ordered to a position on the extreme right, on the south bank of Chickamauga Creek. General Wright was mistaken in the position of the enemy, who were posted in heavy force on the north bank of the creek. Before the troops were aware of the immediate presence of an enemy, they received a volley of musketry from the opposite bank. LaFayette Clark, of Company D, Sixteenth Tennessee Regiment, was killed, and Lieutenant W. C. Womack was severely wounded.

General Wright withdrew his brigade out of range of the Federals, who had the advantage of position, and established his lines on better ground.

The Confederate lines were now pressed at all points. Hooker carried the Confederate position at Lookout Mountain on the left in the forenoon, and the Confederates had withdrawn to the brow of Missionary Ridge. The Federals massed their forces and moved up to the western base. The engagement continued through the afternoon along the center, while all was comparatively quiet on the flanks. About sundown the Federals prepared for a desperate assault upon the Confederate center, and massed their forces at the foot of the ridge at a place known as Moore's House. Under a heavy cannonade, they began the ascent of the ridge. The Confederates resisted with all their power, but the Federals had been so heavily re-enforced, and the Confederates had been weakened by the absence of Longstreet's corps and other troops sent to different points, until the defenses on the brow of the ridge at many places were a mere skirmish line. This was too weak to withstand the heavy columns of the enemy, which now came up the hill in full force. The fight raged furiously for a while, but the Confederate line was broken and the enemy gained the summit of the ridge.

General Bragg was in the thickest of the fight, and tried to rally his men when his lines gave way. Finding his forces inadequate to the work of regaining this part of the line, he ordered a retreat. The Confederate stores at Chickamauga Station were destroyed to prevent their falling into the hands of the enemy, and the army retreated to Ringgold. From this point the Confederates continued the retreat to Dalton, where they remained through the winter and early spring months.

General Bragg was now relieved of the command of the army and his place was filled by General Joseph E. Johnston, who became a great favorite with the army. The soldiers built cabins to shelter themselves, and in a short time the whole army was made comfortable for the winter. Furloughs were granted to the men to visit their homes, and a general quiet reigned in each army during the remainder of the winter.

While stationed at Dalton, Jeff. Davis conceived the idea that it would have a beneficial effect upon the army to intermix troops from different States in the different commands. This caused a buzz of discontent among the Tennessee troops. By this arrangement, Cheatham's division was to be changed so as to be composed principally of troops from other States. The Tennessee troops were unwilling to give up their old division commander, who was equally averse to the idea of giving up his old brigades and regiments. In this emergency General Johnston sympathized with the Tennesseans, and succeeded in having the order revoked before it was put to a practical test.

During the winter there was very little done in military circles. In February a Federal column came out from Vicksburg and was met by the army of General Polk, assisted by Forrest's cavalry. This was a mere raid that came out as far as Meridian and returned to Vicksburg. Johnston sent a part of his command to assist Polk. As soon as the Federals became aware of this they moved out on Buzzard Roost Gap, near Dalton. Johnston succeeded in driving them back. The Federals withdrew from Meridian and the re-enforcements from Johnston's army returned from Meridian to Dalton.

CHAPTER V.

GEORGIA CAMPAIGN—BATTLES AROUND ATLANTA.

The Federal authorities now resolved to concentrate the bulk of their Eastern Army upon Richmond and their Western Army upon Atlanta. Grant was now made commander in chief of the armies of the United States, with head-quarters with the Eastern Army. Sherman was placed in command of the army that was to move upon Atlanta. Each army moved on the same day. Sherman moved upon Dalton early in May, and appeared before Rocky Face Ridge. The Confederates met him at the ridge, and a lively skirmish was kept up for a few days, until the Federals succeeded in turning Johnston's left flank by way of Snake Creek Gap, and he was forced to fall back upon Resaca on the night of May 13; and on the morning of the 14th had his army in position before the Federals came up. As the Federals advanced on Resaca on the evening of May 14, they presented a grand and imposing spectacle. Their forces were massed into three columns. As they came up through an open field their ranks closed up into a solid phalanx, and appeared as so many living walls of blue. Their arms glistened in the sunlight, and the columns advanced as steadily as though they were on dress parade. The artillery kept pace with the columns, and their skirmish lines advanced in front at their regular distance. As the columns advanced, the Confederate skirmish lines withdrew gradually, and kept up a continual fire on their retreat until the Federals arrived at the foot of a long hill that lay parallel to the Federal lines. At this point the guns from the fort at Resaca poured forth a tremendous shower of shot and shell into the ranks of the advancing Federals, and the movement was peremptorily checked. The Federal artillery was quickly wheeled into position, and a heavy artillery duel was carried on during the remainder of the evening.

General Cheatham had rearranged his lines and thrown out his skirmishers. The two opposing columns were now in plain view of each other, on opposite sides of a little ravine, and the skirmish lines within a stone's throw of each other. The fighting was brisk on the skirmish lines all the evening. The Confederate artillery sent showers of grape and canister into the Federal lines on the opposite hill-side, and the compliment was reciprocated with interest and dispatch.

While the lines were being arranged, Colonel S. S. Stanton, of the Twenty-eighth Tennessee Regiment, was killed. There were no casualties in the Sixteenth Regiment during the evening, more than a few very slight wounds.

Night came on and the firing ceased. The Confederates fortified their main lines and dug pits for their skirmishers during the night. At daylight on the morning of the 15th, the skirmishing was resumed, and thickened on the right till it merged into a general engagement. During the 15th, this situation remained comparatively the same.

The Federals had been re-enforced to such numbers that they were able to keep Johnston's front engaged, and still keep a reserved line to operate on his flanks. This policy was inaugurated by Sherman at the opening of the campaign, and carefully kept up all through the Georgia campaign to the fall of Atlanta. This forced upon Johnston the necessity of withdrawing his army to a better position every time he found his flanks endangered. The Federals finding themselves unable to force the position at Resaca, attempted to turn Johnston's left flank again, and he withdrew to Calhoun.

In the retreat, Johnston kept his army in the shape of the letter Z, with one part fronting and engaging the enemy, while the remainder of the line was retreating in shape to cover the retreat of the supply trains, and at the same time to be available in the event of being pressed.

From Calhoun, Johnston retreated to Adairsville on May 17. On the evening of the 17th, Wright's brigade was placed in the rear to hold the enemy in check during further retreat. The Federals were pressing the Confederate rear, and about four o'clock in the evening appeared at a large mansion by the roadside. This mansion had eight sides, and from the house to the right of the road the Federal cavalry came up with considerable dash. The Fifty-first Tennessee Regiment, under Lieutenant-colonel Hall, was placed on the skirmish line near the house, and the brigade was formed about six hundred yards to the rear. A severe brush was carried on between the skirmish lines during the evening. The Sixteenth had no casualties, though the Twenty-eighth Tennessee Regiment lost two men.

At this place Colonel Donnell left the Sixteenth Regiment permanently on account of injuries received at Chickamauga, and his place was filled by Captain Randals.

On the 17th, Johnston withdrew his army from Adairsville to Kingston, and on the night of the 18th encamped near Cass Station. It was determined to give battle near the town of Cassville, a few miles from the station. The Confederate lines were established on the morning. of the 19th. Sherman was prompt to time with his whole army, and his lines were established at an early hour, with his artillery in position for immediate action. The opposing phalanxes were facing each other, with scarcely a mile intervening. Johnston's army had been strengthened by the arrival of Polk's, corps from Mississippi. This re-enforcement had come up during the engagement at Resaca. Johnston had determined to engage the enemy at Cassville, and every arrangement had been perfected accordingly. The Confederates were in line and awaiting the order to attack, which was momentarily expected. The morning was bright and beautiful. The country around Cassville was open and slightly undulating. Each army was busy in its preparations. The columns of the enemy could be plainly seen from the Confederate position; and while all was hurry and dispatch in the disposal of the lines, there was a dull and foreboding stillness that was broken only by the sullen roar of an occasional cannon at some points of the opposing lines. The Confederates moved up a short distance and halted. Suddenly the order came along the lines to "fortify." The order was promptly and speedily obeyed. In less than five minutes every rail and chunk of wood around was piled up along the line as a breastwork for the men. Johnston had discovered some new developments in the position and strength of the enemy in his immediate front. Sherman had attained some advantage during the morning, which the active and watchful Confederate leader was prompt to discover, and on the very moment of giving battle Johnston discovered the sudden and unforeseen disadvantage under which he would be forced to labor, and resolved not to risk an engagement at Cassville. The enemy had massed his heavy batteries on an elevation in Johnston's front, and his artillery was concealed by the timber. As the Confederates moved up this artillery was moved into position, and it developed an advantage to the Federals that rendered the situation so strong that Johnston concluded not to make the attack. Scarcely had the Confederates completed their temporary breastworks of fence rails when the order was given to withdraw the lines, and the Confederates were withdrawn with celerity and promptness, though in remarkably good order. The Confederates fell back to Altoona on the 20th, and on the 21st moved on by way of Ackworth to Big Shanty, and thence across the Etowah River.

Sherman had sent a heavy flanking column on the left of Johnston's lines in the direction of Dallas. Johnston hurried his army across the country and met this movement. From New Hope Church to Dallas the Confederates took position, and the Federals came up on the evening of the 24th. Sherman's forward movement was very determined on this line as he had laid his plans on this place with the intention of gaining Johnston's rear before he could reach Marietta. The Confederate leader was too sharp for this game to be played upon him by Sherman. A line of rifle-pits confronted Sherman on his arrival at Dallas.

As the Federals advanced upon these lines they met

with the most stubborn and determined resistance at the hands of the Confederates. A severe assault was made on the Confederate lines at New Hope Church on the night of May 25, and heavy skirmishing was carried on daily at all parts of the lines from New Hope Church to Dallas during the 25th, 26th, and 27th of May.

The campaign had now become one regular series of skirmishes, with occasional sorties at different points from day to day. The scene of operations was constantly being changed from point to point. Sherman persisted in his attempt to flank Johnston out of every position. Every attempt was successfully thwarted by the ever shrewd and watchful Confederate leader. Sherman found that he could make no movement without encountering a line of Confederate rifle-pits. As the situation demanded the establishment of a new line, the Confederates would defend the line through the day and throw up fortifications at night. The days were devoted to fighting and the nights were spent in fortifying. The Confederates were never off duty. The lines were under fire at all times, and military operations assumed the most active and energetic aspect.

Johnston's lines were changed almost daily, and every new line was promptly fortified. The whole country for miles around was cut up with fortifications. The scene changed from position to position until the Confederate lines were established on Lost Mountain. This mountain was a small mound-like elevation which arose to a considerable height above the surrounding country, which was level. This mountain was about the center of Johnston's lines. In the skirmishes about Lost Mountain the Sixteenth Regiment lost two men, and several were wounded. Private Henry C. Tate, of Company A, and private Andrew Saylors, of Company K, were killed on the 25th. They were both good soldiers and good men.

The campaign was thus vigorously pressed by Sherman and obstinately opposed by Johnston during the latter part of May, and was continued with increased vigor and determination on each side until the fall of Atlanta.

Johnston's army held its position around Lost Mountain until the Middle of June following. On the 14th of June he changed his lines from Lost Mountain so as to include Pine Mountain, a few miles to his rear. Sherman had been operating on Johnston's left for the double purpose of getting the Confederates as far as possible from the railroad, and at the same time to gain, if possible, the Confederate rear. In this manner the scene of operations had thus drifted to the distance of twelve or fifteen miles south-west of the railroad. Sherman finding that every attempt upon Johnston's left had failed, and being thwarted in every demonstration in that direction, now turned his attention to Johnston's right with a view of turning his position on the railroad. Thus operations gradually bore back in the direction of the railroad until the Confederate lines included Pine Mountain on the left. From Pine Mountain the movements of the enemy could be plainly seen in every direction, and on this account signal corps were placed on its summit.

On the morning of the 14th, General Johnston, together with several of his corps commanders, was on the summit of Pine Mountain viewing the movements of the enemy. This group was discovered by the enemy, who fired a rifle shot from one of their batteries into its midst. The shot passed through the body of General Polk, killing him instantly. It seemed that the Federals had learned the signals of the Confederates. The death of General Polk was known along the Confederate lines in a few minutes. Strange as it may appear, the Federals knew it almost as soon as the Confederates. Developments afterward showed that a certain Lieutenant Fluke, of the United States Signal Service, had made a study of the Confederate signals and had been so successful as to be able to read the Confederate signals on Pine Mountain, as the death of General Polk was signaled to the army immediately after its occurrence.

On the 15th, General Johnston withdrew the left wing of his army one and a half miles and established a new line, which he hastily fortified. There was very severe skirmishing all along this line, which was kept up the entire day.

On June 16 the Sixteenth Regiment lost two men. William Lowry, of Company E, and Samuel Baker, of Company I, were killed on the skirmish line. The skirmishing continued brisk, and some charges were made in General Johnston's lines during the day.

It rained almost incessantly during the 18th, 19th, 20th, and 21st of June. Johnston had now moved his lines till his right wing included Kennesaw Mountain, near Marietta. The Confederate left was extended to cover a flanking column of the enemy. The Confederate lines on the left were quickly established, and Hood's corps made a spirited attack upon the enemy's right on the evening of June 23. The attack was brief. Hood withdrew his column and formed on Hardee's left. The lines along the Kennesaw position were strengthened. Rifle-pits were dug for the main line and ditches for the skirmish line. The opposing armies were often within speaking distance of each other, and the picket fighting was constant during the day. At night there was generally a lull in the picket fighting, each side agreeing upon a truce. Sometimes the pickets would engage each other in friendly conversation. At other times the conversation would commence with taunts and continue until the truce would be broken by a shot. In such cases a brisk fight would be the result.

Sometimes during the night the pickets would agree to meet unarmed at the half-way point between the two stands. In such cases the men would exchange papers, and the Federal would exchange his coffee with the Confederate for tobacco, besides a general trade and traffic in such articles as were possessed by each party respectively. On all such occasions the truce was brief, and at its conclusion each party repaired promptly to his respective position.

On the 24th the skirmishing was heavier all along the lines during the entire day. The weather was hot and sultry. The men had become quite inured to hardships. The health of the Tennessee troops continued good. The men were supplied abundantly with plain though substantial food, and they bore up bravely under the continued hardships and toils which this campaign entailed upon them.

Throughout the 25th and 26th were heavy skirmishing and various demonstrations all along the lines. On the morning of the 27th General Sherman massed his troops in Johnston's front on that part of the line occupied by Cheatham's division on the left and Cleburn's division on the right. The Federals came on in several parallel columns. The Confederates awaited their approach until within a few rods of the works, when they opened with artillery and infantry upon the advancing enemy, whose ranks were cut down at a fearful rate. Nothing daunted by the broadside of grape and canister from the Confederate batteries and the storm of bullets that were hurled through their columns from the rifle-pits, the Federals pressed on until their front had reached the works and a hand-to-hand fight ensued. At one point the enemy succeeded in planting his colors upon the works of the Confederates, but were shot down as fast as the works were scaled. The Confederates stood their ground in front and the batteries on the flanks poured such a murderous cross-fire into the Federal columns that they were forced to fall back to their intrenchments. The battle was brief, though furious. The assault was spirited and determined. The loss to the Federals was very severe. General Harker was slain, and their killed and wounded covered the ground in front of the Confederate works. The Confederate loss was small. Private Joshua W. Carter, of Company C, Sixteenth Tennessee Regiment, was killed on the picket line, and a few were wounded and captured.

Sherman was now pressing Johnston's position severely, and having failed in his attempt to carry the Confederate position at Kennesaw by storm, the old game of flanking was resorted to by the Federal general. The Confederate left was withdrawn a short distance on July 2, and on the 3d Johnston withdrew his whole army behind Marietta. On the morning of the 4th the Federals entered Marietta with great enthusiasm.

The two armies remained confronting each other on the Chattahoochie, near Marietta, and engaged in various skirmishes and sorties daily until June 17, when the Confederates fortified their lines and prepared for a stubborn and determined resistance.

General Johnston had been removed from command by the Confederate authorities, and his place was filled by General J. B. Hood, who was at the time a corps commander. The authorities at Richmond had become impatient and dissatisfied because Johnston did not engage the enemy at Cassville, and especially because he had fallen back from his stronghold at Kennesaw Mountain. They could not realize the disparity of numbers and strength between the opposing armies. It was not to be expected that Johnston, with an army constantly on duty and worn out by a constant campaign without relief, could turn upon an army of double his numbers and superior equipments and drive it back from the country.

General Johnston was a wise and prudent commander, who knew his own strength and the strength of the enemy that opposed him. He had confronted an enemy thus flushed with a series of brilliant successes and supplied with every convenience and appliance of modern warfare, and, with an inferior force and with inferior arms and ammunition, he had disputed every inch of his advance and checked every movement that was attempted by the enemy upon his lines. Thus had he disputed Sherman's advance, and by skillful maneuverings he had engaged his front daily, and, with a comparatively small loss to his own army, he had inflicted a severe loss to the enemy, to the extent of several thousand men. He had withdrawn his army carefully from place to place as his flanks were exposed, and with a front to the enemy at all times he protected the withdrawal of his supply trains and his wounded, and let nothing fall into the hands of the enemy. In this retreat, Johnston had accomplished one of the greatest military achievements of modern warfare, and his brilliant genius and practical skill in the work of handling and maneuvering large armies justly placed him in the list of the greatest military chieftains of the age; yet he was to be superseded and his place filled by General Hood—a good soldier and a brave man, but possessed of more courage than prudence, and more valor than discretion.

On the morning of the 18th the Confederates were moved out of their breastworks and hurled upon the Federal lines. The loss was fearful, and nothing practical was accomplished. The Confederates lost many brave and good men. R. M. Safley, of Company H, Sixteenth Tennessee, was severely wounded by a shot through the lungs. Lieutenant John Akeman of the same company fell in this fight, having received four wounds, either of which was mortal. Private A. J. Agent, of Company I, Sixteenth Tennessee Regiment, was killed on the field. The other regiments suffered greatly. The Confederates were repulsed in this attack, as the Federals were intrenched and had greatly superior numbers. The two opposing armies were in the immediate presence of each other all the time and under a continual fire.

General Hood arranged his columns for another attack upon the enemy, and on July 20 threw his whole army upon Sherman's fortified position with all the fury and desperation at his command. The losses were heavy on both sides. The battle was a severe and desperate one. Many of the boys of the Sixteenth Tennessee were severely, and some mortally, wounded.

On July 21, Wright's brigade was moved farther to the right of Hood's lines. Private William Etter was killed on the evening of the 21st while on picket duty. On the morning of July 22, Cheatham's division attacked the enemy's left on that part of the line occupied by McPherson's division. The Federals were driven back at this point and General McPherson was killed. The Confederates carried the Federal position and captured quite a number of prisoners. As in the preceding engagements, the losses were heavy on both sides, though, considering numbers engaged, the losses of the Confederates were greater. The Sixteenth Tennessee lost many valuable men. Grundy Gibbs, of Company C, was killed in this engagement. James C. Biles, of Company C, received two severe wounds during the battle of the 22d, and Wright S. Hackett, of Company C, fell mortally wounded and died within a few days. The other companies and regiments suffered severely. Mr. Hackett was a man beloved and respected by his comrades and all who knew him. At the beginning of the war he was first lieutenant of his company and served in that capacity till the reorganization at Corinth, when he resigned his commission as an officer and entered the ranks of his company as a private. Concerning his noble qualities and many virtues, the Atlanta papers of August 9, 1864, printed the following correct and just tribute:

THE LATE WRIGHT S. HACKETT, ESQ.

WRIGHT'S BRIGADE, CHEATHAM'S DIVISION,
August 12, 1864.

Mr. Editor:—Death, so fond of a shining mark, in his bloody march on the 22d of last month, grasped the vitals of many of the heroes in this veteran army—among them, Wright S. Hackett, Company C, Sixteenth Tennessee Infantry. The painful intelligence of the fatality of his wound, as announced in the *Rebel*, has reached his companions, and a wail of universal lamentation arises from the ranks his presence so long honored.

While it may be wrong to particularize in these remembrances of our valiant dead, where all so nobly die, yet the character of this "bright but fleeting star" was such as to insure from the public a sympathetic tear by a brief rehearsal of the associations antecedent to the calamitous event of his death.

Born in the mountainous region of East Tennessee, of fine physical form, stout and active, with remarkable intellectual promise, he arose in the morning of life to high honors as a literary scholar and a graduate at law. He had but embarked upon his professional career, with a mind well stored with knowledge in all its departments, when that trump, whose martial notes have almost robbed Tennessee of her bed of future glory, awakened the fire of his enthusiastic bosom, and enrolled him in the list of the champions of Southern rights.

During the first year of the war he participated in the arduous campaigns of Western Virginia and North Mississippi, in the capacity of first lieutenant, until the reorganization of the army at Corinth. At that time he was unanimously chosen captain of his old company, which position he flatly but positively refused. Unlike a large number of officers I have known, he did not seek to avoid conscription, but after a visit home, designed to be brief, though protracted by a severe attack of fever which left him almost at the grave, he rejoined his comrades as a private in the ranks. Often entreated to accept the position of an officer—any he might wish—he refused them all alike, positively declaring his determination to do duty as a private throughout the war, which rank he filled up to the time of his death with great credit to himself and his command.

In the gallant charges of his brigade on July 22 he was ever with the foremost in that rapid march to victory; and the field was nearly won, when, some distance ahead of his lines, reconnoitering in front, he fell, shot through and through by a minnie ball. He spoke in cheerful tones of his misfortune and left the field, expressing strong hopes of recovery. But alas! a few days ago he died at Catoosa hospital.

The heart beats quick, the breath is short, and the moist eyes of men who fear not battle, respond to this plaintive tale. The surface of the outside world seems ruffled with never a care, but the large circle of his acquaintances is stricken with grief. He was what we may call a private hero in every sense of the word. With superior mental endowment and most unexceptionable social qualities, with friends without number, and ample capacity to command, the hand of fame and the flatteries of fortune tempting upward to earthly glory, still true to his nature he renounced them all.

In camp-fire consultations his opinion always preponderated; his standard of honor and cleverness was the rule of his messmates, and his merry laugh and gloom-dispelling jokes were sure antidotes to all affections of the blues. Esteemed as a friend, faithful and ready; exalted as a soldier and man, we all loved him. A grateful and admiring people lament great men like Sidney Johnson, Stonewall Jackson, and Leonidas Polk, for the chair of a chieftain is empty; and a like feeling drapes the hearts of Wright S. Hackett's friends. All recognized him an embryo chieftain. Genius sanctioned his earthly advent, fame stamped her image on his brow, and the proud bark of childhood rode on the deep of praise and power. Cut down on the theater of glory, the soaring aspirations of a noble mind obliterated by sudden and unexpected death, his spirit has gone out with the far unknown. His form, once so full of life and vigor, is crumbling in decay; the joy of his smile is lost to us forever; but the memory of his pure patriotism, generous heart, and lofty and refined emotions, are endurable as eternity itself.

> These shall resist the empire of decay,
> When time is o'er and worlds have passed away:
> Cold in the dust the perished heart may lie,
> That which warmed it once can never die.   VIX.

DEATH OF PRIVATE WRIGHT S. HACKETT.
From the Chattanooga Rebel, August 9, 1864.

Died, in this city, on last Saturday, Wright S. Hackett, Esq., a private of the Sixteenth Tennessee Regiment, Wright's brigade, Cheatham's Division, of a wound received on the 22d ultimo in front of Atlanta.

Mr. Hackett was in every sense a remarkable character, and his untimely decease will leave a pang in many hearts who had learned to respect and love him. He was about twenty-six years old, was a lawyer of rising merit in Tennessee, and was one of the best soldiers, most thorough gentlemen, and worthy men that the service afforded. He was as gentle as a child, and as simple-hearted and pure in his tastes and affections; as modest as a young maiden just budding into womanhood; as devoted to duty and his country as any hero of ancient or modern times who has been celebrated in song and story; as fearless as the Roman legionary, and as true as the north star. This is no mere language of eulogy; it is the deliberate judgment upon his character of all who have been associated with him, in and out of the army.

W. S. HACKETT.

He uniformly declined promotion, being convinced that the private station is the post of honor. This was done through no affectation of a contempt for office, but always with modesty and firmness.. He was twice tendered promotion as captain of his company, and twice received the commission as adjutant of his regiment, all of which he promptly declined. At the battle of Murfreesboro he was clothed with temporary command of the regiment by Colonel John H. Savage, commanding the regiment, who was suddenly called to manage a detachment that was being flanked by the enemy. This was a rare and most signal compliment to his ability and capacity for leadership, which was enthusiastically accepted by the regiment, who followed him immediately afterward into a charge by which the enemy was driven back and the detachment of two companies relieved from the danger of capture.

Mr. Hackett's crowning quality was his high moral excellence. His morals were as pure as the philosopher or Christian could enforce. To an intellect of great clearness and force he added the highest virtue and the most exemplary habits and principles. He was an industrious student even in the army. To his love for study was due most of that disposition to avoid promotion, which rendered him a conspicuous example of unselfishness. He knew that the cares of position would interfere with the pursuit of his studies, and hence he preferred to drill and fight in the ranks, where he could discharge the duties of the patriot soldier without the multiplied cares that would fall to his lot as an officer. Such a soldier is a model whose excellences should be held up to our young Confederacy for imitation. Rome, nor Greece, nor our Revolution of '76, ever produced a purer model.

His remains lie in the cemetery at Griffin, bedewed with the tears and laureled with the honors of all who shall come to know his character of patriot, soldier, and man.

RETREAT FROM ATLANTA.

Hood withdrew his forces in good order and retreated seven miles to Lovely Station. Here he drew up his lines and hastily fortified his position. Sherman's army followed in rapid pursuit, and under a heavy cannonade he pushed his picket lines to a close proximity to Hood's position. The lines thus confronted each other and picket fighting was kept up continually till September 5, when the engagement became general. The battle was perhaps not so severe as some of the preceding engagements around Atlanta. The losses on both sides were about the same. The casualties of the Sixteenth Tennessee Regiment were Joseph Brown, of Company K, killed, and H. C. Paine, of Company I, mortally wounded.

The fight closed in the evening, with each army in its original position, no advantage having been gained by either. The armies thus lay confronting each other, with heavy cannonading and picket fighting, during the 3d, 4th, 5th, and 6th of September, with slight casualties on both sides.

On the morning of September 7, the Federals disappeared from Hood's front, and the Confederates followed back five miles in the direction of Atlanta.

The Federal army entered Atlanta September 2, 1864. Hood had been completely flanked out of the position by Sherman in the campaigns resulting in the battles of Jonesboro and Lovejoy Station. The Federals had gained their great objective point, and had captured the Gate City of the South, which contained the principal store-houses and work-shops of the Confederacy. The leading object of the Federals accomplished, and the shattered remnant of the Confederate army being thus cut off from its resources in every respect, the collapse of the Confederacy was a mere matter of time. Hood saw that defensive operations were no longer feasible, and resolved to throw his army upon the north side of the Tennessee with the hope of gaining recruits and supplies, and also expecting that, if he could cut off Sherman's communications with his base of supplies, he would be forced to retire from

Georgia. Accordingly, the Confederate commander put his army in shape for an active aggressive campaign upon the enemy's rear.

Sherman detached Thomas's corps to operate against Hood in these movements, and with the rest of his army he inaugurated his celebrated "March to the Sea," which he accomplished without opposition. This campaign from Atlanta to the sea was attended with a degree of devastation scarcely expected of General Sherman, yet he claimed it as a military necessity to lay waste the country and impoverish the people; further, that the Confederacy might not be able to utilize this section by gathering up supplies from it to feed its armies.

Sherman had left garrisons at all the principal points from Dalton to Atlanta, and fortifying and garrisoning the latter place, he left his sick and wounded here, and, cutting himself loose from his communications, made his march to the sea.

Hood had matured his plans to attack the most salient points of Sherman's line of communications thus abandoned. On September 19 the Confederates marched about twenty miles and encamped at Palmetto Station, on the West Point road. There was a general consolidation of companies and regiments at this time, and the result was a large list of supernumerary officers. The Sixteenth Tennessee Regiment had suffered a long list of casualties in killed, wounded, and missing. The effective force of the regiment was reduced to so small a number that the remnant of the ten original companies was scarcely enough to make three good companies by consolidation. Companies A, D, and E were consolidated and placed under the command of Captain Frank M. York. Companies B,

C, and H were consolidated and commanded by Captain John Lucas Thompson; and Companies F, G, I, and K were consolidated and commanded by Captain Ad Fisk. The regiment was thus consolidated into three companies, and the officers of the other companies were relieved of command and placed on the list of supernumeraries. The other regiments were similarly consolidated. The Eighth, Tenth, and Twenty-eighth Regiments were now consolidated into one regiment and commanded by Colonel John H. Anderson.

President Davis visited the army here and addressed the men several times. He was listened to with great attention, and his remarks were well received. Several changes were made. Hardee left to take command of the District of South Carolina, and General Frank Cheatham took command of the corps. General Stephen D. Lee retained the command of Hood's corps, and General A. P. Stewart was kept in command of ours (Polk's old corps).* General Hood had by this time perfected his plans for a march through Georgia, over the ground where we had fallen back before Sherman.

About the last of September the reorganization of the army was completed and we started north, striking the Georgia Central Railroad near Marietta. This was the road which Sherman depended upon for his supplies. "To destroy is a soldier's joy." Here was property belonging to our friends, but this was no concern of ours. The orders were to tear up the tracks, and at once the work was begun. Huge fires of ties were built, rails laid across them, the center heated to a red heat, when they were carried over to the trees and bent until the ends met. In some cases the rails were twisted around the trunks of the trees, forming a ring; and in every way possible destroying their usefulness. We continued this work until we reached the vicinity of Allatoona, when, on the morning of October 5, we formed line of battle and sent a demand to General Corse, commanding the Federal forces, to surrender. To this he refused compliance, so we were ordered by General French to assault the works.

The fortifications of Allatoona, as near as can be remembered from hasty glances at them during the fight, consisted of, first, a line of rifle-pits for skirmishers; next, a strong abatis and an infantry parapet with two six-pounder guns firing through embrasures; next, in rear, was a strong inclosed fort about twelve feet high, surrounded by a ditch too deep for escalade.

When the assault opened the Federals stood right up to their work, and we, for a few seconds, had what the boys called " a hot time." Our Texas friends in the second line—Ector's brigade—caught up and went over with us. As our boys swarmed over the parapet the bayonet was freely used by both sides, officers firing their pistols, and many throwing sticks and stones. This melee was quickly ended by the surrender of most of the defenders, very few of whom reached their large fort in the rear. All this time our own batteries were silent. They had been ordered to a hill on our right to enfilade the position, and why they did not open fire was, and still is, a mystery.

This was, for the time engaged, the bloodiest fight we were ever in, and our loss was heavy. Corse's men fought like demons.

We now received and replied to a hot fire from the big fort, and soon stopped their artillerists from looking through their embrasures, silencing their guns. At this point General French ordered the line to fall back.

This order was disregarded, but a second peremptory order soon came, and was reluctantly obeyed.

Wright's brigade was now commanded by Brigadier-general John C. Carter, formerly Colonel of the Thirty-eighth Tennessee.

Hood now moved upon Dalton, which was defended by a fortification manned by negro troops. Hood invested the place, and the colored garrison surrendered. The Sixteenth Tennessee Regiment was in the brigade that took charge of the fort and the prisoners.

Proceeding from Dalton, Hood marched through the Buzzard Roost Gap of Taylor's Ridge, a few miles west of Dalton, and thence by Cedar Town across Sand Mountain to Decatur, and invested the place. From Decatur the march was continued to Gadsden, a small town on the Coosa river, and thence to Tuscumbia, arriving October 30, 1864. The march had been a long and severe one, and the men were worn out and exhausted. The army remained at Tuscumbia till November 8, when orders were received to march, the men knew not where. A bridge having been built over the creek, the troops were crossed over in the night. The rain was incessant. The night was dark, the roads muddy, and the weather cold and disagreeable. Having crossed over, the men went into camp and remained till November 11, when the march was resumed in the direction of the Tennessee river. Arriving near its banks, the camp was established and a pontoon was thrown across the river. On the 13th, Hood crossed the Tennessee at Florence with his army and moved on through a fertile, though fearfully desoated, country. Winter was now setting in with its severest rigor, and many of the men were barefooted and destitute of many other articles of clothing. The men bore their hardships and privations with heroic fortitude, and, regardless of the inclemency of the weather, the muddy roads, and their general want of necessary supplies and comforts, they stood ready and willing to act further and suffer more in the defense of their cause, which they conscientiously believed to be right and just.

CHAPTER VI.

BATTLES OF FRANKLIN AND NASHVILLE.

On November 22, Hood moved a portion of his army back to Florence for the purpose of guarding his supply trains on the march. The men waded the snow and mud, and passing the State line by way of Waynesboro, encamped on the night of the 24th. Proceeding on the 25th, they made a rapid march in the direction of Franklin, and camped on the evening of the 26th one and one half miles from Columbia, in Maury county, Tennessee. Proceeding on the morning of the 27th, they appeared in front of a Federal force in the evening, after a march of twenty miles. The Federals were reported to be retreating on the morning of the 28th, and orders were received to be in readiness to march at a moment's notice. On the 29th the Confederates moved at daylight, and marched two miles up Duck River, where a crossing was effected, and the march was pushed with vigor through hills and hollows with the view of getting beyond the enemy and forcing a surrender. The enemy having the advantage of better roads, made his escape and took a stand at Spring Hill. After a slight resistance at Spring Hill the Federals moved on rapidly to Franklin. Hood pressed on, after making a march of seventeen miles without roads, and encamped for the night within four miles of Franklin. The enemy was drawn up in plain view. Hood arrived in their immediate front before

Franklin about 3 P.M. on the 30th. A line of battle was formed, and about 4 o'clock he struck their outer line of works. The fight was the most desperate of the war. The Confederates assaulted the outer line with desperate force, and after a hand-to-hand contest the Federals finally yielded this line and took position behind the inner works. Every approach to the inner works was obstructed in every manner known to civil warfare.

It was now near sundown. The Confederates came up to the work of death in a cool and fearless manner. Working their way through the different species of obstructions, the inner works were assaulted, and as darkness began to envelop the scene the work of carnage was desperate almost beyond description.

The Federals held their ground with a tenacity unknown to former conflicts. The Confederates press on with a reckless daring and determination, utterly regardless of all opposing obstacles. Night had now closed its mantle over the scene, and the conflict raged the more furiously. Many a gallant soldier of each army fell at the feet of his more successful antagonist.

In this manner the fight lasted until about one hour after dark. The enemy retreated, and the Confederates took possession of the works. The Federals retired to Nashville during the night and took position behind their fortifications. The losses on both sides were fearful. The Confederates lost many valuable officers and men—among whom were Brigadier-general John C. Carter and Major-general P. R. Cleburne. The losses of the Confederates were, in proportion to numbers engaged, greater than that of the Federals.

The Sixteenth Regiment had been consolidated into three companies, neither of which was full, and the ranks, reduced by sickness and the casualties of other campaigns since its consolidation, did not number more than a hundred effective men when it entered the battle. Its losses were sixteen men killed, besides a large per cent. of wounded. The killed were: Lieutenant F. M. Pettit, Lieutenant James Green; privates John B. Womack, A. J. Kersy, John Driver, Howard Cantrell, William Wilhoit, William Thompson, George Donnell, A. N. Pepper, C. M. Jordan, John Brown, Thomas Hooper, Samuel Lusk, Pleasant Templeton. N. B. Hambrick.

The morning of December 1 was spent in caring for the wounded and burying the dead. The battle-ground was strewn with the dead and dying of both sides. Hood made the best disposal of his wounded that his facilities would permit, and such attention was paid to the dead and suffering of the enemy as the time and circumstances would allow.

On the morning of December 2, Hood moved onward with his army in pursuit of Thomas in the direction of Nashville. Leaving Franklin about 9 o'clock in the morning, the march was kept up till in the afternoon, when the spire of the Capitol could be seen in the distance. A halt was now made and the army encamped for the night. On the morning of the 3d the Confederates took position on the Murfreesboro pike and were drawn up in line of battle. The guns from the Federal defenses began to shell Hood's lines at a rapid and furious rate, yet he held his position here with little change for four or five days. The weather had become intensely cold. A heavy rain set in, which was followed by sleet and snow. The Confederates had no tents or shelter of any kind. Many of the soldiers were barefooted, and their clothing was thin and scant. They had become dependent upon the country through which they passed for supplies, for the Confederate base had been destroyed. The situation was desperate in the extreme, yet the men stood ready to suffer even more than they ever had suffered, with the hope of gaining their State capital and rescuing their homes from the possession of the enemy. The future was all dark to them, yet they remembered the dark days of the Revolution, when the hopes of the Colonies were even more gloomy than theirs. Their object and aim were to gain possession of the capital of Tennessee, and while they paused not to consider their inability to hold the place, if they even succeeded in taking it, they left it all to the wisdom and discretion of their commanders, and stood ready, in the midst of hunger and privations almost without parallel in history, to renew the conflict to the last and sacrifice their all upon the altar of principle and in behalf of a cause which they believed to be right.

Matters remained thus until December 15, when General Hood issued orders to his soldiers to be in readiness for action at a moment's notice. The Federals had been heavily reinforced, and were threatening his left wing. Wright's brigade was sent around to the left, where the enemy came out in force and drove back both the flanks of Hood's army. Wright's brigade formed on the left in time to check the movement of the enemy in that quarter for a while. It was now dark, and the action was suspended for the night. The Confederates fortified their lines through the night and prepared themselves for action at any moment the enemy might force it upon them.

Early in the morning of December 16 the enemy advanced upon the Confederate's position with spirit and determination. Cheatham's division held its ground on the left throughout the greater portion of the day. Late in the afternoon a heavy reinforcement of Federal troops came in from the Cumberland river and were hurled against Hood's lines with all the impetuosity of fresh troops, and the Confederates began to waver. They were worn out with constant action, and seeing the tide turning against them with such tremendous force, the disheartened and dejected soldiers lost much of the spirit that had ever characterized them. They felt that all was lost, and that the issue of the war was to be decided in this battle. The Federal columns came on, and the Confederates fought with all the nerve and daring of troops on the eve of a decisive action. The Federal lines, strengthened by the arrival of so many fresh troops, became too powerful for the resistance of the Confederate lines in their front. Hood's lines were taxed to their utmost strength at the beginning of the battle, and having no reserves to throw upon their weaker points, were wholly unable to longer withstand so powerful an onslaught. The lines wavered about the center for a while and finally giving way, the exultant Federals pressed in at the break thus made and exposed each wing of the Confederate lines to the greatest danger of capture. The result was a hasty retreat on the part of the Confederates, which partook much of the nature of a rout. The losses on both sides were moderate compared with those at the battle of Franklin. Many of the Confederates were captured, and, without shoes or blankets, were taken on freight cars to Northern prisons during the rigors of midwinter, and they bore the privations bravely. Arriving at prison, they were supplied with shoes and other clothing by the Federal authorities, and survived the struggle. Hood withdrew his army to Franklin on December 16. Halting at Franklin, provisions were issued to his men, and on the following morning the march was resumed in a southerly direction to Rutherford Creek. The enemy was in hot pursuit. At Rutherford Creek Hood's forces engaged the advance-guard of the Federals. The engagement here was of small dimensions, and Hood continued his retreat to Columbia. Arriving at Columbia on the night of December 19, he encamped his army and remained till the morning of the 21st, when his march was resumed and continued from point to point until he finally arrived in North Carolina, where his forces were joined to those of General Joseph E. Johnston, who now assumed command, and Hood was known in military circles but little more during the remainder of the war.

The Confederate forces were now composed of the remnant of three armies: The Army of Virginia, commanded by General Lee; the Army in North Carolina, commanded by General Johnston; and the Army of the Trans-Mississippi Department, commanded by General Dick Taylor. The destiny of the Confederacy was dark and unpropitious, and its doom was sealed. Its armies, reduced by the casualties of war and by desertions, had dwindled down to a mere handful of worn-out veterans, who, though knowing that the cause was lost and all their highest hopes and brightest anticipations had proved to be mere illusions and permanently put to flight, they felt that they had invested their all in the sequel, and many were ready and willing to follow the fortunes of the sinking Confederacy to the last throes of its expiring agonies, and offer themselves as a final sacrifice upon its funeral pile. There were others who had long since beheld the hopelessness of further resistance, and had been governed accordingly, especially among the troops from the border States who had families. Many of these men, who had made good soldiers and fought bravely on many battle-fields, and whose scars told that they had stood where danger was thick and heavy, began to leave the army during the last year and a half of the war. These men, as they had made good soldiers in war, were equally as good citizens in the walks of peace. After the battle of Franklin, many of the Tennessee troops went to their homes and abandoned the service permanently. They had been true and reliable soldiers, and they felt it their duty to take care of their families when they saw that further resistance in behalf of the Confederacy was unavailing. While many of the bone and sinew of the Confederate army thus abandoned the struggle, in doing so they did what they believed to be their duty under all the circumstances.

Hood's army had been reduced largely outside of the results of the casualties of war. Some of the soldiers went home from Chattanooga, some from other points, and many went home from Franklin. They had all made good soldiers during their stay.

THE LAST REORGANIZATION.

At Smithfield, North Carolina, all the Tennessee troops were consolidated into one brigade of three regiments and placed under the command of General J. B. Palmer. The Eighth, Sixteenth, Twenty-eighth, Thirty-eighth, and Fifty-first Tennessee Regiments were consolidated with a part of Maney's brigade into one regiment and placed under the command of Colonel Fields. The old Sixteenth was consolidated into two companies, one of which was commanded by Captain Hill, of General Carter's staff, and the other was placed under the command of Captain Frank York. A. F. Claywell was adjutant of the consolidated regiment, and made out its last official report soon after its consolidation. The surrender followed in a few days.

The three armies, thus reduced by the usual casualties of a four years' war, were now reduced to the last extremity, and the final collapse of the Confederacy was a mere matter of time. Hood's army had gone through all the vicissitudes of desperation in its campaigns from Marietta to Atlanta, from Atlanta to Nashville, and thence on the retreat to North Carolina. Like the early historic adventure of De Soto, it was a visionary attempt to accomplish something that partook of the romantic in its conception, though grand and magnificent in theory. The end proved the impracticability of the theory. Lured on by the fairy dreams that involved the accomplishment of impossibilities, the Confederate leader wandered from place to place, driven by the imperative edict of stinging want, and forced to the humiliating resorts of desperation, finally arrived in North Carolina with the broken and shattered remnants of a once powerful army; but reduced by death, disease, and desertion, until this once magnificent army of the Confederacy's pride and boast was but the mere shadow of its former self. Yet its ranks were composed of men who had been tried on so many hard-fought battle-fields, and in endurance, in courage, in fidelity to trust, and devotion to principle, they had stood a multitude of the severest tests. In no instance had they ever been found wanting. Braver men never lived. Truer men never drew the blade. This phalanx, the remnant of Hood's army, was placed under the command of the old chieftain whom they loved and honored. The men rejoiced at the change. They knew the courage and prudence, as well as the superior skill, of General Johnston; and while they had followed Hood through all his wanderings of rashness and indiscretion, they respected his bravery and devotion to the cause he had vowed to defend. The gallant old Sixteenth Regiment had been with Hood's army through all its trying vicissitudes and its historic campaigns. From Dalton to Atlanta, from Atlanta to Nashville, and from Nashville and Franklin through all its wanderings, to the surrender at Greensboro on April 26, 1865. Its dead lie sleeping upon every battle-field from Cheat Mountain to the Mississippi, and from the Mississippi to the Atlantic and the Gulf. Its sick and wounded surrendered a large per cent. of their number to the demands of the destroyer, Death, and their bodies lie sleeping in their narrow homes in the far-off lands of the stranger, along with their comrades who surrendered their lives upon the battle-fields. While they had surrendered the comforts and endearments of a quiet and happy domestic life to bare their bosoms to the invader and offer up their lives upon the altar of their country in behalf of a cause and principle which they believed to be right and just, their memory will ever live in the hearts and and be enshrined in the affections of their surviving comrades, and all who may appreciate the exalted and noble qualities of fidelity to duty and devotion to principle.

The dead, the maimed, and diseased, at the time of the surrender, constituted two thirds of its original number, inclusive of its recruits. Its effective total was scarcely a fifth. This gallant remnant fought bravely until the time came when they could fight no longer; and when they were surrendered by their superior officer they laid down their arms with the dignity of men who had fought a good fight, and accepted the generous terms which their gallantry elicited at the hands of their adversaries. Vanquished in arms, but not in spirit or principle, they accepted the situation like men; and as they had defended their cause through a four-years' war upon the principle of integrity and honor, they bestowed the same sterling qualities in faithfully and conscientiously complying with the terms of their surrender and the observance of the stipulations of their parole of honor. Thus the gallant old "Sixteenth," in company with the other regiments of the Confederacy, laid aside the implements and paraphernalia of war and donned the happy and quiet habiliments of peace. As they had been faithful, valiant, and true in all the phases of their duty as soldiers, so they became equally faithful, industrious, energetic, and honorable in the quiet walks of peace. Many settled down at their childhood homes and threw all their energies into the work of recuperating and regaining their lost fortunes. Others, including young men, emigrated to the South-west—to Texas, Missouri, Arkansas, and California—and engaged in agriculture. Others went to the North-western cities and engaged in business. Within twelve months after the surrender, members of the old Sixteenth could be found scattered through the North-western cities and over the Western and South-western States, all intent upon business with a view to regaining their losses. Years passed by, and many of them returned to the land of their nativity. The men, after the war, were generally industrious, frugal, and honorable, and made successful business men and good citizens.

Twelve years after the close of the war and the surrender of the Confederate armies, there was a re-union of the old Sixteenth Tennessee at McMinnville. About three hundred of the survivors of the regiment met in McMinnville on the public square, and proceeded to the Fair Grounds, where they enjoyed a sumptuous dinner prepared for the occasion. The rolls were called by companies, and every man, as his name was called, answered, if present; if absent, he was accounted for if living or dead. If living, his place of residence was given; if dead, the place and manner of his death was made known. Speeches were made by Colonel John H. Savage, Colonel T. B. Murray, and Captain J. J. Womack.

The following account of the re-union appeared in the McMinnville *New Era*, of October 11, 1877:

THE REUNION OF THE SIXTEENTH REGIMENT AT McMINNVILLE, ON FRIDAY, OCTOBER 5, 1877.

A reunion of Savage's regiment was held in McMinnville on Friday, October 5, 1877. The day was pleasant, and the assembly a vast one, numbering between three and four thousand. A more orderly and well-behaved crowd never assembled in our town. No drunkenness, no boisterous or loud talking, no quarreling or fussing of any kind; and this feeling pervaded the entire assembly throughout the day. The remains of the regiment were formed on the public square at 10 o'clock, and marched to the Fair Grounds under the stars and stripes, headed by Colonel Savage, mounted on a spirited white horse. As the regiment filed out on our streets with its four hundred or less men in ranks, thoughts of the day when it left our depot in 1861, full of life, and its ranks numbering over a thousand souls, filled the minds of all who witnessed that occasion, and the absence of so vast a number from its ranks on its return filled the hearts of those present with remembrances of the noble dead, and the springfountain of affection burst its bounds and filled the eyes of hundreds with the silent tear of love and affection for the memory of those who sleep in the silent and unmarked graves of the various battle-fields in which the noble old regiment participated. It was a pleasant occasion, and even the sadness lent additional charms and bound the remnant in closer bonds of eternal friendship and fraternal feelings. Arriving at the Fair Grounds, the welcome address was delivered by Colonel Savage, in which he said:

"*Soldiers of the Sixteenth Tennessee Infantry, C. S. A., Friends and Comrades, Ladies and Gentlemen:*—It is my pleasant duty, under the direction of our Committee of Arrangements, to extend to all of this large assembly, whether citizen or soldier, rebel or federal, a cordial welcome. What is said or done here to-day we are willing for the world to see and hear; but nothing will be said or done intended in the least to wound the feelings of a single human heart.

"The sound of hostile cannon and the shout of contending armies are heard no more within our borders, and much better would it have been for the American people if deadly hate and bitter words had been banished far away at the same time.

"The war came—it is not my purpose now to say who brought it on, or who was right or who was wrong, or whether misfortune or misconduct of rulers caused the result. The historians, long after we have slept in the grave, will write and settle these questions. It is enough for me to say, comrades, that we who still live, and our dead brothers in arms, many of whom to-day sleep upon lonely mountain or in some desolate plain, in graves unmarked and unknown to human eye, and our mothers and fathers, our kindred and neighbors, then believed we were right. We 'lost the cause,' and now submit to the victor as become gallant soldiers, but neither armies of artillery have power over the mind.

"We are here to-day to honor the dead. They fought for

principle—not for fame, power, plunder, or party. They offered themselves a sacrifice to the god of battles to maintain the constitution *as it was;* but we, the living, must obey it *as it is.* They sought to rule nobody but themselves, which they claimed the right to do without molestation from kings or armies. For four long years, almost without pay, upon scant rations, badly armed and clad, the Southern soldiers stood against more than double their numbers, sustained by Europe as a recruiting station, and by a greater expenditure of money than any the world has ever known before—*courage, patriotism*, and a *sense of duty*, being the only bonds that held the Southern soldiers in the ranks. The memory of brave men who fell in such a cause may live for ages—indeed it may never die. It is not always the fame of the conqueror that lives longest and shines brightest upon the pages of history. But this subject is delicate, and perhaps enough has been said in that direction; and what has been said is intended for no other purpose than to show that there is nothing in the past to shadow the fame or conscience of the Confederate soldiers.

"And now, comrades, as your old commander, who shared with you many dangers, and who never ceased to care for your honor and welfare, I hope I may say without offense to any that your deeds upon the field entitle you to share in the honors and misfortunes of the lost cause, and proclaim you the equal of the best regiment in the service. It is right that we should meet in tears for the heroic dead—*we* never should forget them, and they deserve to be remembered by the country. To live in the memory of the world and of those we love is a heavenly instinct—man's most powerful incentive to good. I remember a French general (Dessaix) who won for Napoleon a great battle, falling mortally wounded in the last charge. His last words were, 'I die with the regret only that I have not done enough to be remembered by my country.' Our young brothers, bright, buoyant, and brave, fell upon disastrous battle-fields. They have no inheritance in the land; the only thing earthly that yet remains to them is the affection and remembrance of their brothers in arms and of the people in defense of whose rights they offered up their lives. This reunion to-day means that their memory shall not perish like brutes of the field, for they were men with immortal spirits. Our government, with public money, builds imposing monuments over the federal brave, but we are forced to humbler methods. We intend to call the roll to-day and hope to account for each soldier, the living and the dead; and when the rolls are completed we intend to print them and give to each living soldier, or to his representative when dead, a copy to be kept as a perpetual memento of the part their kindred and neighbors bore in the great war. It is my duty to thank this large and attentive audience for their presence here to-day. It shows that their hearts are with the soldiers still. And ladies, I know I utter the sentiments of every soldier when I say, a thousand thanks to you for your presence and assistance at this meeting. It is hard to believe that any cause is wrong that is approved by your smiles. I may well liken woman to a good angel sent from heaven to bind up the wounds and shed eternal tears over the follies and misfortunes of man. We now call the roll to see who still lives, and who has gone from us forever."

The regiment was formed in line, and the orderlies called the rolls of their respective companies, carefully noting the history, so far as known, of every member of the regiment, giving the present residence, so far as known, of the living, and the time, place, and manner of death of the dead. These rolls will be published, as promised by Colonel Savage, so soon as they are perfected.

At the conclusion of the remarks by Colonol Savage, Colonel Thomas B. Murray was loudly called for, and responded in an impromptu speech of ten or fifteen minutes in one of his happiest strains, in which he said that he had not come there to speak, but to grasp his old comrades by the hand and talk over the trials of the days that tried men's souls. He said the occasion brought sadness to his heart. He had left here on May 1, 1861, with 108 of the noble sons of Warren—the sons of the best men in Warren county. He looked around him to-day and saw many familiar faces; he also saw many vacant seats. He asked where were the Thompsons, the Mauzys, Webbs, Smartts, Yorks, Marberrys, Spurlocks, Hacketts, and many others too tedious to mention. They were the pride and chivalry of the land. They had fallen in defense of what they believed right, and he had an abiding confidence that they had met their reward in a better land.

He said he and his comrades believed the South took up arms, not for slavery, but for the doctrine of State's Rights, upon which a republican government depends in this country. They had failed in arms, but had triumphed on an appeal addressed to the intelligence of the people. That a Republican President was to-day administering the government on democratic or State's rights principles. He denied that he rebelled against the stars and stripes that floated over him—he was as true to them as

LIEUTENANT-COLONEL T. B. MURRAY.

Grant or Sherman. He cared nothing for flags except so far as they represented principles. He would follow the stars and stripes as far as he did the stars and bars, so long as they were the emblem of principle. He described the condition of the half-fed, half-clothed Confederate soldiers in March, 1865, in and around Richmond, their ranks decimated by hunger and by sickness, and nothing but defeat and ruin staring them in the face. He described the Confederate ship as it went down; and the faithful soldier, in the last hours of the struggle, folding his arms and going down with the cause for which he had sacrificed so much, and asked the question, What government could not trust such men when they had plighted their faith? He then addressed the ladies, and told them what their sex had suffered for religion and liberty, and how faithful they were to the lost cause. He expressed the hope that these reunions would be continued as long as the old Sixteenth could muster as many as a corporal's guard; not to encourage rebellion, but to promote fidelity to principle.

Captain J. J. Womack was next called for, who in response, briefly alluded to the organization of his company as the first organized in the Mountain District, and to its perils and privations in common with the other companies of the regiment during the war, and then passed rapidly over the history of the times to the beginning of the present administration.

He declined to dwell upon the unfortunate administration of General Grant, preferring to speak of the present as that from which the country, the *whole* country, had something to hope for. He expressed strong confidence in President Hayes, and believed that under his administration, wisely and patriotically begun, the entire country would, in the near future, enjoy far greater prosperity than it had since 1860. He rejoiced to hear the President of the United States announce that the soldiers in the recent war between the States, Confederate and Federal, were *equally* justifiable in the part they took in that unfortunate struggle. He believed this the true ground for all to take—the only ground upon which all could agree—and if it had been taken when the Confederate army surrendered, and Southern people had been recognized as peers, and not as vassals, the country might have been financially and socially far in advance of its present condition. In closing, he thanked the mothers, wives, and sisters, for their care and sympathy while on the tented fields, and the assembly for the invitation to address them.

At the conclusion of the address by Captain Womack, Colonel J. W. Clift, ex-Federal, addressed the audience in a happy manner, and was followed by W. V. Whitson, Esq., of Forrest's cavalry, and Professor W. M. Janes, of Georgia. At the conclusion of these addresses, Colonel Savage dismissed the large crowd, which immediately repaired to town, after having spent a pleasant day, and one that will always be remembered in the kindest feeling.

CHAPTER VII.

MUSTER ROLLS.

COMPANY A.

OFFICERS.

L. N. Savage, Captain.
Iraby C. Stone, First Lieutenant.
John K. Ba'n, Second Lieutenant.
R. B. Anderson, Third Lieutenant.
G. W. Witt, First Sergeant.
G. L. Talley, Second Sergeant.

R. M. Magness, Third Sergeant.
T. B. Potter, Fourth Sergeant.
J. W. Harris, First Corporal.
L. G. Bing, Second Corporal.
M. L. Cantrell, Third Corporal.
Samuel M. Philips, Fourth Corporal.

PRIVATES.

William Adcock.
E. K. Adcock.
Isaac Adcock.
Benjamin Atnip.
E. L. Atnip.
John Atnip.
Larkin Bain.
R. W. Banks.
James Bing.
W. H. Bing.
Phineas Bozarth.
Joseph H. Bozarth.
James Bozarth.
J. A. Briggs.
W. H. Cunningham.
J. H. Cantrell.
U. E. Cantrell.
J. R. Cantrell.
James Cantrell.
John Cantrell.
John Cantrell.
M. L. Cantrell.
James Cantrell.
I. D. Cantrell.
W. H. Cantrell.
L. D. Cantrell.
B. M. Cantrell.

D. W. Cantrell.
Leonard Cantrell.
W. C. Cantrell.
Thomas Cherry.
Isaac Congo.
John W. Colwell.
Watson Cantrell.
Isaac Cantrell.
Peter Cantrell.
P. G. Cantrell.
A. M. Cantrell.
George P. Cautrell.
Martin Cantrell.
June Driver.
W. L. Driver.
Isaiah Driver.
C. B Davis.
Meredith Duwese.
D. C. Doller.
Thomas Dozier.
Martin Delong.
Watt Eastham.
H. C. Eastham.
J. B. Fisher.
S. M. Fulton.
Calvin Fowler.
Samuel Hathaway.

Len Hathaway.
W. A. Hallum.
B. M. Hicks.
Dallas Hicks.
William Herron.
T. M. Hooper.
T. A. Hooper.
Dick Hooper.
James Hooper.
Richard Jones.
J. W. Johnson.
E. S. James.
John James.
W. L. Judkins.
Ben Judkins.
F. E. P. Kennedy.
James Koger.
Pomp Kersey.
A. J. Kersey.
Felix Kersey.
Calvin Kersey.
Enoch League.
Enoch Lockhart.
John Lafever.
John Mason.
Bud Miller.
L. D. Moore.
John Moore.
W. C. Moore.
J. A. Moore.
John Martin.
W. P. Martin.
Thomas Martin.
W. B. Martin.
Robert Martin.
Jasper Martin.
Reuben Meeks.
R. W. McGinnis.
Elisha McGinnis.
G. W. Maynard.
J. M. Pertle.

Charles Pullin.
Robert Pullin.
W. C. Potter.
O. D. Potter.
Thomas Potter.
J. D. Philips.
Samuel M. Philips.
David Pittman.
Robert Rowland.
Jesse Redman.
Ben Rowland.
Dick Richardson.
W. Richardson.
T. J. Richardson.
James Rigsby.
W. G. Stevens.
John Stevens.
J. M. Stevens.
W. B. Sweeney.
A. Simpson.
A. J. Smith.
Burdine Smith.
Noah Smith.
Henry Scawelle.
H. C. Tate.
J. R. Thompson.
Fielding Turner.
Garrison Taylor.
Ross Unchurch.
John Van Hosser.
L. R. Witt.
W. Walls.
John Womack.
P. G. Webb.
I. C. Webb.
D. B. Worley.
W. M. Womack.
W. M. Wilmoth.
John E. Warren.
J. B. Wilkinson.
B. C. Wilkinson.

KILLED.

Capt. L. N. Savage, Murfreesboro.
Lieut. R. B. Anderson, Murfreesboro.
Lieut. G. W. Witt, Murfreesboro.
M. L. Cantrell, Perryville.
Benjamin Atnip, Georgia.
Watt Eastham, Atlanta.
J. H. Cantrell, Perryville.
James Cantrell, Perryville.
W. H. Cantrell, Franklin.
James Driver, Franklin.
Thomas Dozier, Atlanta.
S. M. Fulton, Atlanta.

168   THE SIXTEENTH REGIMENT

W. A. Hallum, Murfreesboro.
T. A. Hooper, Franklin.
F. E. B. Kennely, Perryville.
A. J. Kersey, Franklin.
Felix Kersey, Murfreesboro.
Enoch League, Murfreesboro.
Enoch Lockhart, Murfreesboro.
W. C. Moore, Perryville.

Robert Martin, Franklin.
Robert Rowland, Perryville.
William Richardson, Atlanta.
A. Simpson, Atlanta.
H. C. Tate, Lost Mountain.
P. G. Webb, Perryville.
John E. Warren, Murfreesboro.

DIED IN SERVICE.

Wm. Adcock, Camp Trousdale, 1861.
James Bing, Prison, 1864.
W. H. Bing, Prison, 1864.
William Herron, Georgia, 1864.
Richard Hooper, Georgia, 1864.
James Hooper, S. C., 1862.
J. A. Moore, Home, 1863.

Elisha McGinnis, Unknown.
O. D. Potter, Camp Trousdale, 1861.
Thos. Potter, Camp Trousdale, 1861.
L. R. Witt, Camp Trousdale, 1861.
Wm. Walls, Camp Trousdale, 1861.
Wm. Womack, Huntersville, 1861.
John Womack, Missing, Ga., 1864.

WOUNDED.

Capt. G. L. Talley, Chickamauga.
S. G. Bing, Perryville.
R. M. Magness, Perryville.
Samuel M. Philips, Perryville.
Isaac Adcock, Resaca.
E. L. Atuip, Atlanta.
R M. Banks, Perryville.
B. M. Cantrell, Perryville.
D. W. Cantrell, Perryville.
T. M. Hooper, Perryville.
Richard Jones, Perryville.
Fielding Turner, Perryville.

Peter Cantrell, Murfreesboro.
John Lafever, Murfreesboro.
Garrison Taylor, Murfreesboro.
B. C. Wilkinson, Murfreesboro.
G. W. Colwell, Murfreesboro.
J. W. Johnson, Franklin.
John Mason, Perryville.
W. L. Judkins, Atlanta.
W. C. Potter, Chickamauga.
J. C. Webb, Murfreesboro.
J. R. Thompson, Atlanta.

PROMOTED.

T. B. Potter, Sergeant Major, 1861.
R. B. Anderson, 1st Lieut., 1862.
G. W. Witt, 2d Lieut., 1862.
G. L. Talley, 3d Lieut., 1862, Capt., 1863.

W. C. Potter, 1st Lieut., 1863.
J. C. Webb, 2d Lieut., 1863.
L. R. Witt, 3d Lieut., 1863.

COMPANY B.

OFFICERS.

C. C. Brewer, Captain.
S. G. Crocker, First Lieutenant.
G. W. Turner, Second Lieutenant.
Jo. E. Bashaw, Third Lieutenant.
D. W. Tucker, First Sergeant.
J. H. L. Duncan, Second Sergeant.

L. P. Campbell, Third Sergeant.
M. A. Messick, Fourth Sergeant.
R. C. Carden, First Corporal.
Russel Brewer, Second Corporal.
L. B Campbell, Third Corporal.
A. M. Green, Fourth Corporal.

TENNESSEE VOLUNTEERS. 169

PRIVATES.

Daniel Anderson.
C. R. Alman.
Lytle Adams.
L. J. Butler.
John Brown.
James Brown, sr.
James Brown, jr.
Joseph Brown.
Lewis Burton.
D. C. Burton.
T. B. Butler.
C. H. Butler.
F. M. Boyd.
Thomas Burroughs.
E. M. Bashaw.
J. K. Butler.
Anderson Brown.
G. R. Campbell.
James Carden.
Wiley Calhoun.
J. A. Carden.
F. H. Church.
W. C. Campbell.
W. B. T. Campbell.
W. C. Crocker.
Noah Clay.
Thomas Campbell.
Thomas Douglas.
Osborn Dye.
Lacy Dye.
George Davis.
F. M. Daniel.
William Daniel.
Thomas Daniel.
James Dickerson.
Leroy Dye.
W. L. Ensey.
J. K. Ensey.
J. K. P. Foster.
William Foster.
Dennis Faulin.
W. H. Fisher.
James Fuller.
George Frazier.
Carrol Fultz.
Wiley Ford.
Alexander Farmer.
G. W. Freeman.

John Gaither.
R. E. Garrett.
Henry Herndon.
J. W. Hatfield.
Riley Howard.
I. H. Hawkins.
G. W. Haggard.
J. K. P. Haggard.
James Hawkes.
Isaac Howard.
Wade Henderson.
Elmer Hodge.
Robert Hill.
H. P. J. Hathcock.
Richard Hitson.
James Kilgore.
W. C. King.
Isaiah King.
G. W. Kennedy.
Thomas H. B. Long.
Buck Lowry.
Thomas Lewis.
Alexander Langley.
C G. Lance.
Joseph Massengale.
R. C. Messick.
R. J. Messick.
J. W. Messick.
G. H. Messick.
James McGuire.
U. S. McDaniel.
Griff. Myers.
P. H. McBride.
J. W. Mullins.
Moses Messick.
G. J. Newman.
John Oldfield.
James Popf.
James Paxton.
R. W. Purdom.
Samuel Phelps.
W. A. Powers.
Homer Powers.
Thomas Parker.
Dr. J. B. Ritchey.
J. W. Robinson.
M. D. Record.
G. W. Sain.

A. P. Sherrill.
W. V. Stevens.
Philburn Stevens.
Ezekiel Smartt.
R. J. Smotherman.
Isaac Spangler.
J. A. Smith.
O. P. Tucker.
T. H. Tucker.
Robert Tucker.
J. R. Taylor.
James Taylor.
Merk Thomas.
Robert Vickery.
W. B. Ward.
William Ward.
E. W. Walker.
J. M. Williams.
William Wiser.
Isaiah Wiser.
J. D. Wiser.
Thomas Wiser.
Awris Wilson.
Curtes West.
J. A. West.
Jacob Walker.
Elisha Walker.
John Walker.
William Young.
James Young.
John Young.
Mordecai Yell.
Pierce Yell.
Pleasant Yell.

KILLED.

Capt. C. C. Brewer, in Cavalry (transferred), 1864.
Joseph Brown, Atlanta.
F. H. Church, Murfreesboro.
William C. Crocker, Dalton.
Elmer Hodge, Perryville.
William Wiser, Perryville.
Isaiah Wiser, Perryville.
G. L. Freeman, Ky., (in Cavalry).
Dennis Faulin, Murfreesboro.

DIED IN SERVICE.

Lieut. G. W. Turner, Va., 1864.
Lieut. J. E. Bashaw, Chattanooga, 1865.
Lytle Adams, Prison, 1864.
Thomas Burroughs, Va., 1861.
Noah Clay, Ky., 1862.
Osborne Dye, W. Va., 1861.
G. W. Freeman, Ky., 1864.
J. K. P. Haggard, Unknown.
James Hawkes, Tullahoma, 1863.
Wade Henderson, Camp Trousdale, 1861.
Isaac Howard, W. Va.
Robert Hill, Unknown.
H. P. J. Hathcock, Prison, 1864.
T. H. B. Long, Ga., 1863.
Lieut. T. W. Lewis, Atlanta, 1864.
Alex. Langley, East Tenn., 1864.
R. J. Messick, Ga., 1862.
G. J. Newman, Unknown.
G. W. Sain, Camp Trousdale, 1861.
John Walsh, Unknown.

WOUNDED.

W. C. King, Murfreesboro.
Thomas H. Douglas, Murfreesboro.

PROMOTED.

J. H. L. Duncan, Capt., 1862.
E. W. Walker, 1st Lieut., 1862.
John K. Ensey, 2d Lieut., 1862.
W. H. Fisher, 3d Lieut., 1863.
E. W. Walker, Capt., 1864.
G. R. Campbell, Quartermaster, 1861.
T. W. Lewis, 3d Lieut., 1862.
P. H. McBride, Capt. Cavalry, 1862.
James B. Rickey, Quartermaster, 1863.
Elisha Walker, 3d Lieut., 1863.
James McGuire, 3d Lieut., 1863.

TENNESSEE VOLUNTEERS. 171

COMPANY C.

Officers.

D. M. Donnell, Captain.
Wright S. Hackett, First Lieutenant.
E. C. Reed, Second Lieutenant.
J. M. Castleman, Third Lieutenant.
A. J. Brown, First Sergeant.
Harrison Smith, Second Sergeant.
David Ramsey, Third Sergeant.
John Cope, Fourth Sergeant.
Thomas North, Fifth Sergeant.
L. D. Mercer, First Corporal.
H. H. Faulkner, Second Corporal.
William Wooten, Third Corporal.
Philander Wood, Fourth Corpora

Privates.

S. H. Alexander.
S. H. Allison.
C. B. Alred.
C. G. Black.
Thomas Black.
Thomas B. Biles.
James C. Biles.
Asbury Biles.
W. A. Bell.
Harrison Biles.
Thomas Bonner.
W. J. Bonner.
J. W. Bybee.
Richard Bybee.
A. Blackburn.
Michael Blackburn.
James Blackburn.
E. A. Braxton.
W. T. Brixey.
Calvin Brixey.
W. L. Brawley.
Reese Brewster.
John Brewster.
J. L. Bryant.
William Blanton.
John Cunningham.
J. T. Cannon.
J. B. Carter.
A. F. Claywell.
John Bennington.
George Donnell.
Walter Davenport.
Thomas H. Faulkner.
Robert French.
J. Fallman.
James Gibbs.
Calvin Glenn.
B. T. Groves.
J. H. Greer.
Thomas Greer.
Romulus Gwynn.
L. C. Harp.
R. C. Henderson.
D. B. Hoover.
William Hoover.
W. S. Hill.
J. D. W. Hill.
Peter Hansboro.
W. M. Harding.
J. J. Hensley.
James Hobbs.
John Herriman.
John Hennegar.
Wyatt Hitts.
Dr. Johnson.
D. W. King.
H. J. King.
John King.
Henderson Kidd.
G. Kirby.
James Lytle.
Frank Lytle.
William Lane.
A. B. Marbury.
Ben Marbury.
W. L. Marbury.
Horatio Marbury.
I. N. Mercer.
A. J. Mercer.
W. R. Morrow.
J. K. P. Martin.
Jasper Martin.
Sampson Martin.
Lewis Martin.

Thomas Mulrany.
A. L. Mitchell.
J. N. Mitchell.
John Meadows.
C. R. Morford.
D. C. Mathews.
A. Perry.
Joel Perry.
John Perry.
John Pace.
G. E. Purvis.
Aaron Pepper.
John Pepper.
A. J. Paine.

CAPTAIN D. C. SPURLOCK.

T. M. Reeves.
W. W. Roberts.
W. S. Ross.
James Ross.
E. S. Rowan.
John Rutledge.
A. J. Rayburn.
Elisha Reynolds.
Charles Read.
William Rhea.
M. D. Smith.
Alexander Smith, sr.
Alexander Smith, jr.
J. C. Smith.

TENNESSEE VOLUNTEERS. 173

D. C. Spurlock.
Cicero Spurlock.
C. J. Spurlock.
W. D. Smartt.
E. M. Smartt.
J. K. P. Smartt.
J. C. Smartt.
John Swann.
J. W. Swann.
Martin Stiles.
George Scott.
Samuel Stotts.
Frank Smith.
J. L. Thompson.

W. L. Thompson.
H. S. Thompson.
W. M. Taylor.
H. J. Thaxton.
Joseph Thomas.
Robert Vanison.
Lafayette Vandergriff.
William Vaughn.
C. B. Wilson.
J. B. Wilson.
J. C. Wilson.
William Wallace.
John Walker.
T. C. Wheeler.

KILLED.

Capt D. C. Spurlock, Murfreesboro.
Lieut, E. C. Read, Perryville.
Lieut. W. H. Wooten, Perryville.
Lieut. Cicero Spurlock, Perryville.
Sergt. Thomas North, in Cavalry, (transferred).
Corp'l Philander Wood, Perryville.
Thomas Bonner, Murfreesboro.
Richard Bybee, Murfreesboro.
James Blackburn, Atlanta.
Reese Bruster, Perryville.
Joshua B. Carter, Kennesaw Mt., Ga.

George Donnell, Franklin.
James Gibbs, Murfreesboro.
Thomas Greer, Perryville.
Wright S. Hackett, Atlanta.
Horatio Marbury, Perryville.
A. J. Mercer, in Cavalry, (transferred).
J. K. P. Martin, Murfreesboro.
John Meadows, Franklin.
Aaron Pepper, Franklin.
W. T. Thompson, Franklin.
H. S. Thompson, Perryville.
J. W. Bybee, Murfreesboro.

DIED IN SERVICE.

Harrison Biles, Chattanooga.
John Cunningham, Ga., 1862.
Romulus Gwynn, Grahamville, S. C.
John Herriman, Unknown.
John Hennegar, Unknown.
William King, Camp Trousdale, 1861.

G. Kirby, Unknown.
Louis Martin, Sewell Mountain.
D. C. Mathews, Shelbyville, 1864.
John Pace, Unknown.
John Pepper, Unknown.

WOUNDED.

J. C. Biles, Perryville, Atlanta (2).
J. B. Biles, Kennesaw Mountain.
Mike Blackburn, Perryville.
W. L. Brawley, Murfreesboro.
A. F. Claywell, Perryville.
L. C. Harp, Chickamauga.
W. S. Hill, Perryville.
D. W. King, Perryville.
I. N. Mercer, Atlanta.

W. R. Morrow, Murfreesboro, Chickamauga.
Thomas Marbury, Ga.
C. R. Morford, Perryville.
Charles Read, Perryville.
Alexander Smith, jr., Perryville.
J. L. Thompson, Chickamauga.
T. C. Wheeler, Perryville.

PROMOTED.

D. M. Donnell, Lieut. Col., 1862, Col., 1863.
W. H. Wooten, 3d Lieut., 1862.
E. C. Read, 1st Lieut., 1862.
D. C. Spurlock, Capt., 186?.
Thomas Black, Med. Dept., 1861.
C. G. Black, 2d Lieut., 1863.
A. F. Claywell, Adjutant, 1863.
H. H. Faulkner, Major, 1861.
C. R. Morford, 1st Lieut., 1863.
J. L. Thompson, Capt., 1863.
A. J. Brown, Maj. & A. Q. M., 1861.

COMPANY D.

OFFICERS.

P. H. Coffee, Captain.
Geo. Marchbanks, First Lieutenant.
Wm. W. Mooney, Second Lieutenant.
J. G. Rains, Third Lieutenant.

PRIVATES.

J. E. Anderson.
John Blanks.
Monroe Blanks.
Henry Blanks.
W. R. Bennett.
S. H. Brown.
W. J. Bennington.
H. S. Brabben.
A. P. Bragg.
D. W. Buyars.
Enoch Buyars.
Lafayette Clark.
G. W. Cunningham.
Mithael Cannon.
Walter Cope.
O. B. Christian.
W. B. Christian.
D. W. Campbell.
Gideon Cruse.
Hardeman Cruse.
Walter Cruse.
Stephen Cruse.
Matthew Douglass.
J. P. Douglass.
James Davis.
R. J. Evans.
J. P. Evans.
W. H. Edwards.
M. L. Edwards.
L. D. Elkins.
J. T. Fowler.
James Farless.

J. F. Gaw.
J. W. Greer.
W. T. Greer.
M. V. Gribble.
S. Gribble.
A. P. Gribble.
A. J. Gribble.
S. C. Gribble.
J. A. Gribble.
J. P. A. Hennessee.
Hamp Hennessee.
T. W. Hopkins.
W. L. Hopkins.
J. C. Haston.
J. J. Higginbotham.
Aaron Higginbotham.
Thomas Hutson.
A. J. Higginbotham.
J. J. Logue.
L. E. Logue.
J. K. Lowry.
J. G. Lambert.
J. D. Lusk.
Samuel Lusk.
T. F. Martin.
William Martin.
R. G. Martin.
John Meadows.
John McDaniel.
J. T. Moulder.
John Moulder.
John Mullican.

TENNESSEE VOLUNTEERS. 175

W. W. Mullican.
J. A. McWhirter.
J. B. McAfee.
W. H. Macon.
J. B. Myers.
W. T. McGee.
J. L. McGee.
Richard McGregor.
John McGregor.
W. M. Moulder.
Michael McGeary.
Richmond McGregor.
J. K. P. Nichols.
Patrick O'Keith.
Tim O'Leary.
W. Perry.
W. T. Perry.
William Pinkstone.
W. C Quick.
J. D. Quick.
John Quick.
T. J. Rodgers.

W. H. Rains.
James Rowland.
B. M Rowland.
G. W. Sommers.
J. M. Sommers.
W. L. Smyth.
Lycurgus Smith.
Jerome Smith.
John Tate.
Samuel Templeton.
T. J. Templeton.
John Templeton.
Byars G. Webb.
W. J. Ware.
R. A. Ware.
J. T. Walling.
J. A. Wheeler.
W. H. White.
J. W. West.
T. F. West.
F. M. York.
J. W. Wolcott.

KILLED.

Capt. J. G. Lambert, Perryville.
A. P. Bragg, (transferred to Cavalry), Ala.
Lafayette Clark, Missionary Ridge.
M. L. Edwards, Murfreesboro.
W. T. Greer. Perryville.
S. Gribble, Murfreesboro.
A. P. Gribble, Murfreesboro.
T. J. Gribble, Murfreesboro.
A. J. Gribble, jr., Murfreesboro.

W. Perry, Murfreesboro.
James Rowland, Murfreesboro.
W. F. Smith Murfreesboro.
A. J. Higginbotham, Detached, 1864.
Samuel Lusk, Franklin.
J. K. P. Nichols, Franklin.
W. H. Rains. Unknown.
J. M. Sommers, Perryville.
J. A. Wheeler, Perryville.
J. W. Wolcott, Atlanta.

DIED IN SERVICE.

J. F. Gaw, Camp Trousdale, 1861.
Richard McGregor, Va., 1861.

WOUNDED.

John Blanks, Perryville.
Walter Cope, Murfreesboro.
W. B. Christian, Murfreesboro.
J. P. Douglass, Murfreesboro.
J. C. Haston, Murfreesboro.
J. J. Higginbotham, Murfreesboro.
Aaron Higginbotham, Murfreesboro.
Thomas Hutson, Murfreesboro.
J. D. Lusk, Murfreesboro and Perryville.

Thomas Martin, Murfreesboro and Chickamauga.
R. G. Martin, Murfreesboro.
John McDaniel, Murfreesboro.
J. A. McWhirter, Murfreesboro.
John McGregor, Murfreesboro.
W. T. Perry, Murfreesboro.
W. Pinkston, Murfreesboro.
W. C. Quick, Perryville and Atlanta.
John Quick, Murfreesboro.

Lycurgus Smith, Murfreesboro.
T. J. Templeton, Murfreesboro.
B. G. Webb, Perryville and Franklin.
R. A. Ware, Perryville.
W. H. White, Perryville.
J. F. West, Murfreesboro.
F. M. York, Murfreesboro.

PROMOTED.

P. H. Coffee, Major, 1862.
J. G. Lambert, Capt., 1862.
S. H. Brown, 1st Lieut., 1862.
George Marchbanks, Adjutant, 1861.
J. P. A. Hennessee, 1st Lieut., 1863.
F. M. York, 2d Lieut., 1862, Capt, 1863.
W H. White, 2d Lieut., 1862.

COMPANY E.

OFFICERS.

Thomas B. Murray, Captain.
Alfred P. Smartt, First Lieutenant.
James Hill, Second Lieutenant.
Thomas York, Third Lieutenant.
Moss Mason, First Sergeant.
William Lowry, Second Sergeant.
James Green, Third Sergeant.
Robert Webb, Fourth Sergeant.
Hugh L. Moffitt, First Corporal.
H. J. Christian, Second Corporal.
S. W. Bratcher, Third Corporal.
Duke Blackwell, Fourth Corporal.

PRIVATES.

John Bost.
J. R. Brown.
J. H. Brown.
Asbury Brown.
W. H. Brooks.
Aaron Bouldin.
R. P. Burks.
John Boren.
Harrel Byars.
David Bonner.
Lawson Cantrell.
Samuel Cantrell.
J. C. Corder.
J. R. Countiss.
Peter Countiss.
John Countiss.
W. C. Countiss.
James Christian.
Enoch Cooksey.
Gillam Clark.
Abe Douglass.
Dock Douglass.
Joseph England.
Clark Edge.
Polk Evans.
W. M. Evans.

Newt Fuston.
Reese J. Fuston.
W. J. Fuston.
Joseph H. Goodbar.
John Green.
A. J. Gribble.
R. P. Green.
Elias Green.
W. W. Gourd.
E. H. Green.
D. Holmes.
J. H. Holmes.
Read Holmes.
James W. Hill.
W. M. Hensley.
W. M. Jones.
Isaac Jones.
E. J. Jones.
James Jennings.
Pleasant Jennings.
Dock Jennings.
Tillman Keener.
Lawson Keif.
Nelson Kirby.
Robert Kirby.
James Kirby.

TENNESSEE VOLUNTEERS. 177

Jerry Killian.
W. Lowry.
Polk Lowry.
James Laurence.
George Martin.
Isaiah Moffitt.
William Moores.
John Martin.

William Manning.
John Medley.
Michael Mauzy.
William Mullican.
W. C. Morton.
W. T. Mabry.
Allen Mason.
William Mason.

MAJOR JO. H. GOODBAR.

George McNeeley.
James McGregor.
Riley Nunnelly.
General Nunnelly.
Archie Nunnelly.
O. D. Neal.
John Perser.
Luke Perser.

A. J. Paine.
John R. Paine.
Thomas Potter.
E. W. Smartt.
A. P. Smartt.
John S. Sanders.
Carrol Stepp.
J. R. Skelton.

12

THE SIXTEENTH REGIMENT

J. P. Smartt.
Bryant Stroud.
John Tanner.
Isaac Tramble.
Stephen Tate.
John Van Hooser.
J. Van Hooser.
L. L. Van Hooser.
John Van Hooser.
Fate Van Hooser.
Newt Van Hooser.
Elias Womack.
Jesse Walling.
Robert Webb.
Perry G. Webb.

Rowland Ware.
John R. Womack.
W. C. Womack.
R. R. Womack.
A. M. Womack.
Felix G. Womack.
John S. Womack.
John B. Womack.
John C. Watson.
W. R. Wood.
U. L. Wood.
William Woods.
George Wallace.
Thomas York.
George W. York.

KILLED.

Lieut. James Green, Franklin.
J. H. Brown, Franklin.
John Boren, Perryville.
David Bonner, Murfreesboro.
J. R. Countiss, Perryville.
Lawson Cantrell, Murfreesboro.
James Christian, Perryville.
Abe Douglass, Murfreesboro.
Joseph England, Perryville.
William Evans, Atlanta.
Isaac Jones, Murfreesboro.
James Kirby, Murfreesboro.
William Lowry, Lost Mountain.

Michael Mauzy, Murfreesboro.
Allen Mason, Perryville.
James McGregor, Perryville.
A. P. Smartt, Perryville.
Stephen Tate, Corinth.
L. L. Vanhooser, Unknown.
Elias Womack, Perryville.
Perry Webb, Perryville.
Rowland Ware, Perryville.
John B. Womack, Franklin.
Thomas York, (transferred,) Perryville.

DIED IN SERVICE.

Maj. J. H. Goodbar, Morristown, 1861.
Polk Evans, Meadow Bluff.
Reid Holmes, Warm Springs, Va.
Moss Mason, Prison, Rock Island.

O. D. Neal, Huntersville, Va.
J. P. Smartt, Unknown.
U. L. Wood, (transferred,) Home, 1861.

WOUNDED.

Capt. J. J. Womack, Murfreesboro.
Lieut. Jesse Walling, Murfreesboro.
Lieut. W. C. Womack, Missionary Ridge.
Enoch Cooksey, Perryville.
John Medley, Perryville.
Archie Nunnelly, Perryville.
R. R. Womack, Perryville.
George W. York, Resaca.
W. T. Mabry, Murfreesboro.

G. N. Clark, Murfreesboro.
J. B. Womack, Murfreesboro.
A. M. Mason, Murfreesboro.
Luke Perser, Murfreesboro.
John Perser, Murfreesboro.
Isaiah Moffitt, Murfreesboro.
G. W. Wallace, Murfreesboro.
A. J. Van Hooser, Murfreesboro.
J. S. Van Hooser, Murfreesboro.

PROMOTED.

Thomas B. Murray, Lieut.-col., 1861.
Joseph H. Goodbar, Major, 1861.
J. J. Womack, Capt., 1861.
John R. Paine, Adjutant, 1862.
Jesse Walling, 1st Lieut., 1862.

J. K. P. Webb, 2d Lieut., 1862, Capt. 1863.
B. P. Green, 3d Lieut., 1864.
W. C. Womack, 3d Lieut., 1863.

COMPANY F.

OFFICERS.

H. H. Dillard, Captain.
W. K. Sadler, First Lieutenant.
Holland Denton, Second Lieutenant.
R. A. Young, Third Lieutenant.
M. S. Smith, First Sergeant.
S. W. Brown, Second Sergeant.
B. F. Scudders, Third Sergeant.

James McKinley, Fourth Sergeant.
David H. Bullington, Fifth Sergeant.
H. I. Hughes, First Corporal.
J. M. Null, Second Corporal.
Joel Gabbert, Third Corporal.
J. Y. Crowell, Fourth Corporal.

PRIVATES.

M. M. Anderson.
F. M. Amonet.
Joseph Ballard.
C. M. Ballard.
Samuel Benson.
J. R. Bullington.
Leroy Bullington.
John Bullington.
Josiah Bullington.
Branshaw Boyd.
Obadiah Boyd.
J. A. Boyd.
John Brown.
David Bryant.
W. W. Baldwin.
William Braswell.
W. N. Caruthers.
Crockett Clark.
D. A. Crowell.
Walter E. Chilton.
John Choate.
Jacob Choate.
Meadow Choate.
J. L. Davis.
Van Dillard.
I. C. Eldridge.
G. W. Floyd.
J. H. Fisher.
W. L. Grimsley.

W. F. Grimsley.
Jack Griffin.
Elijah Garrett.
Noah Harris.
Richard Hensley.
William Hoggard.
Henry Harpole.
William Hodges.
J. M. Jackson.
Alexander Jackson.
G. B. Jaquess.
P. H. Leadbetter.
Thomas Laycock.
I. C. Laycock.
J. R. Laycock.
W. H. Maxwell.
D. W. Maxwell.
T. R. Matheney.
J. P. Maberry.
W. T. Moore.
J. F. Moore.
J. R. Murry.
M. J. Nichols.
John Nichols.
Lewis Ollerson.
J. F. Owen.
W. H. H. Ortry.
H. L. C. Pearson.
D. G. Pointer.

180 THE SIXTEENTH REGIMENT

J. J. Richardson.
John Scarlett.
B. L. Scarlett.
A. J. Sutton.
W. H. Sullius.
T. C. Thompson.
John Tolbert.
J. B. Vance.
P. M. Wasson.
Allen Winchester.
William Wiggleton.

R. J. West.
J. M. West.
B. H. Watson.
W. W. Wallace.
A. D. Young.
C. C. Young.
R. R. McDauiel.
Rufus Owen.
William Webb.
Albert Ballard.

KILLED.

M. M. Anderson, Perryville.
John Choate, Murfreesboro.
Jacob Choate, Murfreesboro.
W. F. Grimsley, Perryville.
William Hodges, Chickamauga.
Alexander Jackson, Perryville.
J. C. Laycock, Murfreesboro.
James Murray, Murfreesboro.
John Brown, Murfreesboro.
Joseph Y. Ballard, Murfreesboro.

J. R. Murray, Perryville.
J. F. Owen, Jonesboro, Ga.
Lieut. D. G. Pointer, Perryville.
Capt. J. B. Vance, Perryville.
T. C. Thompson, Perryville.
R. J. West, Atlanta.
Lieut. W. W. Wallace, Murfreesboro.
Rufus Owen, Atlanta.
William Webb, Franklin.
Albert Ballard, Murfreesboro.

DIED IN SERVICE.

David H. Bullington, Tupelo.
Bransford Boyd, Nashville, 1861.
T. R. Matheney, Huntersville.

W. T. Moore, Dublin, Va.
John Tolbert, Millboro.

WOUNDED.

B. F. Scudders, Perryville.
H. I. Hughes, Perryville and Murfreesboro.
Joseph Ballard, Murfreesboro.
John Bullington, Perryville.
Josiah Bullington, Perryville.
John Brown, Perryville.
W. W. Baldwin, Perryville.
W. N. Caruthers, Perryville.
J. H. Fisher, Cheat Mountain.

M. J. Nichols, Perryville.
John Nichols, Perryville and Murfreesboro.
Lewis Ollerson, Perryville.
W. H. H. Ortry, Atlanta.
H. L. C. Pearsons, Perryville.
J. J. Richardson, Perryville.
P. M. Wasson, Murfreesboro.
William Wiggleton, Murfreesboro.
I. M. West, Atlanta.

PROMOTED.

H. H. Dillard, Major, 1862.
John B. Vance, Capt., 1862.
D. G. Pointer, 3d Lieut., 1862.
W. W. Baldwin, 2d Lieut., 1862.

W. W. Wallace, 1st Lieut., 1862.
F. M. Amonett, Capt., 1863.
M. J. Nichols, 3d Lieut., 1863.
J. F. Owen, 3d Lieut., 1863.

COMPANY G.
OFFICERS.

P. C. Shields, Captain.
A. T. Fisher, First Lieutenant.

W. L. Woods, Second Lieutenant.
James R. Fisher, Third Lieutenant

PRIVATES.

Jasper Adcock.
H. P. Adcock.
William Allen.
A. J. Allen.
Benjamin Atnip.
John Atnip.
Alfred Bain.
Peter Bain.
Isaiah Bain.
John Bain.
Peter Bain.
Henry Bain.
C. Bain.
J. L. Britton.
M. Blount.
W. M. Clenny.
Joseph Cantrell.
C. W. Cantrell,
William L. Cantrell.
Meredith Carter.
Darius Clark.
Phineas Clark.
Jefferson Clark.
H. B. Cope.
William A. Cotton.
Ben Capshaw.
Zil Cruse.
T. A. Cotton.
T. A. C. Denton.
John Denton.
D. L. Dunham.
L. R. Dunham.
P. C. Duncan.
John Donnell.
R. N. Earles.
Gabriel Elkins.
John Fisher.
L. B. Fisher.
J. P. Fisher.
Peter Franks.
A. Fisk.
W. J. Farris.
Lawson Fisher.
M. L. Fisher.
L. B. Fisher.
P. B. Franks.
R. Grissom.
Grundy Gibbs.

G. W. Gilbert.
L. W. Gilbert.
William Gleeson.
William Goodson.
E. M. Greenfield.
James Helton.
Lawson Helton.
J. L. Hudson.
Jesse Hudson.
Thomas Hodge.
Moses Hutchins.
Ben Hutchins.
C. M. Jordan.
Lawson Knowles.
Robert Love.
Levi Lassater.
Isaiah Lassater.
Monroe Moore.
Ransom Moore.
Dimmon Moore.
Lawson Moore.
Wallace McPeak.
John McManus.
John Meggerson.
O. D. McGown.
James Mullins.
James North.
A. Norris.
Thomas Pollard.
F. M. Pettit.
Thomas Pettit.
Albert Pickering.
Jasper Roberts.
James Roberts.
G. W. Roberts.
William Roberts.
James Roberts, jr.
Dock Roberts.
Joseph Ray.
Casson Robinson.
C. G. Rankhorn.
H. L. P. Sanders.
L. H. Stockton.
Wiley Sanders.
Lawson Smith.
J. R. Swindle.
J. J. Stanley.
C. G. Stacy.

Nathan Troglin.
Lee Troglin.
Adolphus Wiggins.
J. W. Wiggins.
Tilmon Wiggins.
F. M. Wright.
S. L. Walker.
O. D. Walker.

Alexander Walker.
Seth F. Wright.
D. W. Warst.
Austin Webb.
James Wright.
Deskin Wright.
Andrew J. Youngblood.

KILLED.

Isaiah Bain, Perryville.
C. Bain, Perryville.
J. L. Britton, Murfreesboro.
W. S. Cantrell, Perryville.
Darius Clark, Perryville.
H. B. Cope, Perryville.
P. C. Duncan, Perryville.
Lawson Fisher, Perryville.
Grundy Gibbs, Atlanta.
J. L. Hutson, Perryville.
Monroe Moore, Perryville.
Ransom Moore, Murfreesboro.
Jasper Roberts, Perryville.

Dock Roberts, Perryville.
J. W. Wiggins, Perryville.
Thomas Hodges, Murfreesboro.
F. M. Wright, Perryville.
Thomas Pollard, Atlanta.
S. L. Walker, Perryville.
B. L. Jordan, Franklin.
Zil Cruse, Murfreesboro.
Lee Troglin, Murfreesboro.
Lieut. F. M. Pettit, Franklin.
James N. Cantrell, Murfreesboro.
John Fisher, Murfreesboro.

DIED IN SERVICE.

Lieut. W. M. Clenny, Ga., 1861.
Peter Atnip, Va.
C. W. Cantrell, Ga.
David L. Dunham, Prison.
E. M. Greenfield, in Camp.
James Hilton, Prison.
James Mullin, Prison.

L. H. Stockton, Perryville.
John Donnell, Mississippi.
Dimmon Moore, Murfreesboro.
Wallace McPeark, Huntersville, 1861.
D. W. Marsh, Camp.
J. J. Allen, Ky.
William Gleeson, Vicksburg, Miss.

WOUNDED.

William A. Cotton, Perryville.
P. B. Franks, Murfreesboro.
William Roberts, Corinth.
Lawson Knowles, Perryville.
Adolphus Wiggins, Perryville.

William Gleeson, Perryville.
C. G. Rankhorn, Kennesaw Mountain.
Andy Youngblood, Murfreesboro.

PROMOTED.

A. T. Fisher, Capt., 1862.
W. L. Woods, 1st Lieut., 1862.
A. Fisk, 2d Lieut, 1862, Capt., 1863.
W. M. Clenny, 2d Lieut., 1862.

F. M. Pettit, 2d Lieut., 1863.
P. B. Franks, 3d Lieut., 1863.
Lawson Smith, 2d Lieut., 1862.

COMPANY H.

OFFICERS.

L. H. Meadows, Captain.
H. L. Simms, First Lieutenant.
W. G. Etter, Second Lieutenant.
B. J. Solomon, Third Lieutenant.
James M. Parks, First Sergeant.
R. B. Hayes, Second Sergeant.
W. P. Ray, Third Sergeant.
R. B. Bess, Fourth Sergeant.
Carrol Fultz, First Corporal.
Jerome Safley, Second Corporal.
F. M. Perry, Third Corporal.
William G. Reese, Fourth Corporal.

PRIVATES.

Adrian Anglin.
Tip Anglin.
John Akeman.
George Akeman.
Samuel B. Baker.
F. M. Barker.
J. S. Brown.
John Brown.
John H. Brown.
G. T. Brown.
W. S. Bullen.
Absalom Brown.
Russell Brown.
Jackson Brown.
John Bess.
Wiley Bess.
Russell Bess.
Alius Bess.
Mitchell Campbell.
Samuel Cartwright.
John Countiss.
John Christian.
W. B. Christian.
C. W. Clendennon.
J. N. Clendennon.
Jackson Clendennon.
Isaac Cunningham.
Jacob Curtis.
Wiley Curtis.
Martin Curtis.
T. Coldwell.
W. Coldwell.
Leonard Daniel.
T. J. Davis.
John Davis.
James Dodson.
P. A. Earles.
R. R. Etter.
George H. Etter.
William Etter.
John Etter.
J. P. Etter.
William Furren.
Joseph Furren.
David Fultz.
M. P. Hayes.
H. L. Hayes.
Obadiah Hennessee.
Mart Hennessee.
J. C. Hughes.
Aaron Hughes.
William Hughes.
B. J. Hill, jr.
William Hennessee.
Rad Hill.
James Johnson.
James Jones.
Isaac R. Jones.
A. J. Jordan.
Houston Lynn.
James Lockhart.
Joseph Lockhart.
James McDaniel.
A. McDaniel.
A. J. Moore.
William Mitchell.
J. A. Miller.
J. H. Mooney.
John Murphy.
W. R. Martin.
Alpha Martin.
G. C. McCraw.
M. E. C. Mobley.
F. M. Moffitt.

The Sixteenth Regiment

Sam McCorkle, sr., (Fiddler.)
Samuel McCorkle, jr.
Stephen McCorkle.
David Miller.
William Overturf.
Alexander Pursley.
Henry Powell.

Edward Pursley.
Joseph Pace.
H. Pennington.
Elijah Poe.
G. W. Parks.
Wills Roberts.
Marshal Roberts.

CAPTAIN JAMES M. PARKS.

Isaac Roberts.
Levi Rodgers.
James Rowan.
W. N. Russell.
W. H. Russell.
C. M. Rutledge.
R. M. Safley.

Jefferson Savage.
Jesse Savage.
James Slaughter.
B. J. Slaughter.
Allen Smith.
J. N. Smith.
B. F. Smith.

TENNESSEE VOLUNTEERS. 185

Andy Smith.
Jackson Smith.
John Scott.
Levi Sides.
William Tallent.
Henry Turner.
Simms Vickers.
J. J. Vickers.
A. D. Ware.

J. C. Waldo.
John Willis.
William Willis.
Harmon Willis.
A J. Woodlee.
W. C. Woodlee.
Isaac Walker.
J. C. Watson.

KILLED.

Capt. J. M. Parks, Chickamauga.
Leiut. John Akeman, Altanta, four wounds.
Serg't R. B. Hayes, Perryville.
Serg't W. P. Ray, Perryville.
Corp'l Jerome Safley, Perryville.
Samuel M. Baker, (transferred;) in Cavalry.
John H. Brown, Franklin.
John Countiss, Perryville.
Isaac Cunningham, Perryville.
Martin Curtis, Perryville.
William Etter, Atlanta.

B. J. Solomon, transferred to Cavalry.
John Etter, Murfreesboro.
Obadiah Hennessee, Perryville.
Martin Hennessee, Perryville.
Isaac R. Jones, Murfreesboro.
Alpha Martin, Cheat Mountain.
Edward Pursloy, Murfreesboro.
Henry Pennington, Murfreesboro.
J. N. Smith, Perryville.
B. F. Smith, Murfreesboro.
B. J. Slaughter, in Cavalry, (transferred).

DIED IN SERVICE.

Russell Bess, Camp Trousdale, 1861.
N. J. Hill, jr., Home, 1861.
James Johnson, Pocotaligo, S. C.
William Mitchell, Huntersville, Va.
J. A. Miller, Huntersville.
G. C. McCraw, Camp Trousdale.
Isaac Roberts, Warm Springs, Va.

James Rowan, Home.
Jefferson Savage, Shelbyville, 1863.
Jesse Savage, Atlanta, 1863.
James Slaughter, Atlanta.
Jackson Smith, Home.
Isaac Walker, Home, 1861.

WOUNDED.

Capt. J. M. Parks, Murfreesboro.
G. T. Brown, Pocotaligo.
W. G. Etter, Perryville.
H. L Hayes, Perryville.
Carrol Fultz, Perryville.
R. R. Etter, Perryville.
G. W. Parks, Perryville.
J. S. Brown, Murfreesboro.
W. S. Bullen, Murfreesboro.
T. J. Davis, Murfreesboro.
J. C. Hughes, Murfreesboro.
M. P. Hayes, Murfreesboro.

James Jones, Murfreesboro.
A. J. Jordan, Murfreesboro.
W. N. Russell, Murfreesboro.
W. G. Etter, Chickamauga.
C. M. Rutledge, Chickamauga.
J. C. Watson, Chickamauga.
R. R. Bess, Atlanta.
J. P. Etter, Atlanta.
R. M. Safley, Atlanta.
Rad Hill, (transferred to Fifth Tenn.)
G. H. Etter, in Cavalry, (transferred).
J. H. Mooney, in Cavalry (transf'red).

PROMOTED.

J. M. Parks, Capt., 1862.   H. L. Hayes, 2d Lieut., 1862.
W. G. Etter, 1st Lieut., 1862, Capt., 1863. John Akeman, 3d Lieut., 1862.

COMPANY I.

OFFICERS.

Harmon York, Captain.
Green B. Johnson, First Lieutenant.
Mortimer B. Wood, Second Lieutenant.
A. T. Seitz, Third Lieutenant.
Philip Shockley, First Sergeant.
G. M. Cummings, Second Sergeant.
Ben Randals, Third Sergeant.

James K. Hillis, Fourth Sergeant.
John Grissom, Fifth Sergeant.
Samuel Fleming, First Corporal.
William Jones, Second Corporal.
James Worthing, Third Corporal.
William B. Wood, Fourth Corporal.

PRIVATES.

A. J. Agent.
John Baker.
Samuel Baker.
Peter Baker.
Silas Y. Ballard.
Cyrus Billingsley.
John Boyd.
William Boyd.
R. C. Boyd.
C. H. Clark.
William Creeley.
Denny Cummings.
Joseph Cummings.
Joseph Denny Cummings.
John L. Cummings.
George W. Drake.
J. K. P. Douglas.
J. B. Foster.
John Graham.
G. W. Groves.
James Green.
N. B. Hambrick.
Pleas Harrison.
W. B. Haston.
Samuel Haston.
John Hankins.
Jacob Hayes.
T. A. Head.
W. H. Head.
I. T. Hillis.
W. R. Hillis.
Isham Hollansworth.
Isaac Howard.
Levi Johnson.
A T. Jones.
James Martin.
Stephen Martin.

Isham Martin.
Neil McClure.
W. C. McBride.
G. W. McBride.
Mathew McBride.
George W. Miller.
Martin Mitchell.
Mark Mitchell.
James Mitchell.
William Mitchell.
S. D. Mitchell.
B. F. Morgan.
William Morgan.
James Moore.
D. C. Moore.
Miles Moore.
John A. Myers.
Nero Owens.
Joseph Pace.
W. R. Paine.
H. C. Paine.
Samuel Parker.
Bryson Parsley.
William T. Passons.
E. T. Passons.
James Passons.
A. J. Passons.
George W. Miller.
John Patton.
Simon Philips.
Samuel Porter.
Solomon Porter.
T. A. Priest.
Marion Priest.
Larkin Priest.
D. C. Randals.
Henderson Rhodes.

TENNESSEE VOLUNTEERS. 187

Jeff C. Rodgers.
W. W. Rawlings.
Thomas Rawlings.
Jackson Rolls.
John Smaller.
W. J. Smith.
G. W. Sparkman.
Nelson Sparkman.
Elvin Sparkman.
Peter Shockley.
Hickman Shockley.
John J. Steakley.
James C. Steakley.
A. C. Stype.
Joseph Stype.
George W. Stype.
F. M. Stype.

Marion Thomasson.
A. F. Thompson
W. J. Underwood.
John Underwood.
Joseph Walker.
Joshua Worley.
Rufus Ward.
D. C. Ward.
Samuel Worthington.
W. T. Worthington.
Silas R. York.
A. C. York.
John E. York.
William Wilson.
W. T. Thurman.
W. R. Wood.
U. L. Wood.

KILLED.

Serg't John Grissom, Corinth.
Corp'l William Jones, Perryville.
Corp'l William B. Wood, Perryville.
A. J. Agent, Atlanta.
Samuel Baker, Lost Mountain.
S. Y. Ballard, Detached.
William Creeley, Corinth.
N. B. Hambrick, Franklin.
Isham Hollinsworth, Murfreesboro.
Levi Johnson, Perryville.
James Moore, Perryville.
D. C. Moore, Murfreesboro.
H. C. Paine, Lovejoy Station, Ga.
Marion Priest, Murfreesboro.

Henderson Rhodes, Murfreesboro.
Thomas Rawlins, Murfreesboro.
Samuel Parker, Perryville.
G. W. Sparkman, Perryville.
Peter Shockley, Perryville.
Wiley B. Haston, Perryville.
John J. Steakley, Perryville.
James C. Steakley, Perryville.
Frank M. Stype, in Cavalry, (transferred.)
John E. York, Perryville.
Simon Phillps, Perryville.
Philip Shockley, Transferred.

DIED IN SERVICE.

G. W. Drake, Huntersville.
J. B. Foster, White Sulphur Springs.
Pleas Harrison, Bath Alum Springs.
John Hankins, Bath Alum Springs.
W. R. Hillis, Camp Trousdale.
Isaac Howard, Corinth.

W. J. Smith, Bath Alum Springs.
Marion Thomasson, Tullahoma.
Joshua Worley, Atlanta.
William Wilson, Nashville.
U. L. Wood, Home, (discharged.)

WOUNDED.

Sol Porter, Murfreesboro.
Lieut. S. D. Mitchell, Perryville.
John Smaller, Perryville.
Cyrus Billingsley, Perryville.
Lieut. Denny Cummings, Perryville.

James Passons, Resaca.
W. T. Worthington, Murfreesboro.
Samuel Worthington, Murfreesboro.
S. R. York, Murfreesboro.

PROMOTED.

John Boyd, 3d Lieut., 1861.
Ben Randals, Capt., 1862, Maj., 1865.
James Worthington, 1st Lieut., 1862.

S. D. Mitchell, 2d Lieut., 1862.
Denny Cummings, 3d Lieut., 1862.

COMPANY K.

OFFICERS.

Daniel T. Brown, Captain.
S. B. McMillan, First Lieutenant.

James Revis, Second Lieutenant.
W. D. Turlington, Third Lieutenant.

PRIVATES.

John Austin.
T. J. Bradford.
James Brown.
John Basheers.
Simeon Baker.
R. D. Baker.
R. L. Bronson.
J. D. Bozarth.
Robert Burnett.
Hugh Carrick.
Samuel Carrick.
Dock Carr.
G. W. Collins.
James Collins.
C. C. Cash.
John Castille.
S. W. Cantrell.
Logan Cantrell.
Marshall Cope.
Elbridge Cope.
Tip Cope.
James Cope.
Andrew Cope.
T. R. Cooper.
Jimmy Cottair.
James Clark.
Nick Cook.
John Downey.
Vance Davis.
W. B. Davis.
D. W. Dinges.
W. L. Dibrell.
Perry Epps.
Henry Emmett.
William England.
Jubal Early.
Samuel Eastland.
Silas Farley.
Thomas Farley.
Thomas Farmer.
Simon Frazier.
R. D. Fancher.

J. K. P. Fancher.
J. E. Ford.
Hosea Gist.
Jesse Gross.
H. L. Gracy.
Gardner Green.
Alexander Glenn.
P. L. Hensley.
Trent Hampton.
John Hudgins.
J. L. Heard.
E. M. Irving.
A. T. D. Irving.
Henry Jones.
Henry James.
W. R. Jett.
George Johnson.
Thomas Knowles.
Jasper Knowles.
William Knowles.
John Kirby.
Alexander Kirby.
Zachariah Lay.
Benjamin Lack.
Thomas Lisk.
John Lowry.
William Lowry.
William Lafferty.
J. W. McConnell.
A. D. McKinzie.
Daniel Martin.
George Martin.
W. B. McManus.
Frank Marchbanks.
Joseph Mitchell.
G. W. Nelson.
Durgan Nash.
Alexander Oakes.
Bryson Parsley.
Thomas Purtle.
Elijah Quillen.
James Revis.

TENNESSEE VOLUNTEERS. 189

William M. Revis.
J. E. Rotan.
Alexander Rawlston.
J. E. Shockley.
T. H. K. Shockley.
Samuel Scott.
Robert Snodgrass.
Samuel Snodgrass.
Andrew Saylors.
W. G. Simms.
James Smith.
George Shanks.
Monroe Stacy.
Thomas Taylor.
Hiram Taylor.
A. J. Turlington.
John Turlington.

T. J. Templeton.
Green Templeton.
Pleas Templeton.
Sylvester Humphrey.
Alexander Vass.
George Worley.
Joshua Worley.
John Webb.
Lawson Webb.
William Wilhoit.
James Wilhoit.
Stephen Williams.
John Warren.
Joseph Wilson.
J. H. Whitley.
J. T. Walker.

KILLED.

James Brown, Greensboro, N. C.
Simeon Baker, Perryville.
Hugh Carrick, Chickamauga.
James Carlin, Murfreesboro.
Marshall Cope, Murfreesboro.
James Clark, Perryville.
J. E. Ford, Perryville.
Daniel Martin, Perryville.
F. Marchbanks, in Cavalry, (transferred.

Alexander Oaks, Perryville.
T. H. K. Shockley, Detached.
Robert Snodgrass, Ga.
Andrew Saylors, New Hope Church.
Pleas Templeton, Franklin.
George Worley, Murfreesboro.
Joshua Worley, Murfreesboro.
William Wilhoit, Franklin.
Stephen Williams, Ky.

DIED IN SERVICE.

John Bashurs, Prison.
Logan Cantrell, Huntersville.
Elbridge Cope, Shelbyville.
Vance Davis, Greenbrier, Va.
Jubal Early, Prison.
Silas Farley, Chattanooga.
Thomas Knowles, Huntersville, Va.

John Kirby, Ga.
Zack Lay, Unknown.
George Martin, Tullahoma, Tenn.
Thomas Purtle, Lewisburg, Va.
William M. Revis, Unknown.
George Shanks, Tullahoma.
Sylvester Humphreys, Home.

WOUNDED.

William Lowry, Murfreesboro and Atlanta.
John Castile, Murfreesboro.
H. L. Gracy, Perryville.
Gardner Green, Chickamauga.
E. M. Irving, Va.

Jasper Knowles, Perryville.
William Laferty, Dallas, Ga.
James Revis, Murfreesboro.
T. J. Templeton, Murfreesboro.
James Wilhoit, Murfreesboro.

PROMOTED.

Daniel T. Brown, Major, 1862, Lieut.-col., 1863.
W. T. Turlington, Capt., 1862.

J. Edward Rotan, 2d Lieut., 1862.
William Lowry, 3d Lieut., 1862.
W. G. Simms, 3d Lieut., 1863.

RECAPITULATION.

Showing the number of men enlisted in the Sixteenth Regiment Tennessee Volunteers, and the total casualties from 1861 to 1865, by companies.

COMMAND.	Number Enlisted.	Number Killed.	Number Wounded.	Number Died of Disease.	Total Casualties.	REMARKS.
Field and Staff	3	......	3	1	4	
Company A	147	27	23	14	64	
Company B	143	9	2	20	31	
Company C	143	22	16	11	49	
Company D	110	18	26	2	46	
Company E	125	24	18	7	49	
Company F	92	21	18	5	41	Not including conscripts.
Company G	115	25	8	14	47	
Company H	129	23	21	14	58	
Company I	120	26	9	11	46	
Company K	120	18	10	14	42	
Total	1247	213	154*	113	479	

* This report includes only the severely wounded.

SKETCHES
OF
OTHER TENNESSEE REGIMENTS.

CHAPTER VIII.

THE EIGHTH REGIMENT OF TENNESSEE VOLUNTEERS.

This regiment was composed of volunteer companies from the counties of Lincoln, Moore, Marshall, Overton, Jackson, and Smith, of which Lincoln county furnished four companies, Marshall county one, Jackson county two, Overton county two, Smith county one, and contained the following number of men respectively:

1. Captain McKinney's company, 100 men.
2. Captain Higgins's company, 78 men.
3. Captain Bryant's company, 98 men.
4. Captain Moore's company, 104 men.
5. Captain Hall's company, 78 men.
6. Captain Gore's company, 97 men.
7. Captain Armstrong's company, 80 men.
8. Captain Buford's company, 62 men.
9. Captain Myers's company, 89 men.
10. Captain McHenry's company, 91 men.

The companies were organized into a regiment at Camp Trousdale, in Sumner county, Tennessee, May 29, 1861, and officered as follows:

FIELD AND STAFF.

ALBERT S. FULTON, Colonel;
WILLIAM L. MOORE, Lieutenant-colonel;
W. B. BOTTS, Major;
C. C. MCKINNEY, Adjutant;
L. W. OGLESBY, Quartermaster;
ALBERT EWING, Commissary;
Dr. J. W. GRAY, Surgeon;
Dr. GRANVILLE B. LESTER, Assistant Surgeon;
Rev. DAVID TUCKER, Chaplain.

The companies were officered as follows:

1. CAPTAIN McKINNEY'S COMPANY.
[Lincoln County.]

Rane R. McKinney	Captain.
N. M. Bearden	First Lieutenant.
T. W. Raney	Second Lieutenant.
A. M. Downing	Third Lieutenant.

2. CAPTAIN HIGGINS'S COMPANY.
(Lincoln County.)

George W. Higgins	Captain.
Christopher Griswell	First Lieutenant.
E. S. N. Bobo	Second Lieutenant.
David Sullivan	Third Lieutenant.

3. CAPTAIN BRYANT'S COMPANY.
(Marshall County.)

James L. Bryant	Captain.
James P. Holland	First Lieutenant.
T. F. Brooks	Second Lieutenant.
B. B. Bowers	Third Lieutenant.
T. E. Russell	First Sergeant.

TENNESSEE VOLUNTEERS. 193

4. CAPTAIN MOORE'S COMPANY.
(Lincoln, now Moore, County.)
William Lawson Moore..................................Captain.
William J. Thrash..........................First Lieutenant.
Thomas H. Freeman..................................Second Lieutenant.
W. L. Shoftner..................................Third Lieutenant.

5. CAPTAIN HALL'S COMPANY.
(Lincoln County.)
A. M. Hall..................................Captain.
C. C. McKinney..................................First Lieutenant.
Theophilus W. Bledsoe..................................Second Lieutenant.
C. N. Allen..................................Third Lieutenant.

6. CAPTAIN GORE'S COMPANY.
(Jackson County.)
William Gore..................................Captain.
A. B. Botts..................................First Lieutenant.
James Eaton..................................Second Lieutenant.
A. W. W. Brooks..................................Third Lieutenant.

7. CAPTAIN ARMSTRONG'S COMPANY.
(Jackson County.)
L. T. Armstrong..................................Captain.
(We were unable to procure the names of the other officers of this company.)

8. CAPTAIN BUFORD'S COMPANY.
(Smith County.)
William J. Buford..................................Captain.
(We were unable to procure the names of the other officers of this company.)

9. CAPTAIN MYERS'S COMPANY.
(Overton County.)
Calvin E. Myers..................................Captain.
Columbus Marchbanks..................................First Lieutenant.
W. W. Windle..................................Second Liutenant.
W. C. Hickey..................................Third Lieutenant.

10. CAPTAIN McHENRY'S COMPANY.
(Overton County.)
Tim S. McHenry..................................Captain.
Joseph Wright..................................First Lieutenant.

Andrew Dale	*Second Lieutenant.*
Robert Parker	*Third Lieutenant.*

Captain William L. Moore having been elected lieutenant-colonel of the regiment, William J. Thrash was made captain of Moore's company, and William Bonner was elected first lieutenant.

The Eighth Tennessee remained at Camp Trousdale in camp of instruction under General Zollicoffer until July, when it was sent, with other Tennessee regiments, to Haynesville, East Tennessee, from which point the regiment was placed in a brigade with the Sixteenth and assigned to Loring's division of Lee's army. This brigade was commanded by Brigadier-general Daniel S. Donelson, and the Eighth and Sixteenth Tennessee Regiments remained in this brigade without change to the close of the war.

The Eighth Regiment of Tennessee Volunteers was composed of hardy, able-bodied men, and participated in the memorable campaign of Western Virginia under Lee. At the battle of Cheat Mountain this regiment bore a prominent part. On the night previous to this engagement this regiment was in line of battle within a few hundred yards of the enemy's encampment, having successfully gained the rear of the position. In the affair the evening before, Captain Bryant's company was a part of the front guard that secured the capture of the enemy's picket line, by which Donelson's brigade was enabled to gain the rear of the Federal stronghold on the Huttonville pike. In all the campaigns of Western Virginia this regiment bore a prominent part, and for endurance and daring it proved itself the equal of any regiment in the service.

Donelson's brigade was ordered with Lee to the coast of South Carolina in December, 1861. The Eighth and

Sixteenth Tennessee Regiments thus accompanied General Lee to his new field of labors. At the battle of Coosaw River or Port Royal Ferry, January 2, 1862, the gallant old Eighth performed well its part. In this battle the regiment lost its first men in action. Having been placed within range of the Federal gunboats, the regiment suffered principally from the shells from the enemy's heavy guns.

After the battle of Coosaw River, matters remained quiet on the coast of South Carolina during the remainder of the winter and the early spring months. After the battle of Shiloh, the Eighth Tennessee was sent to Corinth to the support of General Beauregard, who was at that time threatened with an overwhelming force of the enemy, by which the whole Mississippi Valley was endangered, and the Confederacy was about to be cut in twain. Upon the arrival of the regiment at Corinth in April, 1862, the men were all in good health and eager for active service. How well and to what extent their wishes were gratified the sequel will show.

The men of this regiment had enlisted for twelve months, and their period of enlistment was about to expire. They expected to be discharged during the following May, and wanted to participate in at least one big battle before they went home. They knew that they were to be held to the close of the war by virtue of the conscript act which had recently passed the Confederate Congress; yet many thought they would have some privileges in the matter, and were discussing the branch of service they would enter at the expiration of their period of enlistment. At all events, they expected to get a chance to go home.

While the boys of the regiment were revolving these

things in their minds, the mighty army of the advancing foe was steadily approaching nearer and nearer, and securing every step of its advance by the strongest fortifications. A regular siege was now in progress, and under the very guns of an advancing foe the regiment was ordered to reorganize under instructions from the War Department. The commissioned officers were allowed to resign and go home, if they chose to do so, and the only privilege left the private soldiers was to submit to what many considered to be an outrage upon their liberties, while others looked upon the matter as a military necessity, and accordingly accepted the situation as the best and only thing that could be done in order to preserve and maintain the strength and efficiency of the service. The regiment was reorganized on May 8, 1862, the day set apart for the reorganization of the whole army. Many entered into the measure under protest, and some deserted, though quiet was soon restored, and the men became reconciled to the situation. Some of the commissioned officers were re-elected; others were elected to higher offices, and others went home. Of the latter class, many joined the cavalry or entered other departments of the service, while some were fully satisfied with one year's experience in war and not only failed to re-enter the service, but were to some extent so indifferent to the cause as to appear tender-footed on the issues ever afterward. It was thus in all the regiments. The patriotism of a few men completely exhausted itself during the first year, and they appeared fully inclined to cancel the contract into which they at first entered with so much enthusiasm.

By the reorganization and promotion of the officers of the Eighth Regiment Tennessee Volunteers many vacancies were filled from the ranks, and, in fact, after the reorganization of the regiment it was better officered than before; and this was the situation of the different regiments of the army. The first officers were good men, though they were 'selected" more through their standing and influence in private life than through their efficiency. The standard of qualifications was elevated at the reorganization, and the true competency of the aspirant was the only currency that secured his commission. In this manner the regiment was officered, principally, with young and middle-aged men. The events of the following years of the war showed how well they were qualified to perform the duties assigned them.

The officers elected at the reorganization of the Eighth Regiment Tennessee Volunteers were as follows:

FIELD AND STAFF.

WILLIAM LAWSON MOORE, Colonel;
JOHN H. ANDERSON, Lieutenant-colonel;
C. C. McKINNEY, Major;
JOHN D. TOLLEY, First Lieutenant and Adjutant;
Dr. —— COLLINS, Surgeon;
Dr. GRANVILLE B. LESTER, Assistant Surgeon;
RANE R. McKINNEY, Quartermaster;
WILLIS STONE, Commissary;
Rev. M. B. DE WITT, Chaplain.

Dr. S. E. H. Dance, who had been assistant surgeon in Turney's First Tennessee Regiment, and had served in the Army of Northern Virginia until after the battle of Sharpsburg, was, during the following year, promoted to the rank of a full surgeon, and assigned to duty in the Eighth Regiment Tennessee Volunteers, through the request of Colonel Moore and Adjutant

Tolley, to fill the position vacated by Dr. Collins. Dr. Dance assumed the duties of surgeon of the Eighth Regiment Tennessee Volunteers on the eve of the battle of Murfreesboro, and continued with the regiment until the close of the war.

The company officers of the regiment elected at the time of the reorganization were as follows:

CAPTAINS OF COMPANIES.

Company A, Captain WILLIAM BURFORD;
Company B, Captain W. G. CHOWNING;
Company C, Captain W. H. BLAKE;
Company D, Captain JOHN SHOOK;
Company E, Captain N. M. BEARDEN;
Company F, Captain JAMES CULLOM;
Company G, Captain WILLIAM SADLER;
Company H, Captain T. J. DAVIS;
Company I, Captain J. M. McAFEE;
Company K, Captain WILLIAM J. THRASH.

After the reorganization, the Eighth Regiment remained at Corinth during the siege, and retreated with the army to Tupelo. It accompanied its brigade throughout the Kentucky campaign, and participated in the battle of Perryville. It was by the side of the Sixteenth Regiment Tennessee Volunteers in all its campaigns and marches, and the history of the one regiment is virtually the history of the other. The men of the two regiments were warmly attached to each other, and on the march and in the camp many amusing incidents occurred in which the men of one or the other or both of these regiments were principal actors. There was one peculiar characteristic of many of the men of the two regiments, and that was a harmless insubordination at times when there was no danger. The men *would* forage, and no guard could be placed so strong, and with instructions so strenuous and rigid, as to withstand the sagacity and cunning of a member of the Eighth or Sixteenth Tennessee Regiment. They acquainted themselves with the country for miles on either side of the line of march, and were always up with their command at night, laden with the fruits of the tramp in the way of chickens, vegetables, and not unfrequently a few canteens of whisky. The men would not pillage or plunder the people, but would pay for what they procured, with here and there a few exceptions. In each regiment there were a few men who could find a still-house if it was within twenty miles of the line of march, and could go to it and be in camp at night against supper time. When any of the boys procured whisky, they would divide with their comrades, and a general jollification would sometimes ensue; but the closest scrutiny of the brigade and regimental officers could seldom, if ever, locate the evil, or ascertain who procured, or was in possession of, the whisky.

The most amusing incident of this kind occurred at Sparta, while Bragg's army was on its way to Kentucky. In the counties of Van Buren, White, Warren, and DeKalb were the homes of the most of the boys of the Sixteenth Tennessee Regiment. As a result, many of the boys broke ranks and went home, but got with the regiment at Sparta the next morning, where the army encamped for twenty-four hours. The boys of the Sixteenth were loaded down with good things to eat. Their people had come to camps through the day and brought them many luxuries, including a good supply of apple brandy and corn whisky. The old Sixteenth was lively and jolly. Toward evening they had got with the Eighth Tennessee, and not only divided with the boys, but showed them the way to where more was to be had, and they went after it. By night the two regiments were on an equal footing in mirth and hilarity. General Donelson knew the drift of events, and to cut off the supply of whisky from the boys, ordered a strong guard to be put out around the brigade, and instructed the officers of the guard to pay particular attention and see that not a single man was allowed to go out of the brigade encampment except by explicit authority from brigade head-quarters. An officer of the Eighth Tennessee was brigade officer of the day, and to him was assigned the duty of putting out the guard around the brigade. Getting the guard properly mounted after dark, he started out to post them. Placing a man at a designated point, he moved on, posting his sentinels very close together, as he thought. As the detail would move on to the next post, the last sentinel posted would fall in on the rear and move on with the rest. In this way the officer of the day made the circuit of the brigade and had the same number of men he started with. Not finding the sentinel first posted, he moved on to the next post and found it vacant. In this manner he continued around the brigade again, but failed to find the sentinels anywhere. When he saw that he had the original number of sentinels he started out with, he concluded that there was something mysterious about it, and procured an ax with which he blazed the trees at the places where he posted his sentinels, so that he could the more easily find his first starting-point in the darkness. In this manner he made the circuit of the brigade again, and his detail had not diminished at all. General Donelson was becoming wrothy by this time, and sent out to know *what was the matter that the brigade guard could not be posted.* Some officers went to his tent and told him that many of the men were in the neighborhood of their homes and were having some fun; that there was no danger, and the men knew it— that every man would be in place at the proper time. This appeased the General for the time being, and the brigade guard was dispensed with. In the morning, every man was at his post and ready for the march.

The men of the Eighth and Sixteenth Regiments would have their fun and would forage, but when emergencies would arise, they could be found right at their posts, and they *would stay there* till the trouble was over.

In the Kentucky campaign, Colonel Moore's Eighth Regiment encamped at his old home on the evening before the battle of Perryville. On October 8, when Polk's corps was ordered to the right below Perryville, as the army approached the Chaplin Creek, the Eighth and Fifty-first Tennessee Regiments were detached from the brigade, with a section of Carnes's battery, and sent to the extreme right under Colonel Wharton of the Texas Rangers. This movement was for the purpose of gaining the rear of the enemy's left wing. The movement was successfully accomplished, by which the enemy was confused and swung back upon his main line almost simultaneously with the approach of Maney's brigade. This detour on the right at such an opportune moment enabled Maney's brigade to hurl back the force in its front, but at a fearful cost of life. The Federal line being broken, retreated to the brow of a hill about six hundred yards distant and reformed. The Confederates pressed their opportunity and gained a decided victory.

In this battle, Adjutant John D. Tolley, of the Eighth Tennessee Regiment, was wounded while standing on the premises where his father was born, and the house was set on fire and burned by the enemy's shells.

In the affair with the enemy on the extreme right, at the battle of Perryville, the Eighth Tennessee did valuable service, though its losses were not so heavy as that of other regiments of the brigade who attacked the enemy in front. The action of the Eighth and Fifty-first, with the section of artillery, had much to do in deciding the issue of the day. The officers and men of the expedition performed their parts well.

The regiment retreated with Bragg's army from Kentucky, and appeared with its brigade before Murfreesboro in December, 1862. Having recruited its ranks, its numbers were full and the men were in good health and fine spirits.

The Confederate army under General Bragg was composed of two corps, commanded respectively by Lieutenant-generals Polk and Hardee. Hardee was in command of the left wing and Polk was in command of the right wing of the Confederate forces. On the morning of December 31, Hardee attacked Rosecrans's right wing and turned it upon its main line. The attack was made at daylight, and was attended with the best of consequences in Hardee's front. Polk was expected to act in concert with Hardee, and make his attack simultaneous with the attack on the Confederate left. For some cause Polk's action was hindered, by which the enemy had ample time to rearrange and strengthen his lines in Polk's front. The advance was finally ordered on the extreme right, and the enemy being strongly posted in a well-chosen position, was not so easily dislodged. The battle raged throughout the day, and the issue seemed doubtful. Night closed upon the scene with a victory in Hardee's front. While the ground in front of Polk's corps had been stubbornly contested, and was strewn with the dead and dying, each party had maintained its ground at fearful cost. On the following day the Federals had gained and fortified an eminence on the Confederate right, from which it was found impracticable to dislodge them. The result was a retreat from Murfreesboro. The Confederates withdrew to Shelbyville and Tullahoma, and the Federals remained about Murfreesboro during the remainder of the winter and the following spring months.

In the battle of Murfreesboro, the Eighth Tennessee suffered heavier losses than in any engagement during the war. Among its valuable officers who fell in this battle was its regimental commander, Colonel William L. Moore. Colonel Moore was a native of Lincoln county, Tenn., and was the son of General William Moore, who was a soldier under Jackson. Colonel Moore was born near the town of Mulberry, in Lincoln county (now Moore county), May 5, 1830. In his boyhood he received a good education, having the benefit of good schools, and as he approached the age of manhood, he was placed in school at Danville, Ky., the home of his grandparents, where he completed his education; after which he engaged in the mercantile business at Harrodsburg with Collins Moore, who was his uncle. In the year 1853, he was married to Miss Neet, of Woodford county, Ky. After his marriage he remained at Harrodsburg for two years, when he removed to his paternal home on account of the declining years of his father, who had called him hither to look after a large business. Here he resided until the breaking out of the war between the States, when he enlisted a company of his neighbors, and was elected to the captaincy of the same. The company was from

COLONEL WILLIAM L. MOORE.

the village of Mulberry and vicinity, and was known as "The Mulberry Grays."

Colonel Moore was elected lieutenant-colonel of the Eighth Tennessee Regiment in May, 1861, and at the reorganization was elected colonel. A kind officer, a brave soldier, and a Christian gentleman, he was loved by his men, whom he led with characteristic coolness and gallantry in the affairs with the enemy at Cheat Mountain and Port Royal Ferry, at Perryville and Murfreesboro. In the last-named battle, on December 31, 1862, he gave his life to the cause he had espoused, and fell with his face to the foe. His horse had been shot from under him but a few moments previously, and in falling he was caught under its body. Extricating himself with difficulty, he had merely gained his feet and spoken a cheering word to his men, when a ball from the enemy pierced him in the breast and he fell. His death was almost instantaneous. The battle was raging fearfully at the time, and the slaughter on both sides was terrible. The Eighth Tennessee suffered severely in this battle. Its killed and wounded amounted to more than half its numbers in the carnage of the first day's fight, when the regiment lost its gallant leader.

Captain Bearden was also slain, he and nine of his men falling by the same shot from the enemy's cannon. One single shell exploded in their midst, and ten lives were the fruit of its unerring aim.

Colonel Moore's death was lamented by a large circle of relatives and friends, who had known his sterling qualities from childhood, and by his comrades in arms, who knew him but to love him.

Tullahoma Lodge, No. 262, Free and Accepted Masons, passed the following resolutions of respect to the memory of Colonel Moore, as reported by the committee appointed by the lodge for the purpose:

TRIBUTE OF RESPECT.

TULLAHOMA LODGE, No. 262.

The committee to whom was referred the drafting of resolutions to the memory of our much-lamented brother, William Lawson Moore, report that he was born in the county of Lincoln, State of Tennessee, on the 5th day of May, 1830, and suddenly fell on the field of battle, on the 31st day of December, 1862, in the thirty-third year of his age.

He entered the Southern army in April, 1861, and was unanimously elected captain of his company; and on being attached to the Eighth Regiment Tennessee Volunteers, was unanimously elected lieutenant-colonel, and, at the reorganization of the army, under act of Congress, he descended to the ranks, from which he was called to the command of his regiment by its unanimous voice.

His modesty forbade his seeking office, and his gallantry forbade his declining its duties. His men loved him. He commanded their affections and their arms. In time of trial and emergency his regiment was looked to with confidence and emulation. At Corinth his horse was shot from under him. He held his command on foot, receiving a painful wound in the hand. In duty, he was fearless; in authority, he was calm; and in emergency, he was brave. He nobly distinguished himself in his successful charge of the enemy at Perryville, Ky., and the noted battle of Murfreesboro on the last day of the eventful year 1862. He held his command at the very furnace of the conflict; his horse fell from under him; he leaped to his feet with three wounds upon his body, unknown to all but himself, calling on his men, "Forward, my brave boys!" when a ball penetrated the vital breast and he spoke no more. He fell, but he fell forward, and his noble spirit fled. The pen of the historian of that bloody conflict is now ascribing to the prowess and gallantry which he displayed the repulse of the enemy and capture of the spoils.

Those qualities which endear his memory to all who knew him, are not restricted to his short military career. That is rather a history of his death than of his life, and he fell before he had seen the harvest of what he had sown, or finished what he had well begun.

He was one of Tennessee's favorite sons. In all the different relations of life which he sustained, are written the essays of the honest man, the good citizen, the generous neighbor, the kind father, the fond brother, the loving husband, and his fidelity to the Christian faith. In the death of so valuable a citizen, we deplore his loss and sympathize with the common heart; and, as a brother of our mystic order, we feel with deepest sense the breach of fraternal ties.

Clustered around this scene hang the wreaths of mourning in their most melancholy significance. In the midst of circumstances favorable to the hope of many peaceful years, with one fell blow he is stricken down. The suddenness, the place, the time, and manner of his death—the many relationships which clung around, and the many bereaved hearts, conspire to checker the scene. He was the uncle and guardian of an orphan minor, the only brother of five doting sisters, and the father of four interesting children, never to hear his instructing voice or see his smiling face again; the only son of an aged father, grown gray with the buffetings of many years, who had laid his last weighty cares upon his shoulders; and still more sad, the husband of a loving wife, whose affections, charities, and social qualities entitle her to hopes more bright than the altar of mourning, and a destiny more serene than the desolate beach of a troubled sea. The fact that he was the participant of her joys, the support of her hopes, and guide through the cloud and the storm, is a consideration that widens the avenues of sorrow and disappointment.

He snatched from the camp and the march a few fleeting hours to mingle once more with the pleasures of home, with his family and friends, and to share the greetings of a happy Christmas, but the parting hour made haste. Lighted by a brightened sky, joy had perched upon the pinions of pleasing expectations, cheered by the hope of meeting again. Added to all this, to make the sadness more intense, his nephew, W. H. Holman, a young man who bore with him the award of esteem from all who knew him—the only son of a deceased sister—belonging to his command, was also present, participating in the social festivities of the happy circle, and mingling with the solicitudes which fluttered around the omens of the future. But, oh! how deep the pain to tell! They both fell, bleeding offerings upon the altar of war, on the same field and on the same day. The sun which rose upon their buoyant spirits, set upon their dead bodies, cold and lifeless in the gore of battle. Their remains were gathered up and deposited in the same cemetery, on the same day, in two distinct graves, consecrated with the sighs and tears of assembled relatives and friends.

Perhaps there were no two men whose sudden death and irreparable loss could affect so deeply so many hopes and anxieties. Death pursues with a smiling face and strikes his deepest blow where fondest expectations meet. One item in connection with the subject of this memoir is that the very spot which gave him birth, the very garden that nourished his infancy to manhood, has opened her bosom to receive him back, to hold him in her embrace, as the chosen hostage, to the day of retribution.

Resolved, That in the death of Colonel William Lawson Moore society has sustained an irreparable loss, but should cherish his good qualities as a bequeathed inheritance, to imitate his example and emulate his virtues.

Resolved, That we deplore his loss and condole with the bereaved; our balm is too stale to heal affection's wounds so deep, but we would commend them to the God in whom we trust, who "healeth the broken in heart and bindeth up their wounds."

Resolved, That we tender to the surviving widow and her four little ones our best wishes for their happiness. We cannot take away their afflictions, but will help bear them; and that they be furnished a copy of these proceedings by the secretary.

Resolved, That we wear the usual badge of mourning for thirty days.
Jo. C. HOLT,
E. C. McLOUGHLIN,
J. GRIZZARD,
Committee.

A true copy. Attest:
J. GRIZZARD, Secretary Tullahoma Lodge, No. 262.

After the death of Colonel Moore, the command of the Eighth Regiment Tennessee Volunteers devolved upon Lieutenant-colonel John H. Anderson, who was made colonel of the regiment, and remained with it to the close of the war. Colonel Anderson was an able and gallant officer, and a man highly respected and honored, not only by the men of his regiment, but by all who knew him. He commanded the Eighth Regiment through the battle of Chickamauga, and his official report of the part performed by his regiment in that battle is furnished in another part of this work.

At the battle of Missionary Ridge, the brigade under Brigadier-general Marcus J. Wright was placed on the extreme right of the Confederate line of defense. This point was threatened by a heavy force of the enemy, who was trying to cut off Bragg's communications and destroy his stores at Chickamauga Station. The task assigned to Wright's brigade was an arduous one, as the Confederate line of defenses, already weakened by the withdrawal of troops for the East Tennessee campaign, was now lengthened so far that in many points it was a mere skirmish line, and with no reserves, and no means of concentration at any point. The brigade passed the day in front of an enemy many times its number, while the battle raged furiously on the left and center. The operations on the right were confined to maneuverings principally, in which the brigade encountered the enemy in the forenoon on the opposite side of Chickamauga Creek. This being to some extent a surprise, and the ground unfavorable to defense, General Wright withdrew his brigade to a more eligible position. In this affair with the enemy across the creek there were some casualties among the Tennessee troops, but comparatively few in number.

After the battle of Missionary Ridge, General Wright was assigned to duty at Atlanta, as commander of the district and post. Colonel John H. Anderson, of the Eighth Tennessee, was then placed in command of the brigade, a position he filled until after the army was established in its winter quarters at Dalton. The staff officers were retained, and afterward the brigade was placed under the command of Colonel John C. Carter, of the Thirty-eighth Tennessee. Colonel Carter was subsequently commissioned a brigadier-general, and commanded Wright's brigade, in its engagements, to the battle of Franklin, in which he lost his life.

Colonel Anderson commanded the Eighth Tennessee throughout the Georgia campaign, and after its consolidation with other regiments he commanded the consolidated regiments to the time of the surrender.

Colonel Anderson was born in Wilson county, Tenn., near the town of Lebanon, August 6, 1831. His ancestors came from Virginia. His parents, Frank Anderson, jr., and Eleanor T. Anderson, resided in Wilson county. Colonel Anderson received his early education in the schools at Lebanon, and afterward was a student of Irving College, in Warren county. Before the war he was a merchant. When the war broke out in 1861, he enlisted a company for the State service, and was elected captain of the same. This company was a part of the Tenth Tennessee Regiment, and its first service was at Fort Henry, on the Tennessee river. At the fall of this place, the Confederates retreated to Fort Donelson. The Tenth Tennessee was in the battle at this place, and was surrendered with the garrison.

A few days after the surrender Captain Anderson succeeded in making his escape, in company with General Bushrod R. Johnson, and reported to General Albert S. Johnston at Decatur. General Bushrod Johnson was assigned to the command of a brigade, and Captain Anderson was assigned to duty on his staff. In this capacity he fought through the first day's battle of Shiloh. General Bushrod Johnson having been wounded during the first day's fight at Shiloh, Captain Anderson was assigned to duty on General Cheatham's staff, in which capacity he served through the second day's fight, and remained a member of Cheatham's staff till the beginning of the Kentucky campaign, when he was promoted to the rank of lieutenant-colonel, and assigned to duty in the Eighth Tennessee Regiment by order of General Bragg, having been promoted to lieutenant-colonel for gallantry displayed on the field of Shiloh.

Colonel Anderson was with the Eighth Tennessee at the battles of Perryville and Murfreesboro. During the last-named battle Colonel W. L. Moore, the commander of the Eighth Tennessee, was killed, and Colonel Anderson was promoted to the command of the regiment as a full colonel.

At the battle of Missionary Ridge, General Wright became indisposed and turned over the command of the brigade to Colonel Anderson, who continued as its commander until the return of Colonel Carter to the army shortly before the opening of the Georgia campaign. Colonel Carter now commanded the brigade and Colonel Anderson returned to the command of his regiment.

When the army arrived before Atlanta, Colonel Anderson was again placed in command of the brigade. He led the brigade in the battle of Peach Tree Creek, July 20; also in the different battles around Atlanta. He commanded the brigade much of the time from the battle of Missionary Ridge till after the battle of Franklin, when he was placed in command of Gist's brigade of South Carolina and Georgia troops, and served in this capacity to the surrender of the Confederate armies.

During the war Colonel Anderson received two wounds, one in the leg, at the battle of Shiloh, and the other in the shoulder, at Chickamauga. He was engaged in the following battles: Fort Henry, Fort Donelson, Shiloh, Perryville, Murfreesboro, Chickamauga, Missionary Ridge, Resaca, New Hope Church, Kennesaw Mountain, Peach Tree Creek, battles around Atlanta, Jonesboro, Franklin, Nashville, Bentonville, N. C., in all of which he distinguished himself as a brave soldier and good commander.

The Eighth Tennessee Regiment was engaged in all the battles of the Georgia campaign, and sustained heavy losses in killed and wounded. It accompanied the army in the Tennessee campaign after the fall of Atlanta, and participated in the battle of Franklin and the battles around Nashville.

It suffered severely in these battles, and left upon the field many of its bravest and best men. In the battle of Franklin, Brigadier-general John C. Carter, commanding Wright's brigade, was killed while leading his men in the thickest and hottest of the fight.

Following its command from Nashville to Mississippi, thence to North Carolina, where the last battle was fought, the Eighth Regiment Tennessee Volunteers surrendered on May 27, 1865, in common with the rest of the army, and accepted the generous terms offered by their stronger and more successful adversary. Laying down their arms, they donned the habiliments of peace, and, weary and covered with many scars of combat, they returned to their homes and applied themselves to the work of recuperating their lost fortunes with the same zeal and assiduity that had characterized their action as soldiers on so many arduous campaigns and on so many hard-fought battle-fields. The men accepted the situation in good faith, and as they had been zealous and honorable as soldiers, they now exercised the same noble qualities, with all the embellishments available to the paths of peace. Though seemingly unpleasant at first, with a race elevated to their political equals, and whom they had always known as their slaves and inferiors in every respect, the situation was at first disagreeable, yet time wore away prejudices. The white man treated the colored man with courtesy and kindness, and soon learned him that his best friends were those best acquainted with his nature and habits, and the colored man became the firm and fast friend of the Southern white man. Terms of amity and mutual interest sprung up between employer and employe, and the old soldiers made rapid progress in thrift and prosperity.

Many of the members of the old Eighth came home at the close of the war possessed of nothing but their lives and their honor. By industry, economy, and honorable dealing many have accumulated bountiful stores of this world's goods, and are possessed of handsome fortunes. Yet the number of survivors at present is comparatively small, when we consider the number who went out with the regiment in 1861 and the small number who surrendered in 1865. Nearly one fourth the original number sleep upon the different battle-fields from the Potomac to the Mississippi and the Gulf. In the four years of war more than two thirds of the members of the Eighth Regiment felt the missiles of its enemy's guns, and many of the survivors carry honorable scars. The long list of casualties have a claim upon our affections and our memory. We cherish their memory. We cannot forget them.

The following muster-rolls give the members of the regiment by companies, with the casualties of some of the companies:

COMPANY A.

OFFICERS.

J. L. Bryant, Captain.
J. P. Holland, First Lieutenant.
B. B. Bowers, Second Lieutenant.
T. F. Brooks, Third Lieutenant.
T. E. Russell, Orderly Sergeant.

PRIVATES.

W. C. Andrews.
D. A. Bethune.
W. M. Bethune.
J. F. Biggers.
J. W. Biggers.
R. W. Biggers.
W. T. Blackwell.
T. E. Brents.
J. S. Brooks.
Wiles Busset.
J. R. Butler.
W. L. Carrier.
Monroe Cauley.
Joe Cauler.
G. W. Causby.
J. B. Collins.
Jones Collins.
George Crabtree.
J. H. Darnell.
Joel Dodd.
W. S. Dodd.
J. D. Dyer.
George Foster.
Thomas Franklin.
W. F. Gulley.
J. Haislip.
J. H. Haislip.
J. W. Haislip.
O. P. Hill.
J. N. Hitchman.
W. L. Hitchman.
D. P. Hogan.
J. A. Hogan.
Milton Largen.
R. H. Largen.
J. M. Luna.
M. V. Luna.
R. H. Luna.
William Luna.
E. Malone.
W. A. Malone.
H. N. Maulden.
A. M. Meadows.
J. A. Morris.
J. M. McAfee.
J. A. McCrory.
R. J. McCrory.
W. H. McCrory.
J. M. Nichols.
A. J. Patterson.
W. H. Peach.
W. H. Pearson.
M. Petty.
H. M. Pyles.
E. F. Rambo.
G. W. Russell.
J. C. Sanders.
W. J. Shaw.
R. A. Shaw.
R. J. Shaw.
J. Stilwell.
P. H. Tally.
D. E. Tally.
J. J. Tally.
J. N. Tally.
J. G. Troop.
J. F. W. Wakefield.

COMPANY B.

Officers.

A. M. Hall, Captain.
C. C. McKinney, First Lieutenant.
T. W. Bledsoe, Second Lieutenant.
C. N. Allen, Third Lieutenant.

Privates.

N. B. Bates.
W. H. Blake.
L. D. Blake.
George W. Blake.
Thomas Blakemore.
Anderson Blakemore.
James Blakemore.
Henry Blakemore.
T. O. Blacknall.
John Y. Blacknall.
John Bradford.
Jack Branson.
W. D. Bonds.
S. S. Bonds.
John Bonds.
John Brewer.
Green Brewer.
C. M. Buchanan.
James Buchanan.
J. J. Bonner.
John Brown.
Patrick Boyles.
Elisha Blackwell.
Thomas Caldwell.
Martin Capps.
H. K. Carty.
George C. Carmack.
James Clark.
William Cole.
James Cumberland.
J. J. Cummings.
William Craig.
John Davis.
Jo. Darnell.
James Darnell.
D. T. Eastland.
E. W. Ellis.
A. S. Fulton.
William Freeman.
W. H. Gammell.
C. W. Gill.
James Gulley.
F. W. Glidewell.
John Gilbert.
Cullen Gilbert.
Wash. Gilbert.
John T. Green.
John R. Greer.
John M. Hall.
Harrison Hall.
T. F. Harris.
Thomas Hannaway.
Eli Hannaway.
Thomas G. Hester.
William Hardin.
William Isom.
Thomas Jeter.
William Jeter.
Samuel Jeter.
George B. Keller.
N. B. Koonce.
H. C. Lambert.
Samuel J. Leonard.
H. C. Locker.
Robert Locker.
B. E. Malear.
William McKauts.
J. G. McEwen.
E. R. McEwen.
C. B. Metcalfe.
Robert Matthews.
H. B. Matthews.
W. H. Merritt.
Thomas Millard.
Jesse Mitchell.
Joseph Moore.
James Mauldin.
James Morton.
R. A. Morrison.
Jacob Moore.
John Nichols.
William Nichols.
Frank Nichols.
Henry Nichols.

Briggs Nichols.
Claiborne Pigg.
Lewis Peach.
William Pitcock.
George W. Porter.
William Quarles.
Randall Quarles.
James Rives.
William Rives.
B. T. Roach.
J. K. Robinson.
William M. Roseboro.
William Saunders.
E. M. Scott.
John Scott.
A. B. Scott.
N. B. Scott.
Alex. Scott.
Herbert Smith.
J. E. Sorrells.
Harvey Sorrells.
W. T. Watson.
David Watson.
John Watson.
David Wells.
Newton Wells.
Wyatt Woodruff.

PROMOTED.

W. H. Blake, 1st Lieut., 1861, Captain, 1862.
W. H. Bonds, 1st Lieut., 1862, Captain, 1863.
T. O. Blacknall, 2d Lieut., 1862.
A. S. Fulton, Colonel, 1861.
John M. Hall, 3d Lieut., 1861, Captain, 1862.
A. M. Hall, Regimental Surgeon, 1861.
B. E. Malear, 1st Lieut., 1861, Captain, 1861.
J. G. McEwen, 3d Lieut., 1863.
C. C. McKinney, Major, 1862, Lieut.-col., 1863.
C. B. Metcalfe, 3d Lieut., 1863.

KILLED.

Lieut. T. O. Blacknall, Murfreesboro.
Cullen Gilbert, Murfreesboro.
Eli Hannaway, Murfreesboro.
John Scott, Murfreesboro.
Newton Wells, Murfreesboro.
John Nichols, Chickamauga.

WOUNDED.

Capt. W. H. Blake, Murfreesboro.
John Y. Blacknall, Murfreesboro.
Lieut. W. D. Bonds, Murfreesboro and Chickamauga.
S. S. Bonds, Murfreesboro.
John Bonds, Murfreesboro.
C. M. Buchanan, Chickamauga.
H. K. Carty, Chickamauga.
George C. Carmack, Murfreesboro.
J. J. Cummings, Franklin.
Thomas Hannaway, Murfreesboro.
H. C. Lambert, Murfreesboro.
Samuel J. Leonard, Murfreesboro.
Lieut. C. B. Metcalfe, Chickamauga.
W. H. Merritt, Atlanta.
W. M. Roseboro, Murfreesboro.
A. B. Scott, Murfreesboro.
N. B. Scott, Perryville and Murfreesboro.
J. E. Sorrells, Murfreesboro.
Harvey Sorrells, Murfreesboro.
David Watson, Murfreesboro.

DIED IN SERVICE.

Capt. W. H. Blake, wounds, Murfreesboro, 1862.
J. D. Freeman, disease, Murfreesboro, 1862.
Thos. Hannaway, disease, Prison, 1863.
Alex. Scott, disease, Atlanta, 1863.
John Watson, disease, Hospital.

DISCHARGED.

James M. Buchanan, Pocotaligo, S. C., 1862.
J. J. Bonner, 1862.
Lieut. T. W. Bledsoe, 1861.
William Craig, 1862.
W. H. Wells, 1862.

TENNESSEE VOLUNTEERS. 217

RESIGNED.

Lieut. C. N. Allen, Tupelo, Miss., May 8,.1862.
Col. A. S. Fulton, Tupelo, Miss., May 8, 1862.
Surgeon A. M. Hall, Mumfordville, Ky., Sept., 1862.

COMPANY C.

OFFICERS.

R. R. McKinney, Captain.
M. M. Bearden, First Lieutenant.
T. W. Raney, Second Lieutenant.
A. M. Downing, Third Lieutenant.
R. D. Hardin, First Sergeant.
W. J. King, Second Sergeant.
E. J. Bearden, Third Sergeant.

J. W. Rawls, Fourth Sergeant.
W. C. Bright, First Corporal.
J. H. Fletcher, Second Corporal.
D. C. Dewitt, Third Corporal.
J. H. Short, Fourth Corporal.
W. B Blair, Drummer.
E. F. Jones, Fifer.

PRIVATES.

Doe Anderson.
A. C. Beech.
James Billings.
W. J. Bland.
John Blankenship.
F. F. Blankenship.
J. K. Branson.
H. C. Brian.
J. S. Brown.
J. H. H. Burns.
J. M. Byers.
E. M. Carpenter.
J. F. Caughran.
J. C. Colbert.
A. J. Commons.
J. P. Doller.
Robert Daniel.
C. M. Dozier.
F. M. Downing.
Michael Doyles.
G. W. Dunn.
Peter Flannigan.
J. W. Fleming.
Naris Flint.
J. H. H. George.
W. B. George.
Thomas Gee.
H. H. Gray.
J. H. Gray.
J. H. Griffis.
W. J. Grubbs.
J. J. Gully.

W. H. Hamilton.
J. T. Halbert.
J. A. Hall.
D. C. Harbison.
J. W. Henderson.
J. R. Hovis.
B. T. Howell.
Samuel Howell.
Solomon Howell.
J. W. Jamerson.
John Kelly.
Michael Kennedy.
C. G. Key.
Manley Key.
J. H. Locker.
J. J. Maddox.
N. G. Maddox.
Leonard Marburry.
J. A. Meesber.
J. C. Maroney.
S. F. McAmm.
—— McAllister.
Henry McDaniel.
J. Y. McDaniel.
J. M. McFerrin.
E. J. Philips.
A. H. Puckett.
E. P. L. Parr.
F. C. S. Parr.
W. J. Raney.
J. F. Sandlin.
John Satterfield.

William Simmons.
Eli Simmons.
Stephen Smith.
Lewis Spray.
N. P. Steadman.
W. B. Stewart.
John Sullivan.
W. S. Thomas.
F. M. Thornton.
J. P. Loon.

W. T. Vickers.
A. L. Walker.
Thomas Warren.
William Watson.
J. M. Welgart.
H. W. Womack.
T. N. Womack.
J. K. P. Wallace.
O. Walker.

Promoted.

Lieut. M. M. Bearden, Captain, 1863.
Corp'l W. C. Bright, Captain, 1864–5.
J. S. Brown, Captain, 1863.
Norris Flint, Captain, 1862.

Killed.

Dock Anderson, Murfreesboro.
Capt. M. M. Bearden, Murfreesboro.
Lieut. T. W. Raney, Kennesaw Mt.
A. C. Beach, Murfreesboro.
Capt. J. S. Brown, Resaca, Ga.
J. F. Caughran, Murfreesboro.
Capt. Norris Flint, Chickamauga.
G. W. Dunn, Murfreesboro.
T. H. Griffis, Murfreesboro.

W. J. Grubbs, Murfreesboro.
J. A. Hall, Murfreesboro.
J. W. Henderson, Murfreesboro.
—— McAllister, Murfreesboro.
Eli Simmons, Murfreesboro.
A. L. Walker, Murfreesboro.
H. W. Womack, Murfreesboro.
O. Walker, Murfreesboro.

Wounded.

J. M. Byers, Murfreesboro.

Died in Service.

W. J. King, unknown.
J. F. Blankenship, Atlanta, Ga.

J. W. Jamison, West Virginia.
Manly Key, Chattanooga.

COMPANY D.

Officers.

Calvin E. Myers, Captain.
Columbus Marchbanks, First Lieutenant.
W. W. Windle, Second Lieutenant.
W. C. Hickey, Third Lieutenant.

A. L. Windle, First Sergeant.
C. C. Carr, Second Sergeant.
Robert Boles, Third Sergeant.
J. J. Tompkins, Fourth Sergeant.
Robert Cash, First Corporal.

Privates.

Arkley Allen.
Benjamin Allen.
John D. Anderson.
E. L. Armstrong.
Alex. Armstrong.
Cross Armstrong,
Cull Armstrong.

J. A. Anderson.
Hamilton Brown.
Mack Brown.
Trib. Bledsoe.
James Bilberry.
Harvey Brown.
Martin Bilberry.

John Bell.
Jeff Boles.
Porter Christian.
John Crabtree.
Charles Callahan.
J. C. Coleman.
W. M. Copeland.
Lee Copeland.
John Copeland.
James Cope.
Reuben Clark.
Wash. Carmack.
Jack Copeland.
George Coake.
J. J. Cullom.
Erasmus E. Cullom.
John Callahan.
S. B. Dillon.
D. T. Dillon.
Wesley Elum.
James Elum.
J. K. P. Eldridge.
S. B. Evans.
George Finley.
George France.
Ambrose Grace.
J. K. P. Gilliland.
Allen Gilliland.
Jack Garrett.
J. R. Hancock.
Van Huddleston.
Simon Huddleston.
Louis Huddleston.
Frank Harrison.
John Hall.
John Hickey.
Burrell Jones.
Cain Jones.
A. P. Kines.
Ed. Little.

Zeke Long.
W. B. McCally.
James McKinney.
Laurence Morris.
William Morris.
William O'Neal.
John Orsburn.
High Patrick.
Robert Philips.
Samuel Potcet.
*Roland Quarles.
John Quarles.
Thomas Ray.
Huston Ray.
M. V. Richardson.
A. W. Richardson.
Joseph Richardson.
Mike Speck.
John Speck.
Ben Speck.
Jack Sells.
Nick Stephens.
Dade Stephens.
Miles Stephens.
Hilry Smith.
T. P. Staggs.
Thomas Stewart.
Wilburn Stewart.
Payton Smith.
Elijah Stephens.
William Selby.
Burton Swift.
James Simpson.
Asa Shoemaker.
Jo. Williams.
A. R. Wilson.
G. W. Warren.
John Wallace.
William Wallace.

PROMOTED.

J. J. Cullom, Capt., 1862. E. F. Cullom, Lieut., 1862.

KILLED.

Benjamin Allen, in Cavalry.
Simon Huddleston, in Cavalry.
Louis Huddleston, in Cavalry.
High Patrick, in Cavalry.
Nick Stephens, in Cavalry.

Miles Stephens, in Cavalry.
Robert Philips, Murfreesboro.
John Copeland, in Cavalry.
Payton Smith, Clarksville, Tenn.
James Cope, Franklin, Tenn.

Ed. Little, Murfreesboro.
Jack Garrett, in Cavalry.
Jack Copeland, in Cavalry.
Elijah Stephens, in Cavalry.
George Finley, Franklin, Tenn.
John Bell, Perryville, Ky.

Capt. J. J. Cullom, Kennesaw Mount.
Lieut. E. E. Cullom, Atlanta.
Cross Armstrong, in Cavalry.
Cal. Armstrong, Celina, Tenn.
Burrel Jones, South Carolina, 1861.
John Callahan, Murfreesboro.

WOUNDED.

William O'Neal, Perryville.
John Speck, Perryville.

Lee Copeland, Perryville.
John Hall, 3 wounds, Murfreesboro.

DIED IN SERVICE.

John Crabtree, Virginia, 1861.
Charles Callahan, Virginia, 1861.
Samuel Poteet, Virginia, 1861.
J. K. P. Eldridge, Home, 1863.
John Quarles, Warm Springs, Va.

Reuben Clark, Charleston, S. C., 1862.
John D. Anderson, Home, 1861.
Harvey Brown, Burkesville, Ky., 1864.
John Hickey, West Va., 1861.
Burton Swift, Murfreesboro.

COMPANY G.

OFFICERS.

Geo. W. Higgins, Captain.
W. C. Griswell, First Lieutenant.
David Sullivan, Second Lieutenant.
E. S. N. Bobo, Brevet Second Lieutenant.
Jo. G. Carrigan, Orderly Sergeant.
M. C. Shook, Second Sergeant.

T. L. Williamson Third Sergeant.
Francis Wells, Fourth Sergeant.
M. C. Cotton, First Corporal.
W. B. McKenzie, Second Corporal.
M. S. Dollins, Third Corporal.
T. H. Clark, Fourth Corporal.

PRIVATES.

J. R. Ashley.
Jesse Armstrong.
Thomas Armstrong.
William Armstrong.
Elias Ashby.
J. R. Brewer.
J. B. Brown.
J. N Bell.
G. W. Borough.
Jesse Broadaway.
A. P. Clift.
John Cunningham.
C. H. Carrigan.
W. T. Crenshaw.
F. M. Colter.
T. H. Curtis.
Henry Cummings.
Jackson Dollins.
Milton Dollins.

J. G. Epps.
J. N. Epps.
A. C Freeman.
W. J. Freeman.
R. F. Fox.
J. W. Fincher.
Wm. Fuller.
W. H. Gibson.
G. A. N. Green.
Alfred Hale.
G. W. Hale.
W. C. Hall.
Richard Hall.
C. C. Hall.
L. Hamby.
H. F. Hudson.
W. B. Hudson.
J. L. Hudson.
J. B. Headricks.

TENNESSEE VOLUNTEERS. 221

J. G. Harrison.
Joe Hines.
W. H. Ingle.
James Jolly.
J. D. King.
Jeff. King.
J. W. Leonard.
John McKenzie.
M. P. Moore.
J. F. Moore.
J. A. F. Moore.
James McKenzie.
J. E. Mills.
Chas. Miller.
Amos Morris.
M. F. Pylant.
James Pearson.
G. A. F. Pylant,
W. D. Prosser.
J. Reece.
T. J. Rives.
T. J. Robinson.

J. B. Shook.
John Sisk.
G. W. Smith.
Doake Small.
L. P. M. Small.
J. W. Sullivan.
W. M. Smith.
James Steelman.
D. Tucker (Chaplain).
Wm. Thompson.
*David Thompson.
Patrick Thompson.
Isom Wells.
James Wells.
T. J. Wells.
W. L. Waid.
M. J. Wright.
John Willett.
T. A. Yant.
M. P. Yant.
J. L. Yant.

KILLED.

Joseph Hudson, Perryville, Ky.
Capt. M. C. Shook, Murfreesboro.
Meredith Yant, Murfreesboro.
J. L. Yant, Murfreesboro.
Robert F. Fox, Murfreesboro.
Wm. Armstrong, Murfreesboro.
James McKenzie, Murfreesboro.
Wesley Wade, Murfreesboro.
John G. Epps, Murfreesboro.
Milton Dollins, Murfreesboro.
James Steelman, Murfreesboro.
Alfred Hale, Murfreesboro.

Wm. Fuller, Murfreesboro.
Lemuel Small, Murfreesboro.
Jas. W. Leonard, Missionary Ridge.
J. D. Ingle, Resaca, Ga.
Marion F. Pylant, Resaca, Ga.
Jackson Dollins, Atlanta.
J. B. Shook, Atlanta.
G. A. N. Green, Newnan, Ga.
Jas. D. King, Franklin.
Jas. Wells, Franklin.
Doake Small, by cars, in Georgia.

COMPANY H.

OFFICERS.

William L. Moore, Captain.
William J. Thrash, First Lieutenant.
Thomas Freeman, Second Lieutenant.
W. L. Shoftner, Third Lieutenant.
William J. Bonner, First Sergeant.
John W. Sullivan, Second Sergeant.
Albert H. Boon, Third Sergeant.

John T. Reese, Fourth Sergeant.
Moses B. Shores, Fifth Sergeant.
Wm. H. Robertson, First Corporal.
Wm. H. Holman, Second Corporal.
John F. Whittaker, Third Corporal.
M. L. Mead, Fourth Corporal.

PRIVATES.

Joseph Broughton.
James C. Bright.
William A. Blackwell.
John E. Blackwell.
Thomas Brown.
H. L. W. B. Boon.
Alexander Brady.
Robert M. Boaz.
Wiley H. Carrigan.
John S. Carrigan.
Joseph Call.
James C. Clark.
William T. Clark.
Alsa M. Carter.
Stephen Cook.
L. W. Davidson.
M. M. Dean.
James H. C. Duff.
George D. Daniel.
John Eslick.
John A. Eaton.
Isaac V. Forrister.
Nathaniel S. Forrister.
W. M. Franklin.
L. A. Farrer.
Thomas H. Freeman.
Enoch Glidewell.
P. H. George.
David S. George.
Riley Gattis.
Isaac V. Gattis.
George W. Gattis, jr.
William B. Hurst.
James C. Hague.
Eli Honey.
Junius Honey.
James Hachel.
Richard G. James.
P. M. James.
Stephen Johnston.
John J. King.
George C. Logan.
L. B. Leftwitch.
Arch H. Lee.
H. D. Lipscomb.
W. M. Montgomery.
W. H. Martin.
Joseph S. Mooney.
Alexander A. McAfee.

John D. McLean.
Rufus A. Morehead.
James L. Morehead.
George F. Miller.
Preston Y. Mitchell.
E. M. Ousley.
John B. Parker.
Aaron Parks.
Joel Parks.
Elisha T. Parks.
James C. Pitts.
Joel A. Pitts.
Patrick A. Raby.
John R. Raby.
Benj. H. Rives.
John C. Raney.
Robert Reese.
Calvin Rennegar.
William Rennegar.
William A. Rutledge.
William D. Seals.
James S. Seals.
William H. Sebastian.
William L. Shoftner.
Chris. C. Shoftner.
Newton M. Shoftner.
G. W. Shellings.
George W. Street.
Asa Street.
Joseph P. Stacy.
John B. Steagall.
Robert F. Steagall.
Joseph Sullinger.
John D. Tolley.
John B. Thomasson.
Daniel J. Waggoner.
George A. Waggoner.
George W. Waggoner.
George W. Waggoner, jr.
Felix M. Waggoner.
Daniel N. Waggoner.
Marcus D. L. Whittaker.
L. J. Whittaker.
Edward D. Whitman.
James W. Whitman.
J. M. D. Wilson.
William A. Woodard.
Elijah W. Yates.

TENNESSEE VOLUNTEERS. 223

RECRUITS.

Green B. Ashby.
Cullen Bailey.
Benjamin Broughton.
W. N. Bonner.
Hiram Beaver.
Elisha B. Brown.
Brittain F. Carrigan.
Wilson R. Call.
A. B. Carter.
Willis A. Carter.
W. B. Carter.
John P. Cooley.
D. A. Crane.
John W. Cashion.
James Cashion.
Madison Copeland.
W. P. Davidson.
W. R. Duke.
William Eslick.
Isaac Evans.
W. R. Evans.
Aaron Glidewell.
George W. Gattis, sr.
W. H. Gattis.
Elijah L. Hester.
Andrew J. Hudlow.
William N. Johnston.
John H. Leftwitch.
B. D. Morgan.
George W. McAfee.
Jacob C. Morgan.
James F. Massey.
John F. M. Mills.

Ellis Mills.
F. M. Moyers.
James W. Mitchell.
James Marr.
James M. Major.
William Norvall.
Benjamin J. Noles.
John W. Neela.
John Owens.
W. F. Oliver.
William Panther.
James Pearson.
E. B. Raby.
J. W. Robertson.
Samuel Rowes.
Joseph M. Sebastian.
James Sullenger.
W. A. Sullenger.
Samuel C. Strong.
Henderson Speck.
W. J. Taylor.
Nathaniel Tucker.
Francis Tucker.
George H. Waggoner.
Felix Waggoner.
Henry A. Waggoner.
Riley Waggoner.
Stephen P. Wiles.
John C. Waid.
W. H. Webb.
John Ward.
Thomas B. Yeaters.

PROMOTED.

Lieut. Granville B. Lester, Assistant Surgeon, 1861.
Capt. W. L. Moore, Lieut.-col, 1861, Col., 1862.
Lieut. W. J. Thrash, Capt., 1861.
Serg't William J. Bonner, 3d Lieut., 1861.
William A. Rutledge, 3d Lieut., 1862.
John D. Tolley, Ordinance Serg't, 1861, 1st Lieut. and Adjutant, 1862.
J. D. McLean, 2d Lieut., 1862.
J. G. Call, 3d Lieut., 1863.
M. B. Shores, 2d Lieut., 1862.
John Sullivan, 3d Lieut., 1863.
George W. Street, 3d Lieut., 1864.

KILLED.

Capt. Wm. J. Thrash, Murfreesboro.
James Sullinger, Murfreesboro.
Joseph Sullenger, Murfreesboro.
Benjamin Morgan, Murfreesboro.
Frank Johnson, Murfreesboro.
George Steelman, Murfreesboro.

Newt Shoftner, Murfreesboro.
Lieut. J. G. Call, Resaca.
W. L. Davidson, Chickamauga.
George Davidson, Kennesaw Mountain.
William Martin, Franklin.

Joseph Stacy, Franklin.
Lieut. George Street, Franklin.
P. Y. Mitchell, Franklin.
Alexander Brady, Franklin.
John Reese, Franklin.
Benjamin Knowles, Murfreesboro.

WOUNDED.

L. A. Farrar, Murfreesboro.
W. J. Taylor, Murfreesboro.
James Hague, Murfreesboro.
Lieut. M. B. Shores, Murfreesboro.
M. D. L. Whittaker, Murfreesboro.
John Whittaker, Murfreesboro.
N. S. Forrester, Murfreesboro.
F. R. Moore, Murfreesboro.
W. T. Clark, Murfreesboro.
J. E. Waggoner, Murfreesboro.
Benjamin Parker, Murfreesboro.
Enoch Glidewell, Murfreesboro.
John Reese, Murfreesboro.
Lieut. John Sullivan, Murfreesboro.
Collins Bright, Murfreesboro.
Lewis Davidson, Murfreesboro.
Berry Leftwitch, Murfreesboro.
Brittain Carrigan, Murfreesboro.
B. A. Raby, Perryville.

Lieut John D. Tolly, Perryville.
H. L. W. Boon, Perryville.
Lucus Whittaker, Resaca, Ga.
Alexander Crane, Chickamauga.
Stephen Johnson, Chickamauga.
George Street, Chickamauga.
Aaron Parks, Chickamauga.
John Whittaker, Adairsville, Ga.
Lieut. M. B. Shores, Adairsville, Ga.
M. M. Dean Adairsville, Ga.
Stephen Johnson, Peach Tree Creek.
William Martin, Peach Tree Creek.
M. M. Dean, Peach Tree Creek.
P. Logan, Peach Tree Creek.
J. D. Wilson, Franklin, Tenn.
P. Logan, Franklin, Tenn.
Jeff King, Franklin, Tenn.
Wilson Call, Franklin, Tenn.
John Raby, Franklin, Tenn.

DIED IN SERVICE.

J. J. Gaddis, Knoxville, 1861.
James Morehead, Warm Springs, Va.
J. A. Eaton, Warm Springs, Va.

Rufus Morehead, Corinth, Miss., 1861.
J. V. Oliver, Corinth, Miss., 1861.

COMPANY K.

OFFICERS.

William Gore, Captain.
A. B. Botts, First Lieutenant.
James Eaton, Second Lieutenant.
A. W. W. Brooks, Third Lieutenant.
D. M. Haile, First Sergeant.
T. G. Settle, Second Sergeant.
L. M. Gipson, Third Sergeant.

B. P. McClelland, Fourth Sergeant.
T. C. Settle, Fifth Sergeant.
John Van Hooser, First Corporal.
S. L. Hall, Second Corporal.
G. M. Ray, Third Corporal.
Joseph Lipsheets, Fourth Corporal.
N. B. Young, Musician.

PRIVATES.

J. P. Abner.
J. M. Allard.
Z. H. Bryant.
John M. Burriss.

E. M. Brown.
G. W. Brown.
J. L. Brown.
J. H. Brown.

TENNESSEE VOLUNTEERS.

William Buchannon.
R. A. Cox.
Daniel Cox.
B. F. Clark.
Jacob Case.
William Case.
H. Carter.
W. S. Cassety.
L. M. Cason.
J. J. Coake.
John De Jarnett.
Lan Dudney.
Len Darwin.
A. G. Denton.
W. G. De Shields.
William Engle.
W. A. Fax.
Kendrix Fax.
B. B. Fax.
B. A. Fax.
W. B. Fax.
Suel Gordon.
Samuel Gordon.
R. H. Gaines.
R. J. C. Gailbreath.
W. A. Gailbreath.
Matthew Gipson.
J. R. Harrison.
George Harrison.
A. B. Haile.
W. T. Haile.
T. S. Haile.
A. G. Haile.
S. L. Hall.
Jack Hambert.
Peter Huff.
H. C. Huff'hines.
Sam E. Hare.
W. H. Jarman.

William Keith.
J M. Keith.
O. Kirby.
L. Law.
Thad Law.
Abdelenimus Law.
B. H. Lawson.
J. M. Morgan.
P. F. Morgan.
H. T. Minor.
W. C. Minor.
W. J. Mansel.
J. B. Mansel.
J. W. Meaders.
J. F. McClure.
Wm. M. Poston.
T. J. Poston.
C. C. Price.
Warren Pharris.
A. D. Pleasants.
John S. Quarles.
L. W. Rawley.
P. J. Rawley.
Matthew Rogers.
Wade Ransom.
H. H. Roberts.
Wm. Sadler.
A. Stafford.
J. C. Smallin.
W. S. Stone.
C. N. Tinsley.
John Whittaker.
George Whittaker.
Bish. Walker.
G. S. Wheeler.
T. J. Williams.
L. Washburn.
Zeb. M. Young.

PROMOTED.

William Sadler, Captain, 1862.   John S. Quarles, Captain, 1863.

KILLED.

Abdelenimus Law, Knoxville (by cars) P. F. Morgan, Atlanta, July 22, 1864.
Capt. Wm. Sadler, Murfreesboro. S. L. Hall, Murfreesboro.
Lieut. D. M. Haile, Murfreesboro. Joseph Lipsheets, Franklin.
R. H. Gaines, Murfreesboro. J. L. Brown, Chickamauga.
Jack Hambert, Murfreesboro. A. G. Denton, Murfreesboro.
William M. Poston, Murfreesboro. R. H. Gaines, Murfreesboro.

R. J. Gailbreath, Murfreesboro.
J. M. Keith, Port Royal, S. C.
J. F. McClure, Franklin.

T. J. Poston, Atlanta, July 22, 1864.
H. H. Roberts, Chickamauga.

WOUNDED.

Capt. John S. Quarles, Murfreesboro.

DIED IN SERVICE.

William Buchanan, in prison.
H. Carter, West Virginia, 1861.
Lan Dudney.

W. A. Gailbreath, Tupelo, Miss., 1862.
Bish. Walker, Tupelo, Miss., 1862.
P. J. Rawley, West Virginia, 1861.

THE FIFTH REGIMENT TENNESSEE VOLUNTEERS.

This regiment was subsequently known as the Thirty-fifth Regiment Tennessee Volunteers, and was composed of volunteer companies from the counties of Warren, Cannon, Grundy, Sequatchie, Bledsoe, and Van Buren, viz.:

Company A, Grundy county, Captain Hannah, commanding.

Company B, Warren county, Captain John W. Towles, commanding.

Company C, Warren county, Captain Charles M. Forrest, commanding.

Company D, Warren county, Captain W. T. Christian, commanding.

Company E, Van Buren county, Captain W. Burrell Cummings, commanding.

Company F, Warren county, Captain Ed J. Wood, commanding.

Company G, Cannon county, Captain James H. Woods, commanding.

Company H, Warren county, Captain John Macon, commanding.

Company I, Bledsoe county, Captain L. L. Dearman, commanding.

Company K, Sequatchie county, Captain W. D. Stewart, commanding.

The companies were organized into a regiment at

Camp Smartt, near McMinnville, Tenn., September 6, 1861, by the election of Ben J. Hill colonel commanding. The field and staff officers of the regiment were as follows:

COLONEL BEN J. HILL.

BEN J. HILL, Colonel;
JOHN T. SPURLOCK, Lieutenant-colonel;
JOSEPH BROWN, Major and Adjutant;
Dr. W. C. BARNS, Surgeon;
Dr. J. W. WOOTEN, Assistant Surgeon;
Dr. J. M. BELL, Assistant Surgeon;

Captain O. F. BREWSTER, Quartermaster;
Captain JAMES S. GRIBBLE, Commissary;
Rev. DAVID P. RITCHEY, Chaplain.

The regiment, after organizing, remained in camp of instruction at Camp Smartt for three weeks, when it was sent to Camp Trousdale, thence to Bowling Green, Ky., and placed in Brigadier-general P. R. Cleburne's brigade, of General Albert Sidney Johnston's army. Remaining at Bowling Green until the battle of Fort Donelson, it accompanied its brigade in the evacuation of Tennessee, and participated in the great battle of Shiloh on April 6 and 7, 1862.

Colonel B. J. Hill, the commander of the Fifth Regiment Tennessee Volunteers, was a native of Tennessee, and resided at McMinnville at the breaking out of the war between the States in 1861. Previous to the war he was engaged in the mercantile business at McMinnville, where he had resided for a number of years. In 1855, he was elected a member of the State Senate, and represented his constituents with characteristic ability. At the breaking out of the civil war he espoused the cause of his Southern brethren, and enlisted in the Fifth (afterward the Thirty-fifth) Regiment Tennessee Volunteers in September, 1861, and was chosen its commander by the unanimous voice of its members.

As a citizen, he was respected and honored, by all who knew him, for his enterprising spirit and for his sterling integrity. He was steadfast and immovable in his determinations, and was kind and generous to a fault. As a soldier, he possessed all the requisite qualities of a commander. He possessed a degree of obstinate determination that baffled opposition and recognized no opposing obstacles. Infusing this spirit into the soldiers of his command to a remarkable degree, his regiment acted a distinguished part in the various battles of the Western Army, beginning at Shiloh. In this battle, Colonel Hill led his regiment in the thickest of the fight, and for his gallantry, and the gallantry of his regiment, he was mentioned in honorable and commendatory terms by General Cleburne, whose high appreciation and firm friendship seemed to have its origin on this occasion, and ever afterward Colonel Hill was a favorite of his brigade commander.

In the battle of Shiloh, the Fifth Tennessee Regiment carried into the engagement 369 guns. The regiment suffered severely in the engagements of each day. The brigade (Cleburne's) to which the regiment belonged numbered 2,750 men, out of which 1,000 were killed and wounded, and 32 were missing. The Fifth Tennessee captured about 100 prisoners during the two days' engagement.

The following is the official report of Colonel Hill, of the part the Fifth Tennessee bore in the battle:

REPORT OF COLONEL BEN J. HILL, FIFTH TENNESSEE INFANTRY.

HEAD-QUARTERS FIFTH TENNESSEE REGIMENT, }
CAMP NEAR CORINTH, MISS., April 15, 1862.}

Sir:—In compliance with your request, I have the honor to make the following report, showing the positions occupied by my command during the eventful scenes of the 6th and 7th instant, at Shiloh, in Hardin county, Tenn.:

My regiment was detailed to do picket duty on Saturday night, the 5th, and was thrown out within three or four miles of the enemy's encampment. At daylight Sunday morning we were ordered to advance, with the balance of your brigade, the Sixth Mississippi, Colonel Thornton, on my right, and the Twenty-fourth Tennessee, Lieutenant-colonel Peebles, on my left.

We advanced some three miles, when our pickets commenced a sharp and lively skirmish. We continued to advance and drove them before us to within five hundred yards of the Federal encampment, when they opened a terrible fire upon our column. A deep ravine, full of green briers and grape-vines, separated us from Colonel Thornton's regiment. My right was exposed to a severe flank fire from a battery and from musketry and other small arms. We were at the foot of a long hill, upon which the enemy were hidden. Captain Hannah, Company A, and several others were killed at this place, and many wounded.

The Fifteenth Arkansas, Lieutenant-colonel Patton, was in advance of us, and deployed as skirmishers, but was soon called in to sustain the Twenty-fourth Tennessee on the left, which it performed gallantly and promptly.

The firing was constant and continuous for half or three quarters of an hour, when one of the aids of General Beauregard came to me and said that the battery on the right must be charged and silenced at all hazards. I gave the word and my brave boys promptly responded to it. We charged, dispersed the enemy, and silenced the battery. As the enemy retreated my marksmen had better opportunity for trying their skill, and well did they improve it, as was proven by the number of the enemy who there fell. We continued on at double-quick for near a mile, crossing their first encampment, and formed a line of battle at the foot of the next hill.

At this time the Twenty-third Tenneseee, Lieutenant-colonel Neill, and the Sixth Mississippi, Colonel Thornton, constituting the right wing of your brigade, getting separated, you had to go to their aid.

I was then directed, as senior colonel, to take command of all the troops on my left by one of General Beauregard's staff, which I did, and formed them in line of battle to keep back the enemy's right wing. Then with two Louisiana regiments on the left of your brigade, the Texas Rangers on the extreme left, on Owl Creek, a battery in our rear, the Louisiana cavalry as pickets, and the Fifteenth Arkansas, Lieutenant-colonel Patton, as skirmishers, we advanced at once, driving the extreme right of the enemy for at least a mile before us. They halted at their third encampment and gave us a stubborn fight. The Fourth Kentucky and a battalion of Alabama troops were here, on our right, sheltered under the brow of a hill. They had been giving the enemy a hot fire, but ceased as we came up. My regiment then opened a terrible fire upon the enemy, and kept it up alone for a short time, when the Twenty-fourth Tennessee joined with us in firing upon them. Colonel Freeman, commanding a Tennessee regiment, with a squadron of cavalry, then moved rapidly to the left, and opened fire upon their right flank. This, in conjunction with our fire in front, told with terrible effect, and they retreated, leaving many of their dead and wounded behind them. We pursued them and had just formed on the fourth hill, and in sight of their fourth encampment, when you returned to cheer us with your presence and to supply us with ammunition.

The remainder of the evening and during the next day, Monday we fought under your immediate command. It is unnecessary for me to enumerate and recite the many charges and the many incidents that occurred on Monday, as you were in command and witnessed them all.

In conclusion, I beg leave to say that my men, though inexperienced, fought well and bravely, and never failed to charge, or rally, when I commanded them to do so. As far as my observation went, all the Tennessee troops fought well. So it was with the Arkansas troops, the Mississippi, the Kentucky, and the Alabama troops on the left. All of them fought nobly and gallantly and against great odds. My regiment captured about one hundred prisoners during the two days' fighting.

With great respect, your obedient servant,

BEN J. HILL,
Colonel Commanding Fifth Tennessee Regiment, Prov'l Army.

Brigadier-general P. R. CLEBURNE, Commanding Second Brigade.

HEAD-QUARTERS FIFTH TENNESSEE REGIMENT,
PROVISIONAL ARMY,
CAMP HILL, MISS., April 25, 1862.

Sir:—In obedience to Special Orders, No, —, of date the 21st inst., in relation to the number of men of this regiment engaged in the battles at Shiloh on the 6th and 7th inst., I have to report as follows, to wit:

Number detailed as infirmary or hospital corps	29
Number detailed to go with artillery	6
Number detailed to go with sappers and miners	1
Number detailed as wagon-guard	3
Number detailed to guard ammunition	2
Total detailed	41
Number of non-commissioned officers and privates engaged	328
Number of company officers (commissioned)	33
Number of field officers	3
Number of staff officers	5
Total engaged	369

In reply to that portion of the order which refers to the individual action of the officers and men of this regiment on the battle-field of Shiloh, I have to say, the officers and men of the regiment fought well and acted with great coolness and bravery. Considering their inexperience, such was the conduct of most of them on the field.

In Captain Forrest's company (C), private Samuel Evans displayed great coolness and courage. After being severely wounded, the ball passing through the cheeks, he refused to go to the rear, but remained and fought for a considerable length of time, cheering on the men and loading and shooting as fast as he could.

In Company B, commanded by Lieutenant B. H. Womack, privates John D. Smith, Douglas Briers, and J. T. Pennington are mentioned as having distinguished themselves by their bravery and daring.

In Company D, commanded by Lieutenant R. C. Smartt, private John Roberts, a very young soldier, behaved with the greatest coolness and bravery throughout the whole action. He was frequently in advance of his company, was knocked down twice by spent balls, and his gun shattered to pieces. He is but fifteen years old, but displayed the coolness and courage of a veteran.

In Company F, Captain Edward J. Wood, Lieutenant C. C. Brewer is spoken of in the highest terms for cool bravery and gallant bearing. Following the lead and imitating the example of his captain, one of the bravest of the brave, he was ever at the head of the men, his gallant captain only in advance, cheering them on to the conflict, and ever and anon dropping one of the Yankees as his eye would chance to light upon him. Privates Abe Boren and Isaac L. Ray, of the same company, also greatly distinguished themselves, and are spoken of in the highest terms by their comrades and their captain.

Lieutenant George S. Deakins, of Captain W. D. Stewart's company (K), was also conspicuous throughout the engagament for coolness and gallant behavior. . . . .

It is, no doubt, invidious to single out instances of this kind. Officers and men all did well, considering that they were raw and inexperienced, and they were out Saturday night, the whole regiment, on picket duty, and consequently unrefreshed.

Respectfully submitted,   B. J. HILL,
Colonel Commanding Fifth Tennessee Regiment, Prov'l Army.

Major POWHATTAN ELLIS, jr., Assistant Adjutant-general, Second Brigade, Third Army Corps.

The Fifth Tennessee remained with the army during the siege of Corinth, and on May 28, 1862, was on the picket lines when Halleck was pressing the Confederate lines so severely on the eve of the evacuation of Corinth. Being ordered by General Cleburne, on the morning of May 28, to storm the Federal position at Shelton Hill, in front of Corinth, Colonel Hill charged with his gallant regiment into a perfect gauntlet of Federal columns which were concealed behind a hedge of plum bushes; and before he was aware of the fact that the regiments which were ordered to support him on his flanks had failed to advance to the charge, he rushed to the very muzzles of the enemy's cannon and dislodged the enemy from their position, yet the fire of artillery and musketry was so severe in his front and on his flanks, that he was forced to fall back to his original position immediately after the accomplishment of one of the most daring and gallant achievements of the war. For this heroic act, Colonel Hill and his regiment were complimented by General Beauregard in general orders read to the troops of the entire army.

After the evacuation of Corinth, the regiment accompanied its brigade in the Kentucky campaign, and fought bravely in the battles of Richmond and Perryville. At Murfreesboro and Chickamauga it sustained the exalted reputation it had so justly won on all former battle-fields.

When the Confederate forces fell back to Dalton in 1863, Colonel Hill was made provost-marshal-general of the Army of Tennessee by order of General Joseph E. Johnston. In this capacity Colonel Hill served the Confederacy until January, 1865, when he was commissioned a brigadier-general, and assigned to duty in the command of cavalry. In this capacity he operated principally in North Alabama until the close of the war, when he surrendered his command at Chattanooga to the Federal authorities. Colonel Hill always claimed that his was the last command on the east side of the Mississippi to surrender to the Federal authorities.

At the close of the war General Hill returned to his home at McMinnville, and found that his home and his property had suffered greatly from the ravages of war. Gathering up the fragments of a shattered fortune, he adjusted his liabilities, and, in partnership with his brother, he again entered the mercantile business in his native town. In a few years he closed out his business and entered the profession of law, in which capacity he acted during the remainder of his life.

Shortly after the close of the war his health began to fail. The hardships, the exposure, and the excitement of a four years' war had told severely upon his nervous system. He had led his regiment in forty-two battles and skirmishes, and during the whole period of his military service missed but a few days from duty. After an active, brilliant, and useful life, he died at his home in McMinnville, Tenn., January 5, 1880, at the age of fifty-four years. Thus closed the life and labors of Benjamin Jefferson Hill, the commander of the Fifth Regiment Tennessee Volunteers, afterward brigadier-general of cavalry, in the service of the Confederate States.

CARNES'S BATTERY.

Carnes's battery was assigned to General D. S. Donelson's brigade shortly after the battle of Shiloh, in April, 1862, and continued a part of this brigade after the promomotion of General Donelson to the position of major-general, when the brigade was commanded by Colonel John H. Savage, temporarily, and permanently by Colonel Marcus J. Wright, who was made a brigadier-general about this time. This battery was with the brigade in all the engagements from Corinth to Chickamauga, and the warmest feelings of amity existed between it and the officers and men of the infantry of the brigade, especially the Eighth and Sixteenth Tennessee. Captain Carnes, the commander of this battery, always told his brigade commander that he was never uneasy about his front, and wanted no troops in his rear to be killed by shells thrown at his guns; if he would place the Eighth and Sixteenth Tennessee on either side of his battery he would have no uneasiness about being sustained on the flanks. This battery did a considerable amount of desperate fighting at close quarters, and was generally supported by the Eighth and Sixteenth Tennessee. In every instance these were the regiments of the brigade which the battery always preferred, and the brigade commander always respected this preference by a compliance with the wishes of the captain whenever it was practicable to do so. As Captain Carnes operated his guns mostly at close quarters with the enemy, he always threw a great deal of canister shot into their ranks, which had the effect to demoralize and often stampede the enemy in his front. The captain having proved the efficacy of canister in large quantities while at close quarters, he always kept an extra supply on hand and dealt it out lavishly upon the enemy to his great consternation. This policy greatly pleased the chief of artillery of Bragg's army, old Colonel Oladowski, who became a firm and fast friend to Captain Carnes, whom he always jokingly called his "canister-shot" captain.

As Carnes's battery was with Donelson's brigade during the greater portion of the war after the battle of Shiloh, and it was recruited from time to time from the ranks of the Eighth, Fifteenth, Sixteenth, Twenty-eighth, Thirty-eighth, and Fifty-first Tennessee Regiments, a few items of its history will be given, together with a history of its commander, Captain W. W. Carnes.

The battery was organized by Captain W. H. Jackson (afterward General Jackson of the cavalry). The nucleus of this battery was a few German members, and the guns of the "Steuben Artillery" of Memphis, before the war. The men were enlisted as "regulars," and taken from various places, so that scarcely ten men were from the same county, and they were always kept under the discipline and rules of the regular service.

At the battle of Belmont. Captain Jackson was mounted and afterward promoted to colonel, and placed in command of the Seventh Tennessee Cavalry, and was subsequently made a brigadier-general.

CAPTAIN W. W. CARNES.

When Captain Jackson was promoted, W.W. Carnes was made captain of the battery. Captain Jackson, who was now colonel and afterward brigadier-general of cavalry, was a graduate of West Point, and was lieutenant in the First Mounted Rifles till the war commenced.

Captain W. W. Carnes was a young man of excellent literary and military attainments. He was in the graduating class at the United States Naval Academy when the war commenced, and at the time he was made captain of this battery he was only twenty years old, and was beyond a doubt the youngest captain of artillery in the Confederate States Army. When assigned to Donelson's brigade the officers of the battery were as follows:

> W. W. Carnes, Captain;
> L. G. Marshall, First Lieutenant;
> Lewis Bond, First Lieutenant;
> R. E. Foote, Second Lieutenant;
> James M. Cockrill, Second Lieutenant.

Milton Brown, jr., was for a while attached to the battery as supernumerary second lieutenant, but was subsequently assigned to duty elsewhere.

The battery was composed of six guns, consisting of four six-pounders and two twelve-pound howitzers, while under Captain Jackson, and till after the battle of Shiloh, when all eight-gun batteries were reduced to four guns. This left a second lieutenant more than was needed, and Lieutenant Foote was assigned to duty elsewhere. About this time Carnes's battery was assigned to Donelson's brigade at Corinth. Its officers were then as follows:

> W. W. Carnes, Captain;
> L. G. Marshall, First Lieutenant;
> Lewis Bond, First Lieutenant;
> James M. Cockrill, Second Lieutenant.

As above stated, Captain Carnes was educated at the United States Naval Academy. Lieutenant L. G.

Marshall, who was the oldest officer in the battery, was a man of very superior education, was well known as a man of letters, and was connected with a leading Memphis paper when the war commenced.

Lieutenant Lewis Bond was a citizen of Brownsville, and a recent graduate of Harvard University.

Lieutenant J. M. Cockrill was from Nashville, and a son of Sterling Cockrill of that city.

These officers remained with the battery until after the battle of Chickamauga. The only change in the officers of the battery up to this time was the promotion of Sergeant A. Van Vleck to the position of second lieutenant upon the recommendation of his commanding officer for good conduct upon the field. Lieutenant Bond was assigned to General Jackson's cavalry command as ordnance officer. Lieutenant A. Van Vleck was a native of New York, and had been in the South about nine years when the war commenced. He joined this battery at the breaking out of the war, and came from the vicinity of Tracy City, Tennessee. He proved a good and faithful soldier in every position he filled in the service. He fell at the battle of Chickamauga.

The first active service in which this battery participated on the field, after its assignment to Donelson's brigade, was performed at Perryville, Kentucky, October 8, 1862. Being engaged in a heavy artillery duel in the forenoon in front of General Wood's command, the battery was considerably cut up, and Captain Carnes was ordered to refit and await orders. While thus awaiting orders, the scene of operations began to rapidly change to the Confederate right wing. Polk's corps was hurried rapidly down the Chaplin Creek to the right of Perryville, and soon became furiously

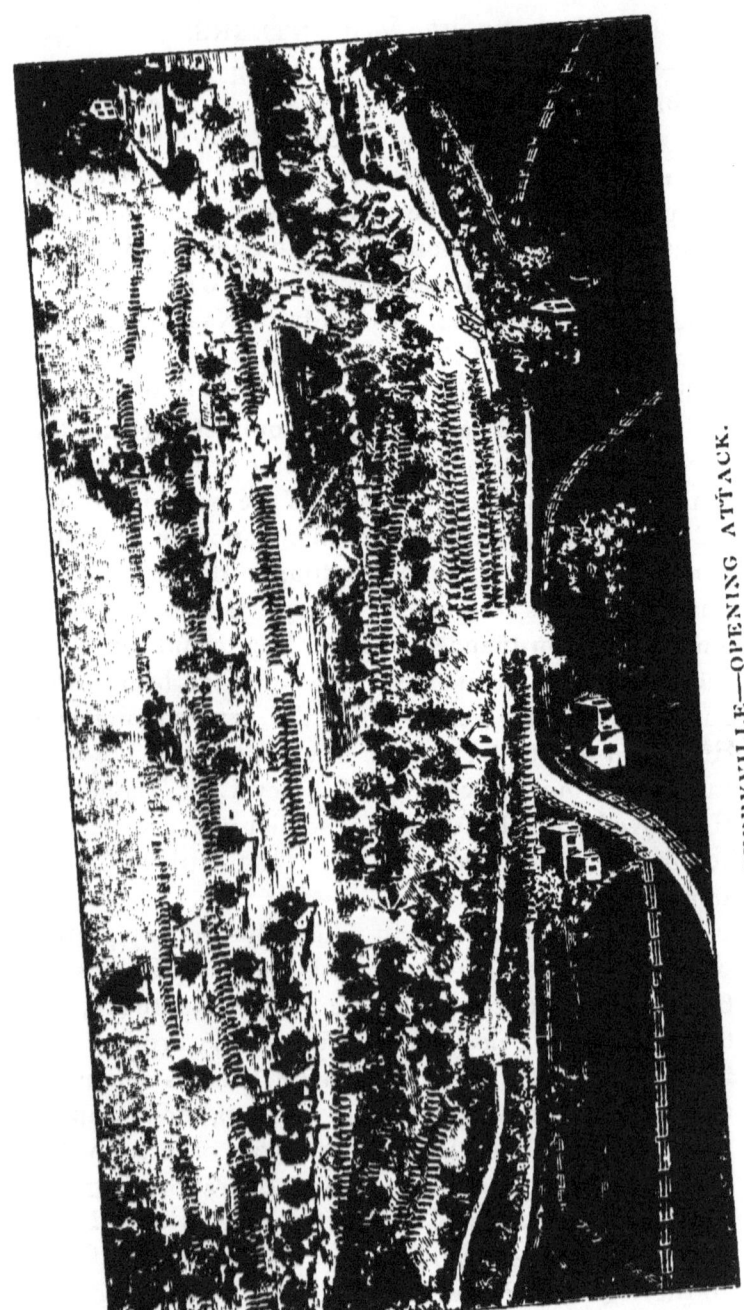

PERRYVILLE—OPENING ATTACK.

engaged in an attack upon the whole Federal left wing. Proceeding to the scene of operations, Captain Carnes found General Cheatham, who told him there was no place where he could be put into action at that time, but to await orders. The battery had already been engaged in a lively engagement, but the position on the right where the brigade was engaged was inaccessible to artillery, as the Federals were posted near the brow of a bluff, and there was but one road that led up to it, and that was a very narrow one on the extreme right. This road was cut out of the side of the bluff, and was held near its brow by a heavy Federal force. Captain Carnes was ordered to remain and await orders until he could be used. Meanwhile Polk's corps ascended the bluff by brigades and rushed forward to the attack. The battle on the right became desperate. In a little while Colonel Wharton, of the Texas Rangers, came up in hot haste and said that he could find a place for the battery to do some splendid work. At the same time Major Martin, of General Donelson's staff, came up with two regiments—the Eighth and Fifty-first Tennessee—that had been detached from Donelson's brigade. After a hasty consultation, these two regiments and a section of the battery went with Colonel Wharton, making a detour to the right toward the enemy's rear. The rear of the Federal left was attacked after a manner planned by the daring Colonel Wharton, of the Texas Rangers. This attack was made upon a fresh line of the Federal forces that had been but recently placed there as a reserve. This line, not knowing the strength of the saucy party attacking them, and confused at the suddenness of the attack and the abundance of musketry and canister shot so unexpectedly hurled into their ranks, stampeded, and their front line giving back about this time from the desperate onslaught of Maney's and Donelson's brigades, the whole Federal left was turned at this point, and the slaughter of the enemy was sudden and terrible. The Confederate columns were now moved up, and the first position of the Federal lines had been broken. The field was practically won by the Confederates.

After the battle of Perryville and the return of the Confederates to Tennessee, Captain Carnes was incapacitated for duty, owing to sickness and a wound received in the engagement of October 8. Accordingly, he was sent on furlough to Macon, Georgia, in order to receive medical treatment. Here he recuperated and was captured *permanently*, not by Federal bayonets, it is true, but by the smiles and charms of a beautiful and charming young lady to whom he was married shortly after the close of the war.

Rumors of a prospective battle near Murfreesboro caused Captain Carnes to rejoin his battery before the expiration of his leave of absence. He found his battery encamped with its brigade in front of Murfreesboro. Soon after his return the battery went with the brigade on a memorable march in a snow-storm to Lavergne, between Murfreesboro and Nashville. The great battle of Murfreesboro was fought shortly afterward. In this memorable engagement Carnes's battery did excellent service. The battery was operated in front of the Cowan House and in the cedar brake on Wednesday, and on the following day was detached from the brigade and assigned to a position on the hill to the right of the Nashville pike, in front of Stone's River. This position was a peculiarly critical and dangerous one, and the battery was here supported by a

Mississippi brigade—its own brigade (Donelson's) held the ground it had gained on Wednesday.

After the retreat from Murfreesboro to Shelbyville, the battery was camped with its brigade at Shelbyville, and afterward at Tullahoma. On the retreat to Chattanooga, in July, 1862, the rains were almost incessant, and when the Confederates arrived at the Tennessee river, near the mouth of Battle Creek, they found that their pontoons had been broken by the freshets of the previous days and the Tennessee river was much swollen. The pontoon had broken in the middle, and a part of the bridge was found on each side of the river. The engineer officers were at a loss to manage it. At the suggestion of General Cheatham, Captain Carnes was directed to take charge of the work, and by using the knowledge of ropes, water, and boats acquired in the United States Navy, he quickly replaced the bridge, over which the retreating army passed in safety. For this, Captain Carnes was highly complimented by Generals Cheatham, Hardee, Walthall, and others, who witnessed the work from the bank of the stream.

The battery participated in all the movements of the brigade up to, and including, the battle of Chickamauga. In this latter engagement the battery, with the brigade, was thrown unexpectedly upon the enemy's breastworks, and through a misunderstanding of orders from division head-quarters, the brigade and battery each thought that Walker's division was in their front, and that *they* were advanced as a support to him. In this manner the whole column moved within a few paces of the enemy's lines. Before the mistake was discovered, the battery was in position. The undergrowth being thick, and it being very difficult to ascertain the true position of the enemy, who was posted on an advantageous and elevated position and could see the position of the Confederates, the fire became general, and the battery received a severe fire of grape and canister at very short range. The Confederates at this part of the line were forced to fall back a short distance. The battery had sustained a fearful loss during the few minutes it took to rectify the mistake. Having lost most of its horses and many of its men, Captain Carnes was unable to bring off his guns when the line fell back, and they fell into the hands of the enemy. Hood's division of Longstreet's corps attacked the enemy on the left of Wright's brigade a few minutes afterward, and drove them back. In this charge Hood recaptured the guns of Carnes's battery.

In the battle of Chickamauga on Saturday evening, the battery entered the action with an effective total of seventy-eight men. Of this number thirty-eight were killed and wounded. The battery also lost forty-nine horses in this brief action of Saturday evening. Among the killed was Lieutenant A. Van Vleck, who received three wounds within fifteen minutes, the last shot causing instant death. Also private Lane, a gallant soldier and a veteran of the Mexican war, laid down his life in the battle.

Owing to the used-up condition of the recaptured guns and the loss of horses and men, it was impossible to operate the battery, and the men being temporarily assigned to other duty, Captain Carnes was assigned to staff duty under Lieutenant-general Polk, who was a particular friend. When Colonel Walter, of Mississippi (who was General Bragg's chief of staff,) learned that Captain Carnes felt mortified over the temporary loss of his guns to the enemy in the engagement of Saturday evening, he went with General Bragg on Sunday morning to show him the ground occupied by the battery at the time of its capture. General Bragg was pleased with the work that Captain Carnes had performed under great difficulties, and complimented him for the good work his battery performed until it was captured. So well was the commanding general pleased with the ability of Captain Carnes as an artillery officer that he caused him to be promoted to the command of a battalion of artillery.

After the battle of Chickamauga Captain Carnes received a thirty-days' furlough in order to refit his battery, being allowed to select from guns out of the fifty-nine pieces of artillery captured by the Confederates at Chickamauga. On his return from Atlanta with the new battery, new horses were given him, and half the men of Scott's battery were assigned to Carnes's battery, with one of Scott's lieutenants to take the place of Lieutenant Van Vleck, who was killed at Chickamauga. Captain Carnes was placed in command of a battalion of four batteries in Stevenson's division. His own battery being assigned to that division was commanded by Captain L. G. Marshall, who had been a first lieutenant all the time while the battery was commanded by Captain Carnes. From this time to the close of the war the battery was separated from the brigade.

About this time the artillery of the army was organized into battalions and regiments, and managed apart from the infantry command. Captain Carnes continued in command of a battalion of artillery until early in 1864, when he was assigned to duty in the Confederate Navy under a commission of lieutenant in the regular navy of the Confederate States, in which capacity he served to the end of the war.

Carnes's battery was a part of Donelson's brigade during the greater part of two years. Its commander, Captain W. W. Carnes, was a young officer of more than ordinary ability. He was honored by his men and the officers and men of the brigade, and by all who knew him. He was a gallant and zealous officer, and a gentleman of sterling integrity and honor. He always operated his guns in every engagement where it was possible to plant his battery, and where he could not operate his whole battery he would bring up a section, or even one piece, into action, if he could possibly get it on the ground. This was the case in many of the smaller engagements in which the brigade participated. At Perryville, at Murfreesboro, and at Chickamauga, the battery operated all its guns, and at close quarters, with the enemy. In each of these engagements it rendered valuable assistance to the brigade and to the whole army. The soldiers of Donelson's brigade cherished the warmest feelings of friendship and good-will toward the officers and men of this battery, which was reciprocated in full. There was no envy, and rivalry, or jealousy, as was often the case between the infantry and other branches of the service. The brigade exercised a warm feeling of interest and pride in their battery, and always showed it. As the guns would move out from camps with the infantry columns to take its position with them, the battery was always greeted with loud and long-continued cheers. The Eighth and Sixteenth regiments made heavy details to recruit this battery in the later years of the war, and these regiments became so attached to Captain Carnes and his men that they considered them almost the same as members of the same company or regiment with them.

As an officer Captain Carnes was a rigid disciplinarian, and conducted every feature of his military life to a mathematical accuracy. Having been educated at the United States Naval Academy and brought up under the rigid rules of the navy in reference to obeying orders, he always made it a point to hold strictly to his instructions. When he was ordered to hold a place as long as he could he made it a rule *to stay there*. He considered that his only means of measuring his ability to hold a position to which he had been assigned was to stick to it till relief came or he had orders to leave it. This was the case at Chickamauga where he was placed by a mistake, not his own, in the very mouths of the enemy's cannons mounted upon breastworks. Here he worked all his guns, and dealt death and destruction to the enemy till half of his men and most of his horses were shot down. When he was ordered to withdraw his battery he found that he had neither men nor horses sufficient to take off his guns, and, as has been before stated, they fell into the hands of the enemy. This was the only retrograde movement that he ever made from the field during his command of artillery.

Captain Carnes was a gentleman possessed of many good qualities. He always admired a fine horse, and was always mounted upon one of the fleetest and best horses in the army, and in the tilts and equestrian exercises at jumping, etc., he always excelled, and was the best horseman in Cheatham's division.

Captain Carnes was a citizen of Memphis, Tennessee, at the breaking out of the war, and was attending the United States Naval Academy at Annapolis. Espousing the cause of the Confederacy in the first stages of the conflict, he continued in its service as has been briefly stated, and was among the last to surrender.

In 1866, he was married at Macon, Georgia, to the lady whom he formerly met at this place in 1863. In 1867 he settled in Macon, and has resided there up to the present time. As he was a faithful, gallant, and true officer and soldier in war, and was honored and loved by his men, he possesses the same good qualities, together with all the embellishments of a true and honorable gentleman in the quiet walks of peace.

WRIGHT'S BRIGADE.

When General Donelson was assigned to duty in East Tennessee, with the rank of major-general, General Wright, who had been previously promoted to the rank of brigadier-general, was placed in command of Donelson's brigade. His commission was dated December 13, 1862, and his first assignment to duty under this commission was in the command of a Kentucky brigade in Hardee's corps.

General Wright was assigned to duty as commander of Donelson's brigade by virtue of the following order:

Special Order, } Head-quarters Army of Tennessee, }
No. 25. } Tullahoma, Tenn., January 31, 1863. }

II. Brigadier-general Marcus J. Wright is hereby relieved from duty in Hardee's corps, and will report to Lieutenant-general Polk for command of Donelson's brigade.

By command of General Bragg.
    George William Brent, A. A. G.

Brigadier-general Marcus J. Wright entered the service as lieutenant-colonel of the One Hundred and Fifty-fourth* Regiment Tennessee Infantry, in the Provisional Army of Tennessee, April 4, 1861; was made lieutenant-colonel and acting adjutant-general June 10, and was commissioned brigadier-general December 13, 1862. He commanded a battalion of the One Hundred and Fifty-fourth Regiment and Steuben Artillery at Fort Wright, on the Mississippi river near Randolph, Tenn., April 29, 1861. He was commander of the Post at Columbus, Ky., from February to March, 1862, and commanded the conscript camp at McMinnville, Tenn., from September to December 12, 1862; was assigned to the command of Hanson's Kentucky brigade January 11, 1863, and was assigned to the command of Donelson's brigade February 1, 1863. He commanded the brigade in the battles of Chickamauga and Missionary Ridge; was assigned to duty as commander of the District and Post of Atlanta in 1863; was commander of the Post at Macon, Ga., in 1864, and commander of the District of North Mississippi and West Tennessee from February, 1865, to the close of the war.

Wright's brigade was composed of the Eighth, Sixteenth, Twenty-eighth, Thirty-eighth, Fifty-first, and Fifty-second Tennessee Regiments, Murray's Tennessee Battalion, and Carnes's Battery of Tennessee Artillery. This brigade was a part of Cheatham's division, Polk's corps, Army of Tennessee.

The following constituted the members of General Wright's staff, with the date of their appointment and the period of their service:

---

*This regiment was numbered on the old list.

J. T. Beverage, Captain and A. C. S., February, 1864.
W. H. Browning, Chaplain, February, 1864.
Laurence L. Butler, Major and Acting A. A. G., December, 1863.
Henry L. Elcan, Major and A. Q. M., January 20, 1863.
James H. Elcan, Captain and Acting A. D. C., February, 1863.
Alexis Gardenhire, Acting A. D. C., April, 1863.
Eugene T. Harris, First Lieutenant and A. D. C., January 20, 1863.
Minor Harris, First Lieutenant and A. I. G., 1863-5.
Charles Hays, Major and Acting A. I. G., January, 1863.
James R. Howard, Colonel and Acting A. D. C., 1863.
Hilton S. Jones, Major and Chief Surgeon, 1863-4.
Edward F. Lee, Captain and A. I. G., September, 1863, to November, 1864.
Andrew J. Paine, Captain and Ordnance Officer, 1863-4.
William Pierce, Captain and A. I. G., 1863.
H. Y. Riddle, Captain and Acting A. A. G., December, 1863.
W. L. Richardson, Lieutenant and Provost Marshal, March, 1863.
Charles Smith, Vol. A. D. C., January, 1863.
T. E. Starke, Captain and A. I. G., January 21, 1863.
W. A. Thompson, Captain and A. C. S., December, 1864, to February, 1865.
John P. Trezevant, Major and A. C. S., January 20, 1863.
Leon Trousdale, Captain and A. A. G., January 20, 1863.
W. C. Whitthorne, Brigadier-general and Acting A. D. C., September 19 and 20, 1863.
Sydney Womack, First Lieutenant and A. I. G., January 9, 1863.

Shortly after the assignment of General Wright to the command of the brigade, General Cheatham addressed him, through his adjutant-general, Major John Ingram, asking him for the names of two Tennesseans of the brigade who fell at the battles of Perryville and Murfreesboro, who were conspicuous for their gallantry on the field. General Wright forwarded the names of Captain B. H. Holland, of the Thirty-eighth

Tennessee, and Colonel W. L. Moore, of the Eighth Tennessee, who fell at Murfreesboro, as shown by the following correspondence:

> HEAD-QUARTERS WRIGHT'S BRIGADE,
> CHEATHAM'S DIVISION, POLK'S CORPS,
> ARMY OF TENNESSEE, April 16, 1863.
>
> *Major:*—I have the honor to acknowledge the receipt of your note of the 13th inst., informing me that the major-general commanding directs me to furnish the names of "two Tennesseans of the brigade who fell at Murfreesboro and Perryville conspicuous for their gallantry," for the purpose of making appropriate inscriptions on the guns of Maney's brigade.
>
> I respectfully forward the names of Colonel William L. Moore, of the Eighth Regiment Tennessee Volunteers, and Captain B. H. Holland, of Company C, Thirty-eighth Regiment Tennessee Volunteers, both of whom were killed at the battle of Murfreesboro, and both of whom were conspicuous for their gallantry displayed upon that ever-memorable field.
>
> I am, sir, respectfully your obedient servant,
>
> MARCUS J. WRIGHT, *Bigadier-general Commanding.*
>
> Major JOHN INGRAM, A. A. G.

General Wright was a clever, genial gentleman, quiet and urbane in his habits, and was a good soldier. His promotion to the rank of brigadier-general over Colonel Savage was not agreeable to the greater portion of the brigade, though they had no animosity against him as a man. They regarded him as a gentleman, but at the same time they felt that the promotion should have been given to Colonel Savage, who was at the time the senior colonel of the brigade. The men knew Colonel Savage as a commander and had confidence in him. Of Colonel Wright they knew comparatively nothing, and were disappointed when he was placed in command of the brigade. General Wright did comparatively little, however, in procuring this promotion. He was popular with the governor and State authorities, some of whom, it was said, were far from being admirers of Colonel Savage. Some old campaign spleen was between them and him, and the feud, though partially dissembled, dated back for several years previous to the beginning of the war. Many of Colonel Savage's friends were of opinion that some of the State officers were in concert with the governor, and their programme seemed to be to see that Savage was promoted no further. Seeing that there would be a promotion for General Donelson in the near future, they procured for Colonel Wright a commission as brigadier-general in advance of any vacancy. When the vacancy *did* occur, they had a brigadier ready to take charge of Donelson's brigade.

General Wright received the commission some time in advance of Donelson's promotion. The authorities treated Colonel Savage with great injustice in this transaction. *They* were the parties who did the wrong, and were the proper subjects of reproach. General Wright accepted the commission which *they* procured for him. That the authorities made a mistake in this action was apparent to many who were in the brigade. Colonel Savage was the superior of General Wright in many respects as a commander. Savage was best qualified for a field commander, while Wright had not a superior as a district or post commander. This was demonstrated in the sequel. General Wright's record as commander of the Post at Columbus, Ky., at McMinnville, Tenn., Charleston, Tenn., and at Dalton, Macon, and Atlanta, Ga., and the District of North Mississippi, is creditable to him as an officer, and in that capacity he was without a superior in the Army of Tennessee. As lieutenant-colonel of the One Hundred and Fifty-fourth Tennessee, General Wright had a good record, and distinguished himself in several battles.

General Wright did what most young officers would have done in accepting the promotion thus procured for him. In this war "rank" was every thing. The Southern soldiery delighted in promotion, and few indeed would have declined the commission of a brigadier.

Though Colonel Savage declined to serve under General Wright, for reasons explained in his farewell address to his regiment, there was no ill will between them, and there ever afterward existed a warm friendship between these two officers.

As an officer, General Wright was kind and courteous. There was little of the pomp and display usual to the commander of a brigade. He was in every respect a gentleman. On account of bad health, his stay with the brigade was brief, during which time his command was in the battles of Chickamauga and Missionary Ridge. Under the chapter of "Official Reports" can be found General Wright's official report of the conduct of his brigade in these two battles.

Since the war General Wright has resided much of his time in Washington, where he has had charge of the war records.

SEVENTEENTH REGIMENT TENNESSEE VOLUNTEERS.

This regiment was composed of companies from the counties of Franklin, Bedford, Marshall, Jackson, and Putnam, and was organized at Camp Trousdale in May, 1861. The field and staff officers, at the time of the organization, were as follows:

 Taz W. Newman, Colonel;
 T. C. H. Miller, Lieutenant-colonel;
 A. L. Landis, Major;
 —— Kincheloe, Adjutant;
 Watt W. Floyd, Quartermaster;
 W. C. Collins, Commissary;
 John W. O'Neal, Sergeant-major;
 W. F. Callahan, Quartermaster-sergeant;
 Thomas Harrel, Commissary-sergeant;
 Dr. Watt Gentry, Surgeon;
 Dr. —— Whitfield, Assisant Surgeon;
 Rev. E. B. Chrisman, Chaplain.

The regiment was composed of the following companies:

COMPANY A—Bedford County.

J. D. Hoyle	Captain.
T. B. Terry	First Lieutenant.
Robert Campbell	Second Lieutenant.
Joseph Hastings	Third Lieutenant.

COMPANY B—Bedford County.

W. A. Landis	Captain.
U. C. Harrison	First Lieutenant.
H. M. Kimsey	Second Lieutenant.
Math Cortiner	Third Lieutenant.

TENNESSEE VOLUNTEERS.

COMPANY C—Marshall County.
R. C. Williams..Captain.
J. C. Davis..First Lieutenant.
F. M. Orr...Second Lieutenant.
W. M. Bryant...Third Lieutenant.

COMPANY D—Franklin County.
T. H. Finch...Captain.
G. W. Corn...First Lieutenant.
William Lee..Second Lieutenant.
W. H. Cardin...Third Lieutenant.

COMPANY E—Franklin County.
Albert S. Marks..Captain.
William Newman...First Lieutenant.
James Grant..Second Lieutenant.
T. H. Cole..Third Lieutenant.

COMPANY F—Marshall County.
R. H. Hunter...Captain.
John Bigger..First Lieutenant.
William Wallace..Second Lieutenant.
James Hunter...Third Lieutenant.

COMPANY G—Bedford County.
James Armstrong...Captain.
Thomas H. Watterson..First Lieutenant.
Thomas Cleveland..Second Lieutenant.
Thomas Woods...Third Lieutenant.

COMPANY H—Marshall County.
R. H. McCrory...Captain.
W. H. Holden..First Lieutenant.
G. W. Collins..Second Lieutenant.
—— Sanders..Third Lieutenant.

COMPANY I—Franklin County.
J. A. Matthews...Captain.
G. W. Ingall...First Lieutenant.
—— Anderson..Second Lieutenant.
—— Stewart..Third Lieutenant.

COMPANY K—Jackson County.

S. B. McDearmon..Captain.
W. W. Cowan...................................First Lieutenant.
R. B. Montgomery.........................Second Lieutenant.
G. W. Montgomery..........................Third Lieutenant.

The Seventeenth Regiment was placed in Zollicoffer's command, which was composed of the following regiments: Fifteenth Mississippi, Colonel Statum; Eleventh Tennessee, Colonel Raines; Seventeenth Tennessee, Colonel Newman; Nineteenth Tennessee, Colonel Cummings; Twentieth Tennessee, Colonel Battle; which operated in Kentucky and East Tennessee during the first year of the war, and was in the battles of Rock Castle and Fishing Creek, after which it joined the army of General Albert Sidney Johnston, in whose command it operated during the campaign of North Mississippi.

On May 8, 1862, the Seventeenth Regiment was reorganized at Corinth, in accordance with an act of the Confederate Congress and orders from General Beauregard. The regimental officers at the reorganization were as follows:

ALBERT S. MARKS, Colonel;
WATT W. FLOYD, Lieutenant-colonel;
JAMES C. DAVIS, Major;
J. B. FITZPATRICK, Adjutant;
D. B. SHOFTNER, Sergeant-major;
JAMES LITTLE, Ordnance-sergeant;
B. H. McCRORY, Quartermaster;
T. H. FINCH, Commissary;
Dr. W. M. GENTRY, Surgeon;
Dr. ALFRED JONES, Assistant Surgeon;
Rev. A. B. MOORE, Chaplain.

The company officers were as follows:

COMPANY A.
F. B. Terry..Captain.
J. D. Floyd..First Lieutenant.
J. H. Hastings..Second Lieutenant.
Robert Campbell......................................Third Lieutenant.

COMPANY B.
U. C. Harrison..Captain.
H. M. Kimsey...First Lieutenant.
—— Hight...Second Lieutenant.
—— Miles..Third Lieutenant.

COMPANY C.
F. M. Orr..Captain.
J. W. McCrory..First Lieutenant.
R. H. Armstrong....................................Second Lieutenant.

COMPANY D.
H. C. Carden..Captain.
G. W. Corn...First Lieutenant.
W. L. Elzy...Second Lieutenant.

COMPANY E.
John R. Handly...Captain.
J. Tipps...First Lieutenant.
M. W. Black..Second Lieutenant.
G. W. Waggoner......................................Third Lieutenant.

COMPANY F.
J. D. Cooper...Captain.
R. P. McCullough....................................First Lieutenant.
William Byars..Second Lieutenant.
Lee Cathey..Third Lieutenant.

COMPANY G.
Thomas H. Watterson.....................................Captain.
Matt Scruggs..First Lieutenant.
Joel Peay...Second Lieutenant.
John Scott (resigned)..................................Third Lieutenant.
John Henslee (elected to fill vacancy)..........Third Lieutenant.

COMPANY H.

—— McAdams (resigned)..........................Captain.
G. W. O'Neal (promoted)..........................First Lieutenant.
T. P. Tolley (promoted)..........................Second Lieutenant.
A. L. Elzy (promoted)..........................Third Lieutenant.
Z. W. Ewing (promoted)..........................Third Lieutenant.

COMPANY I.

William Clark..........................Captain.
J. W. Bolton..........................First Lieutenant.
—— Looney..........................Second Lieutenant.
—— Kelley..........................Third Lieutenant.

COMPANY K.

G. W. McDonald..........................Captain.
James P. Byrne..........................First Lieutenant.
M. L. Poe..........................Second Lieutenent.
J. D. McKinley..........................Third Lieutenant.

At the time of the reorganization the Seventeenth Regiment was a part of Hawthorn's brigade, Cleburne's division. The brigade was composed of the following regiments: Twenty-third Tennessee, Colonel Neil; Fifth Confederate Tennessee, Colonel Pickett; Thirty-third Alabama, Colonel Adams; Seventeenth Tennessee, Colonel Marks.

The Seventeenth Tennessee remained at Corinth until the evacuation, and accompanied Bragg's army in the Kentucky campaign, and participated in the battle of Perryville, and afterward in the battle of Murfreesboro.

From the time of its organization to the battle of Murfreesboro, its campaigns amounted to a total of 3,597 miles, of which it

Marched.................................... 1,532 miles.
Traveled on cars............................ 1,665 "
Traveled on steamboat....................... 400 "

Total .... 3,597 "

The following register of its marches was kindly furnished us from the diary of Private S. G. Ferguson, of Company I, who was a good soldier, and died in prison at Point Lookout, Md., in December, 1864, having been captured at the battle of Missionary Ridge in November, 1863:

ACCOUNT OF THE MARCHES OF THE SEVENTEENTH REGIMENT.

DATE.	LEFT.	ARRIVED AT.	DATE.	DISTANCE.	HOW TRAVELED.
May 10, 1861	Camp Anderson, Tenn	Camp Harris, Tenn	May 10, 1861	40 miles	Cars.
May 27, 1861	Camp Harris, Tenn	Camp Trousdale, Tenn	May 27, 1861	140 miles	Cars.
July 23, 1861	Camp Trousdale, Tenn	Camp King, Tenn	July 26, 1861	483 miles	Cars.
Aug. 3, 1861	Camp King, Tenn	Russellville, Tenn	Aug. 4, 1861	80 miles	March.
Aug. 5, 1861	Russellville, Tenn	Cumberland Gap, Tenn	Aug. 8, 1861	42 miles	March.
Aug. 14, 1861	Cumberland Gap, Tenn	Camp Bridgman, Tenn	Aug. 15, 1861	35 miles	March.
Sept. 10, 1861	Camp Bridgman, Tenn	Cumberland Gap, Tenn	Sept. 12, 1861	35 miles	March.
Sept. 14, 1861	Cumberland Gap, Tenn	Camp Buckner, Ky	Sept. 14, 1861	12 miles	March.
Oct. 3, 1861	Camp Buckner, Ky	Retr'rned to Camp Buckner	Oct. 5, 1861	60 miles	March.
Oct. 16, 1861	Rockcastle, Ky	Rockcastle, Ky (fighting)	Oct. 21, 1861	65 miles	March.
Oct. 21, 1861	Rockcastle, Ky	Cumberland Gap, Tenn	Oct. 31, 1861	77 miles	March.
Nov. 1, 1861	Cumberland Gap, Tenn	Camp Zollicoffer, Tenn	Nov. 3, 1861	40 miles	March.
Nov. 7, 1861	Camp, Zollicoffer, Tenn	Poplar Creek, Tenn	Nov. 8, 1861	38 miles	March.
Nov. 9, 1861	Poplar Creek, T-nn	Camp Zollicoffer, Tenn	Nov. 11, 1861	38 miles	March.
Nov. 16, 1861	Camp Zollicoffer, Tenn	Watsburg, Tenn	Nov. 19, 1861	42 miles	March.
Nov. 27, 1861	Watsburg, Tenn	Mill Spring, Ky	Nov. 30, 1861	100 miles	March.
Jan. 20, 1862	Mill Spring, Ky	Columbus, Tenn	Jan. 26, 1862	80 miles	March.
Feb. 5, 1862	Columbus, Tenn	Carthage, Tenn	Feb. 9, 1862	40 miles	March.
Feb. 16, 1862	Carthage, Tenn	Murfreesboro, Tenn	Feb. 19, 1862	86 miles	March.
Feb. 28, 1862	Murfreesboro, Tenn	Shelbyville, Tenn	Mar. 1, 1862	27 miles	March.
Mar. 4, 1862	Shelbyville, Tenn	Fayetteville, Tenn	Mar. 5, 1862	27 miles	March.
Mar. 8, 1861	Fayetteville, Tenn	Athens, Ala	Mar. 10, 1862	30 miles	March.
Mar. 12, 1862	Athens, Ala	Decatur, Ala	Mar. 12, 1862	17 miles	March.
Mar. 19, 1862	Decatur, Ala	Tuscumbia, Ala	Mar. 19, 1862	40 miles	Cars.
Mar. 24, 1862	Tuscumbia, Ala	Iuka, Miss	Mar. 24, 1862	52 miles	Cars.
April 8, 1862	Iuka, Miss	Corinth, Miss	April 8, 1862	22 miles	Cars.
May 29, 1862	Corinth, Miss	Baldwin, Miss	May 31, 1862	40 miles	March.
June 7, 1862	Baldwin, Miss	Tupelo, Miss	June 8, 1862	25 miles	March.
July 28, 1862	Tupelo, Miss	Mobile, Ala	July 29, 1862	250 miles	Cars.
July 30, 1862	Mobile, Ala	Montgomery, Ala	Aug. 1, 1862	450 miles	Steamboat.
Aug. 3, 1862	Montgomery, Ala	West Point, Ga	Aug. 3, 1862	87 miles	Cars.

Aug. 4, 1862	West Point, Ga.	Atlanta, Ga.	86 miles	Cars.
Aug. 4, 1862	Atlanta, Ga.	Chattanooga, Tenn.	138 miles	Cars.
Aug. 5, 1862	Chattanooga, Tenn.	Tyner Station, Tenn.	10 miles	Cars.
Aug. 18, 1862	Tyner, Tenn.	Camp Stringer, Tenn.	15 miles	March.
Aug. 28, 1862	Camp Stringer, Tenn.	Sequatchie Valley, Tenn.	28 miles	March.
Sept. 1, 1862	Sequatchie, Tenn.	Pikeville, Tenn.	25 miles	March.
Sept. 3, 1862	Pikeville, Tenn.	Sparta, Tenn.	45 miles	March.
Sept. 7, 1862	Sparta, Tenn.	Glasgow, Ky.	82 miles	March.
Sept. 15, 1862	Glasgow, Ky.	Munfordville, Ky.	27 miles	March.
Sept. 20, 1862	Munfordville, Ky.	Bardstown, Ky.	50 miles	March.
Oct. 6, 1862	Bardstown, Ky.	Perryville, Ky.	37 miles	March.
Oct. 9, 1862	Perryville, Ky.	Camp Dick Robinson, Ky.	27 miles	March.
Oct. 13, 1862	Camp Dick Robinson, Ky.	Rockcastle, Tenn.	50 miles	March.
Oct. 16, 1862	Rockcastle, Tenn.	Knoxville, Tenn.	136 miles	March.
Oct. —, 1862	Knoxville, Tenn.	Bridgeport, Ala.	150 miles	Cars.

In the battle of Murfreesboro the losses of the Seventeenth Tennessee amounted to 246 in killed and wounded. In this battle Colonel Marks lost his right leg, and the whole field and staff, except Lieutenant-colonel Floyd, were either killed or wounded. In the battle of Chickamauga the losses of the Seventeenth were, killed, 20; wounded, 57; captured, 70—total, 147.

After the battle of Chickamauga, and before the battle of Missionary Ridge, the Seventeenth Tennessee Infantry was detached from the Army of Tennessee, and became incorporated into the army commanded by General Longstreet in upper East Tennessee, and during the campaign of 1863-4, under his command, it participated in the siege of Knoxville, the battle of Bean's Station, beside a number of minor engagements at various points in East Tennessee during the winter of 1863-4. The regiment had several men killed and wounded in that campaign, and suffered great hardships by reason of the want of food and clothing and the long marches in the severe winter weather.

In May, 1864, the regiment was removed to the Army of Virginia, and immediately upon its arrival at Petersburg, it engaged the Federal forces under General Butler, and as the object was to delay his march on Richmond until General Beauregard could re-enforce the inferior Confederate force, it was engaged for a number of days in fighting the enemy at every eligible point, so as to retard General Butler's advance. Finally, the enemy occupied the fortification at Drury's Bluff, and General Beauregard arriving at this conjuncture, the enemy were assaulted, and the Seventeenth Regiment being among the first to carry the fortifications in its front, and pressing the enemy closely, had both of its flanks uncovered, and by reason of this fact sustained a severe loss in killed and wounded. Among the killed was Lieutenant-colonel Floyd.

The enemy being repulsed at all points and Petersburg being uncovered, the Seventeenth returned there, and from this time to the close of the war it was constantly engaged in repelling the assaults of the enemy in the works around Petersburg and Richmond, as exigency required, until the evacuation of Richmond and Petersburg. In the many engagements it had with the enemy, the loss in killed and wounded was great. It participated in the battle of Hatcher's Run, in February, 1865, and by a gallant and successful charge upon the enemy, it gained much credit in that engagement. It was one of the last regiments to leave the defenses around Petersburg, and it did not retire until it had repeatedly repulsed the enemy on its front, and was nearly entirely enveloped by the enemy. In this engagement it lost a number in killed and wounded, and one half the survivors were captured.

From Petersburg the regiment marched to Appomattox, and there, with the army of General Lee, was surrendered, April 9, 1865.

THE ELEVENTH REGIMENT TENNESSEE VOLUNTEERS.

This regiment was made up of companies from the counties of Dickson, Hickman, Humphreys, Robertson, and Davidson. The regiment was at first commanded by Colonel James E. Raines, and after the promotion of Colonel Raines, was commanded by Colonel George W. Gordon. The following are the names of some of the officers of this regiment: Captains James Long, William Green, James Mallory, Joseph Pitts, Samuel Godshall, Richard McCann, Van Weems, William Thedford, Hugh Lucas, T. P. Bateman. These gentlemen were commanders of companies in the Eleventh Tennessee. Dr. Maney was surgeon of this regiment, and the Rev. Fountain E. Pitts was its chaplain.

This regiment served under Zollicoffer, and was a part of Raines's brigade, Colonel Raines having been promoted to brigadier-general. After the death of Zollicoffer, the Eleventh Tennessee was under General E. Kirby Smith about Cumberland Gap. It was in the battles of Murfreesboro, Chickamauga, and all the battles of the Georgia campaign. It also participated in the battles of Franklin and Nashville, and was surrendered with Johnston's army at Greensboro, N. C., at the close of the war.

We have been unable to obtain any of the muster-rolls of this regiment, or any list of its casualties. It was composed of good men and they fought well. Its losses in the different battles were very severe, showing that it always went where danger was thickest. The original commander of this regiment, General Raines, was killed at the battle of Murfreesboro.

THIRTY-THIRD REGIMENT TENNESSEE VOLUNTEERS.

This regiment was made up of companies from West Tennessee, principally from the counties of Obion, Weakley, and Madison. The regiment was originally commanded by Colonel A. W. Campbell, who was promoted to the rank of brigadier-general in 1864. Warren P. Jones was lieutenant-colonel of the regiment, and was killed at the battle of Resaca. Newton Paine was major. Among the officers of the regiment we have the names of the following:

Captain HENRY HICKMAN,   Captain HUTCHINSON,
Captain BEDFORD,   Captain LACY,
Captain W. F. MARBURY,   Captain COCHRANE,
Captain W. B. MCWHIRTER,   Captain MOROD,
Captain GEORGE WILSON,   Captain MORRIS.

Captain McWhirter was killed at the battle of Chickamauga.

We have been unable to obtain any rolls of the companies or any list of the casualties. The regiment belonged to Cheatham's division of Polk's corps, and fought through the war. As it followed Cheatham, it went where there was hard fighting. The gallant old Thirty-third was a splendid regiment.

SEVENTH KENTUCKY REGIMENT, RUST'S BRIGADE.

This regiment was organized at Camp Burnett, Kentucky, September, 1861, and was composed largely of Tennesseans, though many were resident Kentuckians. The regiment was placed in General Cheatham's brigade. After General Cheatham was promoted to major-general, the brigade was commanded by Colonel Rust, who was made a brigadier-general.

Colonel Charles Wickliffe was the original commander of this regiment, and was a gallant officer as well as a good man. At the battle of Shiloh Colonel Wickliffe was killed, and his regiment suffered severely. The old Seventh was a gallant regiment. After the death of Colonel Wickliffe, it was commanded by Colonel Crossland. It was subsequently transferred to Buford's division of Forrest's cavalry, where it served to the close of the war.

The Seventh Kentucky did much hard fighting, both as infantry and cavalry. Colonel Crossland was as brave an officer as ever was placed in command of men. His daring exploits are prominently recorded in the history of Forrest's cavalry.

Colonel Wickliffe, the original commander of the Seventh Kentucky, was a prominent citizen of Ballard county, and warmly appreciated by his people. Since the building of the Jackson route of the Illinois Central Railroad, a town has sprung up on its line six miles south of Cairo, in Ballard county, Ky., on the east bank of the Mississippi. This town has grown rapidly and commands a flourishing business. Two parallel lines of railroad pass it—the Illinois Central, leading to Jackson, Tenn., and the Mobile and Ohio, leading to Mobile. The country around is fertile and the people are comfortable and prosperous.

The town was named WICKLIFFE, in honor of the departed hero of the gallant old *Seventh Kentucky*, and is at present the county-seat of Ballard county.

SKETCHES OF OFFICERS.

CHAPTER IX.

CAPTAIN D. C. SPURLOCK

Was the son of James Spurlock, one of the oldest and most enterprising business men of Warren county. He was born near McMinnville. His early life was devoted to work in connection with his father's business, and he received a respectable education at home. He was a leading member of the Cumberland Presbyterian Church at McMinnville, and was noted for his upright and consistent life, and for his piety and integrity. He was in every respect an exemplary man, and was loved by his associates and respected by all who knew him.

Upon arriving at his majority, Captain Spurlock engaged in the mercantile business in McMinnville, which occupation he followed successfully till the beginning of the war in 1861. At this time he enlisted as a private in Captain Donnell's company, of the Sixteenth Regiment, and served in this capacity through the Cheat Mountain campaign, during which he was called, on account of his most excellent business qualities, to the position of quartermaster of the regiment. In this position he proved himself eminently qualified, and filled the office with credit to himself and satisfaction to all concerned.

At the reorganization of the regiment, he resigned his position as quartermaster and returned to the ranks of his old company, who, appreciating his merits and good qualities, called him to their command by their unanimous voice. Accepting the position so strongly urged upon him by his comrades, he commanded his company (C) in all the campaigns of the regiment up to the time of his death.

In the battle of Perryville, his younger brother, Lieutenant Cicero Spurlock, of his company, fell in the opening of the fight. At the battle of Murfreesboro, December 31, 1862, Captain Spurlock was among the slain in the fearful carnage of the first day's fight. His aged father and mother had come to Murfreesboro shortly before the battle, and were stopping with Mr. Miles, at the Miles House, when the battle came up. On the night before the first day's fight, Captain Spurlock obtained a short leave of absence from his command in order to call upon his parents at the hotel. Captain Miles, who witnessed the meeting and the parting of parents and son on this eventful night, describes the scene as deeply affecting. After a brief meeting, he bestowed a parting kiss upon each of his aged parents, who, in return, bestowed upon him their parting blessing and an assurance of their prayers. The son, who, though arrived at mature years, and laden with the honors of those who had associated with him so long, showed on this occasion that respect, and honor, and love for his father and mother that had shone so brilliantly in childhood, and which the cares and allurements of more advanced years could not obscure. With much tenderness and love, he bid adieu to his father and mother, and this was the last time they ever saw him alive.

On the following morning the great battle opened. In the midst of its fearful carnage, Captain Spurlock fell at the head of his company. He fell at his post, with his face to the foe. He yielded up a glorious life to the cause he loved, and his loss was deplored by his comrades as that of a brother. His remains were brought off the field and conveyed to McMinnville, where loving hands administered the last sad service, and where loving hearts bow down in deference to the memory of one so brave, so kind, so pure and good; whose life had been one bright record of kindness and usefulness, upon which had been centered so many worthy and noble deeds.

CAPTAIN JAMES M. PARKS.

Captain James M. Parks was the son of Carrol Parks, a substantial and respected farmer of Warren county, Tennessee. His ancestors came from North Carolina at an early period and settled in Warren county.

In his boyhood Captain Parks labored on his father's farm, and as he arrived at his twentieth year he was placed in Irving College, where he remained as a student until the breaking out of the war between the States. At this time he enlisted in Captain L. H. Meadows's company, and was elected orderly sergeant at its organization in May, 1861. He was elected captain of this company at Corinth in May, 1862, at the reorganization of the regiment, and served in this capacity to the day of his death. Throughout his whole military life Captain Parks was much respected for his upright, exemplary life, and for his many sterling qualities, both as a gentleman and a soldier. He was with his company through all its marches and in all its battles to that of Chickamauga, when he received a fatal wound on the evening of the first day's fight. He was pierced by a grape-shot through the upper portion of his left breast, the missile ranging in the region of the heart, and he lived but a few hours. His company and regiment lamented his loss as that of a brother.

Captain Parks was in every respect a worthy young man. Kind and respectful to all, he won the good-will and respect of all who knew him. His daily walk and conversation was without spot or blemish. Upright, circumspect, and conscientious in all things, he possessed the respect and confidence of his superiors, as well as those who were under his command. In his seventeenth year, Captain Parks made a profession of religion and became a member of the Baptist Church at Hebron, in the vicinity of his home. He was an upright, pious, and exemplary young man at home, at school, and in all the walks of domestic life. When he entered the army, those Christian graces which he cherished with so much prayerful care in his previous life never yielded to the temptations of army life. He cherished those graces with more watchful care. It was the motto of his daily life in the army that "religion is the same in the army as at home," and requires even more at the hands of its votaries.

Captain Parks was buried on the battle-field of Chickamauga, near the spot where he fell. After the close of the war his remains were removed by his father from the battle-field to the church-yard at Hebron, where they now rest, and the spot is marked by a marble which records the time and place of his death.

COLONEL JOEL A. BATTLE.

Joel A. Battle was born in Davidson county, Tennessee, September 19, 1811.

His father was originally from North Carolina, and his mother, Lucinda Mayo Battle, being the owner of large estates in that county, he, by inheritance, became the possessor of much landed property.

COLONEL JOEL A. BATTLE.

He was left an orphan at an early age. His education was limited, there being no good schools near him. He was much beloved by his elders, his reverence for the aged being remarkable even in his childhood.

In his nineteenth year he was married to Miss Sarah Searcy, of Rutherford county, Tennessee. Two years after this marriage his wife died, leaving an only son.

Shortly after his wife's death he raised a company near his home and enlisted in the Florida War.

After his return home from the war he met Miss Adeline Sanders Mosely, a lady remarkable alike for her native refinement and her firm Christian character.

Six years after his first marriage he was united to Miss Mosely, at her home near the Hermitage.

As a quiet farmer, he lived with his growing family at the home of his ancestors for many years.

In 1835 he was elected brigadier-general of the State militia, and in 1851–2 represented Davidson county in the Legislature, having, with the Hon. Russell Houston, been chosen representative for that session of the General Assembly.

He was a zealous Whig, but no partisan spirit prevented his earnest devotion to the public interests and his constant adherence to the principles of right and justice.

As a friend he was unwavering in his attachments. His determination and success in overcoming obstacles that came in his way was unsurpassed.

He was a soldier in the late war, serving as colonel of the Twentieth Tennessee.

The first engagement in which his regiment was engaged was at Barboursville, Kentucky. By a ruse the colonel commanding, as he charged the enemy, impressed them with the idea that he had artillery, which was not the fact. The charge was successful, and the enemy fled.

At Fishing Creek Colonel Battle's regiment did noble duty. General Zollicoffer, commanding the brigade to which this regiment belonged, fell early in the action. Colonel Walthall, of the Fifteenth Mississippi, was next in command. The Confederates being suddenly overwhelmed by numbers were forced to fall back. The Twentieth Tennessee, after suffering a heavy loss in killed and wounded, and being cut off from the Fifteenth Mississippi by a flank movement of the enemy, came near being captured, but made a successful retreat, Colonel Battle in command.

Joel A. Battle, jr., a gifted son of Colonel Battle, was seriously wounded in the left breast, and was brought off the field on the back of a fellow soldier.

Many were the hardships these soldiers endured in this, their first disastrous defeat, and they often refer to the watchful care their commander had for them midst these trying reverses.

General Breckinridge, to whose division the Twentieth Tennessee was attached, often spoke with pride of his confidence in the bravery and steadfastness of the noble Twentieth Tennessee. As a mark of his esteem he presented to this regiment a handsome flag made of his wife's wedding dress. At Shiloh the Twentieth was in the heat of the battle. Colonel Battle had three horses shot from under him. On the first day his oldest son, William, was killed. The father's heart was made sad by the loss, and he clung the more tenderly to his other boy, who, still suffering from the wound received at Fishing Creek, rode with one arm in a sling, doing active service through the day as adjutant of the regiment. The second day of the battle of Shiloh is remembered by the soldiers of the Twentieth as the bloodiest day of the war. After such fighting as was never surpassed, the Federals, being heavily reinforced, the Confederates were compelled to move back. When under the cover of night they reached their tents, inquiries were made for missing ones. One of Colonel Battle's men said to him, "Joel is shot and has fallen as we fell back." The father went back to hunt for his boy, and was captured in an exhausted state when he had gone but a little distance. The body of his brave and gallant son was found the next morning, and buried by some of his fellow students * of Miami University.

Colonel Battle was held as a prisoner of war for a long while. After his exchange he was made Treasurer of the State of Tennessee under Governor Harris, his health being too feeble to again enter the service. After the war was over, he came to Nashville to seek in some way to better his then depleted financial condition. Being energetic and attentive to business, he managed to maintain his family by his own exertions.

In 1872, Governor John C. Brown conferred upon General Battle the appointment of Superintendent of the State Prison, which position he occupied until the time of his death. After the commencement of his administration as superintendent, important changes were inaugurated in the control and discipline of the prison, believed by those most conversant with the affairs of that institution to have been a great improvement on the old system, both for the good of the prisoners and the interests of the State.

He died in Nashville, August 23, 1872. His remains, as they were carried to the old family burying-

---

* Lieutenant W. H. Chamberlain, Captain R. N. Adams, Sergeant John R. Chamberlain, Adjutant Frank Evans, private Joseph Wilson—all of the Eighty-first Regiment Ohio Volunteer Infantry.

ground, were followed through the city by the members of the "Old Twentieth" on foot.

COLONEL JOHN H. SAVAGE.

The subject of this sketch was born in the town of McMinnville, Warren county, Tennessee, October 15, 1815, and is at present near seventy years of age. He was brought up on his father's farm, near McMinnville, and spent his youth as a farmer. In early life he was a persistent student, and, possessed of great energy and perseverance, he rapidly acquired a good stock of practical information on all general topics, and an ability to wield the same forcibly and to the point. He rose rapidly into prominence while a mere youth, and his influence was forcibly felt in whatever cause he espoused. Possessed of a true and sterling integrity, and a disposition that bestowed all its insight and all its powers to the support and maintenance of the right, Colonel Savage was honored and respected in his boyhood and occupied an exalted position in the esteem and confidence of all who knew him.

In many respects Colonel Savage was a self-made man. Born of worthy parents who were possessed of a sufficiency of this world's goods to make life comfortable and pleasant, yet the educational facilities of the community at that time were limited to such an extent that, aside from the advantage of a free school of two or three months in the year, there were few opportunities of obtaining a finished education at home. Under these circumstances, he made use of every available opportunity to acquire knowledge, pursuing his studies vigorously, and in many instances without the aid of an instructor. In this respect he became a constant reader, a practical thinker, and, in every respect, a practical man. In boyhood, as in after years, he was plain and practical in his opinions and views on any and all subjects, and the energy he brought to bear upon whatever work he attempted to perform, and his enterprises were well considered and attended at all times with signal success. In the year 1836, when Santa Anna and General Sam Houston were engaged in war upon the Republic of Mexico, the latter to establish the independence of Texas, General Gaines was authorized by the government of the United States to enlist volunteers to operate on the Texas frontier to preserve the neutrality of the government of the United States in that war. Colonel Savage enlisted for this service in a company commanded by John B. Rodgers, of Rock Island, Tennessee, and the command proceeded to Nashville, on its way to the Texas frontier. Upon their arrival at Nashville, news was received of the capture of Santa Anna, and the company was disbanded, after being credited with forty days' service. When it was known that the services of this company would not be needed on the Texas frontier, it was announced that volunteers would be accepted to fight the Indians in Florida. General Armstrong was at Fayetteville, receiving volunteers for the Seminole War, and after being discharged from the Texas service it was desired on the part of the company that they should offer their services to General Armstrong in a body and accompany him on his expedition, but for some cause the matter was waived by Captain Rodgers, and no further steps taken in that direction.

The hesitancy of Rodgers being apparent, the men ceased to depend upon him further as a commander in

the proposed expedition, and a portion of the company, consisting of Pleasant H. Price, E. M. Mercer, Jo. Robertson, Samuel G. Smartt, and John H. Savage, met at General Smartt's and proceeded to Fayetteville, Tennessee, where they arrived on July 4, 1836, and offered their services to General Armstrong, and were accepted. The companies being all full, it was found that no one company could receive all of the party. P. H. Price and E. M. Mercer joined Captain Chandler's company of Highlanders, and Jo. Robertson, Samuel G. Smartt, and John H. Savage joined Captain James Grundy's company. Not being pleased with the branch of service thus entered, Colonel Savage a few days afterward secured a transfer for himself and comrades, Mr. Robertson and Mr. Smartt, to Captain Bill Lauderdale's company of spies, a company organized and equipped at Fayetteville for this special branch of the service, and was composed of select men. Colonel Savage fired the first gun of the campaign, and served in this company till the close of the war. Judge Russel Houston, now chief attorney of the Louisville and Nashville Railroad, and Judge Archibald Wright, formerly Judge of the Supreme Court, were both members of this company.

In the year 1837, Colonel Savage commenced the study of law at his home, and advanced rapidly in his studies. He was admitted to the bar in 1839, and practiced in the courts of Warren, White, Van Buren, and De Kalb counties. Faithful to his clients and well versed in the law, he rose rapidly in the profession and received an extensive and lucrative practice. In 1841 he was elected Attorney-general by the legislature, and entered upon the duties of the office in 1842, and his practice was extended to the courts of Fentress,

Overton, Jackson, Smith, and Macon counties. Meanwhile he was an elector for Polk in 1844, and was opposed by the Hon. Thomas L. Bransford, on the Clay ticket. Colonel Savage served as Attorney-general until the year 1847, when he resigned the office and enlisted in the United States army to serve in the war with Mexico. He was commissioned major of the Fourteenth Infantry, and participated in all the battles in which his command was involved. He was severely wounded while leading an assault upon the Mexican stronghold at Molino-del-Rey, and, after this battle, was promoted to the rank of lieutenant-colonel, and assigned to duty in the Eleventh Regular Infantry, composed of troops from the States of New York, Pennsylvania, and Virginia. This regiment was in the same brigade with the regiment of Voltigeurs, of which Joseph E. Johnston was lieutenant-colonel. Remaining with the Eleventh Regiment till the close of the war, Colonel Savage returned to his home and resumed the practice of law at his old home. As a lawyer he had an established reputation among the people of the Mountain District where he was familiarly known. His professional and military life having brought him so prominently and favorably before the people, he was called upon to represent them in the Congress of the United States, to which position he was triumphantly elected. At the close of the term of his election he was urged to make a second race, and was re-elected to a second term and for two subsequent terms, making eight years of service in the Congress of the United States.

Possessed of a large and extensive knowledge of military affairs, both from experience and from a careful study of the histories of ancient and modern wars, Colonel Savage served for several years in Congress on the Committee on Military Affairs, where his sound judgment and practical knowledge was of acknowledged benefit to the law-making power at Washington, and as a member he possessed an acknowledged influence.

Discussing, in 1850, in the Congress of the United States, the question of disunion, Colonel Savage said:

> I trust I am not more fearful than other men. If danger comes I expect to be as ready to meet it as I am now anxious to avoid it. I pray to God that I may never again witness the wild work of destruction, called glorious war. I hope eternal peace may bless the world. With me
>
> > The drying of a single tear hath more
> > Of honest fame than shedding seas of gore.
>
> . . . .
>
> But for the remarks of the gentlemen who have preceded me, I should have thought it no part of my duty to allude to the great question of slavery now agitating the country from center to circumference, and threatening a destiny so dark and disastrous. Sir, I have read somewhere of a fabled magnet, far in the deep blue sea, whose fatal influence withdrew the nails from every vessel that came within its sphere, leaving the proud ship and its prouder masters an inglorious wreck amid the solitude of the ocean. Who cannot see that while this question is unsettled, each hour will be extracted those fastenings that bind this glorious confederacy together, until our proud ship is left a shattered, broken, disunited thing, to sink beneath the surge of time, as others that have gone before, with no voice to record our memory but that which proclaims our folly. . . . But I want no such issue. I love the people of the North. I have always felt that I would peril all that is dear to my native State to protect from lawless violence Massachusetts' humblest citizen or most barren rock. Those of them who know me know that I do. I have never imagined, nor can I imagine, how I could live out of the Union. I have ever hoped that our ship of State, self-poised

upon the billows, would gather the tempest in her sails and fly with lightning speed to the home of transcendent national glory amid the plaudits of an admiring world. And for this I shall still be ready to make any sacrifice except my honor and my right to be free and equal on every foot of land beneath the " stars and stripes."

Having served in the halls of Congress for eight years, embracing four consecutive terms, Colonel Savage was nominated for a fifth race in 1860, and was opposed by William B. Stokes, the candidate of the Know Nothing party. The popularity of Colonel Savage was unbounded among the people of his district, and his record as a member was in every respect satisfactory to his constituents. Yet he had a few dangerous foes, not in the ranks of his competitor, but in the Democratic ranks, who had become jealous of his popularity, and were ambitious to occupy his place. Knowing his popularity, their policy was to humiliate him by defeat and get him completely out of the way. To do this a few leading lights of the party commenced, first, to disparage him in the estimation of the masses, and subsequently came out openly for Stokes, and in this manner his prospects for re-election were curtailed until the election, when he was defeated by a majority of four hundred votes. This defeat was not the result of a dissatisfied constituency, but through the machinations of a few ambitious Democrats who wished to succeed him, but most signally failed in that particular part of the programme.

About this time the storm of war was gathering in the political horizon. The cloud which had been seen for years previously, though scarcely as large as a man's hand, had now spread to such alarming proportions as to begin already to darken the land. Its blighting shadow was being felt in every department of business, and a general distrust seemed to pervade all hearts. The presidential election was over and the Republican candidate elected. The result is familiarly known to the world. War called into action the best blood of the nation. From the Atlantic to the Pacific, and from Canada to the Gulf of Mexico, the general cry was, "To arms!" The institutions of learning threw open their doors and the young men threw down their books and took their muskets instead, and went forth to war. The farmer abandoned the plow, the mechanic his tools, and the field of conflict was the objective point of all. Excitement spread on the wings of the wind, and, in the South, all was forgotten save the raising and equipment of troops. A similar spirit pervaded the Northern mind meanwhile, and the whole country was on the eve of an inevitable conflict. Tennessee at this time was bestowing all her energies in behalf of the South by organizing and arming for the conflict. Colonel Savage organized the Sixteenth Tennessee Regiment of Infantry, and was commissioned colonel of the regiment in the beginning of the war. He led his command in the campaigns of West Virginia during the first year of the war, and subsequently in the campaigns of South Carolina, North Mississippi, through the Kentucky campaign, and the campaigns of Middle Tennessee. At Cheat Mountain he captured a whole company of Federals on picket by dashing ahead of his column into their very midst, and securing their surrender before his troops arrived upon the scene.

At Perryville he led his regiment in the attack upon the extreme right where the battle was hottest, and receiving two wounds early in the engagement, he staid with his command, which fought valiantly to the close of the fight, and whose casualties aggregated considerably over half its number.

With similar gallantry his regiment fought under his leadership at the battle of Murfreesboro, and suffered similar losses. In this engagement, Colonel Savage's only brother, Captain L. N. Savage, acting lieutenant-colonel of the regiment, was mortally wounded.

After the retreat of the Confederates from Murfreesboro to Shelbyville, Colonel Savage resigned his commission as colonel of the Sixteenth Tennessee, bid adieu to his men in a general address, and retired from the service, much to the regret of his men, who loved him as a commander, and in whom they had a confidence so strong and abiding that his place could not be successfully filled.

After the close of the war, Colonel Savage returned to his old home and entered again upon the practice of law. He was solicited by the people to again represent them in the Congress of the United States, an honor that he respectfully declined, on the ground that he had no desire to engage further in public life. Kind and generous in his impulses, a friend to the farmer, a friend to the mechanic, the laborer, and the masses in general, he has the good-will of his people, who honor him in his old age, and as "The Old Man of the Mountains" they are proud of him.

Colonel Savage at his advanced age is in the enjoyment of remarkably good health and a vigorous constitution. He descended from a long-lived family, his father having arrived at a ripe old age at the time of his death, and his mother is now living at the old homestead near McMinnville, in the enjoyment of good health and mental vigor, at the advanced age of ninety-five years.

After a long and eventful life in the service of his country, Colonel Savage is now enjoying the comforts of a handsome competency, the result of his long and arduous labors. He is generous to all, and his hand is always extended to bestow help to the unfortunate and destitute. He has bestowed many valuable contributions to the support of good schools and the promotion of good educational facilities among his people. After a long and eventful life of usefulness, he enjoys the era of good feeling, of peace and prosperity, the ultimate outgrowth of war and devastation, as described by the poet:

> When peace on earth shall hold her gentle sway,
> And man forget his brother man to slay,
> To martial arts shall milder arts succeed
> Who blesses most shall gain the immortal mead;
> The eye of pity shall be pained no more
> With Victory's crimsoned banner stained with gore.
> Thou glorious era, come! Hail, blessed time!
> When full-orbed freedom shall unclouded shine;
> When the chaste muses, cherished by her lays,
> In olive groves shall tune their sweetest lays,
> When bounteous Ceres directs her car
> O'er fields once blighted by the fires of war,
> And angels view in love and wonder joined
> The golden age returned to bless mankind.

He has contributed liberally to schools and Churches in his section of country, and for the amount of his wealth there is not a man to be found in Middle Tennessee who has contributed more to the building and fostering of educational institutions and churches, and other worthy enterprises, than Colonel Savage. The deserving poor have shared liberally of his bounty, and his kindness and generosity are appreciated by his people, all of whom love and honor him.

Colonel Savage in his private and public life has ever shown the admirable traits of firmness and integrity of character; a faithful friend and an uncompromising, though kind and generous, foe. In his military life he was brave and fearless, and would fight to the bitter end, though when his foe gave down, he showed that kindness and consideration for a fallen or prostrate enemy that always characterized the truly brave and fearless man and the true gentleman. At Perryville, being severely wounded and brought to the field hospital, he found a Federal officer of his own rank who was wounded and a prisoner, and whom he had known in public life before the war. To this prisoner he gave every assurance of such attention as it was in his power to bestow, and gave directions for him to have the same attention that was bestowed upon one of his own men.

At the battle of Murfreesboro, when the battle had raged through the day, and Colonel Savage's regiment was severely cut up and had barely escaped capture on the right of the railroad, when forced to fall back with the pressure that hurled back the brigade that had been sent to his support, many of his dead and wounded, and a few others, fell into the hands of the enemy. At night the Federal lines were changed, and Colonel Savage went to the ground where his wounded were left, and with a small detail he proceeded to gather up his wounded, many of whom he succeeded in finding and bringing back to the rear. While here he found a wounded Federal who was suffering severely, both from his wounds and the intensity of the cold. Ordering his men to place him at a designated spot by a fire, he proceeded to the field hospital to see his brother, who was very severely wounded. Remaining with his brother till a late hour of the night, his thoughts ran to the wounded Federal whom he had left between the lines, and he proceeded again to hunt for him, feeling that he would not forgive himself should he suffer him to lay there so severely wounded and let him die of cold. While renewing the search, he was confronted by a squad of armed men who challenged him, and as he could not tell in the darkness to what army they belonged, Colonel Savage here felt that he was in a very awkward position indeed. He began to realize the situation and to reflect on the consequences of being captured in the enemy's lines at this late hour of the night, and, without the object of his movement having being explained, such a capture at such a time and place would have more of the appearance of *desertion* than capture. In this perplexing extremity he returned the challenge, and resolved upon the *dernier* resort of a parley with the armed force in his front. To his great relief, Colonel Savage found it was a part of his own command who had been cut off during the fight in the evening, and were feeling their way through the darkness back to their command. Colonel Savage was recognized by his voice, which was familiar to the whole command; and, after making the wounded Yankee comfortable by placing him by a good fire, all parties returned to the lines unhurt. Thus his kind impulses in behalf of a fallen and suffering foe were the means of rescuing quite a number of his own men who were cut off by the enemy, and whose capture, otherwise, would have been a mere question of time, as the lines had been changed during the night, and the men would have found the enemy on the ground where they expected to find their friends.

While Colonel Savage was a member of the Tennessee Legislature, a bill was pending which denied the benefit of the exemption laws of the State to poor people moving out of it. Colonel Savage opposed the bill in the following remarks:

Mr. Speaker:—I have great respect for the gentlemen of the Judiciary Committee and for the members of this House, but every impulse of my nature rebels against the spirit and policy of this bill. In my opinion it is neither wise, nor humane, nor merciful. The people of these States should be of one blood, one bone, one flesh, and one destiny. Nor am I unmindful of the still broader doctrines taught from on high, that the human race is, or ought to be, a universal brotherhood, in which the poor man or woman, to the remotest bounds of the earth, is our neighbor and our friend.

Not only is this bill wrong in principle, but it requires but little experience or imagination to see that innumerable wrongs and injuries will be imposed upon the unfortunate poor, from which the humanity and mercy of its advocates would shrink back in shame. It is almost certain that men as noble as any on your soil have, in other days, to better their condition, gone to other States, and now, reduced to abject poverty and want, like the prodigal son, would gladly return to friends, and kindred, and the home of their youth. It may be it is your sister or your beautiful daughter, or the daughter of your neighbor, who has been permitted in the bloom of her youth to accompany the man of her choice beyond your borders, has been stricken in her family by sickness, misfortune, and death, who is now a poor widow with infant children, without friends, in a strange land, pale, emaciated, broken down in health as well as pecuniarily. Nature and necessity would present to her unhappy mind the babbling brooks, beautiful flowers, and trusted friends of her former home. She resolves to return to father and mother and kindred friends in Tennessee. Perhaps she has nothing left from the wreck of her husband's fortune but a half-starved horse, mule, or yoke of cattle, a broken-down cart, wearing apparel, household and kitchen furniture. It is death to stay. Hope points her onward, and the journey is begun; but, unfortunately, she is in a State that has followed the example the Judiciary Committee would have us set. Perhaps on the first, or at a later day, before she reaches the State line, at the instance of some merciless and persistent creditor, an officer overtakes her and seizes every article of property, including the scanty allowance of meat and bread for the journey, leaving the poor woman and her children to perish or live on charity. It is more important that men, women and children shall live happy than that the Shylock shall have his pound of flesh.

My understanding of the duties of statesmanship forbids my support of a policy that will often be used as a means to oppress or destroy the poor, and but seldom to defeat the dishonest debtor. Sir, my nature and statesmanship must change before I can support the bill.

CAPTAIN L. N. SAVAGE.

Captain Lucien Napoleon Savage, whose portrait accompanies this sketch, was born near McMinnville, Warren county, Tennessee, April 25, 1837. His father, George Savage, was a native of Shenandoah county, Virginia, and his paternal grandfather owned the land upon which the town of New Market was located, in Shenandoah county, Virginia, and sold the lots upon which the principal residences of the place were built.

Captain Savage's mother was the daughter of Rodham Kenner, a native of Hawkins county, East Tennessee, who was a soldier in the War of the Revolution, and participated in the celebrated battle of King's Mountain.

Mr. Kenner also represented Hawkins county in the General Assembly of Tennessee, which sat in Knoxville in the year 1804. Captain Savage's maternal ancestors were of English descent, having emigrated from Wales, and were of long-lived stock, every branch of the family being remarkable for strong constitutions and more than ordinary longevity.

Captain Savage.

Captain Savage was the only brother of Colonel John H. Savage, and, like his brother, spent his boyhood on his father's farm, where he labored through the spring and summer months and attended the free schools in the fall and winter.

CAPTAIN L. N. SAVAGE.

He subsequently entered Burritt College, where he pursued his studies for a few years, having previously attended the school at Irving College, in Warren county, Tennessee.

Captain Savage thus acquired a good English education, and was well versed in the classics, in mathematics, and history. In 1856 he commenced the study of law, and pursued his studies with consummate vigor. In 1858 he was admitted to the bar, and entered upon the practice of his profession at Sparta, Tennessee, in partnership with T. J. Bradford, Esq., and practiced in the courts of White and De Kalb counties. His brother-in-law, the Hon. A. J. Marchbanks, being Judge of the Circuit Court in the adjoining counties, Captain Savage withdrew his practice from the courts in Judge Marchbanks's circuit on account of the relationship between himself and the Judge. In 1859 he removed to Smithville, in De Kalb county, where he continued the practice of law, and as a young lawyer he rose rapidly in the profession and secured a large practice.

At the beginning of the war between the States, Captain Savage was a resident of Smithville, where he had resided for two years, and had so thoroughly established himself in the confidence and affections of the people that he was called upon by the young men of his county to lead them in defense of the cause which they had espoused, and to which he was a warm adherent. Accordingly, he organized a company of over one hundred young men of De Kalb county, and reported to the governor of the State early in May, 1861, when his company was accepted and mustered into the service of the State. This company was made the first or senior company of the Sixteenth Tennessee Regiment, of which his brother, Colonel John H. Savage, was the commanding officer.

Captain Savage was the senior captain of the regiment, and was by his brother's side in all the campaigns and hard-fought battles in which the regiment was engaged up to the day of his death. At the battle of Perryville, Captain Savage received a severe flesh wound early in the fight, and upon discovering his ability to conceal the wound and go on with his company in the fight, he led his company to the end of the engagement. While he was observed to be lame meanwhile, and for some time subsequently, there were but few of his company or regiment that ever knew that he was wounded.

At the battle of Murfreesboro, Captain Savage was acting lieutenant-colonel of the regiment, and Captain James J. Womack was acting major. The regiment was hotly engaged during the first day's fight on the Confederate right wing, near the railroad. Being fronted by an enemy many times its number, the regiment was pressed severely on its front and flank by an apparently irresistible onslaught of musketry and canister, and the men of the regiment were falling thick and fast. Colonel Savage had ordered the regiment to lie down and take shelter behind a fence that ran parallel with part of the line. The men obeyed the order, and from behind their frail shelter they poured forth a constant and destructive fire into the ranks of the advancing foe. While engaged in this hot and desperate encounter, the Sixteenth Tennessee lost heavily in officers and men, including Captain D. C. Spurlock, Company C; Lieutenant R. B. Anderson, Company A, killed; and Captain James J. Womack, acting major, seriously wounded. In the hottest of this engagement, while the list of the slain was so rapidly increasing under the fearful and constant assault of the enemy, where a handsome monument will soon be erected over them to mark their final resting-place. Though dead these many years, Captain Savage still lives in the hearts and affections of a large circle of relatives, embracing the best families of the country, and by a multitude of friends over the different counties of the Mountain District, who knew him but to love him, and who honor his memory as a worthy citizen, a gallant soldier, an accomplished gentleman, and a good man.

GENERAL F. K. ZOLLICOFFER.

Brigadier-general Felix Kirk Zollicoffer was born May 19, 1812, in Maury county, Tennessee. His father, John Jacob Zollicoffer, moved from North Carolina, and settling in the rich blue-grass lands of Maury county, was a prosperous farmer, who divided his time between attention to his farm duties and literary pursuits. George Zollicoffer, the paternal grandfather of the subject of this article, was a captain in the North Carolina line in the Revolutionary War. The family came to America from Switzerland, and is of ancestry ennobled by a degree of Emperor Rodolphus II., dated October 19, 1528. A member of it named John Conrad Zollicoffer, who was an officer in the French army, threw up his commission (being furnished with a letter from Silas Deane, our first commissioner to the French court), and accepted a commission from the governor of North Carolina, and served in the Revolutionary War until he was taken prisoner, having been afterward released on parole. This old baronial family still preserve a faithful record of their lineage in this country, and it is their custom to keep up a constant correspondence with the American branch of the family. Every marriage, birth, and death, in the male branch of the family, is promptly forwarded and recorded in the genealogical table in Switzerland. The oldest living male member of the family in this country is by courtesy called "the Baron," and is in regular receipt of a yearly annuity from Switzerland.

Having received a good, plain education, General Zollicoffer's energy and spirit of independence led him, at the age of fifteen, to rely upon his own exertions for a subsistence. Accordingly, he entered a printing office in Columbia, Tennessee. Shortly after he was sixteen he formed a partnership with W. W. Gates (since an editor of prominence) and Amos R. Johnson, (who subsequently became a lawyer, and was promoted to the bench in Paris, Tennessee). Here he met with disheartening difficulties, which only served to develop and prove the pluck and indomitable will possessed by him. In some letters, now extant, from his father to him at that time, his high sense of honor, and his determination not to succumb to the outward turn of affairs, were much commended. He also complimented and encouraged him, for "I am highly pleased," he wrote, "with the appearance of your paper, and am proud to think that I have a son seventeen years of age who can edit such an one."

The young firm becoming financially involved, quit in debt, and Zollicoffer sought employment, first in Knoxville, Tennessee, under the veteran editor Heiskell, and subsequently in Huntsville, Alabama, where by hard work, strict economy, and self-denial, he managed to pay off the whole debt contracted at Paris— his partners subsequently repaying him their portion of it. The printing-press upon which their first editorial venture had been made, was, in 1855, discovered by the Whigs of Henry county, from which they had carved a walking-cane, mounted with solid gold, and presented it to Zollicoffer as a testimonial. His literary tastes were very fine, and while still in his minority he was led occasionally to woo the muses in his leisure moments. One of his prose fancies, which abounds in beautiful word-painting, has been preserved to the public amongst the choice selections in Field's Scrapbook. He was said by those who knew him then, to be a model of neatness and youthful manliness. From Huntsville he returned to Maury county, and located in Columbia, taking charge of the *Observer* newspaper. There he, in 1835, formed a happy matrimonial alliance with Miss Louisa Gordon, and in the following year he volunteered as a soldier and served as a commissioned officer with the Tennessee troops in the campaign against the Seminoles in Florida. He returned in 1837, and resumed his connection with the *Observer*, and continued to edit it with marked vigor and ability throughout the memorable campaign of 1840. He had a strong partiality for agricultural pursuits, and published in connection with the *Observer* an agricultural journal which had a considerable circulation, and the columns of which evinced the variety of his attainments and his eminently sound and practical judgment. The great energy, boldness, and ability which he displayed in the management of the *Observer*, made a decided impression upon the leading minds of the Whig party in the State, and in 1841 he was called to Nashville to a place on the editorial staff of the *Banner*, the chief organ of the party. He at once made his power felt, and by his zealous energy contributed greatly to the re-election of Governor

James C. Jones in 1843. After the election his delicate health caused him to lay down the pen; but he was soon called to another field of labor, the legislature having, on the 1st of November following, elected him Comptroller of the State. He was retained in this responsible position until the spring of 1849, when he resigned. He went into the office without any information as to the routine of its business, and without instructions, but his persevering and untiring purpose soon mastered the details of the bureau, and where he found confusion he introduced system and order, and laid down the seals of office, confessedly one of the most reliable and successful comptrollers that had ever served the State.

In August, 1849, he was chosen to represent Davidson county in the State Senate. Here his powers of intellect and self-culture asserted themselves, and the legislation of the session shows that he made his mark in the Senate and became a leader there among some of the finest minds in the State.

The year of 1851 was an important period in the history of the Whig party of Tennessee, and he was again called to the helm to take charge of the *Banner*, in the hope of rallying the slumbering hosts, re-animating their drooping spirits, and overwhelming the Democracy again. The nomination of a candidate for the chief magistracy of the State was eliciting much discussion.

General Zollicoffer favored the nomination of General William B. Campbell, and exerted his influence, which was now second to no Whig leader in the State, in that direction. Devoted to the Whig cause, and equally devoted as a friend to General Campbell, the canvass which followed was a labor of love. He prosecuted it with untiring energy and skill, initiating and carrying out many of the measures which conduced to its success. Even when so ill that he could scarcely sit at his table, he stuck to his post with his invincible spirit and indomitable will, triumphing over the infirmities of his body: A brilliant victory was the result. The canvass was one of the most remarkable in the annals of Tennessee, and its result added immeasurably to the influence of General Zollicoffer. When at its height, General Campbell was prostrated by disease, and as his competitor, General Trousdale, a war-worn veteran, was exceedingly popular, the Whigs were cast down and well-nigh hopeless, but the gallant Zollicoffer sprang to their relief, snatched up the old Whig banner, and bore it until General Campbell recovered. In the following year, that of the presidential contest between Scott and Pierce, he added fresh laurels to his political career.

On April 30, 1853, he received the Whig nomination for Congress in the Nashville district, and severed forever his connection with the press. Throughout the six years in which he served in Congress his votes and acts were in opposition to the party in power, and he won a national reputation as a Southern conservative, and for great ability, strict probity of character, patriotism, purity, and amiability. These qualities gave him great influence as a representative. He was universally esteemed as an honorable, high-minded gentleman, whose fidelity to principle was conspicuous, and who might at all times be relied upon. He sustained himself admirably in debate, and if he did not exceed in the graces of rhetoric and oratory, he was so well fortified with impregnable facts that the readiest and wiliest adversary had to look well to his cause. His encounter with the Hon. A. H. Stephens, of Georgia, the ablest and most adroit representative during the period of his service from the South, was a splendid display of parliamentary and elevated intellectual warfare, and was keenly relished by the members. The distinguished Georgian went out of the contest with a high appreciation of the gallant knight whose lance had won its laurels. They afterward enjoyed the most amicable relations, and became admiring friends—the great statesman on a subsequent occasion being an honored guest at General Zollicoffer's home in Nashville.

An honorable contemporary, who knew him well in Washington city, thus speaks of him: "In his intercourse with men he was very courteous and polite, and exacted the same deportment from others toward himself. In the House he held a high position, and was esteemed for the excellence of his judgment, the integrity of his character, and the firmness with which he adhered to his convictions. He was a very modest, gentle, and dignified man, without pretension, bluster, or bravado; and yet he not only had commanding influence, but challenged the respect of his opponents."

He retired from political life in 1859, and remained a private citizen until he was elected by the General Assembly of Tennessee a commissioner to the Peace Congress. He accepted the appointment, but came home from the conference sad and disheartened.

Soon after the secession of Tennessee, a provisional army was organized by the General Assembly, and Governor Harris tendered to General Zollicoffer the commission of a major-general. He declined the appointment, giving as a reason, " that he would not consent to risk by his inexperience the safety and reputation of his fellow-citizens of the volunteer State." He was, however, appointed to, and accepted, the position of a brigadier-general, which appointment he afterward received from the Confederate government. Early in the summer of 1861, it became known that the Federal army threatened the invasion of East Tennessee by the way of Cumberland Gap. To defeat this movement, the Confederate government sent brigadier-general Zollicoffer, with a force of about two thousand men, by way of Knoxville, to the point of threatened attack.

Kentucky was at this time endeavoring to occupy and hold a neutral position in the civil war. General Zollicoffer, on September 14, telegraphed Governor McGoffin that "the safety of Tennessee requiring, I occupy the mountain passes at Cumberland and three long mountains in Kentucky. For weeks I have known that the Federal commander at Haskins's Cross Roads was threatening the invasion of East Tennessee and ruthlessly urging our people to destroy our own roads and bridges. I postponed this precautionary movement until the despotic government at Washington, refusing to recognize the neutrality of Kentucky, had established formidable camps in the center and other parts of the State, with the view, first, to subjugate your gallant State, and then ourselves. Tennessee feels, and has ever felt, toward Kentucky as a twin sister; their people are as one people in kindred, sympathy, valor, and patriotism. We have felt, and still feel, a religious respect for Kentucky's neutrality. We will respect it as long as our safety will permit. If the Federal force will now withdraw from their menacing position, the force under my command shall immediately be withdrawn."

General Zollicoffer also issued a proclamation, which

GENERAL ZOLLICOFFER. 301

he caused to be distributed over the country, announcing that he came there to defend the soil of a sister State against an invading foe, and that no citizen of Kentucky was to be molested in person or property, whatever his political opinions, unless found in arms against the Confederate government, or giving aid and comfort to the enemy.

About the middle of September he received information that a camp of about fifteen hundred Federals was located near Barboursville, Kentucky, and were threatening his position. Accordingly, on September 19, he dispatched a portion of his command to that point and dispersed the camp with but slight loss. He advanced cautiously in the direction of Somerset, driving the enemy before him. A large force of Federals under General Schœpf was sent forward to meet him. He had purposely permitted a captured Federal officer to overhear a conversation between some of his staff officers, which induced him to believe that Hardee was advancing from Bowling Green with a view to falling on the flank of General Schœpf. This officer was paroled and mounted, and permitted to go forward to join General Schœpf. His information was no sooner communicated to the Federal forces than it produced a panic, and was followed by what is known as the "Wild Cat Stampede." The frightened soldiers retreated at double-quick for miles, while the route of their retreat was covered with broken wagons, knapsacks, overcoats, dead horses and mules, and soldiers who had fallen from exhaustion.

After the expedition, General Zollicoffer moved with a portion of his command to Mill Springs, Kentucky, on the southern bank of the Cumberland river. He soon afterward advanced across the river to Camp

Beech Grove, fortifying his camp with earthworks, which was located in a bend of the river in the shape of a horse-shoe. This was in January, and he was preparing to go into winter quarters. His cavalry force, about 1,200 men, under command of Colonel McNairy, was across the river in his rear. Soon after General Zollicoffer had established his camp, Major-general George B. Crittenden arrived and assumed command. On the night of January 18 a heavy rain fell, causing a sudden flood in Fishing Creek, a large stream about nine miles from the Confederate camp, in the direction of Somerset.

A citizen of the neighborhood named Johnson came into the camp and gave information that two regiments of Federal troops had been cut off by the flooding of the creek. A council of war was held, and it was resolved to move out a force to attack them. Orders were given and preparations made for a movement of the whole division at daylight next morning. Pending these movements (it has since been developed) General Thomas, of the Federal army, had ordered a force of eight or ten thousand men to Somerset, with a view of crossing the Cumberland at Stegall's Ferry, twenty-five miles above Mill Springs, and falling in the rear of Zollicoffer above Monticello, from which direction the Confederates received their supplies. A portion of these troops had taken up their line of march from Columbia to Somerset on the day of the battle of Mill Springs. The four regiments across Fishing Creek were in expectation hourly of a new brigade commander, who had been ordered to assume the command.

On Sunday morning, January 19, 1862, just before the dawn of day, the Confederate troops' moved out through a drizzling rain to attack, as they supposed, two regiments of Federals; advancing nine miles on the Somerset road, the Federal pickets were driven in a half mile in advance of their already-formed line of battle. Near this point General Zollicoffer formed his men. On the left was placed the Twentieth Tennessee, commanded by Colonel Joel A. Battle; on the right, the Fifteenth Mississippi, under command of Lieutenant-colonel Walthall.

The main body of the Confederate brigade was on the left of the Mill Springs road, and in advancing entered a thick forest directly in front. General Zollicoffer, having ordered the advance of his little command, rode forward with several of his staff officers through the forest to inspect the position of the enemy, and passed into the Mill Springs road beyond the Federal line of battle. Discovering his mistake, he endeavored to retrace his route to his own command, but had proceeded only a few hundred yards when he found himself directly in front of the Fourth Kentucky Federal Regiment, under command of Colonel Speed S. Fry. The Federals, who were expecting the arrival of a new brigade commander, mistook General Zollicoffer for their new brigadier, his uniform being enveloped in an oil-cloth overcoat, and he having come from the direction of Somerset, or Columbia. General Zollicoffer quickly discovered his mistake, and, to put a bold front on the matter, rode up to Colonel Fry, and, after the usual salutations, started down the road, accompanied by his staff, in front of Colonel Fry's command, and about thirty feet in advance of it. He had not proceeded far when Major Henry Fogg,* of his

---

* It was said by some persons who were engaged in this battle that it was Major Ewing, and not Major Fogg, who fired the shot.

staff, drew his pistol and fired toward the Federal line. In a moment a volley from the Federal line was discharged, instantly killing General Zollicoffer and Lieutenant Evan Shield, and mortally wounding Major Fogg.

The story that General Zollicoffer was killed by Colonel Fry has gained general belief, but there is very little reason to sustain it. On his body were found two wounds—one made with a musket ball, which was mortal, and another by a pistol shot, which produced a severe, but not a mortal, wound. If Colonel Fry fired, and his ball lodged in General Zollicoffer's body, it was not the missile that caused his death, this having been the result of the musket shot. In the meantime the hostile forces were hotly engaged, the battle lasting from sunrise until about noon. The Confederates fought with a devotion never excelled by soldiers on any battle-field; nearly half of the Mississippi regiment fell in the action, while the mortally wounded of Colonel Battle's command was very great.

Thus fell Felix K. Zollicoffer. A Federal officer who had known him in Washington, and who looked upon him dead on the field, said that " his face bore no expression such as is usually found upon those who fall in battle—no malice, no reckless hate, not even a shadow of physical pain. It was calm, placid, noble. I never looked upon a countenance so marked with sadness. A deep dejection had settled upon it. The lines of care of the mouth were distinct in the droop at the corners, and the thin cheeks showed the wasting which comes through disappointment and trouble."

One of his early friends and associates, who had known him well, thus wrote of him soon after his untimely death: "How he fulfilled the expectation of a people who long entertained such exalted confidence in his courage and capacity, and redeemed the impressions of the thousands of young hearts around him, many of whose first notions of chivalry were derived from his daring, need not be repeated. Up to the hour of his fall, at the head of his troops, whose adoration marks a volume of suggestive eulogy, and answers every question, nothing but an affectionate faith attended him. He was the model and pattern of integrity and manhood. Although a civilian, his military qualifications received the most general trust; what he lacked in experience he could make up in bravery being the prevailing feeling; and this is more than sustained by the circumstance of his death."

One of the most exquisite little poems, called forth by the tragedies of these four years' war, was written by the gifted Henry Flash, to commemorate the death of General Zollicoffer. It is as follows:

"ZOLLICOFFER."

First in the fight, and first in the arms
   Of the white-winged angel of glory,
With the heart of the South at the feet of God,
   And his wounds to tell the story.

For the blood that flowed from his hero heart
   On the spot where he nobly perished,
Was drank by the earth as a sacrament
   In the holy cause he cherished.

In heaven a home with the brave and blest,
   And for his soul's sustaining
The apocalyptic smile of Christ—
   And nothing on earth remaining

But a handful of dust in the land of his choice
   And a name in song and story—
And Fame to shout with her brazen voice,
   "He died on the field of glory."

At his fall a wail went up from over the whole South, each household seeming to feel as if death had crossed its special threshold—and even the enemy appeared regretfully subdued as if they were reluctant to proclaim such a victory, and by tender respect to the inanimate body of the fallen chieftain, sending it by flag of truce to his people and his family, there to receive in burial every honor that a loved and sorrowing city could bestow, showed a sympathy and appreciation of his merits not often bestowed by one hostile army to the head of another. His qualities as a public character were well known, but there was a gentler side to his character known only to those who clustered about his family fireside. To them he was indulgent, confiding, and affectionate. His attachment to his children was strong, deep, and tender, and was repaid by a devotion almost amounting to idolatry, and as beautiful and pure as it was undying. His loving and loved wife had died in 1857.

In the preliminary report of the battle of Fishing Creek, dated Greensboro, Tennessee, January 29, 1862, General G. B. Crittenden says: "I am pained to make report of the death of Brigadier-general F. K. Zollicoffer, who fell while gallantly leading his brigade against the foe. In his fall the country has sustained a great loss. In counsel he has always shown wisdom, and in battle braved dangers, while coolly directing the movements of his troops."

His regular report was made without the benefit of any subordinate reports, except those of General William H. Carroll and Major Horace Rice, of the Twenty-ninth Tennessee, and under peculiarly embarrassing circumstances. General Crittenden has, without intention, made several important mistakes, as any one who will carefully examine the records and testimony in regard to this battle, will readily perceive. The writer has no censure for General Crittenden or for any of the officers and men engaged. Many of the troops had never been under fire, and the greater number of the officers were wholly unfamiliar with military affairs, and every command, without exception, engaged in that disastrous affair, afterward achieved reputation for bravery and soldierly conduct. But in the light of history, it is proper to endeavor to find out and record the real facts of the great events of the late war without partiality or undue censure.

The plan of the battle, as arranged by General Crittenden, appears to have been well conceived, and the reports show that the surprise was complete. Nearly all of the Confederate troops, as before remarked, were raw recruits who had never before been in action, and a majority of the officers were unfamiliar with their duties. The same troops who on that day retreated in disorder, in subsequent engagements fought as bravely and as well as the oldest veterans.

The two commands which, by official reports, were most conspicuous, and bore the heaviest part of the battle on the Confederate side, were the Fifteenth Mississippi Regiment, commanded by Lieutenant-colonel (afterward Major-general) E. C. Walthall, and the Twentieth Tennessee, commanded by Colonel Joel A. Battle.

The Fifteenth Mississippi Regiment, under Lieutenant-colonel Walthall, followed by the Twentieth Tennessee, Colonel Battle, under orders which they had received, moved forward toward the enemy and soon encountered their pickets, who opened a brisk fire, severely wounding Captain C. G. Armistead, who accompanied Colonel Walthall, and a number of others.

The Federal forces were encamped on both sides of the road, having in their front a thick growth of woods averaging half a mile in extent. Fronting this wood were open fields in which there was a slight elevation or ridge. Colonel Walthall moved his command through the open field, crossing the ridge, and met a force of the Federals in the edge of the woods. This force was the Fourth Kentucky Regiment. A fierce encounter at once commenced, and the Fourth Kentucky showing signs of giving way, it was re-enforced by the Tenth Indiana Regiment. Soon afterward Walthall's command was joined by the Twentieth Tennessee Regiment, and the fight continued. This was the most advanced position gained or occupied by the Confederate troops during the entire engagement.

At that early period many of the Confederate troops wore blue uniforms, and General Crittenden had given warning of this, and had adopted a pass-word by which Confederate troops could recognize their own forces. When Walthall was advancing through the open fields toward the woods, his skirmishers told him that the force in his front was the Twentieth Tennessee Regiment, Colonel Battle. The morning was cloudy and the troops in front could not be clearly distinguished. To make sure that he was not firing on friends, he ordered his command to lie down, and, going forward, followed by Lieutenant Harrington (without Walthall's knowledge), he hailed the troops in front, and inquired who they were. The answer was "Kentucky." This was the pass-word which General Crittenden had given out. He repeated his question and received the same answer. Returning to his line, he took the regimental colors and proceeded again to the front, and repeated the question, and receiving the same reply, he unfurled his colors, when a volley was at once opened upon him from the Fourth Kentucky,* killing Lieutenant Harrington, but leaving Walthall untouched. The flag was penetrated by a number of balls and the staff cut in two.

Walthall then ordered his men to open fire, and soon drove their antagonists from under their cover, and caused them to fall back a considerable distance, when they were re-enforced by the Tenth Indiana, and the struggle was renewed; Battle at this time, with the

---

* The following statement is from Dr. Edward Richardson, a well-known physician of Louisville, Kentucky, then surgeon of the Twelfth Kentucky (Union) Infantry:

"My regiment, in company with the First and Second Tennessee Infantry, reached Logan's farm, the scene of the conflict, Thursday, January 16. We had no tents, and were therefore not noticed by Johnson, the Confederate, who reported our numbers to Zollicoffer. We found there in camp upon our arrival the Second Minnesota, Tenth Indiana, and Ninth Ohio. The Fourth Kentucky, under Colonel Speed Fry, with a few hundred of Wolford's cavalry, joined us on Saturday, the 18th. The picket firing began about daylight Sunday morning. It was misty and dark, with occasional showers. The first regiment of infantry which met the rebels was the Tenth Indiana. They were forced back, and were reinforced by the Fourth Kentucky and Second Minnesota. These three, with Stanard's battery, did most of the fighting. By the time my regiment was well in line the Confederates were falling back. I reached the body of Zollicoffer a few minutes after he fell, the spot not being more than twenty feet in front of our line. He was quite dead, and so was Bailey Peyton, who lay near him. His body was penetrated by several pistol balls from the rear, and by a minnie ball which went clear through, from side to side. I have the General's gum coat now, and would like to send it to some of his family."

Twentieth Tennessee, coming up to Walthall's aid, and forming on his right. A fierce engagement ensued at the forks of the road, to which the Federals had been driven, and where the Fourth Kentucky and Tenth Indiana were supported by Wolford's Kentucky Cavalry, and subsequently by the Ninth Ohio Infantry.

The entire Federal line was driven back, but was re-enforced, and a Federal regiment having gained the left of the Fifteenth Mississippi, and the Nineteenth Tennessee Regiment, which was on Walthall's left, having been forced to retire, Colonel Walthall withdrew his command.

On the open space on the left of Walthall's command General Zollicoffer was killed.

The Nineteenth Tennessee Regiment, Colonel D. H. Cummings, re-enforced the Fifteenth Mississippi and Twentieth Tennessee in the heat of the fight, and was engaged with the Fourth Kentucky under cover of the woods, but was subsequently flanked and forced to retire. Rutledge's battery, though placed in position, did not fire a gun, having been ordered to retire without being brought into action. The right of the Federals pressed closely upon the left flank of the Confederates, and suffered comparatively but small loss, owing to the disparity in their arms, the Confederates having mostly flint-lock muskets of old patterns, while the Federals were armed with the latest-improved long-range guns.

When the Confederate line gave way it made its retreat without pursuit from the Federals. Walthall held the right of the Confederate line, until Battle, commanding the Twentieth Regiment, formed on his right, and held General S. P. Carter's brigade in check, until

Carter, pressing on his flank, forced him to retire. The Twentieth Tennessee and Fifteenth Mississippi Regiments left the field together and narrowly escaped capture. Colonel Walthall, finding a regiment of Federals across his line of retreat, and almost surrounded on all sides by a superior force, moved to the rear with his own immediate command and a portion of Battle's regiment, under command of Captain Rice.

Colonel William Preston Johnston, in his life of his father, General Albert Sidney Johnston, reviewing the battle of Fishing Creek, says: "The Mississippi Regiment and Battle's Twentieth Tennessee had borne the brunt of the day. The former had lost over two hundred and twenty men, out of four hundred who had gone into battle. The Twentieth Tennessee lost half as many more, those two regiments suffering over three fourths of all the casualties on that day. They had the advance and were better armed than the other troops. But had they been supported by the remainder of the column with half the valor and determination which the same troops subsequently exhibited on other fields, the result would probably have been different. Their inferior arms, want of discipline, bad handling, and fatigue, sufficiently account for their ill success."

The table of casualties in killed in eight Confederate regiments (some of them very large), including cavalry and artillery, shows one hundred and twenty-five killed, of which forty-four were in the Fifteenth Mississippi Regiment; three hundred and nine wounded, of which one hundred and fifty-three were in the Fifteenth Mississippi Regiment, and twenty-nine missing out of ninety-nine.

In General William H. Carroll's command twenty-eight were killed and forty-six wounded in this brigade.

In the Twentieth Tennessee Regiment the killed were thirty-three, wounded fifty-nine, and missing eighteen. These figures show clearly what commands bore the brunt of the battle.

About a half mile from the point where Colonel Walthall left the field with the remnant of his command, he was joined by Captain H. Rice with a portion of Colonel Battle's Twentieth Tennessee Regiment. These commands moved toward their former camps several miles, where they met a battalion of cavalry which had been ordered to take up the disabled men, and assist them in getting into camp. One company of cavalry remained in the rear of the command a short time after Captain Rice joined Colonel Walthall, but soon passed to the front in the direction of the camp.

From the time that Colonel Walthall and Captain Rice, commanding a portion of Battle's regiment, took the road toward the camp, they did not meet any command of part of infantry, except the short time when the cavalry company moved in the rear. This command had no rear-guard on its retrograde movement, except such as was furnished from its own men.

After crossing the river, Colonel Walthall's command marched in order without straggling, and it preserved its organization perfectly throughout the whole retreat.

In thus recording the eminent services of Walthall's and Battle's commands in the battle of Fishing Creek, no disparagement is intended to the other commands in that engagement. Those who failed to earn laurels on that occasion earned them afterward, and it is deemed due to the truth of history to make the record which is here written.

MAJOR-GENERAL B. F. CHEATHAM.

The following sketch of General B. F. Cheatham is from the pen of ex-Governor James D. Porter, and is copied from the *National Illustrated Magazine:*

B. F. Cheatham was born in Nashville, October 20, 1820. He was the son of Leonard P. Cheatham, postmaster at Nashville under President James K. Polk's administration. His mother was Elizabeth Robertson, the granddaughter of General James Robertson, the pioneer of Middle Tennessee and the founder of the present city of Nashville.

At the breaking out of the Mexican war, in 1846, he was among the first of the young Tennesseans to respond to the call for volunteers. He commanded a company, the Nashville Blues, in Colonel William B. Campbell's (First) Regiment Tennessee Volunteers. He shared its perils and followed its fortunes in the battles of Monterey, September, 1846; Vera Cruz, March, 1847; and Cerro Gordo, April, 1847. At the battle of Monterey his gallantry was conspicuous, and his action then as a youthful captain was significant of his future career.

Judge Robertson, one of the historians of the war with Mexico, states when the order was given for the First Tennessee to assault the fort at Monterey, "Cheatham, catching the order, sprang forward to the charge, crying, 'Come on, men, and follow me!'"

In his subsequent career, as commander of a regiment, brigade, division, and corps, his troops were stimulated by his presence and with the knowledge that he was there to lead them, not recklessly to a fruitless slaughter, but execute orders, whatever might be the cost.

So distinguished were his services in the field, and so marked was the impression his strength of character made upon all, that in March, 1847, he was unanimously elected colonel of the Third Regiment Tennessee Volunteers. On its arrival at Vera Cruz, in November, 1847, it was brigaded by General William O. Butler with Colonel James H. Lane's Fifth Regiment of Indiana Volunteers.

As the commander of this brigade he was intrusted

GENERAL CHEATHAM.   315

with the responsible charge of conveying through a broken country, invested by guerillas, the trains that carried supplies for Scott's army.

At the end of the Mexican war, crowned with honor and beloved by all his comrades, he resumed the pursuits of peace, and with characteristic energy devoted himself to the improvement of his estate.

More than a decade passed, and again there was a call to arms. The old soldier who had followed his country's flag over the embattled plains of Mexico, who, with the joyous glow of youthful enthusiasm, had seen it so often wave in victory, was called upon to draw his sword against it. All the proud memories of early days protested. A loyalty that had been baptized with fire at Monterey and Cerro Gordo cried out against it. But he did not hesitate, though, like Lee, he deeply regretted the necessity that forced upon him a choice of evils.

At the beginning of the late civil war, in April, 1861, he was appointed by Governor Isham G. Harris a brigadier-general in the Provisional Army of Tennessee. After the transfer of the State forces to the Confederacy, he was appointed by President Davis to the same position in the Confederate States Army. On the 8th of March, 1862, he was promoted to the rank of major-general.

In the organization of the Provisional Army of Tennessee, he was active, and established the camp of instruction at Union City, where he trained, disciplined, and equipped one of the finest bodies of troops, of all arms of the service, engaged in the war. While in command of this camp, General Cheatham exhibited other great qualities outside of those of the mere technical soldier. The public mind was in a state of ferment. Liberal men became violent and intolerant. Appeals were made to him daily for the arrest of citizens suspected of disloyalty to the South. These appeals were frequent and persistent, but he had one answer to all: "This is a free country. Men must not be disturbed because of their opinions. If they are not in accord with us, all we can ask of them is to do no act of hostility during their residence inside of our lines. But I will not permit arrests for opinion's sake and when the government of my choice requires it of me, I will abandon her service."

The district commanded by him contained a large per cent. of Union men, and this policy won many of them to our ranks and secured the good will of all.

General Cheatham was one of the most provident of soldiers. He was always on the lookout for clothing, for shoes, and for all possible comforts for his command. The result was that his division was the best equipped one of the Army of Tennessee. If a surplus of any material was assigned to him, it was sent to the rear in charge of a disabled man until it was needed. His hospital stores were the subject of his greatest watchfulness, and were always in readiness. At Chickamauga, when the army began to maneuver for position, his field hospital was located, and it was the only one on the Confederate side approaching completeness. It was so extensive and well arranged that complaint was made at army head-quarters that Cheatham had appropriated the stores of the army, when the fact was he had simply taken care of what had been allotted to him from time to time. The list of killed and wounded at Chickamauga numbered nineteen hundred. There was a place for every one of the wounded at the field hospital—not one was sent to the rear.

They were cared for on the field, and the per cent. of deaths was insignificant.

Cheatham commanded his own division in the fullest sense. He had an eye to the quartermaster, commissary, and medical departments, and was thoroughly conversant with the details and want of each, and regulated them all. The men observed this, and very soon were so identified with him in feeling and sympathy, that they knew no organization but his division, and to this day the veterans of his command will tell you that they belonged to Cheatham's division, never mentioning brigade or regiment. In action he fought them as one organization, and always had their trust and confidence. They learned at the outset of the war that he had no ambition to gratify beyond the discharge of duty, and that he would never sacrifice the life of a single soldier to advance himself.

General Cheatham moved his command to New Madrid, Missouri, in August, and, after a few weeks, under orders from General Polk, he took possession of Hickman, Kentucky, and, in a few days thereafter, occupied Columbus, Kentucky. The autumn of 1861 and the following winter were spent in fortifying Columbus and in the drill and discipline of the troops. The battle of Belmont was fought in November, 1861. General Pillow was in active command of the troops. General Grant captured Pillow's artillery and forced him to fall back. Cheatham was ordered across the river with a command. He reformed several regiments and led them forward to the attack, and gave the Federal troops the impulse to retreat and abandon the field.

At the battle of Belmont, after the Federal forces had been driven from the field, two of General Cheatham's regiments, the One Hundred and Fifty-fourth Regiment Tennessee Volunteers, Colonel Preston Smith commanding, and Colonel A. K. Blythe's Mississippi regiment, having crossed the river and joined him, he was ordered by Major-general Polk to follow up the retreating Federals under General Grant, and attack the gun-boats and transports. After arriving within half a mile of the boats, he came upon a double log house, standing back one hundred yards from the road, then occupied by the Federals as a hospital. At the gate he found two Federal surgeons mounted upon two fine stallions, one a black, the other a gray. Just at this time two officers—one with his overcoat on, the other with his coat on his arm—came out of the hospital and ran toward a corn field and jumped the fence and disappeared in the corn field. When they first ran out of the house twenty or thirty men of the One Hundred and Fifty-fourth Tennessee, who were in front, cocked their guns and commenced aiming at the officers as they ran toward the corn field. General Cheatham immediately ordered them not to fire on any stragglers, as his orders were to follow up and attack the gun-boats. On the next day he met under a flag of truce, where each party was burying the dead, Colonel Hatch, who was at that time General Grant's quartermaster. Colonel Hatch asked General Cheatham if, on yesterday when he was talking to the surgeons at the gate in front of the hospital, he recollected seeing two men run out of the hospital, one with his overcoat on, the other with his overcoat on his arm. The General replied that he did, and that the front company drew their guns upon them, and were in the act of firing upon them when the General ordered them to desist. Colonel Hatch then informed the General that the two men referred to were General Grant and himself. A few days afterward General Cheatham and General Grant met on a steamboat under a flag of truce. General Cheatham asked General Grant if what Colonel Hatch told him in regard to the two officers leaving the hospital was correct. General Grant answered that it was. General Cheatham has always believed that the two fine horses that the surgeons were on belonged to General Grant and Colonel Hatch. He has also believed that General Grant was the last one of the Federals to get on board their boats.

General Cheatham continued his march, and within half a mile came upon the boats. The water being low they were completely hidden under the river banks, nothing being seen but their smoke-stacks.

Lieutenant-colonel Marcus J. Wright, who was in command of the One Hundred and Fifty-fourth Tennessee Regiment, in his report of the battle of Belmont, says: . . . . "We moved from here through a corn field fronting the enemy's fleet of boats. Colonel Smith leading the line until we came to a lane dividing the field, and which led to the enemy's boats, the left wing of the regiment, under General Cheatham, having filed around the field and taken position on the left and up the river. As we passed down the lane I observed an officer mounted, and in front of the boats, and evidently urging the rapid embarkation of the troops. I ordered the men to reserve their fire until Colonel Smith should have placed the leading companies in position on the right, which he immediately did, and a volley of well-directed musketry was immediately opened by the leading companies upon the boats. I ordered the companies in the rear to pass around rapidly and take position in line and commence firing. This order was promptly executed. The fire was at once returned by volleys of musketry from the boats, and rapid discharges of grape, canister and shell from the gun-boats. The fire was kept up on both sides with very little cessation for about an hour, when the boats having succeeded in cutting their cables, moved out under cover of the gun-boats. As the gun-boats ascended the river they continued their fire, and their new position giving them a better range of shot, Colonel Smith ordered us to fall back to the field on the right."

The first gun-boat fight on the Mississippi river was between the Confederate boat "Jackson," under Commodore —— ——, and the Federal boat "Lexington," at Hickman, Ky. General Cheatham was present and engaged in it with a nine-pounder rifle gun, commanded by now Brigadier-general W. H. Jackson, and another company with smaller guns.

The Tennessee Legislature gave him a vote of thanks for service at Belmont.

He commanded a division with great distinction at Shiloh; and at Perryville he was particularly distinguished; also at Murfreesboro, Chickamauga, and Missionary Ridge.

After the battle of Chickamauga, General Bragg dissolved Cheatham's division, and gave him a division of troops from other States, allowing him to retain one Tennessee brigade, upon the ground that so large a body of troops from one State in one division promoted too much State pride at the expense of pride in the Confederate States. When General Johnston assumed command of the army at Dalton, one of his first acts was to restore the old organization.

The order to this effect created unbounded enthusiasm in the division, and with one impulse the men marched to army head-quarters with a band of music and called for General Johnston. General Cheatham escorted him from his room to the front door, and presented him to his command with a heartiness as genuine as it was unmilitary. Placing his hand upon the bare head of the chief of the army, he patted it two or three times; looking at the men, he said, "Boys, this is Old Joe!" This was a presentation speech to captivate the soldiers' hearts—they called their own chief "Old Frank," and it meant that there is another to trust and to love.

In the Georgia campaign his services were just as conspicuous. The repulse of the Federal assault upon his lines at Kennesaw Mountain will always be remembered for its vigor on one side, and for the calm determination and stubborn resistance displayed by the other, made with numbers so superior as to appall any but troops under proper command.

General Cheatham was especially careful of the rights of citizens. Trespasses upon their property were never permitted. He marched his command many hundreds of miles and never permitted the destruction of a fence or the unlawful appropriation of any species of property. Upon one occasion, marching through North Georgia, an aged couple, man and wife, halted him in the early morning as the troops were moving out, and informed him that during the previous night all the sheep owned by them had been stolen by the soldiers. The entire command had camped around them, and they knew not to whom to charge it. The matter was hurriedly investigated—the loss was established. General Cheatham said to the people, "Can you replace the sheep?" The old man replied, "If I had the money I might do so, but it will take two hundred and fifty dollars, and I have not a dollar." There was no one present but the couple, the general, and one other. The story of poverty was a touching one; the general was visibly affected, and, quietly drawing his pocket-book, counted out the money in the hands of the old man, and, mounting his horse, rode away.

During the siege of Atlanta, the commanding general being disabled, Cheatham was taken from Hardee's and placed in command of Stewart's corps, and upon the assignment of General Hardee to the command of Charleston and its defenses, he was placed permanently in command of Hardee's corps, and so continued until its surrender. His assault of the Federal line of works at Franklin, Tenn., with the divisions commanded by Cleburne and John C. Brown, was made with deliberation and with full knowledge of its difficulties; it was executed with steadiness and determination, and with a valor not excelled in modern warfare. He commanded his corps at the unfortunate battle of Nashville, and there and upon its retreat to the south, was the same gallant and watchful soldier.

After the close of the war, March 15, 1866, General Cheatham was married in Nashville to Miss Anna Belle Robertson, a daughter of Colonel A. B. Robertson, for many years a leading citizen and successful merchant of Nashville.

Since the war he has been a quiet, hard working farmer. In 1872, he received the unanimous nomination of the State Convention of the Democratic party for Congressman of the State at large, and was defeated by the independent candidacy of ex-President Johnson, who carried just votes enough to secure the election of a Republican. Two years later he was ap-

General Cheatham.

pointed Superintendent of Prisons by his friend, Governor James D. Porter, and held it for four years in the most acceptable manner. His first act of administration was to abolish the use of the lash, and if he had accomplished nothing more, this single act was enough to commend him to the good opinion of all humane people, but, with the aid of his enlightened assistants, he inspired the convicts to a new life by the practice of human and friendly acts, taught them that they were not entirely friendless, and made them cheerful and ready to perform their tasks without an overseer.

General Cheatham is genial and affectionate and has troops of friends. He is modest and very unpretending. During the late war he never asked for promotion, and has never paraded his performances. If mistakes were made by his subordinates he was always ready to overlook them, and this was the defect in his character as a soldier. On several important occasions he was made to bear the burden of these mistakes, because, in the kindness of his heart, he would not expose their authors. When the part taken by Tennessee in the war is written, he will be named as her representative soldier, and none can dispute his title.

GENERAL WILLIAM A. QUARLES.

The subject of this sketch is a native of Virginia, and was born July 4, 1825. His parents settled near Jamestown at an early period of Virginia's history. In his early boyhood they came to Christian county, Kentucky. General Quarles, at this time, was five years of age. Availing himself of the benefit of home instruction till 1845, he entered the University of Virginia, where he devoted himself to the study of law. In 1848 he was admitted to the bar, and opening an office at Clarksville, Tenn., he became prominent in his profession. As a lawyer, he was eminently successful, and occupied a position among the leading lawyers of the State.

He was an elector on the Pierce ticket in 1852, and was opposed by the Hon. John A. McEwen. In 1858 he was a candidate for Congress on the Democratic ticket, and was opposed by the Hon. F. K. Zollicoffer on the Whig ticket. In this race General Quarles reduced the Whig majority from 1,500 to 275. The district being largely "Whig," General Quarles was defeated.

About this time General Quarles was appointed Judge of the Circuit Court during the sickness of Judge W. W. Pepper, the regular incumbent. Holding this office for over twelve months, he modestly declined any of its emoluments, but allowed them to go to the regular incumbent. He was afterward appointed President of the Memphis, Clarksville and Louisville Railroad, and held this office for several years. In 1858 he was appointed by Governor Harris to the position of Bank Supervisor for the State of Tennessee. He was a delegate to the National Democratic Convention at Cincinnati in 1856, and at Charleston in 1860.

At the breaking out of the war between the States in 1861, General Quarles tendered his services to the Confederate government, then at Montgomery, Ala. The Confederate Secretary of War urged him to remain in Tennessee and induce the Tennesseans to join the cause of the South. He was appointed aid-de-camp to General S. R. Anderson, and his relations as Bank Supervisor made him instrumental in obtaining for the State about four million dollars.

Soon afterward he was transferred from the staff of General Anderson and placed in command of Camp Cheatham, in Robertson county, Tennessee. At this place he organized the Forty-second Regiment Tennessee Volunteers, and was ordered with his regiment to Fort Donelson, participating in the first great battle of the West.

On August 25, 1863, General Quarles was commissioned brigadier-general, and assigned to the command of a brigade which was composed of the following regiments:

Forty-second Tennessee, Colonel J. M. Hulin;
Forty-sixth Tennessee, Colonel R. A. Owens;
Forty-eighth Tennessee (Vorheis's), Colonel William M. Vorheis;
Fourth Louisiana, Colonel S. E. Hunter;
Forty-eighth Tennessee (Evans's), Colonel Henry Evans;
Forty-ninth Tennessee, Colonel W. F. Young;
Fifty-third Tennessee, Colonel J. R. White;
Fifty-fifth Tennessee, Colonel G. B. Black;
Thirtieth Louisiana, Colonel Thomas Shields;
Freeman's Battery Louisiana Artillery.

His command was engaged in the following battles: Fort Donelson, Tenn.; Port Hudson, La.; Jackson,

Miss.; New Hope Church, Ga.; Pine Mountain, Ga.; Kennesaw Mountain, Ga.; Smyrna Depot, Ga.; Peach Tree Creek, Ga; Atlanta, Ga.; Lick Skillet Road, Ga.; and all the battles and skirmishes of the Georgia campaign. In the last-named battle around Atlanta, General Quarles fell severely wounded. His wound was at first thought to be fatal. Here he fell into the hands of that brave and good man, Bishop Quintard, who nursed him and cared for him until he was out of danger. General Quarles soon rejoined his command and was foremost in battle.

Quarles's brigade rendered gallant service throughout the Georgia campaign. At the battle of Lick Skillet Road, near Atlanta, this brigade assaulted the enemy's works and suffered severely. In this assault General Quarles had two different horses shot from under him. When his first horse fell from under him, he was tendered another by a member of his staff. This second horse fell almost immediately after the General mounted. In this engagement Quarles's brigade suffered worse than any other troops. Its casualties in this action were, killed, 76; wounded, 400; missing, 19—total, 495.

The following were the members of General Quarles's staff:

G. Thomas Cox, Captain and A. A. G., October, 1863.
William B. Munford, A. A. A. G.
A. F. Smith, Lieutenant and A. A. A. G.
Stephen A. Cowley Captain and A. I. G., September, 1863.
Thomas L. Bransford, Captain and Ordnance Officer, 1863.
Captain Shute, A. D. C.
Ashton Johnson, Lieutenant and A. D. C., 1863.
Polk G. Johnson, Lieutenant and A. D. C., 1863.
Clarence Quarles, Lieutenant and A. D. C., 1863.
George S. Atkins, Major and A. Q. M., 1863.

G. L. Harris, Captain and A. A. C. S., 1863.
J. Q. Thomas, Major and A. C. S., 1863.
W. R. Poindexter, Captain and A. A. C. S., 1863.
Dr. Thomas Westmoreland, Surgeon, 1863.
Dr. Jackson, Assistant Surgeon, 1863.
Dr. R. S. Napier, Assistant Surgeon.

Of this number, Captain Ashton Johnson was killed at Lick Skillet Road, Ga.; Captains W. B. Munford and Stephen A. Cowley were killed at Franklin, Tenn.; Colonel Bransford and Captain Shute survived the war, though death took them for his own shortly after the close of the struggle. Colonel Polk G. Johnson is at present the only surviving member of General Quarles's staff. He resides at Clarksville, Tenn., and is a lawyer of prominence.

At the battle of Franklin, General Quarles received a severe wound, from which he did not recover for a long time after the close of the war. Upon his recovery, he resumed the practice of law at Clarksville, where he at present resides. He represented the counties of Robertson, Montgomery, and Stewart in the State Senate in 1875. He represented his State in the Democratic National Convention in 1880, and also in 1884.

QUARLES'S BRIGADE.

The following is from the pen of General Quarles, in answer to an inquiry in reference to the history of his brigade:

Limited as this communication must be, it will be impossible for the writer, to do justice to this noble brigade. What we will say will be the rough sketch of the picture rather than a real and life-like portraiture of the service it performed. The space will admit of a mere summary of events, and will necessarily exclude those details so necessary and so important to give grace and soul and a life hereafter to the story of the chronicler.

When I claim for this brigade a position in the front rank of the soldiers of the South—as I shall with perfect confidence claim—indeed, when it is claimed that it was one of the best, if not the best, brigade in the service, I trust it will be understood I make no invidious distinctions, or, in fact, any claim of superior merit; but the excellence of its soldiery was the result, partly accidental arising from inferior opportunity, and partly, it is but just to say, to the first-rate material of which it was composed; for every soldier in its ranks, and every officer having command, was a volunteer. Its muster rolls have the names of but five conscripts on their pages. They rallied to their flag because honestly and earnestly they believed the struggle they were about to make, and did make, was not to dissolve, but to preserve, the Union—a common birthright inherited from revolutionary ancestors—a union of co-equal sovereignties, with a constitution of government of equal rights and equal obligations, and each of these sovereignties, it was believed, was equally bound, in proportion to the relative strength of each, to preserve, guard, and obey the laws of the Federal government within the limits of its constitutional provisions.

To do full justice to the regiments composing this brigade the services of each should be given before it became a part of the brigade organization. Each regiment and the battery (Yates') attached to it, had won honorable distinction in hard-fought battles before it became a part of Quarles's brigade. But this detail of service must necessarily be left to the future chronicler of each component part when its history is written. At Shiloh, at Donelson, at Island No. Ten, and others, they had had their baptism of fire, and even though but a few weeks before, at their quiet homes in the pursuit of a peaceful life, they had exhibited that steadiness of courage in resisting, and readiness and vigor in making, attacks, for which they afterward became so well known in the Army of Tennessee. Indeed, upon the occasion of an application for one or more regiments to act as a support and reserve for this brigade, which, as it happened, was holding the most important, and, at the same time the weakest, part of the line, General Hood, then in command of the army, said in reply: "No, sir. It is unnecessary. Quarles's brigade has never lost a picket line. I will be responsible that that portion of the line will be held." And it is with proud satisfaction that I here say that this just and deserved compliment was equally as applicable to the brigade to the end of the war. They never lost a picket line, or gave way to the enemy, until ordered by their officer, it mattered not what the condition of things or what the superiority of numbers. Hood, "the bravest of the brave," was chary of compliments, but when he believed it was deserved, and the time came to speak, he was ever ready to bear willing tribute of praise. The old soldier who has himself had the experience of the varying fortunes of war, will well understand the high measure of praise this language imparts, and will be ready to look leniently upon the pride and profound gratification with which I—who owe so much to this noble brigade, and who even to this day can number every individual, both men and officers, among my dearest and warmest personal friends—repeat this so fully-merited compliment. But

I am admonished by my fast-increasing lines that I must forbear, hoping at some future time and occasion to do justice to the unexcelled courage, conduct, and merits of the men and officers, inclusive, of the whole, both field and staff, whose enduring courage and uncomplaining fortitude under such privations and hardships as neither the retreat from Moscow nor that of our Revolutionary army to and at the camp of Valley Forge can furnish parallels—and even mark and number these soldiers along with those of whom it may be said: They may have had their equals; they have never been excelled.

I cannot close this article without a word of acknowledgment and deserved tribute to my staff, composed mainly of young and unmarried men. When it became my duty, as it often did, to send them into the very jaws of death, I had at least the poor satisfaction of knowing that if any casualty occurred there would be no widows' tears or orphans' cries to be heard. Their faithful and uncomplaining service, their amiable accomplishments in camp, their high and honorable characters, their unflinching courage on the battle-field, and always ready hand to aid in soothing the wounded or ministering to the sick, made them not only the admiration of all who knew them, but dear to me as if they had been the children of my own loins. Alas! how sadly I write these lines, a poor tribute to my noble boys, now that twenty years have passed away, and along with it so many of them. But one remains on earth of my personal staff—Polk G. Johnson. At the time I appointed him my aid-de-camp—though the position was one of importance—he was but a beardless boy in his teens. His conduct did not disappoint my expectations. Faithful in the discharge of every duty, he was gifted with a versatility that rendered him most useful in taking the place, as he often did, of other staff officers, who, from sickness, wounds, or other casualties, were unfit for service. As assistant inspector-general, assistant adjutant-general, etc., or in his own official position, he was to me invaluable, obedient to his superiors, polite and affable to and with the men—always ready to get between them and the harsh applications of military rule—he tempered discipline with kindness. Cheerful and happy in temperament, he aided greatly in making the dull routine of camp life enjoyable, and never shrank from sharing the hardships or doing his part of the labor of the march and the bivouac. But it was in the battle—when the pickets had fallen back and the lines met, or when the column of attack, with firm and silent march, met the death-bearing storm of battle—shot and shell —that he proved himself "every inch a soldier."

I had read in classic literature of the "guardia certameries" (the joy of the contest), but never realized it till I saw him in battle where death and glory stood hand in hand ready to be wooed and won by the daring and the brave. . . . But my boy aid-de-camp of the glorious hours my subject arouses my memory to recall, is now the man of forty years, as true, as faithful, as ready to do every duty of civil life as of that hour, beloved and respected by all. He fills an office of great importance and trust * with honor to himself and satisfaction to those having business with his office and its court.

---

* Clerk and Master of Chancery Court, at Clarksville, Tenn.

FIFTIETH REGIMENT TENNESSEE VOLUNTEERS.

This regiment was made up from the counties of Montgomery, Stewart, Cheatham, Humphreys, and Robertson, and a company from Jackson county, Ala.

At the organization of the regiment, Colonel Stacker was elected colonel, but resigning on the eve of the battle of Fort Henry, Lieutenant-colonel C. A. Sugg was made commander of the regiment with the rank of colonel, which position he filled with distinction. This regiment was surrendered at Fort Donelson.

During all the spring and summer of 1862 the regiment lay in prison. At last, on September 5, the men left Camp Douglas for Vicksburg, Mississippi, to be exchanged (the company officers had left Johnson Island four days earlier—on the 1st), and on September 17 they were exchanged—officers and men—and once more trod the soil of the Confederacy.

On the 19th they were ordered to Jackson, Mississippi, and there, on the 29th, the regiment was reorganized. The company officers were as follows:

> Company A, Captain W. C. Allen, Montgomery county.
> Company B, Captain George W. Pease, Kentucky.
> Company C, Captain Reed Jackson, Alabama.
> Company D, Captain Sam. Graham, Stewart county.
> Company E, Captain T. E. Mallory, Montgomery county.
> Company F, Captain James Dunn, Stewart county.
> Company G, Captain Sam. Mays, Cheatham county.
> Company H, Captain E. Sexton, Stewart county.
> Company I, Captain Sam. Allen, Stewart county.
> Company K, Captain Curtis, Humphreys county.

On the 24th, an election was held for regimental officers. Colonel Cyrus A. Sugg was elected Colonel;

T. W. Beaumont, Lieutenant-colonel; and Christopher W. Henderson, Major. Lieutenant Williams, of Company H, was appointed Adjutant; J. B. Sugg, Quartermaster; John L. W. Power, Commissary; W. G. Turin, Sergeant-major; and Cave Morris, Ordinance Sergeant. Dr. R. D. McCauley was Surgeon.

Brigadier-general Tighlman being in command of the exchanged soldiers at Jackson, organized a brigade for himself composed of the Seventh Texas, Third, Tenth, Thirtieth, Forty-first, and Fiftieth Tennessee Regiments, and the First Tennessee Battalion, with Bledsoe's First Missouri Battery.

The regiment remained at Jackson, and in that vicinity, until October 8, and was then sent by rail to Corinth to reinforce General Van Dorn. Met that officer's command at Holly Springs, to which place he had fallen back from Corinth. On November 5, the Federals still advancing, the command fell back to Abbeyville, Mississippi, and thence to Grenada, where it remained two or three weeks.

While at Grenada the small-pox broke out. There were seventeen cases, but no deaths. Dr. McCauley having resigned, Dr. R. G. Rothrock, now of Nashville, was ordered by the War Department to report to Colonel Sugg as surgeon.

Here Colonel Gregg, of the Seventh Texas, was made brigadier-general, and ordered to take command of this brigade, which he did, and commanded until being wounded at Chickamauga. Colonel Sugg, of the Fiftieth Tennessee, commanded the brigade during most of the retreat.

On December 24, the whole command was reviewed by Jefferson Davis and General Joseph E. Johnston, and on Christmas-day the regiment left for Vicksburg, and at Chickasaw Bayou, on the 28th, a sharp fight was had with the Federals under General Sherman, and the enemy driven back to their gun-boats. On January 5, 1863, the brigade, under command of General Gregg, was ordered to Port Hudson. On March 14, at night, occurred the terrific bombardment, during which two of the enemy's gun-boats passed up the river, getting between Vicksburg and Port Hudson. The night was dark, but the heavens were lit up with the bursting shells. "It looked," said one of the men, "like the world on fire—judgment-day can't beat it."

On May 2, the brigade left Port Hudson, marching on foot, for Jackson, Miss. Reached Jackson on the 9th, and marched out next day to Raymond, twelve miles. There, on May 12, fought the enemy five hours; Gregg's brigade of only twenty-five hundred held in check ten thousand Federals.

Here General Gregg was deceived by his scouts as to the strength of the enemy. He entered the fight under the impression that he could capture the whole command. The Fiftieth Tennessee being on the left of the brigade was detached and ordered to charge to the rear of battery, but was confronted by a heavy line. After the fight began it was discovered by an officer of the skirmish line that a heavy column of the enemy was in double-quick to the left, doubtless with the intention of getting in the rear of the Confederates. Lieutenant-colonel Beaumont being in command (Col. Sugg being absent on furlough), ordered a retreat, and by skillful maneuvering to the left succeeded in covering this movement and holding it in check, by moving back and charging the enemy.

Colonel T. W. Beaumont commanded the Fiftieth Tennessee. He was wounded in the head and knocked down; two men sprang from the ranks to take him up, but he rose himself, ordered them back into line, and resumed command of the regiment. At this most opportune moment, Dr. Rothrock, having been where he could discover a flank movement of the Federals, and that the Confederates had yielded the field, reached Colonel Beaumont, who was bleeding profusely, and, having dressed his wound quickly, informed him of the situation. Beaumont then withdrew to the road and fell back in good order to Raymond, where he overtook the other regiments of the brigade. So hard fought was the battle that General McPherson with his whole corps did not pursue. The Confederate wounded who were left at Raymond stated that they were not believed when they told the Federals that the Confederates in the fight amounted to but one brigade. At Mississippi Springs the brigade was reinforced by Walker's and Gist's brigades. The Fiftieth Tennessee was stationed on the road to hold the enemy in check until the other troops, with stores, could pass out—truly a post of danger and a post of honor. The Confederates were forced back into Jackson, and on the 14th fell back from Jackson to Canton, Miss. On June 1 the regiment moved to Yazoo City, on the 13th to Mound Bluff Church, and remained there until July 1; on that day broke camp and marched to Big Black river to get in the rear of General Grant, who was besieging Vicksburg.

On the night of the 3d we had orders to cook three days' rations, and be ready to move by 2 o'clock in the morning to cross the river to attack Grant and deliver Pemberton and his troops; but before the hour to march, General Joseph E. Johnston, who was in command of the three brigades, heard of the surrender of Vicksburg, which, though negotiated on the 3d, was not promulgated till the 4th. Johnston withdrew in the direction of Meridian. With such quietness was the evacuation performed that the Federals were not aware until the next day was well spent that the rebels were gone. The regiment suffered the loss of a number of men killed and wounded. While in earthworks the men suffered greatly from heat and want of water; as, in fact, they did in this whole campaign, from the time of leaving Port Hudson. General Grant seemed satisfied as to what had been accomplished and fell back to Vicksburg, and Gregg's brigade was sent to Enterprise to recruit.

On the morning of the 5th, learned of the surrender of Vicksburg, and again fell back toward Jackson, Miss. Reached Jackson on the 7th, and remained in the rifle-pits skirmishing with the enemy until the 16th, then left at night for Enterprise.

At Jackson, Major Robertson, of the Fiftieth Tennessee, in command of the skirmish line, was complimented by General Joseph E. Johnston in an official order, published in all the papers.

In September, 1863, the command was sent by rail to join Bragg in North Georgia. At Big Shanty, near Cartersville, Ga., there was a collision * in which thirteen men of the Fiftieth Tennessee were killed and seventy-five wounded. Captain T. E. Mallory, of Company E, was dangerously, and it was for a long time thought fatally, wounded in this collision.

On September 18, the regiment reached Bragg's army—on the eve of the great battle of Chickamauga

---

* This collision of the cars was at Allatoona Pass, the casualties of which were about one hundred and fifty killed and wounded.

—and the next morning went into the fight. It was nearly annihilated.

The regiment skirmished all day of the 18th. In the evening the enemy made a determined resistance at Chickamauga bridge. About dark the main line was encountered. The men slept on their arms during the night. On the morning of the 19th, Gregg was in the front line with the Fiftieth Tennessee on his left, which was on the left of Bragg's line. General Gregg was wounded during Saturday's fight, and Colonel Sugg was placed in command of the brigade. Lieutenant-colonel Beaumont was killed. Major Robertson was placed in command of the regiment. Colonel Sugg received four wounds, but continued in command all day.

On Sunday morning a brigade of South Carolina troops took position in front of Gregg's brigade and was immediately fired upon from a dense pine thicket. Colonel Sugg hurried to their relief. The men raised a yell, and with a gallant charge dislodged the enemy and drove them to their main line.

During the remainder of September 20, the fight was in an open field. In the evening the enemy posted on a ridge a battery of ten guns, with heavy support. A stubborn fight raged on this part of the line, and the enemy was finally routed, and the guns captured and turned upon them. The Fiftieth Tennessee had been drilled in artillery, and were ordered to work the captured guns. The enemy made one more halt, but were soon dislodged, and the battle was over.

The captured guns, manned by members of the Fiftieth Tennessee, together with Bledsoe's battery, did valiant service. On September 22, the regiment, with its brigade, was ordered in the direction of Chattanooga, and went into camp near Lookout Mountain.

In the battle of Chickamauga General Gregg commanded the brigade until he was wounded, and Colonel Sugg then took command. The gallant Lieutenant-colonel Tom Beaumont was killed, and Major Christopher W. Robertson fell mortally wounded. He was in the twenty-third year of his age. A letter from Colonel Sugg, written October 10, 1863, three weeks after the battle, says: " I occupied the left of the brigade; the troops on my left failed to support me, and I had to sacrifice my regiment, or let the brigade be captured or cut to pieces. The enemy bore down on our left; the regiment stood like heroes, though the killed and wounded were dropping on every side. We held them in check until assistance came, and then, with reinforcements, drove them from the field. We were in it three hours; one hundred and eighty-six went into the fight; fifty-four only came out. Colonel Beaumont and Major Robertson killed; Major S. H. Colms severely wounded; Captain Williams killed; Lieutenants Hayes and Whittey killed; Lieutenant White will probably die; Captains Pease and Sexton wounded; Lieutenant Holmes Wilson severely wounded; Lieutenant Wheatley wounded, and a host of men—among them, Sam and George Dunn and George Hornberger; John Crunk killed; Isbell missing; John Benton, Billy Boiseau, George Warfield, George Hornberger, Bob McReynolds, John Willoughby, Holt, and Franklin, were wounded. Many others were killed and wounded, whose names I cannot recall to mind."

This is the dreadful tale from the pen of the colonel of the regiment, who was destined himself to lose his life in the next general engagement.

The Captain Williams here spoken of as killed was Adjutant Williams, who, at Mound Bluff Church, in June preceding, had been promoted Captain of Company D. Fletcher Beaumont, a brother of Lieutenant-colonel Tom Beaumont, had been appointed adjutant in his stead.

Major Colms, mentioned as wounded, was Maj. S. H. Colms, the commander of Colms's Tennessee battalion, which went into the battle of Chickamauga with the Fiftieth Tennessee, and was afterward consolidated with the regiment.

Here Gregg's brigade was dismembered, and Sugg was ordered to report with his regiment to General Maney. The Fiftieth Tennessee now became a part of Cheatham's division, until the last reorganization in North Carolina on the eve of the final surrender.

At Missionary Ridge, General Cleburne had repulsed several attacks made by the enemy on a part of his line. Maney's brigade had been held in reserve all day, and in the evening had been ordered to report to General Cleburne, who placed the brigade to the relief of this part of the line.

When the brigade arrived, the Fiftieth Tennessee was ordered by General Maney to attack the enemy and charge their works. The charge was made and the enemy was driven down the mountain. This feat was exacted of the Fiftieth Tennessee, it was said, to gratify the curiosity of the commander, who wanted to see how they would "stand the racket," as they had but recently been attached to Maney's brigade. The regiment did its work nobly and to the satisfaction of the commander. It had stood the test nobly in this instance, as it had on all former fields, though at a fearful loss of life. Here the gallant Colonel Sugg, Colonel Beaumont, Captain Mays, and many others, went down, some to death and others so disabled as to be unfit for further duty during the war.

On the left the Confederates had been driven to the top of the ridge and routed, though Maney held his position till ten o'clock at night, and then withdrew in perfect order. On the following day his brigade covered the retreat. The rear was pressed severely by the enemy. At Cat Creek the Forty-first and Fiftieth Regiments were halted and formed in line to receive the attack of the enemy. Colonel Farquaharson, of the Forty-first Tennessee was in command of the detachment. When he discovered the superiority of the advancing lines, and that his flanks were uncovered to such an extent that to be attacked here would result in defeat and disaster, he quietly fell back to the reserve line. Here the Federals came up in force and received a severe chastisement at the hands of the Confederates. Under cover of the night, the Confederates withdrew in the direction of Ringgold, and thence to Dalton.

The Confederates went into winter quarters at Dalton. The Fiftieth Tennessee was stationed at Tilton, between Resaca and Dalton. This was done at the request of some of the citizens, who knew many of the officers and men of the regiment.

While here the Fiftieth Tennessee and Colms's Battalion were permanently consolidated. During the winter the regiment was sent to Meridian, Miss., to reenforce the Confederates against Grant, who seemed to be moving upon Demopolis. Grant having returned to Vicksburg, the re-enforcements were returned to Dalton.

During the following May the Georgia campaign opened at Rocky Face Ridge, in front of Dalton, and about the middle of the month was fought the battle of Resaca.

During the winter preceding the Georgia campaign the soldiers in all the regiments had cultivated the acquaintance of the people in the surrounding country, and among the young men, Dalton and vicinity had quite a social life. Social gatherings were not unfrequent, and occasionally a ball or old-fashioned "shin-dig" was gotten up in the vicinity of the encampment. When the spring campaign opened it had the withering effect of frustrating many congenial associations. Many of the boys had found sweethearts meanwhile, and a few had become partially oblivious of the pledges they had left at home. Every boy had a "gal" in the rural districts somewhere, who would wash and mend his clothing, and bestow various pledges of devotion and constancy, for which the boy would devote in exchange his surplus of sugar and rice and such other articles as were scarce in the Confederacy. When the campaign opened, reams of Confederate paper were written and interchanged. The boys would send a parting message to the girls, and the girls would respond in eloquent, patriotic strains—sometimes stimulating to valor, and at other times in wailing tones of sympathy for the soldier's hard lot. Occasionally the muses would be called up when they were not in shape for company, but it was a day of emergencies. The boys would wear the lines received nearest their hearts. Among the various inspirations, the following was received by a young soldier from his "gal:"

> "'Tis hard for you'uns to fight the Yanks,
> 'Tis hard for you'uns to live in camps;
> 'Tis hard for you'uns and we'uns to part,
> For you'uns have done got we'uns' heart."

The boys with their pockets full of this and similar sentiment, met the "Yanks" at Rocky Face Ridge and stood their ground nobly. In a few days the army retreated to Resaca.

In the neighborhood of Resaca was the residence of Judge Green, a prominent and wealthy gentleman of Savannah. Judge Green had an interesting family, including two beautiful and accomplished daughters. Adjutant Childress and Lieutenant-colonel Pease had become acquainted with this family while encamped at Tilton, and were invited to visit them on the evening of May 14, to eat strawberries. The gallant young officers accepted the invitation, pledging themselves to be on time, but forgetting the proviso that Johnston and Sherman had an entertainment that was liable to come off the same day. The young gentlemen appeared at the house prompt to time, but under adverse circumstances. Their brigade had been ordered to attack the Federal left, and passed through Judge Green's yard in line of battle. As the Fiftieth Tennessee passed through the strawberry patch in line of battle, at a double-quick, Adjutant Childress could not forget his appointment, but stooped down hurriedly and plucked a few strawberries on the run, which he ate as his regiment was going into the fight. The battle was severe, and among the wounded was the surgeon of the regiment—an unusual occurrence in the army. The strawberry festival was indefinitely postponed.

The campaign now thickened and was one daily round of battles and skirmishes, in all of which the Fiftieth Tennessee bore a prominent part—at Dead Angle or Devil's Elbow, on the Kennesaw line, and all the battles around Atlanta. In the Tennessee campaign it bore a conspicuous part. This regiment was in all the battles in which Cheatham's division was engaged, and in every instance proved itself the equal of any regiment in the service.

At the last reorganization, on the eve of the surrender, about forty skeleton Tennessee regiments were consolidated into one brigade of four regiments. In this the old Fiftieth Tennessee lost its identity. It made one company of the Second Regiment, and the adjutant, J. W. Childress, now of Nashville, was placed in command as captain. The field officers of the consolidated regiment were: O. A. Bradshaw, Colonel, formerly of the Fourth Tennessee; Lieutenant-colonel G. W. Pease, of the Fiftieth, was Major; and Dr. R. G. Rothrock, of the Fiftieth, was Assistant Surgeon.

A few days afterward the whole army was surrendered, when the survivors of the Fiftieth Tennessee returned to their homes and donned the habiliments of peace.

COLONEL WILLIAM F. YOUNG, FORTY-NINTH TENNESSEE REGIMENT.

This gallant officer entered the service as captain of Company G, Forty-ninth Tennessee Infantry, at the beginning of the war. The regiment was composed of the following companies:

Company A, Montgomery county, Captain James E. Bailey.
Company B, Dickson county, Captain T. K. Grigsby.
Company C, Robertson county, Captain W. V. Fyke.
Company D, Dickson county, Captain J. B. Cording.
Company E, Montgomery county, Captain J. M. Peacher.
Company F, Montgomery county, Captain D. A. Lynn.
Company G, Montgomery county, Captain William F. Young.

Company H, Montgomery county, Captain Pugh Haynes.
Company I, Benton county, Captain T. A. Napier.
Company K, Cheatham county, Captain William Shaw.

At the organization of the regiment the field officers were as follows:

>JAMES E. BAILEY, Colonel;
>ALFRED ROBB, Lieutenant-colonel;
>D. A. LYNN, Major;
>R. E. DOUGLAS, Adjutant;
>Dr. W. B. WILLIAMS, Surgeon.

The regiment was engaged in the battle of Fort Donelson, where Lieutenant-colonel Robb was mortally wounded. The regiment was surrendered at Fort Donelson, February 16, 1862. The field officers were sent to Fort Warren, the company officers to Johnson's Island, and the privates to Camp Douglas. The regiment was exchanged at Vicksburg, September 17, 1862. The officers met the men at this point, having been exchanged at City Point, Va. The regiment was reorganized and entered the campaign of North Mississippi and Louisiana.

The Forty-ninth Regiment was a part of Quarles's brigade. Captain Young was afterward promoted to the command of the Forty-ninth Tennessee, with the rank of colonel. Concerning the merits of this officer, we have the following from the pen of Polk G. Johnson, Esq., of Clarksville, Tenn.:

"This brave and gallant Confederate soldier lost an arm at Atlanta, in the battle of Lick Skillet Road, July 28, 1864, and had a minnie ball embedded in his large watch over his heart. His regiment suffered terribly. A ball passed through the flag-staff and thirty-two minnie balls through his flag, and over one half were killed or wounded. While being carried from the field two men carrying him—Captain Dunlap, of Dickson county, Tenn., and the other whose name I have forgotten—were killed. The writer buried Captain Dunlap the next day, with Lieutenant Ashton Johnson, of Quarles's staff.

"A humble man, whose parents came from Virginia, he was born in Bowling Green, Ky., March 26, 1830, and moved to Montgomery county, Tenn., in 1832; and from his early youth he engaged in farming—plowing the fields with his own hands and gathering at the harvest-time. Thus his life was spent until called to the war in 1861.

"His good parents, of whom he is justly proud, taught him to believe in God and to discharge his duty always faithfully. He did not forget this teaching, and in all his relations to family, Church, and State, he has been true.

"He was among the first to respond to his country's call in 1861, and among the last to leave it after 'its banner had been furled.' He took part with his regiment in the battle of Fort Donelson, shared their prison life, and was with them ever afterward, except when confined in the hospital from the loss of his right arm at Atlanta.

"He began his military career as a private soldier in Company G, of the Forty-ninth Tennessee; was elected captain of his company at its organization, and ordered to Fort Donelson. Here this regiment was organized, with James E. Bailey, of Clarksville, as colonel, and Alfred Robb, of Clarksville, as lieutenant-colonel, and the other necessary officers.

"The subject of our short sketch afterward was promoted to the colonelcy of the regiment, and has ever retained the confidence and respect of both officers and men of his command.

"After the war he continued his old occupation of farming, and added thereto school-teaching, being unable to do manual labor, which he followed until 1870, when he engaged in the business of auctioneering, and has followed it since. He is a member of the Cumberland Presbyterian Church, and an honest and faithful Christian."

The following are the muster rolls and casualty report of a portion of the companies of the Forty-ninth Tennessee:

COMPANY A.

Officers.

J. E. Bailey, Captain.
T. M. Atkins, First Lieutenant.
R. A. Wilson, Second Lieutenant.
W. H. Burgess, Third Lieutenant.
A. F. Smith, First Sergeant.
John B. Johnson, Second Sergeant.
Robert Bringhurst, Third Sergeant.
L. W. Bourne, Fourth Sergeant.
M. W. Wisdom, Fifth Sergeant.
Stephen Pettus, First Corporal.
Wm. Adwell, Second Corporal.
C. H. Ricou, Third Corporal.
Wm. McKeage, Fourth Corporal.

Privates.

Q. C. Atkinson.
J. C. Anderson.
B. F. Buck.
G. W. Buck.
J. M. Buck.
G. E. Burgess.
Fletcher Beaumont.
Frank Bell.
J. W. Bourne.
J. D. Broomfield.
J. D. Booth.
Montgomery Bell.
C. D. Bailey.
R. T. Coulter.
C. H. Bailey.
L. R. Clark.
L. R. Cooper.
C. R. Cooper.
W. C. Cooper.
Thomas Coulter.
James Clark.
W. J. Carnell.
Cave J. Clark.
George Chisenhall.
John Dolon.
James Davis.
J. P. Damron.
F. M. Drake.
S. R. Cooke.
W. D. Eminizer.
J. B. Edlin.
George Elliott.
J. W. Ferkin.
Thomas Finley.
J. R. Fletcher.
J. T. Farley.
R. C. Goostree.
Daniel Gold.
L. T. Gold.
Granville Grimes.
J. A. Hutchinson.
R. J. Haskins.
S. Hackney.
Wm. Harris

John Harris.
Robert Harris.
James Harris.
Watson Hibbs.
F. E. Heatherington.
W. T. Hargrave.
J. W. Helm.
J. G. Hoskins.
R. G. Halliday.
Polk G. Johnson.
J. S. Jarrell.
Matt. Leggett.
Charles Loftland.
C. M. Lewis.
G. W. Leigh, Jr.
H. G. Marklin.
T. F. McCallister.
James McCarter.
John McCarter.
Milton Misc.
B. McCormack.
Robert Mellon.
John Mellon.
Walker Manson.
John McClintock.
C. P. Moore.
W. B. Munford.
Benjamin McGhee.
W. H. Neblett.
R. H. Neal.
John Orgain.
B. D. Orgain.

Wm. M. Orgain.
J. W. Oglesby.
John O'Brien.
J. L. Pendergast.
Robert Poole.
Thomas Pearson.
Paris Peter.
W. H. Powell.
W. R. Poindexter.
Cave J. Riggins.
Alfred Robb.
Henry Ring.
Alfred Simpson.
Henry Simpson.
Charles Shanklin.
Thomas H. Smith.
G. R. Smith.
D. W. Scott.
J. W. Smith.
W. H. Turnley.
C. L. Thomas.
W. N. Trice.
John Taylor.
Nathan Vick.
James Wells.
T. W. Walthal.
B. F. White.
Albert Walthal.
B. W. Waller.
G. S. Williams.
Polk Wilcox.

KILLED.

J. C. Anderson, Fort Donelson.
Robert Bringhurst, Franklin.
Fletcher Beaumont, Missionary Ridge.
Montgomery Bell, Franklin.
S. R. Cooke, Franklin.
George Elliott, Nashville.
John T. Farley, Fort Donelson.
R. C. Goostree, Lick Skillet Road, Atlanta.
J. S. Jarrell, Franklin.
Matt. Leggett, Lick Skillet Road, Atlanta.
Wm. B. Munford, Franklin.
Alfred Robb, Fort Donelson.
Nathan Vick, Franklin.
Polk Wilcox, Franklin.
R. T. Coulter, Franklin.
R. G. Halliday, Franklin.

DIED IN SERVICE.

C. H. Ricou, Port Hudson, La., 1863.
B. F. Buck, in prison.
Frank Bell, place of death unknown.
J. D. Booth, Port Hudson, La, 1862.
John P. Damron, Fort Donelson, 1862.
James A. Hutchinson, 1862.
Robert J. Haskins, Chicago, in prison, 1862.
Stephen Hackney, Chicago, in prison, 1862.

SKETCHES OF OFFICERS.

Wm. Harris, at home, 1862.
John Harris, at home, 1862.
Robert Harris, at home, 1862.
James Harris, at home, 1862.
F. E. Heatherington, Clinton, Miss., 1862.
J. W. Helm, Port Hudson, La., 1863.
G. W. Leigh, Jr., Atlanta, 1864.
John W. McClintock, Miss, just before close of war.
John Orgain, time and place unknown.
B. D. Orgain, Camp Douglas, 1862.
B. F. White, Camp Douglas, 1863.

WOUNDED.

Lewis R. Clark, Jonesboro, Ga.
Wm. C. Cooper, Franklin.
W. D. Eminizer, Kennesaw Mountain.
John B. Edlin, Kennesaw Mountain.
J. G. Hoskins, Jackson, Miss.
Polk G. Johnson, Atlanta.
Charles Loftland, Fort Donelson and Shiloh.
Walker Manson, Franklin.
Charles P. Moore, Atlanta.
John L. Pendergast, four times, once very severely.
Robert Poole, Atlanta.
Lewis T. Gold, Franklin.
Charles Shanklin, Atlanta.
Thomas H. Smith, Franklin.
G. R. Smith, Atlanta.
A. F. Smith, North Carolina.
John Taylor, Fort Donelson.
C. H. Bailey, Atlanta and Franklin.

PROMOTED.

James E. Bailey, Colonel.
Thomas M. Atkins, Lieut.-colonel.
Robert A. Wilson, Captain.
A. F. Smith, General Walthall's staff.
John B. Johnson, Captain, and A. C. S. Tenth Tennessee.
Robert Bringhurst, Adjutant.
Fletcher Beaumont, Adjutant Fiftieth Tennessee.
Charles D. Bailey, Captain and A. C. S.
R. T. Coulter, Captain Company G.
Lewis R. Clark, Captain Tenth Tenn.
Charles R. Cooper, Lieut.
George Elliott, Lieut. Company H.
R. C. Goostree, Lieut.
Lewis T. Gold, Lieut.
Polk G. Johnson, Lieut., and A. D. C. General Quarles.
Walker Manson, Lieut. Company G.
John L. Pendergast, Capt. Tenth Tenn.
Robert Poole, Lieut. Thirtieth Tenn.
W. R. Poindexter, Captain and A. Q. M.
Alfred Robb, Lieut.-colonel.
Thomas H. Smith, Captain Company H.
John O'Brien, Ordnance Officer.

The company was in fifteen battles, to wit: Fort Donelson, Port Hudson, La.; Jackson, Miss.; New Hope Church, Ga.; Pine Mountain, Ga.; Kennesaw Mountain, Ga.; Smyrna Depot, Ga.; Peach Tree Creek, Atlanta, Ga.; Lick Skillet Road, Atlanta, Ga.; Franklin, Tenn.; Nashville, Tenn.; south of Lynnville; Anthony's Hill; Sugar Creek; Bentonville, N. C.; and in a great many skirmishes.

COMPANY C.

OFFICERS.

M. V. Fyke, Captain.
T. J. Morris, First Lieutenant.
H. V. Harrison, Second Lieutenant.
M. J. Draughan, Third Lieutenant.
James P. Ownly, First Sergeant.
W. E. Maurey, Second Sergeant.
Harry Pepper, Third Sergeant.
William Barnes, Fourth Sergeant.
J. W. Hart, First Corporal.
W. H. Ward, Second Corporal.
William Cannon, Third Corporal.
J. C. Cole, Fourth Corporal.
J. H. Balthrop, Fifth Corporal.

PRIVATES.

W. H. Banks.
J. A. Brigg.
R. H. Bibb.
Charles Campbell.
James Cannon.
T. B. Dalton.
J. W. Dozier.
J. B. Doss.
E. H. Gallaher.
J. W. Grimes.
R. S. Holeman.
Thomas Higgs.
R. H. Hicks.
Samuel Harris.
William Hoffman.
Archie Hamilton.
J. W. Judd.
William Knight.
A. M. Langford.
Jasper Mathews.
Frank Mantle.
W. E. Maurey.
G. W. McGuire.
J. M. Morris.
G. W. Morris.
J. H. Murphey.
H. C. Murphey.
William Orand.
J. W. Percise.
G. W. Porter.
William Patterson.
Hezekiah Porter.
James Prest.
Wiley Powell.
Young Pepper.
L. D. Robertson.
James Robertson.
W. A. Robertson.
Henry Ruffin.
S. F. Solomon.
H. D. Solomon.
M. D. Taylor.
J. M. Thomas.
W. W. Thomas.
J. A. Thomas.
J. H. Turner.
J. H. Toler.
D. H. Wilkerson.
M. L. Watson.
J. B. White.

KILLED.

W. E. Maurey, Franklin.
W. H. Banks, Peach Tree Creek.
J. W. Grimes, Peach Tree Creek.
G. W. McGuire, Franklin.
Wiley Powell, Fort Donelson.
D. H. Wilkerson, Atlanta.

WOUNDED.

H. V. Harrison, Atlanta.
W. E. Maurey, Atlanta.
J. H. Balthrop, Peach Tree Creek.
T. B. Dalton, Atlanta.
Archie Hamilton, Atlanta.
J. M. Morris, Franklin.
James Robertson, by cars.
S. F. Solomon, Franklin.
M. D. Taylor, Atlanta.

PROMOTED.

H. V. Harrison, Captain, 1862.
M. D. Taylor, 3d Lieut., 1862.
William Barnes, 2d Lieut., 1862, 3d Lieut., 1863.

COMPANY E.

Officers.

J. M. Peacher, Captain.
J. W. Broom, First Lieutenant.
J. W. Wall, Second Lieutenant.
W. H. Powell, Third Lieutenant.
S. A. Wall, Third Lieutenant.
R. M. Powers, First Sergeant.

Privates.

R. A. Alley.
Cap Allen.
Perry Allman.
W. H. Burden.
John Burden.
Oliver Burden.
H. C. Bowers.
T. Bowers.
Henry Burks.
Robert Chance.
J. J. Dilling.
J. J. Fletcher.
W. H. Fletcher.
Charlie Ferguson.
William Ferguson.
Jasper Grimes.
H. B. Hunt.
William Horn.
Hiram Hambrick.
A. J. Hambrick.
John Haley.
J. C. Jordan.
Henry Lewis.
Joseph Lyle.
C. H. Lyle.
Hart Nolin.
J. E. Oldham.
Davis Powell.
W. H. Powell.
G. Powers.
Thomas Powers.
E. H. Powers.
John Powers.
F. B. Powers.
R. D. Robertson.
W. Robertson.
J. N. Robertson.
Nathan Roland.
Wash Roland.
J. H. Sugg.
George Wright.
William Weakley.
Peter Williams.

Killed.

S. A. Wall, Atlanta.

Died in Service.

T. Bowers, Camp Douglas.
Davis Powell, Camp Douglas.
Albert Powell, Camp Douglas.
W. H. Fletcher, Alton, Ill.
J. J. Dilling, Fort Donelson.
Hiram Hambrick, on steamboat.

Wounded.

Lieut. J. W. Broom, Franklin.
Lieut. S. A. Wall, Ga., (three times).
Serg't R. M. Powers, Franklin.
A. J. Hamrick, Franklin.
J. E. Oldham, Atlanta.

Promoted.

Lieut. J. W. Wall, Captain.

COMPANY G.

Officers.

W. F. Young, Captain.
James B. Howard, First Lieutenant.
Charles Anderson, Second Lieutenant.
Ross Evans, Third Lieutenant.
B. W. Humber, First Sergeant.
J. S. Meacham, Second Sergeant.
James B. Leigh, Third Sergeant.
Willis Winn, Fourth Sergeant.
James Council, First Corporal.
John H. Morrison, Second Corporal.
N. J. Morris, Third Corporal.
Thos. Jeff. Stone, Fourth Corporal.

Privates.

Houston Adams.
Richard Averitt.
Benjamin Buck.
Joseph Bullock.
Joseph W. Barnes.
Samuel J. Bumpass.
Zebedee Bumpass.
A. J. Caruthers.
Melville Cherry.
Thomas H. Covington.
Thomas R. Coulter.
Edward Darnell.
James H. Dyer.
William Duberry.
E. O. Ferrell.
John Foster.
P. Gibbs.
William Gafford.
Isaac Gafford.
N. W. Lissenbee.
—— Lowry.
A. McNichols.
J. W. Manson.
James Norfleet.
Joseph Norfleet.
William P. Outlaw.
William Oates.
Robert Prewitt.
William Prewitt.
T. G. Barbee. (Pete).
J. D. Riggins.
C. J. Riggins.
Ike Smith.
Taylor Smith.
Joseph Smith.
John Stewart.
John Satterfield.
—— Shelton.
John M. Tyson.
T. J. Taller.
J. R. Wooten.
E. C. Waters.
John Woods.

Killed.

Lieut. James B. Howard, Atlanta. July 28, 1864.
Thos. Jeff. Stone, Atlanta, July 28, 1864.
Joseph W. Barnes, Franklin.
A. J. Cuthbertson, Franklin.
Thomas R. Coulter, Franklin.
James Norfleet, Atlanta, July 28, 1864.
T. J. Barbee, Nashville.

Wounded.

Houston Adams, Franklin.
Melville Cherry, Seven Pines and Atlanta.
Serg't Ross Evans, Franklin.
John H. Howard, Atlanta.
W. N. Lissenbee, Atlanta.
William Prewitt, Peach Tree Creek.
Corp'l N. J. Morris, Atlanta and North Carolina.
John M. Tyson, Atlanta, July 23, 1864.
Col. W. F. Young, Lick Skillet Road, Ga., lost right arm.

DIED IN SERVICE.

Charles Anderson, Johnson's Island.
John H. Morrison, Camp Douglas, Ill.
Richard Averitt, Camp Douglas, Ill.
Benjamin Buck, Camp Douglas, Ill.
Zebedee Bumpass, Camp Douglas, Ill.
Edward Darnell, Camp Douglas, Ill.
Ike Smith, on exchange boat.
T. J. Taller, Camp Douglas, Ill.

PROMOTED.

Capt. W. F. Young, Colonel, 1863.
James B. Howard, Captain, 1863.
Thomas R. Coulter, 2d Lieut., 1862; 1st Lieut., 1863, Cap., 1864.

State of Tennessee, Montgomery County:

The foregoing muster roll of Company G, of the Forty-ninth Tennessee Regiment, is a full, true, and perfect list of the same, so far as my memory will admit of making. The company was organized by me at Palmyra, this county, on December 3, 1861. Upon organization, it was composed of sixty-four men, but as all records have been lost, I can only furnish the above, which is exclusively from memory.

I was promoted to colonel of the regiment in September, 1863. Lieutenants Howard and Coulter were afterward promoted to captains, but both were killed, and I am now the only captain of this company. W. F. YOUNG,

First Captain of Company G, Forty-ninth Tennessee, afterward Colonel of the Regiment.

CLARKSVILLE, TENN., April 17, 1883.

GENERAL ROBERT HATTON.

This gallant officer of the Tennessee Army of the Confederate service, was a citizen of Wilson county at the opening of the war. His record as a citizen and statesman was without spot or blemish. He was a citizen of whom the State was justly proud.

At the beginning of the war he brought out a company from Wilson county, and was made colonel of the Seventh Tennessee Regiment, at its organization, by the unanimous voice of its members. John F.

Goodner was lieutenant-colonel; John K. Howard, major; George Howard, adjutant; Alexander Vick, quartermaster; R. Hawkins, commissary; Dr. Robertson, surgeon; Dr. Fite, assistant surgeon. Upon the resignation of Doctor Robertson, Dr. Fite was made surgeon.

The Seventh Regiment was made up from the counties of Wilson, Sumner, Smith, and DeKalb, as follows:

1. Captain Hatton's company, Wilson county;
2. Captain Howard's company, Wilson county;
3. Captain Goodner's company, DeKalb county;
4. Captain Fite's company, Smith county;
5. Captain Douglas's company, Sumner county;
6. Captain Oakley's company, Wilson county;
7. Captain Anderson's company, Wilson county;
8. Captain Anthony's company, Wilson county;
9. Captain Shepherd's company, Wilson county;
10. Captain Baber's company, Sumner county.

This regiment served in Western Virginia, about Cheat Mountain, during the first year of the war, and was afterward transferred to the Army of Northern Virginia, where it served till the surrender at Appomattox.

We regret our inability to give a full history of this regiment. It was composed of good material, and was officered by the best men that the State afforded. Its record is a bright one. To record in full the unwritten catalogue of its glorious deeds would of itself require volumes.

This regiment was a part of S. R. Anderson's brigade, which was composed of the following regiments: First Tennessee, Colonel Maney; Seventh Tennessee, Colonel Hatton; Fourteenth Tennessee, Colonel Forbes; Eighteenth Georgia, and Baxter's Virginia Battery.

When General Anderson was assigned to another field, Colonel Hatton, of the Seventh, was promoted to the command of the brigade, with the rank of brigadier-general. The Seventh Tennessee was then commanded by Colonel John F. Goodner. After the death of General Hatton, the brigade was commanded by General Archer. This brigade was in the following pitched battles: Cheat Mountain, Seven Pines, Mechanicsville, Cold Harbor, Gaines's Mill, Malvern Hill, Cedar Mountain, Wilderness, Gettysburg, Bristow Station, Chancellorsville, second battle of Manassas, Harper's Ferry, Antietam, Shepherdstown, Mine Run, and all the daily battles and skirmishes around Richmond and Petersburg. In each of these battles the losses of the Seventh Tennessee were very severe. Colonel Hatton had received a commission of brigadier-general on the eve of the battle of Seven Pines, and fell at the close of the first day's fight. His command suffered severely. The enemy was strongly fortified at the edge of a swamp, through which the Confederates had to charge to assault the Federal works. This swamp was nearly knee deep in water in many places, and in passing this swamp many of the severely wounded were drowned before assistance could reach them. General Hatton led his brave boys against the enemy's fortifications. The resistance was obstinate, though the Confederates carried the works after a hard day's fight. At the close of the first day, in the last charge, just as the Federal line yielded and the Confederates gained the works, General Hatton was killed. His last command was, "Boys, follow me!" The loss of General Hatton was a severe blow to the State and to the army.

Colonel Goodner commanded the regiment much of

the time during the remainder of the war. Colonel Fite commanded at the time of the surrender. It is to be hoped that a full history of this regiment may yet be written.

We regret our inability to furnish complete muster rolls and reports of casualties of each company of the gallant old Seventh. The following is a list of most of the members of Company G, as furnished by Sergeant J. H. Bond, of that company. This company was brought out by Captain Shepherd, and was from Wilson county. Its company officers were as follows:

L. G. SHEPHERD, Captain;
J. H. HOBBS, First Lieutenant;
M. M. BOND, Second Lieutenant;
F. GRAVES, Third Lieutenant.

COMPANY G.

PRIVATES.

Bill Allen.
Bill Baird.
Pete Baskings.
Can Balingtine.
George Blankingship.
Huse Bond.
Hart Bradshaw.
Fount Cluck.
Sum Currey.
Frank Currey.
Harris Davis.
Tip Daugherty.
Lus Dement.
John Edwards.
Buck Edwards.
W. H. Edwards.
John Grisam.
Albert Grisam.
Will Grisam.
Bob Gwynn.
Jack Gwynn.
Alexander Hamilton.
John Hobbs.

George Huddleston.
Aaron Hutchins.
Laf Hutchins.
John Harrison.
Will Harrison.
Henry Harrison.
James Harrison.
Cal Ingram.
Tom Jackson.
Hal Johnson.
W. H. Johnson.
Nube Jennings.
Dan Johns.
Ned Jones.
Dock King.
John Kennedy.
Laf Lannom.
Coon Lannom.
Joe Launom.
Fed Lenard.
John Mount.
John McCrary.
James McCrary.

SKETCHES OF OFFICERS.

Cap Nelson.
Burt Ozment.
John Ozment.
Laf Oliver.
James Oliver.
Wiley Pool.
Tom Patterson.
Hue Quisenbury.
Bill Quisenbury.
Tom Rucker.
Brown Rucker.
Alexander Richmond.
James Richmond.
Tom Rice.

Martin Robins.
Luke Robison.
Calvin Simmons.
Eli Sellars.
J. Summers.
Brud Sullivan.
Laf Sullivan.
Bill Sullivan.
Bill Vaughters.
John Van.
Dick Vaughn.
Bill Woodram.
Balie Young.

KILLED.

Wm. Baird, second battle of Manassas.
Hart Bradshaw, Wilderness.
Frank Currey, Wilderness.
Buck Edwards, Seven Pines.
William Grissom, Seven Pines.
Hal Johnson, Gettysburg.
John Ozment, Harper's Ferry.
Tom Rice, Seven Pines.
Calvin Simmons, Seven Pines.
William Sullivan, Shepherdstown.
Baile Young, Fredericksburg.

WOUNDED.

Harris Davis, Seven Pines.
Cal. Ingram, Sheperdstown.
Burt Ozment, Harper's Ferry.
Nube Jennings, second battle of Manassas.
Martin Robins, Wilderness.

DIED IN SERVICE.

Ned Jones, Va.
John Mount, Warm Springs, Va.
Wiley Poole, Warm Springs, Va.
Wm. Woodram, Warm Springs, Va.

PROMOTED.

Capt. S. G. Shepard, Major, 1862, Lieutenant-colonel, 1863.
Lieut.-col. J. F. Goodner, Colonel, 1862.
Capt. John Fite, Major, 1862.
Sergt. J. H. Bond, 1st Lieutenant, 1861, Captain, 1862.
Sergt. J. C. Ingram, 2d Lieut., 1863.
Martin Robins, 3d Lieutenant, 1863.

BRIGADIER-GENERAL WILLIAM McCOMB

Was born in Mercer county, Pa., Nov. 21, 1832. He came to Tennessee in 1854, and from that time until the beginning of the war was engaged in developing the manufacturing interest of Southern Kentucky and Tennessee. He came to Clarksville, Tenn., among strangers, and confined himself so closely to the business in which he was engaged that his acquaintance was not large, but he was highly esteemed by all who knew him. He never engaged in politics, and hence had no influential politicians to urge his advancement; but he was a patriot, and ever ready to serve his country.

When the first call was made for troops by Governor Harris to defend the South, he promptly responded, joining as a private soldier Captain Ed. Hewett's company of the Fourteenth Tennessee Infantry—Forbes's regiment. His military record is remarkable. A private soldier, without strong and influential friends or relatives, and a Northern man by birth, he was elevated to the rank of brigadier-general to command two of the finest brigades ever connected with any army—Archer's and Bushrod Johnson's.

He won this position by gallantry on the field of battle, and did it step by step as follows: In May, 1861, he was elected second lieutenant of his company. In October, 1861, he was appointed first lieutenant and adjutant of his regiment by Colonel William A. Forbes. Was elected major of his regiment at Yorktown in 1862. Was promoted to lieutenant-colonel after the death of Lieutenant-colonel George A. Harrell, who was killed at the battle of Cedar Run. Was promoted to colonel upon the death of Colonel William A.

Forbes, who was killed at the second battle of Manassas. Was appointed brigadier-general by President Davis and confirmed by the Senate in December, 1864, and assigned to the command of the two brigades above mentioned, and ordered to report to Major-general Harvey Heth. He continued in command of the same until the close of the war, surrendering with General Lee at Appomattox Court-house, Va. He was wounded three times during the war—first at Gaines's Mill, slightly; secondly, at Sharpsburg, September 17, 1862, very severely; and lastly, at Chancellorsville, May 3, 1863, very severely. He was in the following battles: Williamsburg, Red House, Seven Pines, Mechanicsville, Gaines's Mill, Frazier's Farm, Malvern Hill, Harrison's Landing, Harper's Ferry, Sharpsburg, Chancellorsville, Wilderness, Spotsylvania, Anderson's, Cold Harbor, Squirrel Level Road, and Petersburg. He was also in the many skirmishes in which his command was engaged. He went to the Army of Virginia early in the war, and was with his command in all the engagements and skirmishes from Cheat Mountain to Appomattox.

During 1866 he was engaged in raising cotton in Alabama. In 1867-8 he was superintendent of the Mississippi and Alabama Turpentine Company, located at Pascagoula, Miss. Since 1869 he has been engaged in farming in Louisa county, Va., and his post-office is Gordonsville, Va.

The following were the members of General McComb's staff—all Tennesseans except Captain Archer, who was a Virginian:

  John Allen, Captain and A.A. General.
  William T. Moore, Captain and A. I. General.
  R. E. McCullock, First Lieutenant and A. D. C.

C. J. Allensworth, Major and A. Q. M.
Polk G. Johnson, First Lieutenant and A. I. General.
James Archer, Captain and Ordinance Officer.

MAJOR-GENERAL WILLIAM B. BATE.

General William B. Bate was born and educated in Sumner county, Tennessee. At the beginning of the Mexican war he was quite a young man, and was residing for the time being in the city of New Orleans. He enlisted for a term of twelve months in this war, and served out his time with distinction. At the close of the period of his enlistment he returned to his home and assisted in raising a company for further service. He was elected to the position of lieutenant of this company, and proceeded with his command to the scene of action for a second campaign, and served to the close of the war. General Bate then returned to his home and was shortly afterward a candidate for the legislature. At this time he was about twenty-one years of age. Being so young, and to a great extent unacquainted with the ways of the political world, his friends were fearful of his chances of election. Yet he made the campaign lively to his competitors, and was elected as representative from Sumner county.

As a debater, General Bate was pleasant and affable, a good reasoner, and a man of dignified bearing and remarkable oratorical powers. As a member of the legislature he was an able and influential member. He soon became a leader in his party.

At the close of his first session as representative he entered the profession of law at Gallatin, and during a portion of his early professional life was editor of a weekly paper. As a lawyer he was remarkable for his knowledge of men. He could read character at a glance, and used this knowledge successfully in the selection of jurymen. In 1854 he was elected to the position of Attorney-general of the Nashville district, and served the State for six years. In 1860 he was a candidate on the Breckinridge electoral ticket, and made a vigorous and spirited campaign.

In the beginning of the civil war he raised and organized the Second Tennessee Regiment, and was elected its commander as colonel. Proceeding with his regiment to the scene of hostilities he served in the campaigns on the Potomac, and led his regiment in the first battle of Manassas. His regiment was afterward transferred to the Western Army under Johnston, and figured prominently in the battle of Shiloh.

In the last-named battle General Bate received a severe wound, and was thereby disabled for the greater portion of the ensuing year. For gallantry displayed on the field of Shiloh he was promoted to the rank of brigadier-general, and placed in command of a brigade. Returning to his command before his wounds had healed, he led his brigade in all the battles of the Western Army.

During the Georgia campaign he was made a major-general, in which capacity he served till the collapse of the Confederate cause.

As a soldier he possessed the essential qualities of a commander. Careful of his men in camp and on the field, he was appreciated by them and loved as a leader. Careful of the rights of citizens, he always looked carefully to the protection of their property and premises when in the vicinity of his encampment. With a profound respect for the moral and religious status of his men, he afforded every assistance to the chaplain, to whom he extended the hospitalities of his tent and table. He was a regular attendant at divine service, and as a commander he showed by example his solicitude for the spiritual welfare of his men and his respect for the Christian religion. As a citizen he is sociable and pleasant, and combines all the sterling qualities of the true gentleman.

General Bate is at present the Governor of Tennessee, to which position he was elected in 1882, and re-elected in 1884. As an occupant of the executive chair he discharges its duties with that ability and integrity that have ever characterized every department of his private and public life.

LIEUTENANT-GENERAL JOHN B. HOOD.

This officer was placed in command of the Army of Tennessee early in July, 1864, and continued in command in the battles around Atlanta and in the Tennessee campaign till after the battles of Franklin and Nashville. His military career was an unfortunate one, and its record is a catalogue of reverses. He was a gallant officer, and was justly entitled "the bravest of the brave," but was lacking in that discretion so necessary to his position at the time he was placed in command, and which in this instance would have been truly "the better part of valor." As the Confederate authorities saw proper to displace the renowned General Joseph E. Johnston with General Hood, a few points in the record of this general's history will be given.

General John B. Hood was born in Owensville, Bath

county, Ky., June 28, 1831, and was brought up at Mount Sterling, Montgomery county, Ky., where he received his early education. He entered upon his collegiate studies at West Point in 1849, and graduated in 1853. He was assigned to duty in the Fourth Infantry, in California, where he served for two years. He was then transferred to the Second Regiment, commanded by Colonel Albert Sidney Johnston, in which R. E. Lee was lieutenant-colonel. Van Dorn, Kirby Smith, Fields, Evans, and Hardee, afterward generals in the Confederate army, were members of this regiment. In 1855, Hood was assigned to the Texas frontier, and in July of the following year was wounded in an engagement with the Indians on Devil River. Shortly after this he was ordered to report for duty at West Point. Having become attached to Texas during his service there, he asked to be retained on the Texas frontier, both as a matter of choice and policy. Owing to the threatening aspect of national affairs, and his sympathy with the South, his desire was to be where he could look after her interests in the impending struggle. The struggle came, as expected. On April 16, 1861, he resigned his commission in the United States Army, and tendered his services to the Confederacy. He was commissioned first lieutenant in the Confederate service and ordered to report to General Lee, in Virginia. General Lee ordered him to report to General Magruder, on the Peninsula. He was immediately placed in command of all the cavalry on the Peninsula, and promoted to captain. On September 30 he was commissioned colonel, and ordered to report to Richmond, where he was placed in command of the Fourth Texas Infantry. This regiment had been for some time disturbed by a faction and could not organize. A portion of its men wanted Colonel Allen, of Texas, to command them, while a portion of the officers were opposed to the measure. Colonel Hood took command of the regiment, and the appointment was satisfactory.

The Fourth and Fifth Texas Regiments were organized into a brigade on November 12, and placed under command of Colonel Wigfall, who had recently been appointed brigadier-general. General Wigfall had been elected to the Confederate States Senate, and resigned his commission as brigadier-general at the opening of the Confederate Congress. Colonel Hood was promoted to the rank of brigadier-general and placed in command of Wigfall's brigade. Shortly afterward he was commissioned major-general and assigned to duty in Longstreet's corps, in which capacity he served till after the battle of Chickamauga, where he lost a leg in the first day's fight.

As soon as General Hood recovered from the amputation of his limb at Chickamauga, he was promoted to a lieutenant-general and assigned to the command of a corps in the Army of Tennessee. In the Georgia campaign Hood's corps occupied the left of Johnston's army. Every retreat in that campaign was the result of Hood's inability to cover the enemy's right. Shortly after the retreat from Kennesaw Mountain, Hood superseded Johnston and took command of the whole army. This measure met the bitter disapprobation of many of the division commanders, most prominent of whom was General Cleburne. The remainder of Hood's military record has been briefly stated in another place. A brave and intelligent officer, he had risen repeatedly, from a lieutenant of the ranks to be commander in chief of a department and army. Yet his last promotion placed him in an unenviable position.

The Confederate resources were exhausted. In the agonies of desperation the armies and people of the Confederacy were hoping against hope, and their only vision of success lay beyond the accomplishment of impossibilities. Hood took command with these facts staring him in the face. He hurled his columns upon the fortifications of the enemy only to be slaughtered and repulsed by their superior numbers. Atlanta was given up, and Hood was in a few months pushing, by a flank movement, upon the outposts of Nashville. At Franklin he made his last blunder. The works of the enemy were assaulted, and after a desperate battle the enemy gave back, though the position could have been easily flanked. These pitched battles from the Chattahoochee to Jonesboro, thence to Franklin and Nashville, involved a reckless and deplorable slaughter of the Confederates. The enemy were masters of the field. They were always prepared for those assaults. The Confederates would move up to the attack with that coolness and steadiness of courage that is without a parallel in history, and were mowed down by the raking of musketry and canister from the enemy's works. They did all that brave men could do. The enemy boasted of their superior numbers, and of Hood's weakness in throwing his columns upon their works to be mowed down as wheat before the scythes, yet

> No vulgar crop was theirs to reap—
> No stinted harvest thin and cheap—
> Heroes before each fatal sweep
>   Fell thick as ripened grain.
> And ere the darkening of the day,
> Piled high as autumn shocks they lay,
> The ghastly harvest of the fray,
>   The corpses of the slain.

The brave Confederates were never found wanting in courage. To them death had no terrors. They approached and embraced it, linked, as it was, hand in hand with glory, waiting to be wooed and won by the daring and the brave.

MAJOR-GENERAL P. R. CLEBURNE.

This gallant officer of the Confederate army was a native of Ireland, and was born at Bride Park Cottage, on the river Bride, county Cork, Ireland, March 17, 1828. This place is about ten miles west of the city of Cork. His father, Dr. Joseph Cleburne, was a physician of considerable note, and was a graduate of medicine from the University of London, and of surgery from the Royal College of Surgeons at Dublin. He was of an old Tipperary family, originally of English stock.

General Cleburne's mother, Mary Ann Cleburne, was the second daughter of Patrick Rouayne, Esq., of Annebrook, on the Island of Cork. This name has been preserved in the family, having passed through four generations. General Cleburne was named after his maternal grandfather, and having been born on St. Patrick's day, he had a double title to the name given him.

When General Cleburne was three years old his mother died. About one year after, Dr. Cleburne married a second wife—Miss Isabella Stewart, the daughter of a Scotch clergyman. This woman was kindhearted and intelligent, and bestowed great care and attention in the education of the step-children thus placed under her charge.

From Dr. Cleburne's first marriage there were four children—three sons and one daughter. Their names, in the order of their ages, were: William Cleburne, Annie Cleburne (now Mrs. Sherlock, of Omaha), Patrick Rouayne Cleburne, and Joseph Cleburne—all of whom, except General Cleburne, are now living.

From the second marriage there were four children, whose names, in the order of their ages, were: Isabella Cleburne, Edward Warren Cleburne, Robert Stewart Cleburne, and Christopher S. Cleburne. Of the latter family only two are now living. Edward Warren Cleburne went to sea, and died of yellow fever, on the coast of Africa, several years ago. The youngest, Christopher S. Cleburne, was a captain in the Second Kentucky Cavalry of Morgan's command, and was killed at the battle of Cloyd's Farm, near Dublin Depot, Va., May 10, 1864, in the twenty-first year of his age. William Cleburne is engaged in civil engineering, and resides in Oregon. Robert S. Cleburne resides in Cincinnati, and is also a civil engineer.

General Cleburne's early education was under the care of a private tutor. At the age of twelve years he was placed in school under a teacher named Spedding, of the Established Church. As a boy he was fond of childish sports and innocent amusements. He had a high sense of honor and a keen sense of disgrace. He was fond of history, poetry, and travels. For Latin and Greek he seemed to have but little taste, though his preference for mathematics was quite prominent. His father possessed a good income from the practice of medicine, and had a farm of two hundred acres. Having a taste for experimental farming, he sunk in this what he made out of his profession, and when he died in 1844, he left but a small estate to divide between his widow and eight children. This caused General Cleburne to look around for some means of support, and he apprenticed himself to Dr. Justice, who kept a drug-store in the little town of Mallow. Had chemical tastes and pharmaceutical studies been the only requirements to advancement in this line of business, General Cleburne, perhaps, would have never been known outside of the little village of Mallow and its vicinity.

MAJOR-GENERAL P. R. CLEBURNE.

The first prerequisite to advancement in the occupation of his choice was a thorough knowledge of Latin and Greek. Unfortunately this was his weakest point, and when he appeared for his preliminary examination at the Apothecaries' Hall in Dublin, he failed to pass the necessary examination. Being eighteen years old at this time, General Cleburne felt his disgrace so keenly that he resolved that his family should never again see a member who had disgraced them, and, without disclosing his intentions to any one, he enlisted in the Forty-first Regiment of foot, then stationed at Dublin, and daily expecting to be ordered to foreign parts. No one of his family or friends knew any thing of his whereabouts for a year. Through Captain Pratt, an officer of the regiment, and son of the Rector of Desartmore—a parish adjoining that of the Cleburne family—his whereabouts were discovered. This captain visited the family, and had General Cleburne thought of this he would have enlisted under an assumed name, as he afterward remarked to his friends. His discharge was procured a year or so afterward, with a portion of the means that had fallen to him, and in company with a sister and two brothers he sailed from Queenstown, November 11, 1849, in the bark Bridgetown, under command of Captain Mills. The vessel landed at New Orleans on Christmas-day.

General Cleburne proceeded immediately to Cincinnati, where he received employment as prescription clerk in the drug-store of a Mr. Salter, on Broadway. The sister and brothers joined him soon afterward. In a short time he located in Helena, Ark., where he followed the drug business, and afterward studied law and formed a partnership at Helena with Judge L. H. Mangum.

When the civil war broke out in 1861, both members of this firm enlisted in the Confederate service, and were together till the death of General Cleburne. General Cleburne was made captain of Company A, Fifteenth Arkansas Regiment, and at the organization of the regiment was made colonel. He was soon afterward promoted to brigadier-general and placed in command of the following regiments: Twenty-third Tennessee, Lieutenant-colonel Neil; Sixth Mississippi,

Colonel Thornton; Fifth Tennessee, Colonel Ben. J. Hill; Twenty-fourth Tennessee, Colonel Mat. Martin; Fifteenth Arkansas, Lieutenant-colonel Patton; Second Tennessee, Colonel William B. Bate.

The above regiments engaged in the battle of Shiloh. The brigade consisted of two thousand seven hundred men, of whom the casualties were one thousand. In his official report of this battle, General Cleburne made honorable mention of the following parties for gallantry displayed upon the field: Privates William Dixon, Fifteenth Arkansas; William Pierce, Fifteenth Arkansas; W. H. Kinney, Fifteenth Arkansas; H. A. Sales, Fifteenth Arkansas; Sergeant T. H. Osborn, Fifteenth Arkansas; Lieutenant Josey, Fifteenth Arkansas; Colonel Ben. J. Hill, Fifth Tennessee; Lieutenant-colonel Peebles, Twenty-fourth Tennessee; Lieutenant R. H. Keeble, Twenty-fourth Tennessee; Captain Ridley, Twenty-fourth Tennessee; Lieutenant-colonel Neil, Twenty-fourth Tennessee. In this battle Colonel Bate, the present Governor of Tennessee, was severely wounded.

General Cleburne was promoted to major-general shortly after the battle of Shiloh, and assigned to the command of a division in Hardee's corps.

The following are the names of the members of General Cleburne's staff, with rank and date of service, as furnished from Confederate archives at Washington, D. C.:

Calhoun Bonham, Major and A. A. G., December, 1862-3.
Irving A. Buck, Captain and A. A. G., December, 1862-3.
C. H. Byrne, Captain and Volunteer A. D. C., December, 1862-3.
J. R. Dixon, Major and A. A. and I. G., December, 1862-3.
J. H. Erskine, M. D., Medical Inspector, 1863.
S. P. Hanly, First Lieutenant and A. D. C., 1862-3.

Charles S. Hill, Captain and Ordnance Officer, 1863.
T. R. Hotchkiss, Captain, 1863.
J. W. Jetton, Second Lieutenant and A. D. C., 1861.
John M. Johnson, M. D., Chief Surgeon, 1863.
W. W. Kirkland, Colonel and Chief of Staff, 1863.
A. S. Landers, Major and A. Q. M., 1861.
R. C. Sanford, Major and A. C. S., 1861.
D. A. Linthicum, M. D., Chief Surgeon, 1863-5.
L. H. Mangum, Lieutenant and A. D. C., 1862-3.
B. F. Phelps, Captain and A. A. and I. G., 1862.
H. Rucker, Signal Officer, 1863.
H. W. Smith, Signal Officer, 1863-4.
N. B. Stubblefield, Sergeant and Orderly, 1861-3.

As a commander General Cleburne was without a superior for talent and for skill in handling troops upon the field. He was in every sense of the word a soldier.

Cleburne's division was with Bragg in his Kentucky campaign, and distinguished itself at Richmond, Ky. While a portion of his command was in the battle of Perryville, the remainder was holding an important position in front of Covington. At Murfreesboro, Chickamauga, and the hundred days' battles of the Georgia campaign, and Hood's Tennessee campaign, this command was distinguished for its effective work and the skill and gallantry of its commander. At Franklin, General Cleburne fell in the heaviest of the charge upon the enemy's works.

The battle of Franklin was an unfortunate affair to the remnant of the Confederate army. Many of Hood's subordinate generals were of opinion that the Federal force at Spring Hill could be captured by flanking the position, and the remainder defeated in detail before it could reach Nashville or be re-enforced. General Cleburne urged the policy of a flank movement, and his counsel partially prevailed. His division succeeded in gaining the rear of the enemy at Spring Hill, and he had his men posted along the pike. While awaiting orders to attack, by which, with little loss, he could have cut off their retreat and forced their surrender, the commanding general seemed to change his pur-

N. B. STUBBLEFIELD.

pose, and through the usual channel ordered Cleburne not to attack the enemy until further orders. Thus Cleburne. after he had placed the enemy virtually in his power by his skillful generalship, was forbidden to strike the blow that was only necessary to secure the victory at small sacrifice and gain Franklin without a struggle. Cleburne was forced to remain all night by the road-side and let the enemy pass within a few hundred yards of his lines, going safely into Franklin. Cleburne was eager to strike the blow, and when he saw that he was denied the privilege he was deeply moved. The battle of Franklin followed the next day.

DEATH OF GENERAL PAT. R. CLEBURNE.

The following is a true and correct account of the last battle and death of Major-general Patrick R. Cleburne, as given by Judge L. H. Mangum, his law partner before the war, a member of his staff, and one of his most intimate friends:

"It is due to history and the memory of General Cleburne, that a correct account should be written as to the part his division performed at Spring Hill and Franklin, and the circumstances attending his death and burial.

"I have read many different descriptions, but never a correct one, of the part taken by Cleburne and his division at those two places. The most of the articles that have been written upon the battle of Franklin read, to those who participated in that terrible slaughter, like a romance; especially so the account of the battle and the death of General Cleburne, written by Mr. E. L. Roberts, and published in a number of Southern papers. A letter published a short time since by Mr. M. Quad, in the Vicksburg *Herald*, is an exception to most of the articles written upon the battle of Franklin and death of Cleburne, and is correct in the main.

"I will write of, and describe, things as they actually

GENERAL CLEBURNE. 373

occurred, and not as I might picture them in my imagination. In doing so I will endeavor, as far as circumstances will permit, in order to write the truth, not to reflect upon the official conduct or military skill of any officer, for that can now do no good, although there was a terrible blunder at Spring Hill that cost the lives of thousands of the best men in the army.

"On the morning of November 29, 1864, Cleburne's division crossed Duck River at Davis's Ford, and, by a circuitous route, marched rapidly to Spring Hill. Cleburne's division was composed of four brigades, viz.: Granberry's Texas brigade, Govan's Arkansas brigade, Lowry's brigade, composed of Alabama and Mississippi troops, and Mercer's Georgia brigade, commanded by General J. A. Smith. The latter brigade was left on duty at Florence, Ala., and did not reach the command until after the battle of Franklin. Late in the afternoon of that day, November 29, Cleburne reached the vicinity of Spring Hill (a village situated on the Columbia and Franklin pike, twelve miles from Columbia and eleven miles from Franklin), being the leading division of Hood's army. Approaching this village on a road running at right angles to the pike, upon Cleburne's division crossing McCutcheon's Creek, a quarter of a mile from the pike, General Hood, in person, ordered General Cleburne to form line of battle to the left of the road, at the foot of a hill, in a corn field, then move forward and take the enemy's breastworks that were just over the brow of the hill, built principally of rail piles. Cleburne executed the command rapidly, and in less than fifteen minutes, took the works and some prisoners. There was not exceeding a regiment of Federals in the works, and those that were not captured ran into Spring Hill. Cleburne's command was now in full view of Spring Hill, and not exceeding three hundred yards from it. His loss in the the charge was four killed and forty-five wounded. The Federals had time to fire but one volley when Govan's and Granberry's men were on the works. A Federal battery on the pike then commenced shelling the command. Govan's and Granberry's brigades, that were in the charge, becoming more or less scattered running after the retreating Federals, Cleburne ordered me to direct General Granberry, who was on the left of the line, to form his brigade along a fence running parallel with the pike, and about two hundred yards from it, so as to be prepared to move on the pike, remarking at the time that he would see Govan. Just then a shell bursted over us and wounded Cleburne's horse 'Red Pepper' in the hip. He reared furiously for a while, and I remained a moment to see if the General was hurt. Upon asking him, I shall never forget his reply and manner, both showing how determined he was to take the pike. 'No; go on, Mangum, and tell Granberry what I told you.' I delivered the order. Granberry in a few minutes had his brigade formed along the fence. I then returned to Cleburne. In the meantime Govan's brigade was formed, and the Federal battery on the pike had retreated. As I reached Cleburne, Colonel Bostwick, assistant inspector general on General Cheatham's staff, rode up with an order from General Cheatham directing Cleburne to remain where he was and not move on the pike until further orders. This was near sunset. But for the order delivered by Colonel Bostwick, Cleburne would have been on the pike and had possession of Spring Hill in less than ten minutes. Then there would have been no battle of Franklin. As ordered, Cleburne's command remained in line of battle till morning, within two hundred yards of the pike, along which the entire Federal army passed that night from Columbia to Franklin unmolested.

"On the morning of the memorable November 30, 1864, after considerable delay, Hood's army moved toward Franklin. It was in the afternoon before the army reached Winston's Ridge—a high ridge some two miles south of Franklin. There a council of war was held, and General Hood, against the judgment of his best generals, decided to attack the almost impregnable works around Franklin, and, what was even worse, to attack them in their strongest point. Cleburne opposed an attack, but he was too blunt and frank to have any influence with Hood. Cleburne considered the removal of Joseph E. Johnston and the appointment of General Hood in his stead as a great disaster to the army and Confederacy, and exceedingly unwise in General Hood accepting the command under the circumstances. Cleburne had too little of the political general about him to conceal his views; hence General Hood had no good feeling toward Cleburne.

"Dr. D. A. Linthicum, chief surgeon of Cleburne's division—who remained behind to care for the wounded of the division in the skirmish of the evening before at Spring Hill—came up and reported to General Cleburne, at General Hood's head-quarters, just after the council of war was over, just prior to the battle; and, after General Cleburne was on his horse, heard General Hood say to him: 'General, form your division to the right of the pike, letting your left overlap the same. General Brown will form on the left with his right overlapping your left. I wish you to move on the enemy. Give orders to your men not to fire a gun until you run the Yankee skirmish line from behind the first line of works in your front, then press them and shoot them in their backs as they run to their main line; then charge the enemy's works. Franklin is the key to Nashville, and Nashville is the key to independence.' General Cleburne smiled and said, 'General, I will take the works or fall in the effort.' The line of battle was formed on the north side of Winston's Ridge, between the ridge and the town, fully one mile from the Federal works. Hardee's old corps, then commanded by General Cheatham, on the left, and Stewart's corps on the right, Cleburne's division on the right of Cheatham's corps, his left guiding on the pike; then Cheatham's old division, commanded by General John C. Brown, his right guiding on the pike; Bate's division on the left of the corps and army. Cleburne marched forward with two brigades in front—Granberry and Govan—Lowry in the rear. In a few moments the command was under a galling fire from the enemy's artillery. The men were ordered not to stop or to fire, but to rush upon the enemy's works. The first line of works in Cleburne's front was easily taken. This line was some two hundred yards in front of the main line of breastworks. Behind this first line Cleburne's command halted a few moments, preparatory to making a charge at the main works. Just at this time I galloped up to Cleburne, who was riding alone immediately behind his division, about the center. Previous to this, Cleburne had ordered me to locate one of his batteries at a certain point. Soon after leaving upon this mission, he sent Captain S. P. Hanly, one of his staff, to locate the battery, and for me to return to him immediately. Upon riding up to him and asking him what he wanted, he replied: 'It is too late,' and directed me to go with Granberry's brigade. He then turned his horse toward the right and galloped up to Govan's brigade. The whole line was then rushing madly for the enemy's works. That was the last time I saw General Cleburne alive.

"The space between the enemy's first line and the main line was about two hundred yards. The ground was level, and I don't think there was a tree or bush between them. The fire and destruction were beyond description. I went up to the works with Granberry's brigade. Generals Granberry and Govan, and their staff, were on foot. About half way between the first and main line General Granberry was killed. I was within ten feet of him, and remember well the last words he spoke:—'Forward, men; never let it be said that Texans lag in the fight.' As he spoke these words, a ball struck him in the cheek and passed through his brain. Throwing both hands to his face he sunk down on his knees and remained in that position until his body was taken off the field after the battle. Better soldiers and braver men were never marshalled than this Texas brigade, and Granberry was, in every way, worthy to command such a brigade of heroes. Well may the Lone Star State be proud of every man in that brigade.

"When I last saw General Cleburne he was going up toward the enemy's works, mounted on a brown mare belonging to Lieutenant Tip Stanton, of his escort, from Natchez, Miss. This mare was killed seventy-five or a hundred yards from the works. Young Brandon, of Mississippi, a member of General Cleburne's escort, dismounted and offered his horse to him. While Cleburne was in the act of mounting, the horse was shot dead by many bullets. Then Cleburne rushed on foot for the works. He must have been killed between where his last horse was shot and the works, about where M. Quad says he found his body next morning.

"The sun was not over half an hour high when the battle began, and did not last exceeding an hour. Cleburne's division never made seven charges, as Mr. Roberts states, but only one. Those of the division that were not killed or wounded reached the enemy's breastworks, but were unable to scale them, so they remained in the ditch dug along the breastwork until the Federals retreated, which was about eleven o'clock that night. By twelve o'clock General Lowry had guards all over town. Men were detailed, and lights procured, to hunt for General Cleburne, but I soon stopped them upon being told by a Confederate soldier that he had been captured and made his escape—that he saw General Cleburne passing through Franklin, a prisoner.

"One, not in the battle of Franklin, might think it strange that such a conspicuous character as General Cleburne should be killed and his death not witnessed by any one; but the fire was so terrific and the smoke so dense that one could not distinguish an object at twenty feet distant. The morning after the battle information came to our head-quarters that General Cleburne's body was found. I immediately went in search of it and found it laid out on the gallery of the McGavock brick house—boots, pocket-book, diary, and sword-belt gone. I afterward found the latter on a soldier, who claimed to have found it. His (General Cleburne's) face was covered with a lady's handkerchief finely embroidered. Who placed his body there I have never been able to ascertain, and never knew who found it until I read M. Quad's letter. General Cleburne received but one wound, and that was from a minnie ball which passed through his body. I procured coffins for Generals Cleburne and Granberry, and Colonel Young, of the Tenth Texas, carried their remains to Columbia for interment, sent a courier ahead to have three graves dug in some suitable place in the country there; reached Columbia late in the evening. The remains of these three heroes lay, during that night, in the parlor of Mrs. Mary R. Polk. While the body of Cleburne was lying in Mrs. Polk's parlor, the following verses were placed upon his coffin, written by the talented and accomplished Miss Naomi Hays, niece of ex-President Polk, who afterward married the late lamented Major W. E. Moore, chief commissary of the Army of Tennessee:

> Fare thee well, departed chieftain!
>   Erin's land sends forth a wail,
> And O my country sad laments thee,
>   Passed so late through Death's dark vale!
> Blow, ye breezes, softly o'er him,
>   Fan his brow with gentlest breath;
> Disturb ye not the peaceful slumber—
>   Cleburne sleeps the sleep of death.
> Rest thee, Cleburne, tears of sadness
>   Flow from hearts thou'st nobly won;
> Mem'ry ne'er will cease to cherish
>   Deeds of glory thou hast done.

"Funeral rites were performed the next day by the Right Rev. Bishop Quintard. The bodies were borne to the cemetery and placed in graves beside General Strahl and Lieutenant Marsh, of his staff. After the burial, I discovered that these gallant men were buried in that portion of the cemetery known as the 'potters' field,' between a row of negroes and Federal soldiers."

I felt very indignant, and so expressed myself. General Lucien J. Polk, brother to General and Bishop Leonidas Polk, was present, and most kindly offered me a lot in the Ashwood Cemetery, six miles south of Columbia, which kind and generous offer I most thankfully accepted. The next day I obtained a detail from the commandant of the post and disinterred Generals Cleburne, Granberry, and Strahl, Colonel Young, and Lieutenant Marsh. I disinterred General Strahl and Lieutenant Marsh at the request of Bishop Quintard. Having only a slight acquaintance with those gentlemen, I did not feel authorized to remove their remains from where their friends had planted them, but did so at the earnest request of Bishop Quintard, who I knew was a warm friend of General Strahl and Lieutenant Marsh. Five graves were dug in Ashwood Cemetery, in a row, where I buried these five noble and gallant soldiers.

"Upon my return to the division, then around Nashville, I stated to General Cleburne's staff where I had buried our general. Captain Hill, ordnance officer, related what Cleburne said to him while riding through Ashwood Cemetery, about which so much has been said and written. Commenting upon the beauty of the grounds, he said: 'It would not be hard to die if one could be buried in such a beautiful spot.' He never expressed himself, as Mr. Roberts said in the Philadelphia *Times*, 'If I fall in the coming fight, bury me here at Ashwood.'

"In 1869, at the request of many friends, and the Ladies' Confederate Memorial Association of Phillips county, Ark., Dr. H. M. Grant, an old friend of General Cleburne, and myself brought the remains of General Cleburne from Ashwood to Helena, and buried them in the Confederate burying-grounds, where, General Cleburne's friends feel satisfied, that could his wishes have been ascertained, he would have chosen to be placed at rest.

"No monument has ever been placed over Cleburne's grave by the Ladies' Confederate Memorial Association of Phillips county. The only marks that show his grave are the marble head and foot stones, brought with his remains from Ashwood, where they were placed soon after the war closed by the ladies of that neighborhood, with this inscription on it:

'Major-general P. R. CLEBURNE,
Of the Confederate Army.
Born in the county Cork, Ireland.
Killed at Franklin, Tennessee, November 30, 1864.'

"Mr. Roberts has been very erroneously informed as to Cleburne's personal appearance and early life. Cleburne was not 'weak and rather wan.' On the contrary, he was six feet high, broad-shouldered, but spare built, very active, had remarkable endurance; large, dark gray eyes; awkward in his manners; very sensitive to the opinions of the world, but a stranger would suppose him indifferent to them; a poor conversationalist; exceedingly absent-minded, except when on duty and the battle-field; perfectly indifferent to danger; possessed of fine literary attainments; very fond of ladies' society, but always appeared embarrassed when in their company. A purer and more honorable man never lived, yet these noble qualities were only known and appreciated fully by his intimate friends. He had, to perfection, that noble trait of character always to make the *amende honorable;* never hesitating to apologize when in the wrong. He illustrated this on one occasion most generously toward General John C. Brown, afterward governor of Tennessee. The Army of Tennessee, retreating from Middle Tennessee to Chattanooga, camped at what was then called University Station—now Sewanee. Early in the morning he filed his division in the road, when he found a brigade marching in front. This annoyed him exceedingly. He galloped to the head of the brigade and asked for the commander. General Brown, whom Cleburne had never met, answered that he was. Cleburne, in a peremptory and insulting manner, upbraided General Brown for violating orders, and ordered him to halt his brigade until his (Cleburne's) division could pass. On returning to the head of his division he met General Hardee, who told him that he had changed the order of march by putting Brown's brigade in front. Cleburne, without saying a word, immediately galloped rapidly back to General Brown, and made to him, in the presence of his men, a most ample apology for what he had said to him. This little circumstance made them warm friends ever afterward.

"Cleburne had never traveled extensively, as Mr. Roberts states; nor was he ever a cornet of British Light Dragoons in India, nor a student of Belles Lettres in Paris. In fact, he was never in that city. When in his 'teens' he ran away from home and joined the British army in Ireland, remaining in the service only a few months, when his family obtained his discharge. His father was a physician in Ireland, where Cleburne graduated in pharmacy, and came to America in 1850, and was first employed in a drug-store in Cincinnati, Ohio. Cleburne was an ardent Whig, a regular reader of the old *National Intelligencer* and Prentice's *Louisville Journal*. He was known in early days in Helena as an 'Irish Whig.' After the organization of the Know Nothing party he became a strong Democrat, and remained devoted to that party to the day of his death. He was an active member of the Episcopal Church, and took great interest in all Church matters, and was for a number of years a member of the Vestry of St. John's Episcopal Church in Helena, Ark.

"Cleburne's career was as remarkable as it was brilliant, and it is to be hoped that the day will not be far distant when a full history of his life will be published."

BISHOP C. T. QUINTARD.

This celebrated divine was a citizen of Nashville at the beginning of the war, and was rector of the Church of the Advent. His ancestors were French Huguenots, who came to America at an early day, and, with the Bayards, the Pintards, and the Jays they formed a colony in New York, which was called New Rochelle.

Dr. Quintard graduated at Columbia College, New York, when quite a young man, and studied medicine and surgery under the celebrated Dr. Valentine Mott, of New York, one of the most renowned surgeons of America. After graduating in medicine at the University of New York, he was appointed one of the assistant physicians of Bellevue Hospital. After remaining in this institution for one year, he removed South and located in Georgia. Here he practiced his profession, and was an able contributor to the medical journals of the day.

In 1851 he was called to the chair of Physiology and Pathological Anatomy in the Medical College at Memphis.

Becoming dissatisfied with secular pursuits, and feeling himself moved by the Holy Ghost to a sublimer work, he commenced the study of theology under the Rt. Rev. J. H. Otey, D.D., LL.D., and was by him admitted to the holy order of deacons in January, 1855. Resigning his professorhip, he commenced the duties of his sacred calling, to which he has ever since arduously and faithfully devoted all his energies and ability.

In 1856 he was ordained priest, and a year after was called to the rectorship of Calvary Church, in Memphis. In 1858 he resigned the rectorship of Calvary Church, and was made rector of the Church of the Advent, at Nashville, which position he filled till 1861, when he was chosen chaplain of the First Tennessee Regiment, many of whose men were members of his Church. At Cheat Mountain, in the autumn of 1861, he was called to act on General Loring's staff, which position he filled till June, 1862, when he rejoined his regiment at Chattanooga on the eve of the Kentucky campaign. Here he was called to take a position on General Polk's staff, which he accepted and filled till February, 1863. During all this time he had faithfully filled the position of chaplain as well as staff officer.

In the spring of 1863, at the request of his fellow chaplains, he was assigned by General Bragg to the charge of the hospitals of Polk's corps. Here he filled the positions of surgeon and chaplain, with the privilege of free travel on all railroads to the different points of his field of labor. In this capacity he served to the close of the war.

Bishop Quintard always attended his men on the field in the event of a pitched battle. He never chose a position of safety in the rear, but advanced to the front with his men, to the very thickest and hottest of the fight, and was ever prompt to render surgical assistance to the wounded and speak words of consolation to the dying.

Throughout the war Bishop Quintard was a very useful as well as a pious and good man. Since the close of the war he has been zealous and faithful in the discharge of every duty pertaining to his position as bishop of his Church. His present residence is Sewanee, Tenn.

REV. JOSEPH CROSS, D.D.

This celebrated divine entered the Confederate service as chaplain of Colonel Bate's Second Tennessee Regiment in 1861. Of his history there is a singular coincidence of dates. He was born in England, July 4, 1813; landed in America, July 4, 1825; joined the Church, July 4, 1826; preached his first sermon, July 4, 1829; was married, July 4, 1834; ascended Mont Blanc July 4, 1857; commissioned chaplain of the Second Tennessee Regiment, July 4, 1861.

Dr. Cross's boyhood was spent in very humble circumstances. His father came to America in 1822 in the hope of bettering his condition, leaving all of his family in England, except one son, who accompanied him. After three years of faithful toil he succeeded in gathering up enough means to bring his family to America, where he had prepared for them a home. During the father's absence in America the health of the mother gave down, and the children were placed upon the parish for support. The three brothers were apprenticed to farmers of the neighborhood, where they remained till funds arrived with which to defray the expenses of the family to America.

Shortly after the arrival of the family in the New World the mother died. The father and children were established in their new home. Here Dr. Cross grew up to manhood, and as he grew up he took an abiding interest in the spiritual welfare of his father's household. At the age of thirteen he commenced holding prayer-meetings with the boys of the neighborhood, and his brothers and sisters were converted. He soon engaged in public exhortations, and preached his first sermon at the age of sixteen. He now felt the want of an education, and proceeded at once to the Oneida Conference Seminary, at Cazenovia. When he arrived at the turnpike gate he had no money, and pawned his knife for his passage through. He soon gained an audience with the trustees, and prevailed upon them to wait for his tuition till he could pay for it by teaching. At the same time he perfected arrangements to pay his board by sweeping the rooms, sawing wood, making fires, and such other work as was needed to be done about the seminary.

During his stay at school he preached every Sabbath in the vicinity. He soon after engaged in teaching, in which he was successful. He had by this time become an able young minister of the Methodist Church. He joined the Conference and bestowed all his energies upon his work of the ministry.

About this time there was a severance of the Church on political issues, and Dr. Cross came South and settled in New Orleans.

By faithful study he had become a learned man, and was called to the chair of *Belles-lettres* in Transylvania University. This was in the year 1847, when New

Orleans was so severely scourged with yellow fever. Embarking upon a steamer, he started to his new field of labor, but was attacked with yellow fever soon after his departure from New Orleans. In this trying hour he would doubtless have died but for the assistance of that good man, Bishop Paine, who happened to be on board the vessel. Bishop Paine nursed him on the voyage to Cairo, and took him ashore and remained with him till he recovered sufficiently to complete his journey to Louisville, and thence to Harrodsburg.

Dr. Cross remained in Kentucky three years. He was then transferred to the Tennessee Conference and stationed at Nashville, where he remained two years. He was next transferred to Charleston, S. C., where he preached four years. At this place the honorary title of Doctor of Divinity was conferred upon him. While at Charleston he wrote several works, and subsequently went to Europe. After his return to America he published an account of his travels. In a short time he was called to a professorship in Spartanburg Female College, and afterward to its presidency.

On the eve of the opening of the war between the States he removed to Gallatin, where he took charge of a Church, and dwelt there until the war commenced. He followed the fortunes of the Confederacy from its beginning to its final collapse. Throughout the war Dr. Cross filled the position of chaplain of the Second Tennessee, and other positions to which he was promoted. As a man of true Christian piety, he was prominent, and for his ability and goodness in the different phases of his work, he was respected, honored, and loved by all who knew him.

Concerning his history since the war the writer knows comparatively nothing.

Official Reports.

CHAPTER X.

Official Report of Colonel D. M. Donnell, Commanding the Sixteenth Regiment Tennessee Volunteers, in the Battle of Chickamauga, September 19 and 20, 1863.

MISSIONARY RIDGE, October 6, 1863.

Captain:—I have the honor to make the following report of the part taken by my regiment, the Sixteenth Tennessee, in the battle of Chickamauga on September 19 and 20:

The line of battle having been formed, we advanced, changing direction slightly to the right, through a corn field and a short distance into the woods beyond, where we found ourselves under a very heavy fire from a battery of the enemy about one hundred and fifty yards in front of the left wing of my regiment. This fire wounded a considerable number of my men, who retired from the field; and at the same time a number of others fell back ten or fifteen paces, to seek protection behind trees. This for a moment induced the belief that the line was giving way, but the men maintained their position, firing as rapidly as they could through the thick undergrowth, which very much obstructed the view of the enemy, for about three hours, when I received an order from Brigadier-general M. J. Wright to retire, which I did. A few moments before I received the order, Strahl's brigade, having relieved Smith's, was in the act of charging the enemy. Having notified Colonel J. H. Anderson, on my left, I com-

COLONEL D. M. DONNELL.

menced moving with Strahl's brigade, but had not advanced more than twenty paces when the order from General Wright, alluded to above, came, and I retired. During this time our loss was sixty-seven wounded.

On the next morning, while lying in line of battle, one man was mortally wounded.*

During this day we changed position several times, and just before night joined in the charge which drove the enemy from his fortifications, thus ending the engagement.

On this occasion the officers and men under my command, with few exceptions, conducted themselves with their usual gallantry. I am particularly indebted to Lieutenant-colonel D. T. Brown, Captain H. H. Dillard, acting major, and Adjutant A. F. Claywell, for the invaluable assistance they gave me in preserving order and inspiring confidence in the minds of the men. Captain Dillard does not belong to my regiment, but is attached to the conscript bureau. Knowing him to be a most excellent officer, and being without a major, I invited him on the evacuation of Chattanooga to act in that capacity. This he has done on the march and in action with marked ability. I cannot speak too highly of his cool gallantry and sound judgment.

I am, captain, yours respectfully,

D. M. DONNELL,
Colonel Sixteenth Tennessee Regiment.

Captain LEON TROUSDALE, Assistant Adjutant-general, Wright's Brigade.

---

* Private William Hodges, Company F.

Report of Captain A. J. Paine, Ordnance Officer of Wright's Brigade.

Number of guns carried into the battle of Chickamauga, and number of rounds of ammunition expended on the field, in Wright's Brigade, Cheatham's Division, Polk's Corps, Army of Tennessee:

REGIMENTS.	No. guns taken into fight.	No. rounds expended per man.	Total No. rounds expended.
Eighth Tennessee	260	$9\frac{1}{4}$	2,400
Sixteenth Tennessee	242	$7\frac{3}{4}$	1,833
Twenty-eighth Tennessee	254	12	3,048
Thirty-eighth Tennessee	264	10	2,640
Fifty-first and Fifty-second Tennessee	232	10	2,320
Total	1,252		12,241

The detail with the ordnance train during the fight were employed chiefly in watching the movements of their respective regiments, so as to know at all times their exact locality, that they might be able to supply them with ammunition at any moment. Their leisure hours were occupied in gathering and transporting to the rear ordnance stores from the battle-field. The brigade carried from the field upward of 1,100 guns, beside a good many accouterments and bayonets. These guns were hauled to the rear for transportation to the railroad.

Very respectfully,   A. J. PAINE,
   Ordnance Officer, Wright's Brigade.
October 18, 1863.

Official Report of Colonel John H. Anderson, Commanding the Eighth Tennessee Regiment Tennessee Volunteers, in Battle of Chickamauga.

CAMPS NEAR CHATTANOOGA, October 3, 1863.

Sir:—I have the honor to make the following report of the part taken by the Eighth Regiment Tennessee Volunteers in the battle of Chickamauga, September 19 and 20:

On the night of the 18th my regiment bivouacked about three and three fourth miles from the battleground, and at daylight on the 19th I was ordered to move forward and cross the Chickamauga River at a ford in the rear of General Walker's division, which was then engaged with the enemy about one and a half miles from the ford. After crossing, we were formed in line of battle in an old field on the bank of the river, in which position we remained an hour and a half, when we were again moved to the front by the right flank, to a position on an eminence about half a mile to the front, when we were again formed into line, in which position we remained but a short time, being annoyed to some extent by one of the enemy's batteries, in position near Lee and Gordon's Mill, about one mile to our left and front. We were then ordered forward to engage the enemy on the left of Major-general Walker's division—who were hotly engaged by the enemy in heavy force—double-quick a distance of about one mile, over a very broken and bushy ground, to the immediate front of the alignment. The correction being made, my command moved upon the enemy, who was posted upon an eminence protected by heavy timber and undergrowth, with two batteries of artillery stationed in commanding positions to enable him to give us a warm reception. I had not advanced far when the enemy opened upon me a heavy fire with artillery and small arms. My men maintained perfect order and moved steadily to the front, to a position

MAJOR H. H. DILLARD,
Sixteenth Tennessee Regiment.

not exceeding two hundred yards from the enemy, when I received an order to halt, and I gave the order to open fire, which order was promptly executed, with, as I suppose, considerable effect upon the enemy, as he commenced giving way in my front. The fire of the enemy at this time was very severe, causing the regiment on my right—the Sixteenth Tennessee, Colonel D. M. Donnell—to retire some distance to the rear, to a position not so much exposed; and a few moments after the Sixteenth retired, the regiment on my left— the Fifty-first Tennessee, Lieutenant-colonel J. G. Hall —retired to the rear, leaving both of my flanks exposed. I immediately dispatched some three different officers to see Brigadier-general Wright for orders, but they did not succeed in seeing him. Having no orders, and believing it my duty to hold my position, if possible, until ordered to the contrary, I maintained and held my position, though subjected to a murderous fire from small arms and artillery, my men standing firmly to their posts and keeping up a continuous fire upon the enemy.

Though with considerable loss in my regiment, I then dispatched an officer to my left to ascertain if there were any of our forces on my left. He returned and reported that there was no support on my left at all, but that the enemy was there in heavy force. There was a force of ours some distance on my right, hotly engaged with the enemy; and seeing no immediate danger from my left, I thought it best to hold my position as long as possible, in order to keep the enemy from turing the left flank of our forces, then engaging them on my right, which I succeeded in doing. I held my position for about two hours, when it was reported that the enemy in heavy force was moving on my left flank, and had opened fire upon me from the left. I then gave the order to retire by the right of companies to the rear, which order was executed slowly and in perfect order, to a position one hundred and fifty yards to the rear, upon an eminence, that I might better observe the movements of the enemy, and keep him from turning my left flank, in which position I was joined by the Sixteenth Tennessee, Colonel Donnell, who moved forward and formed upon my left. In this position I remained a short time, when I observed that the forces on my right were being hotly pressed by the enemy; and still having no order, I moved by the right flank to their assistance, but just before I reached them I received orders from Brigadier-general Wright, through one of his staff officers, to move to the rear about a mile, and join the balance of the brigade and get a supply of ammunition, which order I promptly obeyed.

After being supplied with ammunition, I moved by the flank to the front, with the balance of the brigade, to a position in front of an old field, the opposite of which the enemy was in position. It then being near sundown, we were formed in line of battle and ordered to bivouac for the night. In this position we remained during the night and until about 12 M. of the 20th, when we moved to the extreme right of our lines, and formed a line in support of Major-general Breckinridge's command, who was then engaging the enemy's extreme left, where we remained until about 5 P.M., when we were ordered forward to charge the enemy in his fortifications on an eminence near the Chattanooga road, which order was obeyed with a deafening yell; and we moved forward at a double-quick step, but before we reached them in their position, they abandoned it and fled in great panic and disorder. The firing having ceased, the enemy having fled, and it being then about 7 P.M., we were ordered to bivouac upon the grounds we then occupied, where we remained until the following morning at 9 o'clock, when we were ordered to move on the Chattanooga road about one and a half miles, where we remained until 4 P.M., when we moved forward to our present position.

Although my command had been subjected to a great many hardships and privations — heavy marching through heat and heavy clouds of dust, and the mortification of again being compelled to leave their native State, their homes, and those near and dear to them, to a treacherous, insolent, and unprincipled foe — yet they behaved and fought like true patriots and freemen, who knew their rights and privileges, and were willing to maintain them at all hazards. All honor to our brave dead and wounded, who sleep and have bedewed the battle-ground of Chickamauga with their blood for the cause of freedom and of the South! May the dead live in the memory of every true patriot, and the wounded soon be healed to again join their brothers in arms, and to continue to battle until the last armed foe has been driven from our homes!

I cannot close this report without saying a few words in honor of the brave officers and men of my regiment. They behaved, with but the fewest exceptions, in the most gallant manner, maintaining their position for about two hours under a terrific fire of artillery and small arms, in the very face of a large and overwhelming force of the enemy. Of the field and staff, I would mention Lieutenant-colonel Chris. C. McKinney, Major W. G. Burford, and Adjutant A. J. Murphy, who conducted themselves in the most gallant and soldierly manner, directing and encouraging the men at all times during the action. I have to regret the loss of Adjutant Murphy, who was severely wounded in the arm and shoulder; Captain William D. Bond, severely in the scrotum; Lieutenant N. Flynt, I fear mortally, in the hips; and several valuable officers and men whom it would afford me great pleasure to mention if the length of this report would permit. Accompanying you will please find a report of the casualties of my regiment, all of which are most respectfully submitted.

I am, sir, very respectfully your most obedient servant, JOHN H. ANDERSON,
Colonel Commanding Eighth Regiment Tennessee Volunteers.
Captain LEON TROUSDALE, Assistant Adjutant-general.

Report of Lieutenant-colonel John G. Hall, Fifty-first Tennessee Infantry, Commanding the Fifty-first and Fifty-second Tennessee Regiments, in the Battle of Chickamauga.

IN CAMP NEAR CHATTANOOGA, TENN., October 4, 1863.

Sir:—I respectfully submit the following report as to the action taken by the Fifty-first and Fifty-second Tennessee Regiments, under my command, in the late engagement with the enemy, on September 19 and 20 last:

On the morning of the 19th, in forming the line of battle, I was ordered to take my position and form on the left of the Eighth Tennessee Regiment, Colonel J. H. Anderson commanding. The Twenty-eighth Tennessee Regiment, Colonel S. S. Stanton commanding, formed on my left. I found, on examination, that the Sixteenth Tennessee Regiment, Colonel D. M. Donnell commanding, was formed on the extreme right of the brigade, and that the Thirty-eighth Tennessee Regiment, Colonel J. C. Carter commanding, was formed on the extreme left of the brigade, thus placing me in the center. The line being dressed and the order to load being complied with, the brigade was ordered forward to engage the enemy.

In approaching the enemy's line of battle, I was in doubt whether the battalion of direction was on my right or left. This embarrassed me somewhat in my movements, and when the brigade went into the action, I discovered that in executing an oblique movement to the left, I had gone too far in that direction; that my left was much nearer to Colonel Stanton's right than my right was to Colonel Anderson's left; Colonel Anderson also had gained some ground on me by a movement by the right flank, which I did not discover at the time of its being executed, under the circumstances above stated.

Learning that the general commanding the brigade was on my left, I determined to direct my movements with those of Colonels Carter and Stanton. The position which I held during the engagement was an open glade, almost entirely level, with the exception of a small mound on my extreme left, with but few trees, and but little undergrowth. I saw from the range of the enemy's balls, and from the surroundings of the position which I occupied, that I must necessarily suffer severely in any thing like a prolonged engagement. I determined, however, to occupy the position and to keep the regiments as well prepared as could be done under the circumstances for an advance. I remained in this position about one hour. The fire of the enemy was well directed. We carried into the action 232 muskets. Thirteen men were killed dead on the field, and 132 were wounded—eight mortally.

The officers and men behaved well, loading and firing with great coolness about twenty rounds to the man.

When the order to fall back was being complied with, color-bearer W. M. Bland, who distinguished himself at Murfreesboro, was shot through the head and killed. The colors were immediately seized by Sergeant Troborough, but almost simultaneously with his receiving them, he received a wound from one of the enemy's shots, which caused him to relinquish the colors to private Rivers, who was also wounded and assisted from the field and the colors left.

The regiment having been supplied with ammunition, remained idle until about 4 o'clock in the evening, when we were again ordered in line; but our brigade taking no further part in the engagement, we were ordered some distance to the rear, where we bivouacked for the night.

On the morning of the 20th we were again ordered in line, and gradually moved round to the right, until about 4 o'clock in the evening, when the brigade was formed on the right of Brigadier-general Maney's line. We were still later ordered forward, but did not engage the enemy. Met with no casualties. Encamped for the night on the battle-field, the enemy having been routed and driven off.

Respectfully submitted, JOHN G. HALL,
Lieutenant-colonel Commanding Fifty-first and Fifty-second Tennessee Regiments.

Captain LEON TROUSDALE, Assistant Adjutant-general.

Official Report of Colonel John C. Carter, commanding Thirty-eighth Regiment Tennessee Volunteers, in the Battle of Chickamauga, Sept. 19 and 20, 1863.

IN CAMP NEAR CHATTANOOGA, TENN., Oct. 6, 1863.

Captain:—I have the honor to make the following report in regard to the part taken by my regiment, of Brigadier-general Wright's brigade, in the late battle of Chickamauga, fought on September 19 and 20 last. The brigade was formed in line of battle about 12 M. of Saturday the 19th ultimo. My regiment was on the left of the brigade, Captain W. W. Carnes's battery of light artillery was on the left of my regiment. The brigade was ordered to advance as soon as the line of battle was formed. For a short time I thought that Major-general Walker's division was in our front, and that Brigadier-general Maney's brigade was on my left. I, however, soon discovered that no Confederate troops were on the left, and that the enemy alone in heavy force was in our front. When I was about one hundred and fifty yards from the enemy's line of battle I was ordered by Captain E. F. Lee, assistant inspector-general to Brigadier-general Wright, commanding brigade, to halt my regiment, and was informed at the same time that the command, "Commence firing," had been given. I immediately complied with these orders. My regiment fought for about three hours under a very heavy fire, advancing a little during the time. I cannot say definitely what loss I inflicted upon the enemy. For my own loss I respectfully refer to a report of the killed and wounded already forwarded.

About 3:30 P.M. of the same day I received an order from Mr. E. C. Smith, volunteer aid-de-camp to Brigadier-general Wright, commanding brigade, to fall back. As this order reached me last, my regiment being on the left and the order coming from the right, I believe that the other regiments retired a little before mine did. I do not assert this as a fact, as I could not observe the regiments on the right of the brigade. As soon as I discovered that there were no Confederate troops on my left I immediately requested First Lieutenant L. G. Marshall, of Carnes's battery of light artillery, to turn his guns to the left, as I felt sure the enemy would flank us; that we—the infantry—would attend to the enemy in front.

Almost immediately afterward we were apprised of the fact that the enemy had flanked us, by his fire and by seeing his flanking line.

On Sunday, the 20th ultimo, my regiment, together with the brigade, was ordered to charge the enemy. We complied with the order, but the enemy retreated before we reached him. I must be permitted to speak of the courage and efficiency of the officers and men under my command. Lieutenant-colonel A. D. Gwynne, Major H. M. Cotter, Adjutant R. L. Caruthers, Captain F. Pugh, H. M. Neely, M. N. Nevill, and J. C. Millers, and Lieutenant J. W. Chilcutt, R. B. Koen, and R. Field deserve especial mention. I regret that necessity compelled us to move so rapidly before the line of battle was formed. Our sorrow for the fallen is softened by the fact that our banners waved over the ground upon which they lay, and that shouts of triumph rang upon their ears and lit in death their smiles of hope. We return thanks to God for the victory won. I am, very respectfully,

JOHN C. CARTER, *Colonel Commanding.*
Captain LEON TROUSDALE, Assistant Adjutant-general.

Official Report of Colonel S. S. Stanton, Twenty-eighth Regiment Tennessee Volunteers.

HEAD-QUARTERS TWENTY-EIGHTH TENNESSEE REGIMENT, October 7, 1863.

Sir:—I have the honor to make the following report of the part taken by the Twenty-eighth Tennessee Regiment in the late battle of Chickamauga. The Sixteenth, Eighth, and Fifty-first Tennessee Regiments being formed on my right, and the Thirty-eighth Tennessee Regiment on my left, mine was immediately on the left of the center regiment of the brigade.

Having crossed Chickamauga Creek on Saturday morning, September 19, we were maneuvered furiously for two or three hours, and finally placed in order of battle. Early after noon the entire brigade was ordered forward, with instruction from Brigadier-general Wright that each regiment would cover its front with skirmishers, to be instructed by their respective colonels, to advance with great caution, lest they should fire on a line of friends who, he had been informed, were on our front, and that ours was a supporting line.

Having thrown forward skirmishers, as above ordered, we moved forward some four or five hundred yards rapidly, through a thick woods, some portion of which was densely lined with undergrowth, when, somewhat to our astonishment, instead of friends, who were supposed to be on our front, we found ourselves suddenly in contact with the enemy, not more than one hundred yards distant, who had already commenced fire upon us as we came upon them concealed behind breastworks. Our line, in moving up to this point, had been brought most of the way in double-quick time, therefore the skirmishers had not kept far in advance of the line. The skirmishers were not, therefore, blamable for this sudden contact with the enemy, for the firing came upon the line about the same time that it did upon the skirmishers; hence the enemy got the first fire upon us. But nothing daunted, my brave boys fired promptly at the command, and moved forward a few paces, when they were ordered to fire and load lying down. This order was executed for more than an hour in splendid style, when from an overpowering fire, both of infantry and artillery, from the enemy, who were securely intrenched behind said breastworks immediately on our front, my line was for a moment driven back about fifty yards. It was immediately rallied again under the unceasing fire of the enemy, and much to the credit of my officers and men they moved firmly forward again, and in a moment retook position even in advance of the ground they first held. Here they fought with desperation and unyielding determination, returning volley for volley until from an overwhelming cross-fire from the left, and receiving at this time information that the enemy were flanking our left, and being ordered to move by the left flank to meet said flank movement, my command was accordingly brought to their feet and put in motion by the left flank. By this last movement the men were more fully exposed to the deadly fire of the enemy, and we were ordered to retire; and we did then retire about one hundred and fifty yards. Here they were reformed and were again ready to face the enemy in further combat, when, on the arrival of supporting columns, we were ordered by the right of battalion to the rear. Having replenished our cartridge-boxes and canteens with ammunition and water, we were formed on the right of the position. Nothing worthy of notice occurred after this until late Sunday evening, when we participated in the last charge, which resulted in driving the enemy from his main stronghold. In this we had three more men wounded.

The casualties of this regiment in the entire engagement sums up as follows: killed outright, nine—six more died soon after being moved to the rear; wounded, seventy; making the aggregate loss eighty-five. None are reported missing. We went into the engagement with three hundred and eight men, including field and staff, infirmary corps, provost guard, etc.

Much is due my associate field officers, Lieutenant-colonel D. C. Crook, Major W. G. Smith, and Adjutant W. B. Whitefield for the energy and courage displayed on their part in aiding me to rally and stimulate the men to action, while the sound of musketry, cannon, and shell would have rendered it impossible for one officer to have been heard, or the command extended along the whole line but for this gallant co-operation on their part.

The subordinate officers and men throughout the entire engagement behaved nobly, and showed themselves worthy veterans of the gallant State from which they came, and which they were struggling to regain.

All of which is respectfully submitted.

S. S. STANTON,
Colonel Twenty-eighth Tennessee Regiment.

Captain LEON TROUSDALE, Assistant Adjutant-general.

Inclosure.

ON THE FRONT NEAR CHATTANOOGA, October 6, 1863.

Brigadier-general Wright:—Having learned that Colonel S. S. Stanton has been called on for a report of the part taken by the Twenty-eighth Tennessee Regiment in the action of September 19, upon the banks of the Chickamauga, and believing that he, through modesty, will omit an act of the most daring gallantry on his part, which contributes not only to his own fame, but adds luster to the conduct of the regiment, we beg leave to mention the same. After the terrible onslaught made upon the enemy by your brigade, the Twenty-eighth Regiment, occupying the left center of the same, slightly wavered as if being pressed back by the weight of the immense volume of lead that was poured against it. Our colonel, seeing this, rushed to the front of the line on horseback, seized the standard of the colors, and bearing them to the front, shouted for his men to follow, which they did in the most gallant manner, regaining the ground they had lost. While thus bearing the colors they were riddled with balls, being pierced not less than thirty times. We respectfully ask that this incident be incorporated in and made a part of said report.

Yours respectfully,
D. C. CROOK,
Lieutenant-colonel.
W. G. SMITH,
Major.
W. B. WHITEFIELD,
Adjutant.
W. F. M. BEATTY, R. ROBERSON,
Captain Company H.
J. G. MAXWELL,
First Lieutenant Company K.
W. S. WOODS,
Captain Company G.
O. H. ANDERSON,
First Lieutenant Commanding Company D.

J. R. DONALDSON,
Captain Company A.
G. W. COOK,
Lieutenant Commanding Company F.
JOHN B. HOLMAN,
Captain Company B.
W. H. MITCHELL,
First Lieutenant Commanding Company E.
S. S. DEARMAN,
Lieutenant Commanding Company I.
Z. H. BRYANT,
Lieutenant Company C.

Official Report of Brigadier-general Marcus J. Wright, of Battle of Chickamauga, September 19 and 20, 1863.

HEAD-QUARTERS WRIGHT'S BRIGADE, CHEATHAM'S DIVISION, POLK'S CORPS, ARMY OF TENNESSEE, IN THE FIELD, October 9, 1863.

Major:—I have the honor to make the following report of the operations of my brigade in the battle of Chickamauga on the 19th and 20th ultimo:

On Saturday, 19th ult., at 3:30 A.M., I was ordered by Major-general Cheatham to advance and cross the Chickamauga at a ford known as Byron's Ford, following immediately after Brigadier-general Preston Smith's brigade, and followed by Brigadier-general George Maney's brigade. Immediately after we crossed the ford, heavy firing commenced in our front, which was ascertained to be an engagement between the reserve division of Major-general Walker and the enemy, who was in heavy forces, and was pressing Walker hotly with his largely-superior numbers. My brigade, after crossing, was formed in line of battle in a field in the rear of Brigadier-general Smith. I was ordered to follow immediately upon the rear of Smith when he moved. In an hour Smith moved in the direction of the battle-field, and we followed closely in his rear. After moving into a wood, in a direction inclining down the Chickamauga, another halt was made of half an hour, when I received an order from General Cheatham to forward in a direction nearly at right angles to the road along which we were posted, with that brave and competent officer, General Preston Smith, still on my right. Maney being in my rear in the line of march, I supposed that he would be ordered up to the left, and indeed, in the act of executing the forward movement in the line of battle, I was informed by General Smith that we were a supporting force to Major-general Walker, who was supposed to be in our front. My brigade is composed of the following regiments, which moved in line from right to left in the order named: Sixteenth Tennessee, Colonel D. M. Donnell commanding; Eighth Tennessee, Colonel John H. Anderson commanding; Fifty-first and Fifty-second Tennessee Regiments, Lieutenant-colonel John G. Hall commanding; Twenty-eighth Tennessee, Colonel S. S. Stanton commanding; Thirty-eighth Tennessee, and Murray's Battalion, Colonel John C. Carter commanding; with the battery of light artillery, commanded by Captain William W. Carnes. The men moved up in splendid style, obeying all orders with the alacrity and precision which is their habit on parade. With the information I had received, believing Major-general Walker in our front, I had directed each regiment to throw out skirmishers and to guard against the too frequent and often criminal folly of pouring a fire into the rear of our own comrades in arms when engaged against a foe in front. This order I immediately countermanded when it became quite evident that a most galling fire had been opened by the enemy's batteries and infantry upon my right flank and a portion of the center. This fire continued for some minutes before the left flank was engaged, and was the result of my line of battle being advanced obliquely toward the right, instead of being parallel to the enemy's line. It was certainly due also somewhat to the fact that the Sixteenth Tennessee and the Eighth Tennessee Regiments extending their line into a corn field in open view of the enemy, whose position was concealed by timber and undergrowth, were compelled to advance into the wood in front, thus finding a better and more secure position, and some cover for their men from the murderous fire which they were gallantly sustaining. The center and left, however, soon became earnestly engaged. Having no eligible position for artillery near the center, I was compelled to post Carnes's battery (Steuben artillery) on the left of the Thirty-eighth Tennessee, being the extreme left of my position—supposing, too, at that time, that I would be supported on the left by the brigades both of Brigadier-general Maney and Brigadier-general Strahl. My position was near the foot of a declivity, gently rising toward the left, and presenting on that flank the highest ground on our lines, and therefore the best position for artillery, while that of the enemy was on an eminence rising from the drain or low ground just in our front, many feet above ours, and protected by works probably thrown up the previous night. Immediately after the enemy's fire was opened, I dispatched the order to commence firing to each of the commanding officers of regiments, which was executed promptly, and with coolness and precision. I have reason to believe that the effect of our firing upon the enemy was terrific from the report of a wounded officer who fell into the hands of the enemy and subsequently escaped, and from a careful survey of the battle-ground by some of the men after the action. The enemy opened upon us a cross fire of two batteries and a concentrated shower of musket shot from a greatly superior force, their line extending the full length of a brigade beyond my unsupported left. Our men met the terrible fire which was hurled upon them with constancy, coolness, and undaunted courage, bearing the shock like veterans, and not perceptibly wavering beneath its severity, and returning shot for shot as far as their inferiority of numbers would allow.

After sustaining this fire for three and a half hours— from 12 M. to 3: 30 P.M.—seeing that Brigadier-general Smith, immediately on my right, had withdrawn from the field, and learning from some of my officers that their ammunition was nearly exhausted, I determined to order the brigade to retire. Before, however, I could give orders to execute this movement, a courier informed me that the enemy was flanking my position, which, upon moving in that direction, I distinctly discovered, seeing his line moving through the ravine and undergrowth upon the left flank. I then dispatched orders to the colonels and commander of the battery to withdraw to a hill about a quarter of a mile in the rear. Discovering at this opportune moment a supporting brigade approaching in line of battle, and not being able to move rapidly enough to communicate with General Clayton in consequence of my being dismounted, I requested the colonel commanding the leading regiment to move to my left and protect the men in retiring, which he did promptly and efficiently. At the same time I informed him that the enemy was flanking our position. Each of the regiments were withdrawn slowly and in good order, although all the horses of the battery except three were killed, and one half of the company shot down, either killed or wounded, thus rendering the battery useless to check the advance of the enemy's flanking force. Captain Carnes, First Lieutenant L. G. Marshall, and Second Lieutenant James M. Cockrill, of the artillery, remained with the battery until they received orders to retire, narrowly escaping capture, and gallantly standing at their posts until the last moment. Second Lieutenant A. Van Vleck gallantly died at his post. After retiring from the field, I at once dispatched a staff officer to Major-general Cheatham advising him of the position of the brigade, and informing him of the fact that our ammunition was nearly exhausted, which was promptly supplied.

After 5 P.M. the brigade was again ordered to take position about eight hundred yards to the right of the ground on which we had fought the enemy. Major-general Cleburne's division and Smith's brigade, of Major-general Cheatham's division, at about 6:30 P.M., on our immediate right, made a most gallant and successful movement upon the enemy's position, but my brigade was not ordered to participate in the glorious charge which cost the lives of many brave patriots, and among them the heroic General Preston Smith.

Having bivouacked at this position on Saturday night, on Sunday morning a line of battle was again formed, and held steadily for three hours under a most harassing fire from the enemy's batteries. One man of the Sixteenth Tennessee was severely wounded by a round shot.

About 1 P.M. I was ordered to move the brigade around to the right of our position, following Maney in moving by the right flank. About 6 P.M., Maney being on the left, I was ordered to follow his movements in line of battle. Major-general Walker's division and Brigadier-general Jackson's brigade, of Cheatham's division, were already engaged fiercely in assaulting a fortified position of the enemy, at which a very large force of his artillery had been concentrated. A furious contest was raging with wild and terrible carnage. Though the gallant troops of Walker and Jackson held their position with unsurpassed stubbornness and heroism, yet the enemy, encouraged by the strength, natural and artificial, of his position, and his concentrated forces, was making a most stubborn fight. At this critical moment the two brigades—General Maney's and my own—were precipitated with a deafening hurrah and rapid shock to support our gallant comrades who were contending against unequal odds. The men were in the highest spirits, and moved forward with an animation that I have never seen surpassed. At this time the scene was one of the most animated and exciting that can be imagined. The whole issue of the combat seemed suspended upon a moment's work. The shouts of our gallant patriots presaged success, and every eye was lighted with victory. It came at that propitious moment. The enemy, already daunted by the fierce ordeal through which they had passed from the guns of Walker and Jackson, could no longer bear the trials when the cheers of our reinforced battalions were wafted to them on the evening breeze. They broke in hopeless confusion and rout, precipitately fled before our pursuing columns, leaving their dead and wounded behind them and several pieces of their artillery. Although my brigade did not reach the position in time to fire but a very few guns from the Thirty-eighth Tennessee, yet it is a source of heartfelt satisfaction that the cheers of the men and their impetuous charge assisted in striking a terror into the heart of the foe and in hastening his inglorious flight. In this engagement and that of Saturday the brigade captured seventy-one prisoners, including a captain and two lieutenants. The loss in the brigade was eighty-nine killed on the field, eighty-three missing, most of whom are known to be, and others are supposed to be, in the hands of the enemy, and four hundred wounded. Among the killed I regret to mention Captain J. M. Parks, of the Sixteenth Tennessee; Lieutenant Hainey, of Murray's battalion, attached to the Thirty-eighth Tennessee; Lieutenant W. T. Wade, and color-bearer Bland, of the Fifty-first and Fifty-second Tennessee Regiments; Captain S. B. Whaley, and Lieutenant Craig, of the Twenty-eighth Tennessee; and Lieutenant Van Vleck, of Carnes's battery. Among the wounded were Colonels John H. Anderson and D. M. Donnell; Lieutenant-colonel John G. Hall, and Major Thomas G. Randle; Captains D. C. Puryear, James J. Cullom, and W. D. Bonds; and Lieutenant Cunningham, J. W. Leonard, N. Flynt, and ——— Shaw, of the Eighth Tennessee; Lieutenants Potter, J. F. Owen, James Fisher, and James Worthington, of the Sixteenth Tennessee; Captain W. H. McDonald, Lieutenant H. M. Apple, W. L. Danley, and D. C. Taylor, of the Twenty-eighth Tennessee; Adjutant R. L. Caruthers, Lieutenant J. M. Banks, and W. D. Ridout, of the Thirty-eighth Tennessee; and Captain R. M. Burton, Lieutenants R. P. Billings, W. B. Chester, W. H. White, E. R. Hainey, B. M. Tilman, and W. T. Wade, of the Fifty-first and Fifty-second Tennessee Regiments. All the field officers of the brigade and the officers of the battery acted with such distinguished gallantry that I feel it would be invidious to make a distinction. Company officers and men, with very inconsiderable exceptions that have come to my knowledge, bore themselves with a gallantry and steadiness becoming patriots contending for freedom and all that honorable men hold dear.

I am indebted for valuable assistance during the engagement to my staff officers, Captain Leon Trousdale, assistant adjutant-general; Captain Edward F. Lee, assistant inspector-general; my aid-de-camps, Lieutenant E. T. Harris, and Lieutenant Sidney Womack, and Mr. Charles T. Smith. They each discharged their duties with fidelity and zeal. One of my couriers, Mr. William S. Hill, won the commendations of all, and my warm thanks for his gallantry and alacrity in the discharge of his perilous duties. Brigadier-general W. C. Whitthorne, adjutant-general of Tennessee, volunteered to act as aid-de-camp on the first day's march from Chattanooga, and discharged the various duties that I assigned to him with a promptness, courage, and ability which merited and received my warmest thanks. On the field General Whitthorne conducted himself with conspicuous gallantry.

The infirmary corps discharged their duties with such fearlessness and fidelity as to attract my special observation.

The provost guards also, under their worthy and gallant provost marshal, Lieutenant W. L. Richardson, fully fulfilled the standard of their duties. They lost one killed and two wounded in the engagement of Saturday. I unite with all true patriots of our country in returning thanks to Almighty God, without whose assistance our strength is weakness, for the substantial victory with which he has crowned our efforts.

I herewith transmit the reports of the regimental commanders of the brigade, to which your special attention is respectfully invoked. I regret I cannot accompany them with the report of Captain Carnes, commanding battery, whose absence on business connected with his battery necessarily delays its preparation.

I have the honor to be, Major, very respectfully, your obedient servant, MARCUS J. WRIGHT,
Brigadier-general.

Major JAMES D. PORTER, Assistant Adjutant-general, Cheatham's Division.

Report of Captain Ben Randals, Commanding Sixteenth Regiment Tennessee Volunteers.

HEAD-QUARTERS SIXTEENTH TENNESSEE REGIMENT,
April 9, 1864.

Captain LEON TROUSDALE, A. A. G., Wright's Brigade:

Captain:—I have the honor to make the following report of the part taken by the Sixteenth Tennessee Regiment in the battle of Missionary Ridge, November 24 and 25, 1863:

On the evening of the 24th, the regiment, with the other regiments of the brigade, was marched down the east side of the Chickamauga, Colonel D. M. Donnell commanding. When near the mouth of the river we were fired upon by infantry and artillery—surprised, as none were anticipating an enemy. The same eagerness was manifested by the men to engage the enemy that has ever characterized the men of this regiment. There were but few shots exchanged. The regiment was ordered to fall back under cover of a hill. There was no disorder or confusion among the men. All acted well the part of good soldiers. They were cool, calm, and deliberate.

We were then withdrawn to the bridge across the Chickamauga, with loss of one killed and eight wounded. Here we remained on our arms during the remainder of the engagement.

I am, Captain, very respectfully,

BEN RANDALS,
Captain Commanding Sixteenth Tennessee Regiment.

P. S.—Captain, I have omitted the different changes of position during this time, thinking it unimportant.

Truly, B. R.

Report of Killed and Wounded of the Sixteenth Regiment Tennessee Volunteers, in the Battle of Missionary Ridge, November 24, 1863.

Private G. G. Taylor, Company A, wounded slightly; private Peter Cantrell, Company A, wounded slightly; private Dallas Hicks, Company A, wounded slightly; private T. R. Hooper, Company A, severely wounded in arm; Lieutenant W. C. Womack, Company E, severely wounded in thigh; private Andrew Hawkins, Company E, severely wounded in breast; Sergeant J. M. West, Company F, slightly wounded; private L. Clark, Company D, killed; private E. M. Irwin, Company K, severely wounded in arm.

BEN RANDALS,
Captain Commanding Sixteenth Tennessee Regiment.

A. F. CLAYWELL, Adjutant.

Official Report of Brigadier-general Marcus J. Wright, of the part taken by Wright's Brigade, Cheatham's Division, Polk's Corps, Army of Tennessee, in the Battle of Missionary Ridge, November 24 and 25, 1863.

HEAD-QUARTERS POST, ATLANTA, GA., May 7, 1864.

Colonel JOHN B. SALE, Military Secretary:

Colonel:—Although a report of the operations of my command near Missionary Ridge on the 24th and 25th of November, 1863, has not been officially required of me, yet I have the honor to request that the following report be accepted by the general commanding the Army of Tennessee at that time, as a record of the part taken by my brigade in the battle near Missionary Ridge:

Being under the immediate orders of the general commanding on that occasion, I address this communication to you.

Having been in command of the post at Charleston, Tenn., for some weeks, I was ordered by telegram from Colonel Brent, A. A. G., on the evening of the 23d of November, to move with all expedition by rail to Chickamauga Station *via* Dalton, Ga., which I executed on the first train of cars I could command—leaving Charleston about 4 o'clock on the morning of the 24th and arriving at Chickamauga Station about 8:30 in the morning on the same day. I was also ordered to leave three hundred men at Charleston. In conformity with which, I ordered the Thirty-eighth Tennessee Regiment, commanded by Colonel John C. Carter, and my provost guard, under command of

Lieutenant Richardson, to remain, making an effective force of about three hundred.

Colonel Carter assumed command of the post, and maintained his position under the severest tests to which a soldier can be subjected with the highest constancy, gallantry, and firmness, until pressed by a column of the enemy under General Sherman, numbering fifteen or sixteen thousand, when he reluctantly retreated toward Knoxville, and successfully joined Lieutenant-general Longstreet in East Tennessee, after having destroyed the bridges at Charleston and Loudon behind him. The zeal, ability, and courage with which he conducted his isolated command out of the difficulties which environed him cannot be too highly commended. I refer you to his report, herewith submitted, for a full and accurate statement of his operations.

On the arrival of the other portion of my command, numbering four small regiments, at Chickamauga Station, I was met with an order from Colonel Brent to proceed at once to the mouth of the Chickamauga, to resist any attempt the enemy might make at crossing the river at that point, leaving a regiment to guard the railroad bridge at Shallow Ford. In consequence of the weakness of my command, after mature consideration, the regiment I had posted at Shallow Ford was ordered to withdraw and follow on with the brigade, when the command moved in the direction of the mouth of the Chickamauga. Brigadier-general Polk's brigade being in position at the railroad bridge, General Polk dispatched a force to the Shallow Ford to take the place of the regiment withdrawn by me. I moved up in the direction indicated until I came into a road running parallel and adjacent to the Chickamauga, on the margin of open fields, which gently sloped up toward a line of precipitous hills on the route. It was a very exposed position, but the road passing through this space was the only one practicable for artillery in the direction of the mouth of the creek.

Captain R. F. Kolb, with his battery, had reported to me at the railroad bridge for duty, and was with my command. While marching over this ground, by the right flank, the Eighth Tennessee Regiment, Colonel John H. Anderson commanding, on the right; the Sixteenth Tennessee Regiment, Colonel D. M. Donnell commanding, following; and the Twenty-eighth Tennessee Regiment, Colonel S. S. Stanton commanding, in the rear, the whole line was suddenly assailed with a heavy and galling fire from the opposite bank of the creek, at a distance of not exceeding one hundred yards. The enemy's sharp-shooters were concealed in the undergrowth along the bank and waited, before opening their fire, until the entire length of the line could be commanded by their fire. I immediately ordered the troops to form, advance to the margin of the creek, and fire. This they did promptly and gallantly, returning the fire upon the foe with marked effect, nearly silencing their guns and driving them behind the railroad embankment, where they sheltered themselves and kept up a brisk but desultory fire for several minutes. In the meantime, Kolb, to get his battery in position on a commanding point to the left of my center, which he did promptly, fired a few rounds at the enemy from this point; but ascertaining that a better position might be had on the extreme left, I ordered him to that point, where he proceeded and kept up a brisk artillery duel with the enemy's battery, composed of two three-inch rifled-guns. Captain Kolb's guns were served with the greatest coolness and signal gallantry, for which he is entitled to my thanks and the commendation of the country. His report is herewith filed.

Seeing from the position of the grounds, the obstructions presented by the intervening stream, the overwhelming force of the enemy, and his being sheltered by a railroad embankment; and being advised by Colonel Grigsby, commanding the cavalry, that a large force of the enemy's cavalry had already succeeded in crossing the river above the mouth of the Chickamauga, and moved out in the direction of Tyner's Station, I deemed it best to withdraw my command through the hills to the rear, by the right of companies, which was done in admirable order, and with but little damage from the enemy's artillery fire; Captain Kolb having opened fire upon him from an eligible position, to which he had withdrawn through the woods on a route for his battery which I had reconnoitered to prevent the necessity, if possible, of his battery being exposed to the enemy's fire, in endeavoring to return by the road on which we had approached.

In this action I lost from my command one killed and eleven wounded. My regimental commanders behaved with their usual gallantry, coolness, and skill. My troops displayed the highest qualities of veterans— intrepidity and self-possession — when suddenly attacked by an unseen foe. The horses of my staff and field officers not having arrived from the train, I was necessarily compelled to ride up and down the lines and convey the orders to the different commanding officers in person. My staff rendered me all the assistance that was practicable under the circumstances.

I retired about half a mile into the hills and selected

a high ridge, where I placed my command in position, directing Colonel Grigsby to occupy the right flank with his cavalry, while the left was protected by a precipitous bluff extending to the creek. About 9 o'clock P.M., I received an order from Colonel Brent to move with the command to Chickamauga Station, which I reached in about one hour and a half. Finding three batteries there, I ordered them to be disposed for the defense of the station, and selected a position for my brigade to defeat an apprehended cavalry raid. The men were ordered to rest in their position.

At two o'clock on the morning of the 25th I received an order to return to the railroad bridge. and in the act of executing it, I was taken ill with a severe chill, which was brought on by exposure during the preceding day. I immediately directed Colonel John H. Anderson, senior colonel present, to take command of the brigade and carry out the order, which he promptly did. You are respectfully referred to his report for an account of the subsequent operations of the brigade.

It affords me high satisfaction to express my acknowledgement to Colonel Grigsby, commanding cavalry, and Captain Kolb, commanding battery, who were not of my permanent command, for the valuable assistance rendered my command and the intelligent counsel which they rendered me. Colonel Grigsby's knowledge of the ground and his careful and thoughtful interest contributed materially to the successful maneuverings by which my command was saved from a heavy and useless waste of life. My officers and men of all grades deserve my acknowledgements for their good conduct and admirable coolness, by which we succeeded in developing a very important position of the enemy, and checking any contemplated movement upon the right flank of the army, by which the enemy might have succeeded in gaining our rear, and thus have rendered our reverses most disastrous.

I regret to report that the cavalry of the enemy, commanded by Colonel Long, which crossed near the mouth of the Chickamauga, succeeded in capturing my brigade train, which was *en route* from Charleston to Chickamauga. My brigade quartermaster, learning that a large cavalry force was approaching, had turned his train down the Ringgold road, when the enemy pursued and captured it. The small detail guarding were unable to make any resistance to so overwhelming a force. Major Elean, assistant quartermaster, and several of the men with him, escaped capture. This proved a severe loss to my officers and men, whose personal baggage was in the train, as well as a heavy loss to the government.

All of my staff discharged their duties promptly and with the highest zeal and intelligence, including Captain Leon Trousdale, assistant adjutant-general; Captain E. F. Lee, assistant adjutant-general; First Lieutenant E. F. Harris, assistant aid-de-camp; and Surgeon H. S. Jones, brigade surgeon.

Surgeon Jones was at the head of the column when the enemy's fire opened, and rendered me material assistance in transmitting my orders. His field hospital was established with promptitude under unusual difficulties.

I respectfully refer you to the reports of subordinate commanders for a more minute statement of the operations of their commands.

I am, Colonel, respectfully your obedient servant,
MARCUS J. WRIGHT,
Brigadier-general Commanding.

Forrest's Cavalry.

CHAPTER XI.

This portion of the Confederate Army is worthy of more than a passing notice. It is to be regretted, however, that our limited space forbids a fuller detail of its operations and the many hard-fought battles in which it was engaged. The history of modern or ancient warfare has never recorded more gallant service, or the achievement of more consummate victories in the face of apparently impassable obstructions. Like Stonewall Jackson, if any man could accomplish impossibilities, it was General Forrest. He seemed to laugh at obstacles, and look with contempt upon what would seem to others practically impossible. His career in the four years' war between the States was as romantic as it was brilliant. Its record is full of gallant and glowing achievements, and though the pen of the historian has faithfully portrayed many of his daring exploits, the true merits of this gallant hero have never been fully given.

General Nathan Bedford Forrest was born near Chapel Hill, in what was then Bedford county, Tennessee, July 13, 1831. The place is now a part of Marshall county, on the waters of Duck River. His early life was mixed with hardships and adversity, to some extent occasioned by the death of his father and other members of the family in succession, leaving the family affairs in an embarrassed condition financially, by which young Forrest was thrown upon his own resources early in life, with a limited education. He grew up inured to the hardships of pioneer life, and his manhood developed that determined firmness and unrelaxing energy that characterized his after-life, and rendered his career as a soldier so remarkably famous.

General Forrest was in many respects the counterpart of Stonewall Jackson. He was possessed to a remarkable degree of that disposition that naturally inspired courage and confidence. As a disciplinarian, he was stern, rigid, and exacting, though kind, humane, and generous. As an officer, he was brave and fearless. He appeared perfectly insensible of danger, and never called upon his men to do a thing that he was not willing to do himself. He *led* his men in action, and expected of every soldier the full measure of his capacity to render efficient service, and nothing short of this would render satisfaction. By discipline and association, he infused his own spirit into his command, and every soldier under him soon learned that their legitimate business was TO FIGHT, and to render every blow effective upon the enemy.

General Forrest was of a sober and grave temperament, and always seemed to be in a very deep study. He was to some extent absent minded when off the field, and seldom, if ever, indulged in jest. His whole self appeared to be absorbed in the work he had in hand, in maturing plans of operation, and putting them into execution. As a commander, he was not only busy, but untiring and persistent in the execution of his plans, which were always well matured and successfully carried out.

At the breaking out of the war between the States, General Forrest was a resident of Memphis, where he had served as alderman for several years. He was possessed of a large fortune in landed estates and negroes, as well as stocks and securities. As the war-cloud lowered, Forrest made such disposal of his affairs as was practicable, and entered the Confederate service in June, 1861. At this time a company of "mounted riflemen" were forming at Memphis under Dr. Josiah White. Forrest entered this company as a private, June 14, 1861. This company became a part of the garrison at Randolph, Tenn. In July, Governor Harris called Forrest to Memphis, where he was urged to raise a regiment of cavalry for the Confederate service. General Polk also urged the measure, and Forrest was, accordingly, commissioned a colonel, with authority in accordance with the governor's request.

Colonel Forrest enlisted his men rapidly, and proceeded to Kentucky for the purpose of securing arms and accouterments as well as recruits. In both he was successful. The brilliant career of "FORREST'S CAVALRY" here had its origin. Armed and equipped, the regiment operated upon the Mississippi river during the first year of the war, in which several engagements took place with the Federal gun-boats.

Forrest's Cavalry was first conspicuously known in the affair with the enemy at Murfreesboro in July, 1862. Colonel Forrest had started from Chattanooga on the 6th, with about one thousand men, for the purpose of reconnoitering the position of the enemy about Nashville. As he passed McMinnville, he received reliable information of the situation between that point and Nashville; and learning that a Federal garrison was at Murfreesboro, he resolved to take the place and capture the garrison. He had increased his command to thirteen hundred men by a junction with Colonel Morrison. With this force he left McMinnville in the afternoon of July 12, 1862, and arrived at Woodbury about midnight. The Federals had just been to Woodbury, and had arrested and taken away many of the people to Murfreesboro. The people of Woodbury were in great excitement. The ladies of the place were much affected at the loss of kinsmen, and when Colonel Forrest heard their statement, he assured them in response that they might confidently look for a restoration of their kinsmen by the following sunset, and assured the ladies of his ability to perform the promise.

By five o'clock on the following morning Colonel Wharton captured the pickets on the outskirts of Murfreesboro, and the plan of attack was arranged. The Federals were surprised and captured after some skirmishing. In this affair Colonel Duffield, the Federal commander, was wounded. The Confederate citizens were released and returned to their homes. Forrest was made a brigadier-general soon after this affair with the enemy at Murfreesboro. Continuing his operations in Middle Tennessee, he destroyed the railroad bridges from Tullahoma to McMinnville. The Federals had placed a new garrison at Murfreesboro so strong that Forrest did not attempt the place a second time, but proceeded to the mountains near Altamont, where he rested his command for a while. We next hear of him in various encounters with the enemy in West Tennessee and North Mississippi. Forrest's cavalry seemed to be ubiquitous. The Federals never knew when he would appear upon their flanks or in their rear. In the Kentucky campaign this cavalry did valuable service. On the march from Munfordville, this cavalry harassed the flanks of Buell's army and destroyed the bridges of the Louisville and Nashville Railroad from Munfordville to Nolin. This command picketed the roads from Bardstown to Louisville, Frankfort, and other points. On the eve of the battle of Perryville (September 26), General Forrest was ordered by General Bragg to repair with his command immediately to Murfreesboro, Tenn. The object of this move was to gather recruits, and General Bragg informed General Forrest that such recruits as he might raise were to be under his immediate command.

On September 28, Forrest left Bardstown with his command for Murfreesboro, a distance of one hundred and sixty-five miles. This journey was performed within a period of five days. Forrest assembled his cavalry at Murfreesboro and gathered recruits from different sources until his command was materially strengthened. The Confederates had taken possession of Lavergne, and the forces consisted of several regiments of militia and one regiment of cavalry. These troops were all raw, and the Federal commander at Nashville resolved upon the capture of the place. By a night march, on October 6, the Federals gained position in front and rear of the Confederates, and on the morning of the 7th opened the attack. The Federals were commanded by General Palmer. The Confederates were defeated. The Federals entered Lavergne. The militia gave way in the fight and fled in confusion. The Thirty-second Alabama was the only regiment of veterans on the scene, and this regiment held the enemy in check and prevented the Confederate defeat from becoming a rout. Forrest was at Murfreesboro. As soon as he heard of the disaster at Lavergne, he hurried to the scene with re-enforcements. The Federals had withdrawn to Nashville, and the Confederates re-occupied Lavergne. Pickets were placed on all the approaches to Nashville, and the Confederates pushed their picket lines to the very gates of the city. During the months of October and November, Forrest was busy in arranging his forces for more effective service. Since the battle of Perryville, the Confederates had withdrawn from Kentucky, and were being collected under Bragg in the vicinity of Murfreesboro. The Federals, under Rosecrans (who had superseded Buell), were now being collected at Nashville, and two powerful armies were collected face to face, ready for the sanguinary conflict soon to ensue. The great battles of Murfreesboro came off on December 31 and January 1, following. The Confederates withdrew to Shelbyville after this battle, and Forrest's cavalry was engaged principally in picket duty on the outposts and on the flanks of the army during the remainder of the winter.

Previous to the battle of Murfreesboro, General Wheeler was placed in command of all the cavalry, with his head-quarters at Lavergne. Forrest was ordered with his brigade to Columbia, with a view to future operations in West Tennessee. As soon as his men were properly armed and mounted, Forrest proceeded upon his West Tennessee campaign. A lively and spirited campaign, checkered with many thrilling incidents, was the result. It would be impossible to give the details of the expedition in the space allotted to this narrative. Forrest was in constant encounters with the enemy, in which he was generally victorious. In some instances he encountered such vastly superior numbers that he would be forced to fall back in haste, but his retreats were rapid, and only consummated in order to strike the enemy from an unexpected point.

In April, 1863, Forrest was sent by General Bragg to the relief of Colonel Roddy, who was pressed by two heavy columns of the enemy—one from Corinth, under Dodge, the other from Eastport, under Streight. These two columns were marching upon Tuscumbia, Ala. This was the inauguration of the celebrated "Streight raid," in which Forrest displayed his best generalship, as well as the best fighting qualities of himself and his command. The Federals being so far the superior of the Confederates in numbers, and having gained such decided advantages meanwhile, were pushing their advantages with vigor. The people became alarmed for the safety of North Georgia, and Bragg's communications with Atlanta and Montgomery. Dodge had commenced a retreat with a view to cover the movements of Streight, who was by this time moving with all his might in the direction of Rome. At this juncture Forrest divided his forces, and placed a part under Roddy to follow Streight. The remainder of his force was sent around to the north-east to prevent the escape of Streight's command by a flank movement. The men under Streight were the Fifty-first and Seventy-third Indiana Regiments; Eightieth Illinois, Third Ohio, and two companies of Alabama (Union) cavalry. They had marched from Tuscumbia in the rear of Dodge, who had been sent in advance to divert the attention of the Confederates and disguise Streight's real intentions. The Federals were conducted by native guides, and had succeeded in getting so far that they felt their plans almost accomplished without hinderance. The Confederates gave hot pursuit when the intentions of Streight had fully developed themselves. A running fight now set in. Forrest seeing that Streight intended to avoid an engagement by hurrying on in the direction of Rome, pressed onward and pushed his adversary with all haste and vigor. Dodge had commenced his retreat, and left the country desolate, and a line of smoky ruins marked his path. In the engagements thus far Forrest had captured quite a number of prisoners. Roddy was ordered to take charge of the prisoners and return to Decatur. Detachments were sent out on the flanks of the raiders to guard the passes, and the pursuit was pressed with renewed vigor by Colonels Biffle and McLemore. Forrest with his escort, together with a part of the Fourth Tennessee Cavalry, rushed forward for the purpose of overtaking the enemy and bringing on an engagement. A running fight of some hours was the result. Streight, seeing that an engagement was forced upon him, formed his main line on an elevation about half a mile east of Long Creek. Biffle and McLemore came up and formed their line, having dismounted, and proceeded as infantry. It was near dark when the fight began, and for three hours the contest was stubborn. The Federals gave way slowly, and the Confederates pushed every advantage. At eight o'clock Colonel Biffle was ordered around the Federals for the purpose of attacking the horse-holders. In a short time a brisk skirmish was opened on the Federal rear. The Confederates charged in front, and Streight was forced to fall back in confusion. The loss on the Federal side was fifty killed, with a corresponding number of wounded. The Confederates recovered a section of artillery which had been captured a few days previously, and captured about thirty wagons and teams. The Confederate loss was slight. Streight now realized his situation. The Confederates were pushing him desperately, and had sent detachments around to cut off his escape. Forrest followed up, and by eleven o'clock the pursuit was hastened. The stars were shining and the darkness of the night was to some extent diminished. Shortly after midnight Streight made another stand on the south bank of a creek. The banks were high and steep. Streight was soon dislodged from this position and he resumed his retreat. Forrest now halted and rested his men for a couple of hours and renewed the chase. Streight now turned in the direction of Gadsden, Ala. A running fight occurred again, and Streight, after crossing the Black Warrior, hurried on at a desperate rate with the Confederates at his heels. The Confederates attacked the rear-guard before it had time to cross the river. A running fight was kept up. Streight now resorted to every means available to hinder pursuit. After crossing a deep and rapid stream, the bridge was destroyed. The banks of this creek were high, and a crossing was rendered difficult; yet the Confederates pressed on. The Federals having crossed Black Creek, the bridge was set on fire and destroyed. The current was swift. The banks were high, and to effect a crossing was considered impossible. Forrest was nonplussed when he came to the stream, and paused. It was impossible to ford the stream, and while he was pondering over the situation a little girl came up and presented herself to General Forrest, and told him of an old ford not a great way off. Forrest took the little girl up behind him, and she showed him the way to the ford. The Confederates were soon across and pushing the Federals with their usual vigor. The men safely over the stream, General Forrest sent the little girl home under special escort. The name of this little girl was Emma Sanson. Her mother lived near the bridge, and the Federals in passing her house captured some young men who were at home on furlough. Upon the request of the young lady that her brother be restored, General Forrest assured her that it should be done before ten o'clock on the following morning. After crossing Black Creek, the Confederates pursued the raiders ten miles, and overtook them on Saturday evening, May 2, at a village called Turkeytown. The Federals soon gave way.

In this encounter the Federal colonel, Hathaway, was killed. The Confederate loss was light.

The Confederates were now reduced to about five hundred men. So great had been the zeal of the pursuit that many had become exhausted. The Federals had crossed the Coosa River and destroyed the bridge. The Confederates carried over the ammunition by hand, and in a short time were in hot pursuit. Forrest had sent runners to Rome to notify the authorities of the situation, and requesting that they bring out every available man. Colonel McLemore moved on the right flank and Colonel Biffle on the left, while the militia were in front of the raiders. Forrest now sent an officer with a flag of truce to demand "an immediate surrender of the Federal force, in order to stop the further and useless effusion of blood." Colonel Streight, in reply, asked to communicate with General Forrest in person. The two generals met in the woods and talked the matter over. Streight hesitated to surrender unless assured that he would be surrendering to a force at least his equal in point of numbers. Just at this time a section of artillery came up and was privately instructed to move in a circle. Streight believed that several batteries were moving up and taking position at the limit agreed upon in the stipulations made under the flag of truce. Impressed with this belief, Streight asked of General Forrest how much artillery he had. Forrest replied, "Enough to destroy your command in thirty minutes." Colonel Streight still insisted on knowing the strength of the enemy to whom he was asked to surrender, and held a consultation with his officers. In a quarter of an hour he returned and repeated his desire to be assured that he was confronted by at least an equal force. Forrest replied, "That discussion was entirely useless—that he had known of this movement from its first inception, and prepared for it." Forrest further called Streight's attention to the fact that he (Streight) had a river on his right that was not fordable, a mountain on his left that shut him off from escape, a force in his front with which he was not able to cope, and a force in his rear that had gained strength every day. If he (Streight) failed to surrender he would thus incur upon himself the gravest consequences. Streight clung to his old idea of *equal numbers*, and was in the act of returning to his men, when Captain Pointer invited him to take a drink before parting, and in a pleasant manner suggested that it might be the last he would ever take. The offer was accepted and the two opposing commanders shook hands and separated. Streight had not gone far before he met a white flag from his own men, and he returned with the flag to Confederate headquarters. He announced the desire of his officers to surrender, and proposed to capitulate upon condition that "all were to be held as prisoners of war, and the officers should retain their side-arms and personal baggage." The offer was accepted.

In order to keep the enemy still deceived, Captain Pointer asked of Forrest what disposition should be made of several imaginary detachments of troops. Forrest replied in a corresponding manner, and Captain Pointer would gallop away hurriedly to execute the orders. Streight and his men, 1,466 in all, had surrendered to a very small force, and to disguise this fact Forrest informed Streight "That, as forage was very scarce in Rome, *he would be guarded to that point by only his escort and one regiment.*"

The route of Streight's raid was from Courtland to Moulton, thence to Danville, thence to Mt. Alvis, Blountsville, Walnut Grove, McCluskey's, Bennettsville, Wills's Valley, Gadsden, Turkeytown, King's Hill, to Rome. The capitulation was effected on May 3, 1863, within eighteen miles of Rome, between the Coosa and Chattahooche Rivers, in that part of the county known as "Straight Neck" precinct. Forrest received quite an ovation at the hands of the Southern people for his great victory.

SPRING HILL.

Shortly after the capture of Colonel Streight, Forrest was ordered to Spring Hill, to take charge of all the cavalry in that section. Forrest assumed command on May 16, with head-quarters at Spring Hill. The summer months were devoted to various movements on the flanks of Rosecrans's army. During the latter part of June, Forrest was ordered to Shelbyville, and performed a prominent part in the retreat of the Confederates from Shelbyville to Chattanooga.

CHICKAMAUGA.

At the battle of Chickamauga, Forrest's Cavalry brought on the attack on the right, where they dismounted and performed the service of infantry. Walker's division formed on the left of Forrest, and Cheatham's division on the left of Walker's. In this battle the cavalry did most efficient service.

At the conclusion of the battle and retreat of the enemy, Forrest's Cavalry pursued the enemy across Missionary Ridge, and the Confederate army following, occupied the ridge on the morning of September 21.

During the winter of 1863, Forrest's Cavalry operated in East Tennessee, and engaged in many skirmishes with the enemy.

FORREST A MAJOR-GENERAL.

On December 4, 1863, Forrest was commissioned a major-general and ordered to West Tennessee. His territory was "Forrest's Cavalry Department," comprising West Tennessee and North Mississippi. His command embraced the following brigades and regiments:

First Brigade—Twelfth Tennessee, Lieutenant-colonel J. U. Green; Fourteenth Tennessee, Colonel J. J. Neely; Fifteenth Tennessee, Colonel F. M. Stewart; Sixteenth Tennessee, Colonel Thomas H. Logwood; Seventeenth Tennessee, Major Marshall; Street's and Bennett's Battalions Tennessee Volunteers.

Second Brigade—Colonel Robert McCullock (Second Missouri)—Second Missouri Regiment, Lieutenant-colonel R. A. McCullock; Willis's Texas Battalion, Lieutenant-colonel Leo Willis; Faulkner's Kentucky Regiment, Colonel W. W. Faulkner; Keizer's and Franklin's Tennessee Battalions; Chambers's Battalion (Mississippi), A. H. Chambers; Second Arkansas (remnant), Captain T. M. Cochran.

Third Brigade—Colonel T. H. Bell (2,000 men)—Russell's Tennessee Regiment, Greers's Tennessee

Regiment, Newsom's Tennessee Regiment, Willson's Tennessee Regiment, Barteau's Tennessee Regiment.

Fourth Brigade—Colonel J. E. Forrest—McDonald's Battalion, Seventh Tennessee Regiment, McGuirk's Regiment, Third Mississippi Regiment (State troops), Fifth Mississippi, Lieutenant-colonel Barksdale; Nineteenth Mississippi Battalion.

The Second and Third Brigades were formed into a division, and placed under command of Brigadier-general J. R. Chalmers.

General Forrest established his head-quarters at Oxford, Miss. The Federals at this time were meditating a movement on Meridian, and Forrest was busy in penetrating the designs of the enemy, and using every means at his command to thwart their consummation. As a consequence, there was a constant and stirring movement between the opposing armies, resulting in frequent skirmishes and several hard-fought battles within the boundaries of General Forrest's department.

Later in the spring of 1864, the cavalry command in Mississippi was increased by three regiments of Kentucky infantry, which had been transferred to Forrest's Cavalry Department. These three regiments numbered seven hundred men. These, with others, were organized into the Second Division of Cavalry and placed under command of Brigadier-general Abe Buford on March 8, 1864.

PADUCAH.

To give the details of the daring deeds and glorious achievements of Forrest's Cavalry in this his new field of operations would, of itself, require volumes. Forrest was in constant contact with the enemy. On

March 25, 1864, he made a descent upon Paducah and captured the town, but the Federals were garrisoned in a strong fortress below the town, and the point was also protected by two gun-boats. When the attack was made upon the fortress the Confederates suffered a severe loss and failed to carry the works. Forrest then sent a demand for the surrender of the garrison, and added, "That if it became necessary to take the position by force he would not be responsible for the consequences." This demand was answered by Colonel Hicks with a positive refusal. While the parley was going on, the Confederates were gathering up supplies and stock from the town and vicinity. Forrest reconnoitered the position and declined the idea of any further assault on the ground that the capture of the place would involve a sacrifice greater than the capture would justify, and withdrew from the place.

The threat that was intimated in Forrest's demand for surrender, has been severely criticised by the Northern press, but the demand was made under circumstances in which a little effort was made at intimidation merely—a measure justified in war.

FORT PILLOW.

The next point where Forrest's Cavalry figured, even more prominently than in the "Streight raid," was the affair with the enemy at Fort Pillow, on the Mississippi river. This occurred on April 12, 1864. It appears that the fort was garrisoned by some negro troops and West Tennessee (Federal) troops and a corresponding amount of artillery, all commanded by Major Booth. These Federal Tennesseans were from the surrounding country, and were thoroughly acquainted with the people. Between these and the

Confederate Tennesseans there existed the greatest antipathy. By mutual threats, a desperate state of feeling existed, not only between the *men* but toward the *families* of these people mutually. The Union families were persecuted to some extent by the Confederates of that section of country, and the men of these families were in the garrison at Fort Pillow. These men would come out from the fort, accompanied by negro soldiers, and would insult the women of their Confederate neighbors, and commit various depredations upon the community. In this manner the garrison at Fort Pillow became a terror to the country. Forrest was solicited by a delegation of citizens to look into the matter and punish the offenders. When urged by the ladies of the country, he made a promise similar to his promises at Woodbury and to the ladies at Black Creek when he was after Streight. He assured them that "the matter would receive prompt attention." Faithfully did he execute his promise in this as in the other two instances.

With his usual sagacity and celerity, he invested the fortress on April 12, and planting sharp-shooters under cover at the most advantageous points, he besieged the place. Having carried on an active skirmish for some time with his sharp-shooters, Forrest had now approached to within a few hundred yards of the fort, and having fully ascertained the position and strength of the garrison, he was satisfied of his ability to take the place. Accordingly, he sent Captain Walter A. Goodman, of General Chalmers's staff, with a flag of truce to Major Booth, and a demand for the surrender of the place. The demand was in these words:

HEAD-QUARTERS FORREST'S CAVALRY,
NEAR FORT PILLOW, April 12, 1864.

Sir:—As your gallant defense of the fort has entitled you to the treatment of brave men, I now demand an unconditional surrender of your forces, at the same time assuring you that they will be treated as prisoners of war. I have received a fresh supply of ammunition and can easily take your position.

N. B. FORREST.

To Major L. F. BOOTH, Commanding United States Forces.

In the engagement preceding the demand for the surrender, Major Booth was killed, and the command of the garrison devolved upon Major W. F. Bradford, who was commander of the Thirteenth Tennessee Battalion. This command was very odious to the Confederates, especially those from West Tennessee. Major Bradford replied over the signature of Major Booth, who had been dead for over an hour. Bradford seemed inclined to waive proceedings, and asked an hour for consultation with the officers of the gun-boat in reference to the surrender of the garrison and the gun-boat. General Forrest immediately replied that he had not demanded, and did not ask, the surrender of the gun-boat, but had only demanded the surrender of the garrison, and would give twenty minutes for a decision, and added that "He could not be responsible for the consequences if obliged to storm the place." This clause was added, not through any desire or intention on the part of General Forrest to go beyond the usages of war, but through a knowledge of the inveterate hatred borne by his Tennessee troops toward the Tennessee troops of the garrison, and especially the negro troops; and he felt assured that they would, on this account, be liable to go beyond the bounds of restraint toward the garrison, if he should be compelled to take the place by force.

While this parley was going on, several steamers came in sight, and Forrest, believing that the parley was continued by Bradford to cover the arrival of reinforcements, hastily sent a detachment to occupy the old intrenchments and prevent the landing of troops. This detachment was under command of Captain Anderson, and his instructions were only to prevent the landing of troops during the truce. As the transports approached, Captain Anderson fired a few shots through their pilot-house, and they changed their course. For this act Forrest was charged with violating the flag of truce, but he was only acting to meet such a violation on the part of the enemy. Bradford seemed impressed with an idea that he was not negotiating with Forrest, and seemed anxious to know that this general was actually before him. While yet in doubt about the matter, he sent a reply over the signature of "Booth," in these words: "Your demand does not have the desired effect." When Forrest read this reply, he said: "This will not do; send it back and say to Major Booth that I must have an answer in plain English—yes, or no." Forrest believed that the fort would be surrendered, but in a short time a reply came from the garrison positively refusing to capitulate.

Forrest immediately proceeded to storm the place, and pushed into the Federal works. The negro troops threw down their guns and attempted to run out at a gap with a view of escaping to the gun-boat. Captain Anderson poured a destructive volley into their ranks from the river bank, and the garrison, with its colors flying, ran in confusion about the fortress, and were shot down at will. Forrest came up meanwhile, and ordered his men to cease firing, though the garrison had not surrendered. Many of the wounded had scrambled off to some cabins, which caught fire, and before the Confederates were aware of the situation, this portion of the Federal wounded had been severely burned. Forrest took steps immediately to care for the wounded, after having gathered up his prisoners. The fight was a desperate one, and by the Northern press was looked upon as a massacre. The garrison was slaughtered by the Confederates at a fearful rate, but it was through the persistent stubbornness of a weak and ignorant commander and undisciplined troops in the garrison, that would not surrender when overpowered. Bradford was a weak and unprincipled man, and had negotiated with Forrest in the name of Major Booth, who was killed early in the fight. He had inspired his men with the same spirit of knavery; and had taught them none of the principles of soldiers. The prisoners were taken to Jackson, and thence to permanent quarters. On the way to Jackson, Captain Bradford was found guilty of violating a sacred pledge which he had made under the pretext of going to bury a brother. Colonel McCullock had given him quarters and treated him like a gentleman under this pledge. He attempted to escape during the night and go to Memphis. Being recaptured, Captain Bradford paid the penalty of his treachery with his life.

The prisoners captured at Fort Pillow were as follows:

THIRTEENTH TENNESSEE BATTALION.

COMPANY A.

Sergeant R. C. Gunter, J. Childress, A. J. Knight, J. E. Lemon, J. E. Howell, G. W. Kirk, T. E. Burton, J. B. Phipps, J. Clark, J. Long, C. Swinney, D. Burton, J. Minnyard, J. Berry, J. Halford, W. T. Lovett, M. Mitchell, E. Haynes, A. A. Anthony, V. Y. Mattheny, J. Moore.

FORREST'S CAVALRY.   441

COMPANY B.

A. J. Pankey, R. R. McKie, J. H. Scoby, J. Green, A. McKie, W. G. Bowles, E. Jones, A. J. Crawford, S. Hubbs, G. W. Bowles, T. L. Perry, J. W. Stewart, D. Floyd, W. P. Flowers, J. A. Baker, J. C. Paulk, C. P. Bowles, W. T. Hooser, J. Jones, W. Morrow, C. R. Allen, H. Bailey, J. A. Beatty, D. B. Burress, W. J. Miflin, J. Burrus, W. Woodward, A. H. Barrom.

COMPANY C.

Lieutenant N. D. Logan, H. Corning, W. L. Tate, N. G. Henderson, T. Wheeless, E. Scarborough, J. Bynum, S. Read, J. Clarke, D. Myers, W. Stafford, A. McGhee, F. E. Neeham, J. A. Smith, J. Hann, J. Presley, M. Day, D. F. Hood, F. M. Gammon, J. Jones, L. Hohoer, G. L. Ellis, J. H. Webb, H. C. Moore, W. H. Bolls, A. J. Rice, William Ryder, J. Norman, J. Southerland, A. Middleton, H. S. Morris, J. M. Tidwell, J. M. Knuckles, C. Oxford.

COMPANY D.

C. D. Alexander, S. E. Kirk, B. J. Kirk, F. D. Tidwell, William Hancock, John Taylor, J. W. Brown, T. Woods, B. Johnson, J. Wilson, W. R. Johnson, J. Moer, M. Harper, E. E. Stewart, B. F. Ellison, T. P. Paschal, J. M. Wilson, J. W. Gibson, P. S. Alexander, B. W. King, J. Rumage, J. C. Green.

COMPANY E.

Captain J. L. Poston, J. Smith, J. T. Cockran, A. J. Hall, E. Childress, J. A. Brown, W. G. Poston, O. B. Goodman, S. N. Scarberry, N. C. Cleek, J. Cozart, W. Hines, J. W. Atwine, C. Ellis, A. J. Madlin, A. Carr, J. F. Stamp, R. Richardson, J. A. Haynes, J. M. Smith, T. J. McMurray, J. F. Rolf, J. Shoemate, Henry Clay, J. Arnold, R. Williams, A. J. Sutton, A. Lewis, J. H. Scarboro, T. A. Lunsford, W. J. Scarberry, J. Hodge, H. Jones, W. H. Henley, H. L. Brogden, M. E. Beard, F. Dowling.

MISCELLANEOUS.

Lieutenant P. H. McBride, Johnson's escort; Lieutenant A. M. Hunter, Second U. S. Light Artillery; Captain J. F. Young, Company A, Twenty-fourth Missouri Infantry; W. H. Gibson, S. T. Gibson, J. W. Autring, William Boyer, R. C. Price, and S. M. Price, Steagall's Home Guards; R. B. Springer, Company L, Second Iowa Cavalry; C. E. Pratt, Company A, First U. S. Regular Artillery; H. W. Holloway, Company B, Second Illinois Cavalry; A. Baker, Company I, Fifty-second Indiana Infantry; R. Mullins, Company A, Seventh Tennessee Cavalry; R. H. Stewart, Company C, Seventh Tennessee Cavalry; W. M. Crews, Company D, Seventh Tennessee Cavalry; W. H. Snow, Company M, Seventh Tennessee Cavalry; J. K. Taylor, Company E, Sixth Tennessee Cavalry; T. C. George, Company —, Seventh Kansas Cavalry.

SIXTH U. S. HEAVY ARTILLERY.

(Colored Troops.)

COMPANY A.

Captain C. J. Eppenciter, Lieutenant P. Bishop, Sergeant J. Hennissy, A. J. Hatfield, J. Thompson, Frank Hooper, Tom Norris, Anthony Flowers, Bill Smith, Oliver Jones, Henry Smith, Jenkins Rice, Bill Ward, Monk Moores, Cog Horton, Edmond Trice, Peter Williams, Charlie Williams, Dave Manley, Ray McGhee, Braxton Kirkman, Wilson Johnson, Bill Oats, Solomon Patrick, Henderson Johnson, John Gentry, Sandy Worsham, Wilson Crenshaw, Jim McCauley, Albert Ingram, Jefferson Dobbs, Spott Clayton, Harry Hill, William Gray, Jim Daubridge, Dan Newburn, Dave Oats, Frank Browden, Tom Palmer, Aaron Bradly, David Oats, Henry Smith, Wilson Peyton, David Johnson, Jacob Lumpkin, Moses Wiseman, Lewis Van Eagle, John McHainey, Jim Murrell, Jim Flowers, Sam Baugh, Dick Sallee, Hiram Lumpkin, Jim Pride, John Henry Harper, David Flowers.

RECAPITULATION—*Prisoners*.

REGIMENTS.	Officers.	Men.	Total.
Sixth U. S. Heavy Artillery (colored)	2	54	56
Second Iowa Cavalry		1	1
Thirteenth Tennessee Battalion	3	148	151
Second U. S. Light Artillery	1	1	2
First U. S. Regular Artillery		1	1
Twenty-fourth Missouri Infantry	1		1
Steagall's Home Guards		6	6
Second Illinois Cavalry		1	1
Fifty-second Indiana Infantry		1	1
Seventh Tennessee Cavalry		4	4
Sixth Tennessee Cavalry		1	1
Seventh Kansas Cavalry		1	1
Total	7	219	226

After the battle of Fort Pillow, various movements were made by the cavalry, in which different detachments were engaged with the enemy at various points. During the month of May, Forrest devoted himself principally to gathering up recruits and horses, and in every available manner strengthening his command to the highest possible standard of efficiency. Meanwhile his head-quarters were at Tupelo. At this point he formed his artillery into a battalion and placed it under command of Captain J. W. Morton, chief of artillery. This battalion numbered batteries of four guns each. officered as follows:

First battery, Morton's, four guns; second battery, Thrall's, four guns; third battery, Rice's, four guns; fourth battery, Walton's, four guns.

His other troops consisted of twenty regiments, four battalions, and five independent companies. These troops were distributed with a view to convenience of forage and so as to be available in case of urgent need. Chalmers's division was stationed at Verona and Grenada. Another detachment was placed at Panola, and the Mississippi State troops and Buford's division were stationed at Tupelo.

An expedition was organized to operate in North Alabama to the relief of General Roddy, who was being pressed by the enemy in that quarter. Forrest now resolved to effect a junction with Roddy, and sent him a notice to that effect. About the time of its consummation, a heavy force of Federals were moving out from Memphis and threatening Northern Mississippi. When this fact was ascertained, the expedition was recalled by Major-general Lee, and, on June 5, Forrest resumed his head-quarters at Tupelo. Matters were lively in Northern Mississippi. The enemy moved in the direction of the Memphis and Charleston Railroad, and the cavalry force was being rapidly concentrated at Baldwin, to which point Lee and Forrest started out on June 7, and arrived there on the 8th. The enemy was now at Ruckerville, and preparing to cross the Hatchie River. Subsequent information developed the fact that the enemy contemplated a movement upon Guntown by way of Ripley. Forrest was active in his maneuvering with the intention of giving the enemy battle. His force at his immediate disposal were three brigades, commanded respectively by brigadier-generals Lyon, Rucker, and Johnson. Lyon's brigade was composed of the Third Kentucky, Lieutenant-colonel G. A. C. Holt commanding; Seventh Kentucky, Major H. S. Hale commanding; Eighth Kentucky, Captain R. H. Fristoe commanding; Faulkner's Kentucky Regiment, T. S. Tate commanding. Rucker's brigade was composed of the Eighth Mississippi, Lieutenant-colonel A. H. Chalmers; Nineteenth Mississippi, Colonel W. L. Duff; Seventh Tennessee, Colonel W. L. Duckworth. Johnson's brigade was composed of the Fourth Alabama, Lieutenant-colonel Windes; Moreland's battalion, Major George; Warren's battalion, Captain W. H. Warren; Ferrell's battery, four guns.

With this force Forrest encountered the enemy at Brice's Cross Roads, in the vicinity of Guntown, near the waters of Tishomingo Creek, on June 10, 1864. The forces of the enemy amounted to over nine thousand men, composed of two cavalry brigades commanded respectively by Brigadier-generals Warren and Winslow, and numbered three thousand men. The infantry brigades of Wilkins and Hayes, composed of white troops, and Benton's brigade of colored troops, six thousand strong. The battle was fierce and desperate, and resulted in a complete victory for the Confederates. The colored troops were possessed of an idea that no quarter would be granted them, and when defeated refused to surrender, and sought safety in flight. The Confederates pursuing commanded them to halt, but the negroes, disregarding the commands of their pursuers, continued their flight, and were shot at their very heels. Whether this unfortunate idea was inculcated into the minds of the negro troops by their officers to strengthen their courage and efficiency in action, or was the result of parleys and interchanged threats between themselves and the non-combatants before the battle of Fort Pillow, is not definitely known, From whatever source it emanated its results were deplorable. As at Fort Pillow, the negroes acted with a dogged and reckless obstinacy having no relationship to courage, but partaking more of the nature of animals that were hemmed and refused to be caught. The Confederates expected no quarter at the hands of the colored troops. As a consequence, when the Confederates gained a complete victory and had captured several of the enemy's guns and quite a number of prisoners, the colored troops hurdled in gangs and were shot down before the Confederates, who demanded their surrender, and would have much preferred their surrender to their destruction.

Previous to the departure of the Federals from Memphis the colored troops had taken an oath before General Hurlburt to avenge Fort Pillow, and show the Confederates no quarter. General Forrest having been apprised of this fact addressed the following note to the Federal commander at Memphis:

HEAD-QUARTERS FORREST'S CAVALRY,
IN THE FIELD, June 14, 1864.

General:—It has been reported to me that all your colored troops, stationed at Memphis, took an oath on their knees in the presence of Major-general Hurlburt and others of your command to avenge Fort Pillow, and that they would show my troops no quarter. Again, I have it from indisputable authority, that the troops under Brigadier-general Sturgis, on their recent march from Memphis, publicly, and in many places, proclaimed that no quarter would be shown my men. As they were moved into action on the 10th, they were exhorted by their officers to remember Fort Pillow. The prisoners we have captured from that command, or a large majority of them, have voluntarily stated that they expected us to murder them; otherwise, they would have surrendered in a body rather than taken to the bushes after being run down and exhausted. The recent battle of Tishomingo Creek was far more bloody than it would otherwise have been but for the fact that your men evidently expected to be slaughtered when captured, and both sides acted as though neither felt safe in surrendering even when further resistance was useless. The prisoners captured by us say they felt condemned by the announcements, etc., of their own commanders, and expected no quarter.

In all my operations since it began I have conducted the war on civilized principles, and desire still to do so; but it is due to my command that they should know the position they occupy and the policy you intend to pursue. I therefore respectfully ask whether my men, now in your hands, are treated as other Confederate prisoners of war; also the course intended to be pursued in regard to those who may hereafter fall into your hands.

I have in my possession quite a number of wounded officers and men of General Sturgis's command, all of whom have been treated as well as we were able to treat them, and are mostly in charge of a surgeon left at Ripley by General Sturgis to look after the wounded. Some of them are too severely wounded to be removed at present. I am willing to exchange them for any men of my command you have, and, as soon as able to be removed, will give them safe escort through our lines in charge of the surgeon left with them. I made such an arrangement once with Major-general Hurlburt, and am willing to renew it, provided it is desired, as it would be better than to subject them to the long and fatiguing trip necessary to a regular exchange at City Point, Va.

I am, General, etc.,   N. B. FORREST, *Major-general.*

To this General Washburn replied as follows:

HEAD-QUARTERS DISTRICT OF WEST TENNESSEE,
MEMPHIS, TENN., June 19, 1864.

Major-general N. B. FORREST, Commanding Confederate forces:

General:—Your communication of the 10th inst. is received. The letter to Brigadier-general Buford will be forwarded to him.

In regard to that part of your letter which relates to colored troops, I beg to say that I have already sent a communication on the same subject to the officers in command of the Confederate forces at Tupelo. Having understood that Major-general S. D. Lee was in command there, I directed my letter to him. A copy of it I inclose.

You say in your letter that it has been reported to you that all the negro troops stationed in Memphis took an oath on their knees, in the presence of Major-general Hurlburt and other officers of our army, to avenge "Port Pillow, and that they would show your troops no quarter." I believe it is true that the colored troops did take such an oath, but not in the presence of General Hurlburt. From what I can learn, this act of theirs was not influenced by any white officer, but was the result of their own sense of what was due to themselves and their fellows who had been mercilessly slaughtered. I have no doubt that they went into the field, as you allege, in the full belief that they would be murdered in case they fell into your hands. The affair at Fort Pillow fully justified that belief. I am not aware as to what they proclaimed on their late march, and it may be, as you say, that they declared that no quarter would be given to any of your men that might fall into their hands.

Your declaration that you have conducted the war on all occasions on civilized principles cannot be accepted; but I receive with satisfaction the intimation in your letter that the recent slaughter of colored troops at the battle of Tishomingo Creek resulted rather from the desperation with which they fought than a pre-determined intention to give them no quarter. You must have learned by this time that the attempt to intimidate the colored troops by indiscriminate slaughter has signally failed, and that, instead of a feeling of terror, you have aroused a spirit of courage and desperation that will not down at your bidding.

I am left in doubt by your letter as to the course you and your government intend to pursue hereafter in regard to colored troops; and I beg you to advise me, with as little delay as possible, as to your intentions. If you intend to treat such of them as fall into your hands as prisoners of war, please so state. If you do not so intend, but contemplate either their slaughter or their return to slavery, please state *that*, so that we may have no misunderstanding hereafter. If the former is your intention I shall receive the announcement with pleasure, and shall explain the fact to the colored troops at once, and desire that they recall the oath they have taken. If the latter is the case, then let the oath stand, and upon those who have aroused this spirit by their atrocities and upon the government and people who sanction it, be the consequences.

In regard to your inquiry relating to prisoners of your command in our hands, I state that they have always received that treatment which a great humane government extends to its prisoners. What course will be pursued hereafter toward them must, of course, depend on circumstances that may arise. If your command hereafter do nothing which should properly exclude them from being treated as prisoners of war, they will be so treated.

I thank you for your offer to exchange wounded officers and men in your hands. If you will send them in, I will exchange man for man so far as I have the ability to do so.

Before closing this letter, I wish to call your attention to one case of unparalleled outrage and murder that has been brought to my notice, and in regard to which the evidence is overwhelming.

Among the prisoners captured at Fort Pillow was Major Bradford, who had charge of the fort after the fall of Major Booth. After being taken prisoner, he was started with other prisoners in charge of Colonel Duckworth, to Jackson. At Brownsville, they rested over night. The following morning two companies were detailed by Colonel Duckworth to proceed to Jackson with the prisoners. After they had started and proceeded a short distance, five soldiers were recalled by Colonel Duckworth and conferred with by him. They then rejoined the column, and, after proceeding about five miles from Brownsville, the column halted, and Major Bradford was taken about fifty yards from the road side and deliberately shot by the five men who had been recalled by Colonel Duckworth, and his body left unburied upon the ground where he fell. He now lies buried near the spot, and, if you desire, you can easily satisfy yourself of the truth of what I assert.

I beg leave to say to you that this transaction hardly justifies your remark that your operations have been conducted on civilized principles, and until you take some steps to bring the perpetrators of this outrage to justice, the world will not fail to believe that it has your sanction. I am, General, your obedient servant, C. C. WASHBURN, *Major-general.*

Accompanying this document was this copy of a letter from General Washburn to Major-general S. D. Lee, referred to in the above communication. The letter read as follows:

HEAD-QUARTERS DISTRICT OF WEST TENNESSEE, }
MEMPHIS, TENN., June 17, 1864. }

Major-general S. D. LEE, Commanding Confederate forces, near Tupelo, Mississippi:

General:—When I heard that the forces of Brigadier-general Sturgis had been driven back and a portion of them probably captured, I felt considerable solicitude for the fate of the two colored regiments that formed a part of the command until I was informed that the Confederate forces were commanded by you. When I heard that, I became satisfied that no atrocities would be committed upon those troops, but that they would receive the treatment which humanity, as well as their gallant conduct, demanded. I regret to say that the hope I entertained has been dispelled by facts which have recently come to my knowledge. .

From statements that have been made to me by colored soldiers, who were eye-witnesses, it would seem that the massacre at Fort Pillow had been reproduced at the late affair at Brice's Cross Roads. The details of the atrocities there committed I will not trouble you with. If true, and not disavowed, they must lead to consequences hereafter fearful to contemplate. It is best that we should now have a fair understanding upon the question of the treatment of this class of soldiers.

If it is contemplated by the Confederate government to murder all colored troops that may, by the chances of war, fall into their hands, as was the case at Fort Pillow, it is but fair that it should be truly and openly avowed. Within the last six weeks I have on two occasions sent colored troops into the field from this point. In the expectation that the Confederate government would disavow the action of their commanding general at the Fort Pillow massacre, I have forborne to issue any instructions to the colored troops as to the course they should pursue toward Confederate soldiers that might fall into their hands; but seeing no disavowal on the part of the Confederate government, but, on the contrary, laudations from the entire Southern press of the perpetrators of the massacre, I may safely presume that indiscriminate slaughter is to be the fate of colored troops that fall into your hands. But I am not willing to leave a matter of such grave import, and involving consequences so fearful, to inference, and I have therefore thought proper to address you this, believing that you would be able to indicate the policy that the Confederate government intended to pursue hereafter on this question. If it is intended to raise the black flag against that unfortunate race they will cheerfully accept the issue. Up to this time no troops have fought more gallantly and none have conducted themselves with greater propriety. They have fully vindicated their right (so long denied) to be treated as men. I hope that I have been misinformed in regard to the treatment they have received at the battle of Brice's Cross Roads, and that the accounts received result rather from the excited imagination of the fugitives than from actual facts.

For the government of the colored troops under my command I would thank you to inform me, with as little delay as possible, if it is your intention or the intention of the Confederate government to murder colored soldiers that may fall into your hands, or treat them as prisoners of war, and subject to be exchanged as other prisoners. I am, General, respectfully, etc.,

C. C. WASHBURN, *Major-general.*

To these two communications from the Federal General Washburn, General Forrest replied as follows:

HEAD-QUARTERS FORREST'S CAVALRY, TUPELO,
June 23, 1864.

Major-general C. C. WASHBURN, Commanding United States
 forces, Memphis:

General:—I have the honor to acknowledge the receipt (per flag of truce) of your letter of the 17th inst., addressed to Major-general S. D. Lee, or officer commanding Confederate forces at Tupelo. I have forwarded it to General Lee with a copy of this letter.

I regard your letter as discourteous to the commanding officer of this department and grossly insulting to myself. You seek, by implied threats, to intimidate him, and assume the privilege of denouncing me as a murderer and as guilty of the wholesale slaughter of the garrison at Fort Pillow, and found your assertions upon the *ex parte* testimony of (your friends) the enemies of myself and country.

I shall not enter into the discussion, therefore, of any questions involved, nor undertake any refutation of the charges made by you against myself. Nevertheless, as a matter of personal privilege alone, I unhesitatingly say that they are unfounded and unwarranted by the facts. But whether these charges are true or false, they, with the questions you ask, as to whether negro troops, when captured, will be recognized and treated as prisoners of war, subject to exchange, etc., are matters which the government of the United States and the Confederates States are to decide and adjust—not their subordinate officers. I regard captured negroes as I do other captured property, and not as captured soldiers; but as to how regarded by my government, and the disposition which has been and will hereafter be made of them, I respectfully refer you, through the proper channel, to the authorities at Richmond.

It is not the policy or the interest of the South to destroy the negro; on the contrary, to preserve and protect him; and all who have surrendered to us have received kind and humane treatment.

Since the war began, I have captured many thousand Federal prisoners, and they, including the survivors of the "Fort Pillow Massacre," black and white, are living witnesses of the fact that, with knowledge or consent or by my orders, not one of them has ever been insulted or maltreated in any way.

You speak of your forbearance in "not giving instructions and orders as to the course they should pursue in regard to Confederate soldiers that might fall into (your) their hands," which clearly conveys to my mind two very distinct impressions. The first is, that in not giving them instructions and orders, you have left the matter entirely to the discretion of the negroes as to how they should dispose of prisoners; second, an implied threat to give such orders as will lead to "consequences too fearful" for contemplation. In confirmation of the correctness of the first impression (which your language now fully develops), I refer you, most respectfully, to my letter from the battle-field of Tishomingo Creek, and forwarded to you by flag of truce on the 14th inst. As to the second impression, you seem disposed to take into your hands the settlement which belongs to, and can only be settled by, your government. But if you are prepared to take upon yourself the responsibility of inaugurating a system of warfare contrary to civilized usages, the onus, as well as the consequences, will be chargeable to yourself.

Deprecating, as I should do, such a state of affairs, determined as I am not to be instrumental in bringing it about, feeling and knowing as I do that I have the approval of my government, my people, and my own conscience, as to the past, and with the firm belief that I will be sustained by them in my future policy, it is left for you to determine what that policy shall be—whether in accordance with the laws of civilized warfare or in violation of them. Very respectfully, etc., N. B. FORREST,
Major-general.

After Forrest's brilliant victory at Tishomingo Creek, the fortunes of the Confederacy were rapidly on the wane. The Federal General Wilson was organizing a heavy cavalry force for the purpose of striking Selma and Mobile. Forrest found his forces inadequate to the task of resisting its progress. He met the enemy and disputed every inch of ground. Finding further resistance useless, he surrendered his command to the Federal authorities, near Selma, in the spring of 1865. The other armies of the Confederacy had surrendered. Forrest issued an address to his men, recounting their noble deeds while under his command, and exhorting them, now that further resistance was useless, to accept the situation in good faith, and make as good citizens as they had made soldiers.

REORGANIZATION OF FORREST'S CAVALRY.

Lieutenant-general N. B. FORREST Commanding.

[Commissioned Brigadier-general, July 21, 1862; Major-general, December 4, 1863; Lieutenant-general, March 2, 1865.]

STAFF OFFICERS.

John P. Strange, Major and Assistant Adjutant-general.
Charles W. Anderson, First Lieutenant and Aid-de-camp.
William M. Forrest, First Lieutenant and Aid-de-camp.
Samuel Donelson, First Lieutenant and Aid-de-camp.
C. S. Severson, Major and Chief Quartermaster.
R. M. Mason, Major and Chief Quartermaster.
G. V. Rambaut, Major and Chief Commissary.
George Dashiel, Captain and Chief Paymaster.
Dr. J. B. Cowan, Chief Surgeon.
Charles S. Hill, Captain and Chief Ordnance Officer.
John G. Mann, Captain and Chief of Engineers.

CHALMERS'S DIVISION.

Brigadier-general JAMES R. CHALMERS Commanding.

[Commissioned Brigadier-general February 13, 1862.]

STAFF OFFICERS.

Walter A. Goodman, Captain and Assistant Adjutant-general.
L. T. Lindsey, Captain and Acting Assistant Adjutant-general.
Andrew J. Mills, Captain and Acting Assistant Inspector-general.
George T. Banks, First Lieutenant and Aid-de-camp.
Samuel O'Neill, Captain and Chief Quartermaster.
William F. Avent, Captain and A. Q. M. Pay Department.
John T. Buck, First Lieutenant and Chief Ordnance Officer.
B. S. Crump, Major and Chief Commissary.
Dr. James R. Barnett, Chief Surgeon.

BUFORD'S DIVISION.

Brigadier-general ABE BUFORD Commanding.

STAFF OFFICERS.

Hunter Nicholson, Major and Assistant Adjutant-general.
Thomas M. Crowder, Captain and Assistant Adjutant-general.
D. A. Given, First Lieutenant and Aid-de-camp.
D. E. Myers, First Lieutenant and Assistant Inspector-general.
James L. Lea, Captain and Assistant Quartermaster.
J. R. Finch, Major and Chief Commissary.
John D. Gardner, First Lieutenant and Chief of Ordnance.
Thomas F. Clardy, M.D., Chief Surgeon.
William M. Cargill, Major and A. Q. M. Pay Department.

JACKSON'S DIVISION.

Brigadier-general WILLIAM H. JACKSON Commanding.

STAFF OFFICERS.

E. T. Sykes, Captain and Assistant Adjutant-general.
James C. Jones, First Lieutenant and Assistant Adjutant-general.
T. B. Sykes, Captain and Assistant Inspector-general.
J. H. Martin, First Lieutenant and Aid-de-camp.
W. P. Paul, Major and Assistant Quartermaster.
A. P. Slover, Major and Chief Commissary.
Dr. Arthur Bragden, Chief Surgeon.
Dr. G. A. Hogg, Assistant Surgeon.
Lewis Bond, Captain and Chief of Ordnance.
John Watics, Captain and Chief of Artillery.
William Ewing, Drill Master.

BELL'S BRIGADE OF BUFORD'S DIVISION.

Brigadier-general TYREE H. BELL Commanding.

STAFF OFFICERS.

R. D. Clark, Captain and Assistant Adjutant-general.
T. E. Richardson, First Lieutenant and Assistant Adjutant-general.
J. L. Bell, First Lieutenant and Assistant Inspector-general.
P. A. Smith, First Lieutenant and Assistant Inspector-general.
I. T. Bell, First Lieutenant and Aid-de-camp.
T. P. Allison, Major and Assistant Quartermaster.
J. L. Lea, Captain and Assistant Quartermaster.
D. M. Womack, Captain and Chief Commissary.
A. G. Harris, First Lieutenant and Brigade Commissary.
C. C. Harris, First Lieutenant and Ordnance Officer.

THOMPSON'S* BRIGADE, BUFORD'S DIVISION.

Colonel ED. CROSSLAND Commanding.

STAFF OFFICERS.

C. L. Randle, Captain and Assistant Adjutant-general.
J. P. Mathewson, First Lieutenant and Assistant Inspector-general.
William Lindsey, Captain and Assistant Quartermaster.
J. R. Smith, Major and Chief Commissary.
Robert A. Galbraith, Captain and Aid-de-camp.
F. G. Terry, Captain and Ordnance Officer.

---

* Col. A. P. Thompson, former Commander of this brigade, was killed while leading an attack upon the Federals at Paducah.

FIRST BRIGADE, CHALMERS'S DIVISION.

Colonel ROBERT McCULLOCH Commanding.

STAFF OFFICERS.

John T. Chandler, Captain and Assistant Adjutant-general.
W. J. Vankirk, Captain and Assistant Quartermaster.
J. M. Tyler, First Lieutenant and Acting Inspector-general.
J. J. Guyton, Captain and Chief Commissary.
T. M. Turner, First Lieutenant and Aid-de-camp.
J. J. Hay, Second Lieutenant and Ordnance Officer.
Dr. F. R. Durrett, Chief Surgeon.

RUCKER'S BRIGADE, CHALMERS'S DIVISION.

Colonel E. W. RUCKER Commanding.

STAFF OFFICERS.

John T. Chandler, Captain and Assistant Adjutant-general.
Ferdinand Smith, Captain and Acting Assistant Adjutant-general.
John Overton, jr., Captain and Assistant Inspector-general.
F. B. Rodgers, First Lieutenant and Aid-de-camp.
William O. Key, Major and Assistant Quartermaster.
R. M. Ligon, Captain and Chief Commissary.
Dr. C. K. Caruthers, Chief Surgeon.
C. N. Featherston, Second Lieutenant and Ordnance Officer.

NEELEY'S BRIGADE, CHALMERS'S DIVISION.

Colonel J. J. NEELY Commanding.

STAFF OFFICERS.

V. B. Waddell, First Lieutenant and Assistant Adjutant-general.
Edward Reneau, Second Lieutenant and Acting Inspector-general.
M. K. Mister, Second Lieutenant and Aid-de-camp.
William O. Key, Major and Assistant Quartermaster.
S. J. Alexander, Major and Chief Commissary.
Dr. C. K. Caruthers, Chief Surgeon.

CAMPBELL'S BRIGADE, JACKSON'S DIVISION.

ALEXANDER W. CAMPBELL Commanding.

[Commissioned Brigadier-general May 1, 1864.]

STAFF OFFICERS.

Ferdinand Stith,* Captain and Assistant Adjutant-general.
John Overton, jr.,* Captain and Inspector-general.

---

* Transferred from Rucker's Brigade.

William R. Harris, First Lieutenant and Aid-de-camp.
A. Warren, Major and Assistant Quartermaster.
W. J. Sykes, Major and Chief Commissary.
C. N. Featherston,* Second Lieutenant and Ordnance Officer.

ARTILLERY OF FORREST'S COMMAND.

MAY, 1864.

MORTON'S BATTERY.
(Four Guns.)

John W. Morton. Captain.
T. S. Sale, First Lieutenant.
G. T. Brown, First Lieutenant.
Joseph M. Mayson, Second Lieutenant.
Dr. James P. Hanner, Surgeon.

RICE'S BATTERY.
(Four Guns.)

T. W. Rice, Captain.
B. F. Haller, First Lieutenant.
H. H. Biggs, Second Lieutenant.
Dan. C. Jones, Second Lieutenant.
Dr. Jacob Huggins, Jr., Surgeon.

HUDSON'S BATTERY.
(Four Guns. Originally known as Walton's Battery.)

E. S. Walton, Captain.
Milt. H. Frautham, First Lieutenant.
G. C. Wright, Second Lieutenant.
W. O. Hunter, Second Lieutenant.
R. P. Weaver, Surgeon.

THRALL'S BATTERY.
(Four Guns.)

J. C. Thrall, Captain.
R. S. Anderson, First Lieutenant.
J. C. Barlow, Second Lieutenant.
W. J. D. Winton, Second Lieutenant.
Dr. J. L. Grace, Surgeon.

SECOND TENNESSEE CAVALRY.

C. R. Barteau, Colonel.
G. H. Morton, Lieutenant-colonel.
William Parrish, Major.
Dr. J. M. Hughes, Surgeon.
Dr. J. W. Harrison, Assist. Surgeon.
E. O. Elliott, Quartermaster.
P. A. Smith, First Lieut. and Adj't.
Rev. S. C. Talley, Chaplain.

COMPANY A.

T. C. Atkinson, First Lieutenant.
A. H. French, Second Lieutenant.

COMPANY B.

T. B. Underwood, Captain.
G. W. Smithson, First Lieutenant.
S. B. Wall, Second Lieutenant.
J. D. Core, Third Lieutenant.

---

* Transferred from Rucker's Brigade.

FORREST'S CAVALRY.

COMPANY C.

M. W. McKnight, Captain.
H. L. W. Turney, First Lieutenant.
Samuel Dennis, Second Lieutenant.
J. S. Harrison, Third Lieutenant.

COMPANY D.

William T. Rickman, Captain.
George Love, First Lieutenant.
F. W. Youree, Second Lieutenant.
Ed. Bullock, Third Lieutenant.

COMPANY E.

W. A. DeBow, Captain.
George E. Seay, First Lieutenant.
R. B. Dobbins, Second Lieutenant.
F. J. Carman, Third Lieutenant.

COMPANY F.

John A. Binkley, Captain.
James F. Austin, First Lieutenant.
John E. Demming, Second Lieutenant.
Newson Penell, Third Lieutenant.

COMPANY G.

J. M. Eustis, Captain.
B. G. Moore, First Lieutenant.
A. W. Lipscomb, Second Lieutenant.
J. J. Laurence, Third Lieutenant.

COMPANY H.

B. Edwards, Captain.
J. Bedford, First Lieutenant.
E. Lassater, Second Lieutenant.
T. L. Stubblefield, Third Lieutenant.

COMPANY I.

S. W. Reeves, Captain.
William Lattimer, First Lieutenant.
J. H. Bettick, Second Lieutenant.
W. C. Roberts, Third Lieutenant.

COMPANY K.

O. B. Farris, Captain.
J. H. Neal, First Lieutenant.
F. M. McRoe, Second Lieutenant.
H. Pryor, Third Lieutenant.

FOURTH TENNESSEE CAVALRY.

James H. Starnes, Colonel.
P. C. Haynes, Lieutenant-colonel.
P. T. Rankin, Major.
William H. Davis, Adjutant.
Dr. Edward Swanson, Surgeon.
Dr. Allen E. Gooch, Assistant Surgeon.
Joseph B. Briggs, Quartermaster.
Moses H. Cliff, Commissary.
Rev. William H. Whitsit, Chaplain.

COMPANY A.

Aaron Thompson, Captain.
James C. Candiff, First Lieutenant.
B. F. Boyd, Second Lieutenant.
S. S. Short, Third Lieutenant.

COMPANY B.

J. B. Britton, Captain.
C. C. Rutherford, First Lieutenant.
E. L. Collier, Second Lieutenant.
S. T. Bass, Third Lieutenant.

COMPANY C.

E. L. Lindsey, Captain.
W. E. Donnell, First Lieutenant.
C. C. Hancock, Second Lieutenant.
D. W. Grandstaff, Third Lieutenant.

COMPANY D.

A. A. Dysart, Captain.
W. M. Robinson, First Lieutenant.
F. M. Webb, Second Lieutenant.
John Carpenter, Third Lieutenant.

COMPANY E.

G. W. Robinson, Captain.
W. F. White, First Lieutenant.
W. A. Hubbard, Second Lieutenant.
J. W. Norton, Third Lieutenant.

COMPANY F.

W. S. McLemore, Captain.
J. T. Pierce, First Lieutenant.
S. S. Hughes, Second Lieutenant.
S. C. Tulloss, Third Lieutenant.

COMPANY G.

Andrew McGregor, Captain.
A. J. Duffey, First Lieutenant.
John H. Dice, Second Lieutenant.
E. W. Burwell, Third Lieutenant.

COMPANY H.

J. E. Teague, Captain.
J. W. Johnson, First Lieutenant.
C. G. Pryor, Second Lieutenant.
J. M. Ragen, Third Lieutenant.

COMPANY I.

P. H. McBride, Captain.
J. A. Smotherman, First Lieutenant.
G. L. Freeman, Second Lieutenant.
T. W. Lewis, Third Lieutenant.

COMPANY K.

Francisco Rice, Captain.
J. B. Poston, First Lieutenant.
W. E. Baker, Second Lieutenant.
W. A. Young, Third Lieutenant.

SEVENTH TENNESSEE CAVALRY.

FIELD AND STAFF.

William L. Duckworth, Colonel.
Wm. F. Taylor, Lieutenant-colonel.
C. C. Clay, Major.
Wm. S. Pope, Lieut. and Adj't.
Kenneth Garrett, Quartermaster.
Dr. J. C. Word, Surgeon.
Rev. W. L. Rosser, Chaplain.

COMPANY A.

J. W. Sneed, Captain.
H. W. Watkins, First Lieutenant.
W. L. Certain, Second Lieutenant.
J. D. Mitchell, Third Lieutenant.

COMPANY B.

J. P. Russell, Captain.
H. T. Sale, First Lieutenant.
J. N. Stinson, Second Lieutenant.
Robert J. Black, Third Lieutenant.

COMPANY C.

John T. Lawler, Captain.
W. B. Winston, First Lieutenant.
S. B. Higgins, Second Lieutenant.
A. L. Winston, Third Lieutenant.

COMPANY D.

L. W. Taliaferro, Captain.
H. J. Livingstone, First Lieutenant.
T. J. Mann, Second Lieutenant.
A. A. Johnson, Third Lieutenant.

FORREST'S CAVALRY.

COMPANY E.

W. J. Tate, Captain.
J. P. Statler, First Lieutenant.
H. Harris, Second Lieutenant.
W. C. Mashburn, Third Lieutenant.

COMPANY F.

C. H. Jones, Captain (consolidated with Company E).

COMPANY G.

F. F. Aden, Captain.
J. J. Blake, First Lieutenant.
W. N. Griffin, Second Lieutenant.
James T. Haynes, Third Lieutenant.

COMPANY H.

H. C. McCutcheon, Captain.
J. A. Jenkins, First Lieutenant.

COMPANY I.

J. R. Alexander, Captain.
W. P. Malone, First Lieutenant.
P. A. Fisher, Second Lieutenant.
E. M. Downing, Third Lieutenant.

COMPANY K.

J. A. Anderson, Captain.
J. S. Hille, First Lieutenant.
John Trout, Second Lieutenant.
E. R. Scruggs, Third Lieutenant.

COMPANY L.

Alexander Duckworth, Captain.
———— ————, First Lieutenant.
Frank Pugh, Second Lieutenant.
Wm. Witherspoon, Third Lieutenant.

COMPANY M.

Benjamin T. Davis, Captain.
William Moore, First Lieutenant.
Charles Rice, Second Lieutenant.
J. L. Livingstone, Third Lieutenant.

EIGHTH TENNESSEE CAVALRY.

FIELD AND STAFF.

George G. Dibrell, Colonel.
F. H. Dougherty, Lieutenant-colonel.
Jeffery E. Forrest, Major.
M. D. Smallman, Lieut. and Adj't.
A. C. Dale, Quartermaster.
J N. Bailey, Commissary.
Dr. William C. McCord, Surgeon.
Dr. J. Luke Ridley, Assistant Surgeon.

COMPANY A.

W. W. Windle, Captain.
A. L. Windle, Second Lieutenant.

COMPANY B.

Hamilton McGuinnis, Captain.
Thomas C. Webb, First Lieutenant.
Allen G. Parker, Second Lieutenant.
Levi Maynard, Third Lieutenant.

COMPANY C.

Isaac G. Woolsey, Captain.
William C. Wood, First Lieutenant.
J. W. Pendergrass, Second Lieutenant.
Jackson Davis, Third Lieutenant.

COMPANY D.

Jefferson Leftwitch, Captain.
James W. Revis, First Lieutenant.
William R. Hill, Second Lieutenant.
Wayman Dibrell, Third Lieutenant.

COMPANY E.

William P. Chapin, First Lieutenant.   Lloyd W. Chapin, Second Lieutenant.
Jesse Allen, Third Lieutenant.

COMPANY F.

Josiah Bilberry, Captain.   Thomas H. Webb, Second Lieutenant.
Jefferson Bilberry, First Lieutenant.   —— Herner, Third Lieutenant.

COMPANY G.

Mounce L. Gore, Captain.   Newton Byber, Second Lieutenant.
William Z. Beck, First Lieutenant.

COMPANY H.

James Barnes, Captain.   John S. Rhea, Second Lieutenant.
John Hill, First Lieutenant.   Joseph D. Bartlett, Third Lieutenant.

COMPANY I.

James W. McReynolds Captain.   Simon D. Wallace, Third Lieutenant.
James Walker, Second Lieutenant.

COMPANY K.

Bryan M. Swearingin, Captain.   Elijah W. Terry, Second Lieutenant.
Jesse Beck, First Lieutenant.

NINTH TENNESSEE CAVALRY.

FIELD AND STAFF.

J. B. Biffle, Colonel.   William M. Irwin, Quartermaster.
A. G. Cooper, Lieutenant-colonel.   W. S. Johnston, Commissary.
Roderick Perry, Lieut. and Adj't.   Dr. Henry Long, Surgeon.

COMPANY A.

J. J. Biffle, Captain.   G. Wells, Second Lieutenant.
John W. Hill, First Lieutenant.

COMPANY B.

James Reynolds Captain.   —— Littleton, First Lieutenant.

COMPANY C.

C. F. Barnes, Captain.   P. Brownlaw, Second Lieutenant.
Thomas Helmick, First Lieutenant.

COMPANY D.

Lewis M. Kirk, Captain.   —— May, First Lieutenant.

COMPANY E.

G. J. Adkinson, Captain.   P. Pigg, Second Lieutenant.
James Leftwitch, First Lieutenant.   P. Nichols, Third Lieutenant.

COMPANY F.

J. W. Johnson, Captain.   B. S. Hardin, Second Lieutenant.
J. P. Montague, First Lieutenant.   John Johnson, Third Lieutenant.

FORREST'S CAVALRY.

COMPANY G.

John S. Groves, Captain.
D. B. Cooper, First Lieutenant.
Robert Harris, Second Lieutenant.
Jacob Armstrong, Third Lieutenant.

COMPANY H.

Thomas H. Beatty, Captain.
Denton Pennington, First Lieut.
J. Davis, Second Lieutenant.
M. D. Cooper, Third Lieutenant.

COMPANY I.

Frank Smith, Captain.
B. F. Burkitt, First Lieutenant.

COMPANY K.

R. L. Ford, Captain.
Thomas Hargroves, First Lieutenant.
John Hicks, Second Lieutenant.

COMPANY L.

Robert Sharp, Captain.
Edward Cannon, First Lieutenant.
Robert Clarke, Second Lieutenant.

TENTH TENNESSEE CAVALRY.

FIELD AND STAFF.

N. N. Cox, Colonel.
E. B. Trezevant, Lieutenant-colonel.
William E. Demoss, Major.
E. A. Spottswood, Lieut. and Adj't.
D. H. White, Quartermaster.
J. N. Rickman, Commissary.
Dr. Julius Johnston, Surgeon.

COMPANY A.

W. J. Hall, Captain.
John Pace, First Lieutenant.
J. W. Townshend, Second Lieutenant.

COMPANY B.

W. H. Lewis, Captain.
William Fisher, First Lieutenant.
J. M. Randall, Second Lieutenant.
Thomas Mitchell, Third Lieutenant.

COMPANY C.

W. H. Whitehall, Captain.
A. D. Craig, First Lieutenant.
John Horner, Second Lieutenant.
Thomas F. Lewis, Third Lieutenant.

COMPANY D.

W. J. Robinson, Captain.
W. P. Edds, First Lieutenant.
W. N. Phipps, Second Lieutenant.
W. A. Wray, Third Lieutenant.

COMPANY E.

John Minor, Captain,
Andrew Nesbitt, First Lieutenant.
J. B. Williams, Second Lieutenant.
—— Nesbitt, Third Lieutenant.

COMPANY F.

W. W. Hobbs, Captain.
M. M. Box, First Lieutenant.
J. T. Hobbs, Second Lieutenant.
C. S. Summers, Third Lieutenant.

COMPANY G.

T. S. Easley, Captain.
J. A. McCauley, First Lieutenant.
J. M. Hall, Second Lieutenant.
W. J. Frazier, Third Lieutenant.

COMPANY H.

B. G. Rickman, Captain.
W. H. Coode, First Lieutenant.
E. H. Shepherd, Second Lieutenant.
J. D. Land, Third Lieutenant.

COMPANY I.

Thomas Fletcher, Captain.
Clinton Aden, First Lieutenant.
B. E. Summers, Second Lieutenant.
—— Dodson, Third Lieutenant.

COMPANY K.

Thomas M. Hutchinson, Captain.
J. Utley, First Lieutenant.
W. O. Chapman, Second Lieutenant.
J. O. Pinick, Third Lieutenant.

ELEVENTH TENNESSEE CAVALRY.

FIELD AND STAFF.

James H. Edmondson, Colonel.
D. W. Holman, Lieutenant-colonel.
J. T. Martin, Major.
W. R. Garrett, Lieut. and Adj't.
Dr. J. D. Core, Surgeon.
Dr. W. H. Anderson, Assistant Surgeon.
O. G. Gurley, Quartermaster.
J. D. Allen, Commissary.

COMPANY A.

Charles McDonald, Captain.
(Afterward McDonald's Battalion.)

COMPANY B.

Johnson Nevils, First Lieutenant.

COMPANY C.

T. C. H. Miller, Captain.
W. W. Braden, First Lieutenant.
E. G. Hamilton, Second Lieutenant.
E. F. Raney, Third Lieutenant.

COMPANY D.

John Lytle, Captain.
John L. Carney, First Lieutenant.
N. P. Marble, Second Lieutenant.
I. H. Butler, Third Lieutenant.

COMPANY E.

A. R. Gordon, Captain.
J. M. Edmonson, First Lieutenant.
Robert Gordon, Second Lieutenant.
George Rotherock, Third Lieutenant.

COMPANY F.

P. T. Allen, Captain.
(McDonald's Battalion.)

COMPANY G.

Thomas Banks, First Lieutenant.
David S. Chancy, Second Lieutenant.
A. S. Chapman, Third Lieutenant.

FORREST'S CAVALRY.

COMPANY H.
Chatham Coffee, Captain.
Robert Bruce, Second Lieutenant.
William Durley, Third Lieutenant.

COMPANY I.
T. F. Perkins, Captain.
John C. Bostick, First Lieutenant.
Malachi Kirby, Second Lieutenant.
S. Rozelle, Third Lieutenant.

COMPANY K.
James Rivers, Captain.
William H. Baugh, First Lieutenant.
Robert McNairy, Second Lieutenant.

COMPANY L.
John M. Rust, Captain.
James Ward, Second Lieutenant.

TWELFTH TENNESSEE CAVALRY.
FIELD AND STAFF.
J. U. Green, Colonel.
G. W. Bennett, Major.
R. B. Bone, Lieutenant and Adjutant.
Dr. A. Beatty, Surgeon.
Dr. E. H. Sholl, Assistant Surgeon.
S. F. Cocke, Quartermaster.
Rev. A. G. Burrow, Chaplain.

COMPANY A.
Edward Daley, Captain.
W. H. Crite, First Lieutenant.
R. H. Strickland, Second Lieutenant.
H. L. Massey, Third Lieutenant.

COMPANY B.
W. T. Carmack, Captain.
W. D. Wilder, First Lieutenant.
F. E. Brown, Second Lieutenant.
J. E. Yancy, Third Lieutenant.

COMPANY C.
J. L. Payne, Captain.
William Bell, First Lieutenant.
R. C. Simonton, Second Lieutenant.
C. F. Sullivan, Third Lieutenant.

COMPANY D.
J. G. McCauley, Captain.
J. Appleberry, First Lieutenant.
Wm. M. Parker, Second Lieutenant.

COMPANY E.
C. S. McStusack, Captain.
J. S. Granberry, First Lieutenant.
J. S. Stewart, Second Lieutenant.

COMPANY F.
William Bell, Captain.
John Matthews, First Lieutenant.
James Brooks, Second Lieutenant.
Hiram Prewitt, Third Lieutenant.

COMPANY G.
John Massey, Captain.
W. W. Freeman, First Lieutenant.
Ambrose House, Second Lieutenant.
O. H. Wade, Third Lieutenant.

COMPANY H.

W. M. Craddock, Captain.
J. C. Haines, First Lieutenant.
W. J. Overall, Second Lieutenant.
L. L. Cherry, Third Lieutenant.

COMPANY I.

J. B. Scarborough, Captain.
R. Johnson, First Lieutenant.
William Stewart, Second Lieutenant.
Wm. McKirksill, Third Lieutenant.

COMPANY K.

J. R. McSpadden, Captain.
E. H. Cobbs, First Lieutenant.
J. T. Briggs, Second Lieutenant.
R. A. Williford, Third Lieutenant.

FOURTEENTH TENNESSEE CAVALRY.

FIELD AND STAFF.

J. J. Neely, Colonel.
R. R. White, Lieutenant-colonel.
Gwynn Thurmond, Major.
E. S. Hammond, Adjutant.
H. M. Pirtle, Quartermaster.
Dr. T. H. Turner, Surgeon.
Dr. R. P. Watson, Assistant Surgeon.

COMPANY A.

S. J. Cox, Captain.
M. P. Harbison, First Lieutenant.
J. B. Harris, Second Lieutenant.

COMPANY B.

J. H. DeBerry, Captain.
N. A. Senter, First Lieutenant.
G. Hicks, Second Lieutenant.
John B. Holt, Third Lieutenant.

COMPANY C.

Z. Voss, Captain.
R. J. Strayhorne, First Lieutenant.
W. H. Swinck, Second Lieutenant.

COMPANY D.

L. A. Thomas, Captain.
J. W. Ricks, First Lieutenant.
James Drake, Second Lieutenant.

COMPANY E.

E. M. Jacobs, Captain.
A. R. Emmerson, First Lieutenant.
W. G. Pirtle, Second Lieutenant.

COMPANY F.

W. J. Hall, Captain.
J. M. Moore, First Lieutenant.
M. G. Hall, Second Lieutenant.

COMPANY G.

A. C. Reid, Captain.
W. F. Dillard, First Lieutenant.
J. Robertson, Second Lieutenant.
J. Reid, Third Lieutenant.

COMPANY H.

James Gwynn, Captain.
B. F. Tatum, First Lieutenant.
D. L. Hill, Second Lieutenant.
H. J. Brewster, Third Lieutenant.

COMPANY I.

J. S. Elliott, Captain.
James Laird, First Lieutenant.
John Langley, Second Lieutenant.

COMPANY K.

C. C. Conner, Captain.
A. W. Fleming, First Lieutenant.
W. J. Campbell, Second Lieutenant.

FIFTEENTH TENNESSEE CAVALRY.

FIELD AND STAFF.

F. M. Stewart, Colonel.
T. H. Logwood, Lieutenant-colonel.
Solomon G. Street, Major.
J. L. Barksdale, Adjutant.
John Sheffington, Quartermaster.
Dr. A. B. Tapscott, Surgeon.
Dr. A. Bruce, Assistant Surgeon.

COMPANY A.

P. W. Moore, Captain.
W. R. Griffith, First Lieutenant.
R. S. Van Dyke, Second Lieutenant.
R. T. Gardner, Third Lieutenant.

COMPANY B.

J. L. Garrison, Captain.
John F. Garrison, First Lieutenant.
W. B. Nolley, Second Lieutenant.
W. D. Brown, Third Lieutenant.

COMPANY C.

H. T. Hanks, Captain.
A. B. Henry, First Lieutenant.
J. Ray, Second Lieutenant.

COMPANY D.

T. Nutt, Captain.
L. C. Street, Second Lieutenant.

COMPANY E.

E. L. Hussey, Captain.
G. W. Yapp, First Lieutenant.

COMPANY F.

T. C. Buckhannon, Captain.
J. P. Thurman, First Lieutenant.
F. G. Ferguson, Second Lieutenant.
E. S. Thirman, Third Lieutenant.

COMPANY G.

R. B. Sanders, Captain.
J. M. McCaleb, First Lieutenant.
P. H. Sutton, Second Lieutenant.

COMPANY H.

J. M. Witherspoon, First Lieutenant.

COMPANY I.

P. M. Williams, Captain.
T. W. Allen, First Lieutenant.
R. Y. Anderson, Second Lieutenant.
J. L. Seward, Third Lieutenant.

COMPANY K.

J. A. Williams, Captain.
R. Stone, Second Lieutenant.
V. H. Swift, Third Lieutenant.

McDONALD'S BATTALION.

(Forrest's Old Regiment.)

FIELD AND STAFF.

D. C. Kelley, Lieutenant-colonel. Lieut. E. A. Spottswood, Adjutant.
P. T. Allen, Major. G. A. Cockran, Assist. Quartermaster.

COMPANY A.

T. F. Pattison, Captain. J. A. Powell, Second Lieutenant.
W. J. P. Doyle, First Lieutenant. James Southerland, Third Lieutenant

COMPANY B.

James G. Barbour, Captain. R. L. Ivey, Second Lieutenant.
C. D. Steinkuhl, First Lieutenant. J. W. Alexander, Third Lieutenant.

COMPANY C.

J. C. Blanton, Captain. Samuel Powell, Second Lieutenant.
Charles Balch, First Lieutenant. G. Glenn, Third Lieutenant.

COMPANY D.

W. H. Forrest, Captain. S. B. Soliuan, Second Lieutenant.
T. H. Magee, First Lieutenant. Joseph Luxton, Third Lieutenant.

COMPANY E.

N. E. Wood, Captain. B. A. Powell, Third Lieutenant.
W. J. Redd, Second Lieutenant.

COMPANY F.

J. F. Rodgers, Captain. J. S. Nichols, Third Lieutenant.
C. A. Donglass, Second Lieutenant.

COMPANY G.

W. J. Shaw, Captain. D. A. Autrey, First Lieutenant.

COMPANY H.

J. L. Morphis, Captain. W. J. Morphis, Third Lieutenant.
J. H. Jones, Second Lieutenant.

COMPANY I.

T. R. Bearfoot, Captain. E. Wooten, Second Lieutenant.
J. M. Duncan, First Lieutenant.

COMPANY K.

William Higgs, Captain. J. C. Savage, Second Lieutenant.
J. P. Johnson, First Lieutenant. John Ramsey, Third Lieutenant.

SIXTEENTH BATTALION TENNESSEE CAVALRY.

FIELD AND STAFF.

J. R. Neal, Captain.
Joseph Paine, Major.
Lieut. W. B. L. Reagan, Adjutant.
H. W. McElwie, Quartermaster.

COMPANY A.

James Rodgers, Captain.
F. A. Lenoir, First Lieutenant.
G. A. Montgomery, Second Lieutenant.
W. C. Pride, Third Lieutenant.

COMPANY B.

R. F. Mastin, Captain.
W. N. King, First Lieutenant.
J. T. Vaughn, Second Lieutenant.
J. M. King, Third Lieutenant.

COMPANY C.

W. P. Darwin, Captain.
H. C. Collins, First Lieutenant.
—— Armour, Second Lieutenant.
—— Thomas, Third Lieutenant.

COMPANY D.

F. M. Murray, Captain.
T. H. Masten, First Lieutenant.
—— Campbell, Second Lieutenant.
James Baine, Third Lieutenant.

COMPANY E.

Thomas S. Rambaugh, Captain.
Thomas Williams, First Lieutenant.
William Williams, Second Lieutenant.
W. P. Reed, Third Lieutenant.

COMPANY F.

Mike Stoley, Captain.
E. Etson, First Lieutenant.
—— Monyham, Second Lieutenant.
Moses Anderson, Third Lieutenant.

SIXTEENTH TENNESSEE CAVALRY.

FIELD AND STAFF.

A. N. Wilson, Colonel.
Jesse A. Forrest, Lieutenant-colonel.
W. T. Parham, Major.
Lieut. F. M. Bell, Adjutant.
B. M. Bray, Quartermaster.
Dr. S. H. Caldwell, Surgeon.
Dr. M. D. L. Jordon, Assist. Surgeon.

COMPANY A.

J. A. Russell, Captain.
W. A. McCandless, First Lieutenant.
John Coberne, Second Lieutenant.
T. F. Wilson, Third Lieutenant.

COMPANY B.

Ed. Polk, Captain.
J. C. Shipp, First Lieutenant.
W. B. Malone, Second Lieutenant.
J. R. Glover, Third Lieutenant.

COMPANY C.

J. J. Rice, Captain.
I. J. Galbreath, First Lieutenant.
J. F. Collins, Second Lieutenant.
J. D. Walker, Third Lieutenant.

COMPANY D.

W. H. Bray, Captain.
J. R. Arnold, First Lieutenant.
J. C. Dodd, Second Lieutenant.
J. M. Bray, Third Lieutenant.

COMPANY E.

W. H. Simmons, Captain.
J. P. Reverly, First Lieutenant.
A. J. Baxter, Second Lieutenant.

COMPANY F.

James Stennette, Captain.
S. J. Crowder, Second Lieutenant.

COMPANY G.

J. W. Fussell, Captain.
James Tomlinson, First Lieutenant.
T. R. Mangrum, Second Lieutenant.
T. A. Haynes, Third Lieutenant.

COMPANY H.

J. W. Carroll, Captain.
M. L. Cherry, First Lieutenant.
S. C. Kennedy, Second Lieutenant.

COMPANY I.

J. C. Gooch, Captain.
H. Lassiter, First Lieutenant.
M. H. Goodloe, Second Lieutenant.
J. B. Northern, Third Lieutenant.

COMPANY K.

R. E. Dudley, Captain.
J. F. Looney, First Lieutenant.
W. E. Scales, Second Lieutenant.
A. F. Brooks, Third Lieutenant.

NINETEENTH TENNESSEE CAVALRY.

FIELD AND STAFF.

John F. Newson, Colonel.
D. M. Wisdom, Lieutenant-colonel.
W. Y. Baker, Major.
Lieut. H. T. Johnson, Adjutant.
A. B. Crook, Quartermaster.
Dr. Lockart, Surgeon.
Rev. John Randolph, Chaplain.

COMPANY A.

W. N. Barnhill, Captain.
L. T. Settle, First Lieutenant.
J. C. O'Neill, Second Lieutenant.
H. Clyce, Third Lieutenant.

COMPANY B.

R. M. May, Captain.
M. Hayes, First Lieutenant.
N. T. Buckley, Second Lieutenant.
J. O. Ray, Third Lieutenant.

COMPANY C.

William Wilson, Captain.
William Lee, First Lieutenant.
John Barrett, Second Lieutenant.
Thomas Barrett, Third Lieutenant.

COMPANY D.

T. H. Taylor, Captain.
M. B. Ormsby, First Lieutenant.
D. J. Bowdin, Second Lieutenant.
W. P. Walker, Third Lieutenant.

COMPANY E.

J. B. Michin, Captain.
R. M. Wharton, First Lieutenant.
E. R. Turner, Second Lieutenant.
J. R. Adams, Third Lieutenant.

COMPANY F.

J. R. Damron, Captain.
A. P. Meeks, First Lieutenant.
A. L. Winningham, Second Lieutenant.
W. R. Ledbetter, Third Lieutenant.

COMPANY G.

J. J. Sharp, Captain.
M. T. Shelby, First Lieutenant.
A. Brashear, Second Lieutenant.
R. T. Simmons, Third Lieutenant.

COMPANY H.

J. G. Sharp, Captain.
J. D. Springer, First Lieutenant.
J. M. Wardlaw, Second Lieutenant.
Nathaniel Busby, Third Lieutenant.

COMPANY I.

S. C. McClirkin, Captain.
J. J. Betts, First Lieutenant.
J. M. Bumpass, Second Lieutenant.
S. M. Ozier, Third Lieutenant.

COMPANY K.

W. D. Stratton, Captain.
J. C. Miller, First Lieutenant.
J. J. Lane, Third Lieutenant.
E. W. Dunn, Third Lieutenant.

COMPANY L.

Thomas R. Dick, Captain.
William Hollis, First Lieutenant.
James Stewart, Second Lieutenant.
—— Lockman, Third Lieutenant.

TWENTIETH TENNESSEE CAVALRY.

FIELD AND STAFF.

R. M. Russell, Colonel.
H. C. Greer, Lieutenant-colonel.
H. F. Bowman, Major.
Lieut. A. G. Hawkins, Adjutant.
S. J. Ray, Quartermaster.
Dr. T. C. McNeille, Surgeon.
Dr. J. R. Westbrook, Assist. Surgeon.

COMPANY A.

William Gay, Captain.
J. H. Blackmore, First Lieutenant.
J. N. Gay, Second Lieutenant.
R. H. Goodman, Third Lieutenant.

COMPANY B.

W. H. Hawkins, Captain.
N. W. McNeille, First Lieutenant.
W. H. Courts, Second Lieutenant.
M. B. Dinwiddie, Third Lieutenant.

COMPANY C.

J. T. Mathias, Captain.
J. P. Armstrong, First Lieutenant.
U. S. Halliburton, Second Lieutenant.

COMPANY D.

J. A. Shane, Captain.
J. R. Dance, First Lieutenant.
J. W. Herrin, Second Lieutenant.
G. F. Nelson, Third Lieutenant.

COMPANY E.
W. D. Hallam, Captain.   J. A. Caster, First Lieutenant.

COMPANY F.
J. C. Wilson, Captain.   J. A. Crutchfield, First Lieutenant.

COMPANY G.
J. R. Hibbitts, Captain.

COMPANY H.
J. R. Gardner, Captain.   R. C. McLesky, Second Lieutenant.
A. C. Miller, First Lieutenant.   George Cathy, Third Lieutenant.

COMPANY I.
W. H. Lawler, Captain.

COMPANY K.
M. H. Freeman, Captain.   T. J. Burton, Third Lieutenant.
A. J. Killebrew, Second Lieutenant.

NIXON'S CONSOLIDATED REGIMENT FOURTEENTH AND FIFTEENTH CAVALRY.

FIELD AND STAFF.
G. H. Nixon, Colonel.   Dr. T. H. Turner, Surgeon.
T. H. Logwood, Lieutenant-colonel.   Dr. A. L. Hamilton, Assistant Surgeon.
J. M. Crews, Major.   R. H. Shacklett, Quartermaster.
Lieut. W. W. Bayless, Adjutant.

COMPANY A.
Peter W. Moore, Captain.   W. R. Griffith, Second Lieutenant.
J. L. B. Barksdale, First Lieutenant.

COMPANY B.
Z. Voss, Captain.   W. M. Weatherly, Second Lieutenant.
W. H. Wharton, First Lieutenant.

COMPANY C.
C. A. S. Shaw, Captain.   H. D. Nealson, Second Lieutenant.
H. J. Brewster, First Lieutenant.

COMPANY D.
A. C. Reed, Captain.   W. H. Reid, Second Lieutenant.
C. C. Cowan, First Lieutenant.

COMPANY E.
Calvin Gilbert, Captain.   B. G. Pierson, Second Lieutenant.
J. T. Scott, First Lieutenant.

COMPANY F.
James H. George, Captain.   P. W. Halbert, Second Lieutenant.
J. F. Byers, First Lieutenant.

COMPANY G.

J. R. Voss, Captain.
A. C. Harwell, First Lieutenant.
J. M. Jackson, Second Lieutenant.
G. W. Prior, Third Lieutenant.

COMPANY H.

J. B. Van Houtin, Captain.
J. L. Herren, First Lieutenant.
Eugene Allen, Second Lieutenant.
G. W. Heath, Third Lieutenant.

COMPANY I.

N. J. Vaughan, Captain.
L. Burnett, First Lieutenant.
T. R. Hallowell, Second Lieutenant.

COMPANY K.

R. H. Dudley, Captain.
E. J. Neille, First Lieutenant.
J. L. Dismukes, Second Lieutenant.

We were unable to procure the names of the officers of the remaining regiments of Forrest's Cavalry.

MISCELLANEOUS.

CHAPTER XII.

PRISON LIFE.

During the first two years of the war the prisoners captured by the different armies were generally exchanged within a few months after their capture. This exchange was agreed upon and conducted by the Federal and Confederate governments, respectively, through commissioners appointed and instructed for the purpose. This was fortunate for the prisoners of each army. Aside from the humiliation of captivity and constant surveillance, the prisoner's life is a hard one. There is a lack of respect between captor and captive that is goading and disagreeable beyond description. Every item contributing to comfort in any way appears to be sparingly, grudgingly bestowed—at least the prisoner so regards it. The men of either army who were so unfortunate as to spend any of their time in prison know something of these things.

While an exchange could be readily effected, prison life was of short duration. In the latter part of 1863, the Confederates had a large excess of prisoners over the Federals, and were anxious to exchange them. Colonel Robert Ould, the Confederate commissioner of exchange, made every effort to effect an exchange, but the Federal commissioner declined to negotiate with him. The Federal authorities seemed determined to hold the Confederates permanently, with the view of weakening their armies. The Confederate authorities wanted their men for service in the field, and were wholly unprepared to take care of so many prisoners, both on account of their poverty of supplies and the demand they had in the field for the services of the men necessary to guard them.

The Confederates collected a portion of their prisoners at the Libby Prison, at Richmond, while the others were confined principally at Andersonville, Ga. The Federals established prisons at Camp Douglas, near Chicago; Camp Morton, near Indianapolis; Camp Butler, near Alton, Ill.; and other prisons at Fort Delaware and other points near the Eastern army. To be imprisoned in either of those places seemed to imply an indefinite captivity, for there was a permanent deadlock in the business of exchange.

The largest Confederate prison was at Andersonville, Ga. At this place several thousand Federal prisoners were confined in an inclosure of twenty acres. A tall plank fence surrounded the prison. Upon the walls was a walk for the sentinel, and on the inside a line was established about twenty feet from the wall all around the prison. If a prisoner passed this line he was shot on the spot, and on this account this line was known as the "dead line." A stream of water ran through the prison, from which the prisoners procured water for cooking, drinking, and washing purposes. There were no houses for the prisoners, and they were fed on coarse food, and often in scant quantities. It was far from the desire of the Confederate authorities to treat the prisoners in this manner. It was all that they *were able* to do. They had neither lumber nor nails with which to build quarters for the prisoners. They had nothing but coarse food, and that in scant quantities, with which to feed them. In fact, they cared for their prisoners in the same way that they cared for their soldiers. It was hard, but it was the best they could do. The Confederacy was at this time impoverished in every respect to the uttermost limit.

The Federal authorities, instead of exchanging their prisoners, as was urged by the Confederates, began to complain of the treatment they were receiving at Andersonville, and decided to retaliate upon the Confederates who were confined in Northern prisons. A distressing policy was inaugurated. Rations were cut down to the lowest estimate necessary to sustain life. Thus, in the midst of abundance, the poor Confederate prisoners were forced to languish and starve in Northern prisons for causes of which they were innocent, and over which they never had been able to exercise any control.

Previous to the adoption by the Federal government of retaliatory measures upon Confederate prisoners, the discipline in Camp Douglas was mild and humane. The prisoners were well fed and supplied bountifully with every necessary comfort. The Federal authorities complained of Andersonville, and they adopted retaliatory measures.

A system of the severest oppression, coupled with every manner of indignity, was now inaugurated. The writer was in Camp Douglas for the greater portion of twelve months, and while there saw all the inner working of Northern prison life. Hundreds of Tennesseans were with him, all of whom, if living, remember the events of which we write. While we chronicle these events, there is no disposition in any way to disparage or criminate a people or government against whom we were then at war. We are writing history and dealing with unpleasant facts, for or on account of which we feel no enmity toward any one. The horrors of Andersonville have been exaggerated by prejudiced pens. That the prisoners suffered at Andersonville, no one can deny. They had fallen into the hands of an enemy that was at the time so impoverished as to be unable either to feed them or take care of them, and begged their government, on this account, to take them in exchange for Confederate prisoners. This the Federal government declined to do, and in this manner resolved to submit to the situation and punish innocent Confederate prisoners in retaliation.

"How the Federals treated their prisoners" is a subject that has never yet found its way into print. We speak of our experience at Camp Douglas. The other Northern prisons were conducted in a similar manner.

CAMP DOUGLAS.

This prison was an inclosure of seventeen acres, surrounded by a triple plank wall fourteen feet high, with sentinel walk on the top of the wall. The prison was about four miles from the court-house at Chicago, and was named in honor af Stephen A. Douglas, near whose residence it was established. The prison consisted of barracks arranged in rows, in the manner of streets. There were twenty-one rows. Each row had four barracks, arranged in regular order, with cross streets at the end of each barrack. The buildings were box-houses, on posts four feet high, and each building contained one hundred and fifty men. Some of the buildings were used for hospitals. The prison was a little town of ten thousand inhabitants. It was supplied with water from the hydrants, and the buildings were comfortable. Brigadier-general B. J. Sweet was commander of the post, and the prison was under the command of Captain Welles Sponable. This prison had the "dead line," just the same as Andersonville. If a man passed it he was shot. The men were made to retire at sundown, and were not allowed to talk to one another after they laid down. If the Federals heard any talking at night in the barracks they would shoot into the house through the crowd. This was often done, when several men were shot, not only innocently and unexpectedly, but sometimes mortally. The men were not allowed to walk the cross streets. The prisoners were subjected to the severest punishment for trivial offenses.

Good accommodations were furnished the prisoners for keeping warm. The barracks were tight and had good stoves furnished with plenty of coal. The prisoners were not allowed to sit or stand around the stoves after sundown. They were required to lie in bed till the bugle sounded in the morning for them to get up. The sleeping accommodations were naked bunks, and the prisoners were allowed one blanket each.

The prisoners were allowed to go out at night in their night clothes, but were not allowed to go on a cross street. In cold weather they were allowed to wear their shoes, but were not allowed any other addition to their night clothes. If any prisoner became possessed of a change of garments the excess was taken away from him. Every week the barracks were policed by soldiers who in this way would gather up cart loads of clothing which had been taken from the prisoners in this manner, and take them out of the prison encampment.

Each barrack had a kitchen supplied with a kettle for boiling beef and vegetables. This was the only cooking utensil. A detail was made to boil the beef and issue it out to the men. The prisoner's ration was to each man one half a loaf of baker's bread daily, together with about four ounces of meat and a gill of beans or potatoes. The prisoners were not allowed any vessels of any kind. They made little wooden dishes and spoons in which they received their scanty allowance. There was a sutler's store in the prison that sold a few things at exorbitant prices, and for a long time this sutler's establishment was not allowed to sell any kind of provisions in any shape to the prisoners. The result of this treatment was that many prisoners died of starvation. If a prisoner took sick he was removed to the hospital, where better accommodations were extended to him.

During this period of starvation at Camp Douglas, the prison was visited one day by some distinguished people from England. The prison officers were showing them around in great pomp. When they came to the barracks of Morgan's men, the boys commenced crying out, "Bread! bread! bread!" The British visitors looked confused and the prison officers were greatly exasperated. As a punishment, they ordered that no bread be issued to these men for the next twenty-four hours, and gave orders to all the men of the other barracks not to trade or traffic bread to those men under the severest penalties. The men became desperate. A dog came into the camp with some visitors one day, and was decoyed away from its owner. It was reported that this dog was slaughtered and eaten by Morgan's men. The prison authorities investigated the matter, but without any satisfactory results. The matter passed off quietly. It was evident the dog had been appropriated. In this way the men suffered in Northern prisons for the last year and a half of the war.

When the news came of the assassination of President Lincoln, the prisoner who expressed himself about it in any way was jerked up and severely punished. Some people wanted to kill the prisoners and the whole Southern people when the calamity was made known. The prison was threatened with a mob, but excitement soon abated. The war soon closed. The prisoners were discharged and sent home. The horrors and cruelties of Andersonville have been at least balanced, if not eclipsed, by the cruelties of Northern prisons, of which little has been said or written since the close of the war.

It is not to be expected that prison life possesses any charms or desirable associations. In civilized wars it is destitute of many of the horrors usual among more barbarous people. Captivity is deplorable, because it is at variance with man's highest nature and noblest impulses.

During the prison life at Camp Douglas, the people of Chicago manifested toward the prisoners much sympathy and assistance, not as a political measure so much as a matter of humanity. As the war progressed, the Federal authorities forbade such expressions of sympathy, but the noble ladies of Chicago continued in the good work, prominent among whom was Mrs. Mary Blackburn Morris. This lady was possessed of great wealth, and in its bestowal to the relief of the suffering Confederate prisoners, she endeared herself to the prisoners and to the Southern people. Mrs. Morris died at Louisville, Ky., October 18, 1884. In honor of her memory, the following meeting was held in Clarksville, Tenn., on Friday, October 24, 1884, an account of which was printed in the Clarksville papers of October 28:

MRS. MARY BLACKBURN MORRIS.

In pursuance of the following call, the Confederate soldiers and many of the citizens of Clarksville assembled at the court-house in Clarksville on Friday, October 24, 1884, at 11 o'clock, A.M.:

Our comrades of the Tenth, Forty-second, Forty-ninth, and Fiftieth Tennessee Regiments remember the motherly kindness of this good woman, who ministered to them when prisoners of war at Chicago, Ill., in 1862, and to show their appreciation of her noble action, and grateful remembrance of the same, a meeting of Confederate soldiers is called at the circuit court room, at the court-house in Clarksville, on Friday, at 11 o'clock A.M., October 24, 1884. All citizens—ladies especially—are invited to attend.

Lewis R. Clark, Tenth Tennessee.
R. E. McCulloch, J. J. Crusman, T. D. Johnson, D. F. Wright, Fourteenth Tennessee.
W. A. Quarles, T. A. Turner, E. M. Nolan, Forty-second Tennessee.
J. E. Bailey, T. M. Atkins, R. Y. Johnson, W. F. Young, Thomas H. Smith, Polk G. Johnson, Forty-ninth Tennessee.
Charles W. Tyler, J. L. W. Power, John D. Moore, Fiftieth Tennessee.
William R. Bringhurst, Austin Peay, C. D. Bell, Woodward's Cavalry.
John Minor, Tenth Tennessee Cavalry.
Henry Merritt, H. H. Lurton, Dortch's Cavalry.
F. P. Gracey, Gracey's Battery.

On motion of ex-United States Senator James E. Bailey, colonel of the Forty-ninth Tennessee, C. S. A., Brigadier-general William A. Quarles was called to the chair. Upon taking the chair, General Quarles paid a high tribute to the many virtues of the noble woman whose memory we had met to commemorate.

The chair appointed Lieutenant Polk G. Johnson, Forty-ninth Tennessee, secretary; W. O. Brandon, Clarksville *Tobacco Leaf;* B. M. DeGraffenried, Clarksville *Democrat;* and R. H. Yancy, Clarksville *Chronicle*, assistant secretaries.

The meeting being organized, was opened with prayer by Dr. J. W. Lupton, of the Presbyterian Church.

On motion of Captain Thomas H. Smith, of the Forty-ninth Tennessee, the following committee on resolutions was appointed: Captain Thomas H. Smith, Forty-ninth Tennessee Infantry, chairman; Captain Lewis R. Clark, Tenth Tennessee Infantry; private J. M. Rogers, Eleventh Tennessee Infantry; Major D. F. Wright, surgeon Fourteenth Tennessee Infantry; private T. A. Turner, Forty-second Tennesse Infantry; Colonel James E. Bailey, Forty-ninth Tennessee Infantry; Lieutenant Charles W. Tyler, Fiftieth Tennessee Infantry; Austin Peay, Woodward's Cavalry; Major John Minor, Tenth Tennessee Cavalry; Lieutenant H. C. Merritt, Morgan's Cavalry; Captain F. P. Gracey, Cobb's Battery; T. J. Munford, One Hundred and Fifty-fourth Tennessee Infantry; Captain W. D. Taylor, Price's army, of Missouri; Lieutenant A. M. Trawick, Sixteenth Arkansas Regiment; private T. D. Lucket, Morgan's Cavalry; Captain J. W. Scales, Longstreet's staff.

The committee retired, and, upon their return, reported, through their chairman, the following resolutions:

IN MEMORY OF MARY BLACKBURN MORRIS.

In all the epochs of civilization individuals have arisen equal to the demands of the occasion. Whether it be to lead the councils of nations in the senate, the soldiers in the field, or to lift aloft and protect from corrupting influences the banner of God's holy religion—whatever may be the demand of the occasion, by an influence acting either from within the human heart or mind or without, from the direct interposition of Providence, the individual comes along with it, coeval and co-equal to the duty of the hour.

Not only is this true with reference to men, but woman grows with the demand. Her frail form becomes energized, is braced as with iron nerves, and her gentle spirit puts on the courage and strength of the lion. The demands for such exaltation of human character are not so frequent as to render their number in the history of our human kind very great, but here and there along the roadway of civilization they stand, like the finger-boards of time, at once directing and illuminating the way. It is some revolution in affairs (grand occasions) that give birth to these men and women. We might cull from history a list of such names, but prefer to let our own country and our own womanhood furnish illustration, and that too in the person of her whose memory we have met to honor, and to do this we will have to recur to the past and, to us, some of its familiar history.

On the 22d of February, 1862, the first of the Confederate prisoners of war arrived at Camp Douglas, in the suburbs of the city of Chicago, Ill. These happened to be mainly of the Forty-ninth, Forty-second, and Fiftieth Tennessee Infantry regiments, all of Montgomery county. It happened they were placed in the barracks from which a Federal regiment had that day been sent to the front. Fortunately for our poor fellows, they had, out of their abundance, left here and there crumbs and crusts of bread, and these they eagerly gathered up and greedily devoured.

Strangers, as they supposed, in a strange and distant land, they neither hoped for nor expected relief from the gentle hand of friend, and still less from that of the foe; but after many hundreds had come and gazed upon them as upon so many wild animals captured from the forest or the jungle, the matronly form of a woman, who, their experienced eyes told them, was of our Southland, came in their midst with look and word and deed of sympathy and love.

The form referred to was that of her whom we are met here to-day to honor, whose name, already engraven on our hearts, we would give our humble efforts to place where it of right belongs—on the living annals of the history of the times as one of its great and heroic workers, illustrating and exemplifying human nature in its highest and grandest type.

From the date of the birth of the Saviour of mankind to this hour, no higher evidence of his divine origin has ever been vouchsafed than this—he came as a sacrifice for the good of mankind, as an exemplar for every Christian life. He draws nearest Christ who can reverently and humbly give himself or herself a sacrifice for the good of others, and surely if ever human being did thus put away the things of this world and follow after her Master, she did.

At the date given above, February 22, 1862, she was

the possessor of a luxurious home, in the very front rank of all social life in her circle, with the wealth of a millionaire, her husband honored in the past as the second mayor of Chicago, and the candidate on the Bell and Everett ticket for governor of Illinois, and in the front as judge of their court. Hers was the very acme of human life, with all the sources from which its pleasures are derived in full, present possession. All she had to do to keep what she had and even add tenfold to it, was to keep herself aloof from public affairs and quietly float down the tide of life; but the spirit of her divine Master, "working with her own spirit," bid her make her own sacrifice for the lives of others, and without a murmur or complaint, without a moment's hesitation, she gave it all—social position, luxurious home, wealth, every thing—to comfort and relieve the captive in his chains, and the cause and the land as much her own as if she carried the banner and wielded the sword of the Southern Confederacy.

It was not long after her good offices had been given to the prisoners, before she and her husband became the objects of Federal persecution, till to visit her hospitable home was made a cause of arrest. Soon that home was taken from her, and she, a delicate woman, all unused to hardship, made the inmate of a dark, cold prison, with nothing to feed upon save such prison fare as her own money would purchase. To use the unvarnished and literal truth, they took from her all she had, save one dress, denying her the use of her own private room to make her toilet as they took her off to prison, and she was compelled to make a screen of the body of her faithful maid servant behind which to make the change from her indoor to the one street dress they allowed her to take away with her. All the rest of the wealth of herself and husband they either gave to the *bummer*, or it became a part of that vast and mysterious amount of goods known then, as now, as captured or confiscated goods.

Finally, after long and cruel torture, they sent her with broken health, but unbroken spirit, to her brother, Dr. James Blackburn, of Scott county, Ky., with orders to keep "watch and ward" over her, and expatriate her if she left the limits of Dr. Blackburn's farm. With the courage of a man and the devotion of a woman, she gave her all to the cause. Many of us remember the soothing words and hand of this noble woman in our sickness and suffering, and the words of encouragement and cheer with which she revived and sustained our drooping spirits; and when, as was sometimes the case, disease and death came, no mother's hand ever more softly and gently placed the boy soldier in his shroud and with flowers decked him for the grave.

After the war and the death of her husband, which occurred, we believe, in 1875 or 1876, she came back to the home of her girlhood and the home of her brother, Dr. Luke Blackburn, then governor of Kentucky, and when he retired from office she followed him to Louisville, Ky., where, with his aid and others of like philanthropic character, they erected a sanitarium in which to provide for and treat the unfortunate victims of minds diseased. This was the work most congenial to her quiet, gentle heart. With all of her losses, great as we have seen they were, but a few hours before her death she declared that the only regret she had in dying was that she could do no more for the needy and the helpless.

On October 18, 1884, at the Sanitarium, near Louisville, Ky., with the armor of her good work still on her, Mary Blackburn Morris died in the full possession of all her mental faculties, and the bright jewels of her noble and heroic life crowning her more richly and grandly than kingly crown ever decked a royal head. To us who meet here to-day her life was more even than that of one of the historic characters of her time—to us she was the kindly, gentle ministering spirit, and though gray hairs have blossomed in the heads of the boy soldiers she ministered to at Camp Douglas in 1862, to our hearts and in our memories she was, and is, and will forever be, a second mother; therefore,

Resolved, That the loss of such a person is not only a source of grief to those who stand in the circle of her own family, and with whom we sympathize and to whom we respectfully tender our sincere condolence, but a public calamity, in which society at large sustains a great and irreparable loss.

Resolved, That a copy of these resolutions be sent to the family of the deceased, and that the Clarksville papers and the *Courier-Journal* be requested to publish the same.

In presenting the resolutions, Captain Smith, who was the orderly sergeant of Company A, Fourth Tennessee Regiment, at the time it was carried to Camp Douglas, Chicago, Ill., as prisoners of war, gave a history of its arrival at Chicago and at Camp Douglas, and paid a glowing tribute to the deceased, as also to the other noble women of Chicago who visited the prisoners, nursed the sick, fed the hungry, and clothed the suffering—mentioning the names of Mrs. Philip Larmon, Mrs. J. H. Larmon, Mrs. Marshall, Mrs. Belle Waller, Miss Pet Boone, Mrs. Robb, and others.

Appropriate speeches were also made by the following gentlemen, who seconded the resolutions.

Ex-United States Senator James E. Bailey, Colonel of the Forty-ninth Tennessee; Polk G. Johnson, Lieutenant of the Forty-ninth Tennessee; Judge Charles W. Tyler, Lieutenant of the Fiftieth Tennessee; Lewis G. Munford, of the Clarksville bar.

Judge Horace H. Lurton, of Morgan's cavalry, moved the adoption of the resolutions, which were unanimously carried.

Prayer was then offered by Dr. A. D. Sears, of the Baptist Church, whereupon the meeting adjourned.

WILLIAM A. QUARLES, *Chairman.*
POLK G. JOHNSON, *Secretary.*

When Camp Douglas was first established, the prisoners had kitchens supplied with stoves and cooking utensils, and were supplied with more provisions than they were able to consume. They were also allowed as much clothing as they pleased to possess. The buildings had their floors near the ground, and the prisoners would "tunnel" out. To prevent this the barracks were put on posts, as before stated, and when retaliatory measures were adopted, the stoves were taken away. It is strange to what extent man's ingenuity can be exerted under trying circumstances. One day a young Kentucky lad, who had been clerking in the sutler's store, was missing. Search proved in vain. The lad was gone. It was a regular custom to send out boxes or barrels from the store as soon as emptied. This lad had crawled into a sugar barrel and concealed himself. The barrel was rolled into a cart and dumped out on the yard of a groceryman's establishment in the city. The lad made his escape in this way. At another time a prisoner who staid near the wall had cultivated very friendly relations with a Federal soldier, and succeeded in borrowing his overcoat. At night the prisoner put on the overcoat, and with a frail ladder ascended the wall to where the sentry was walking. He told the sentinel to keep quiet, that he knew where there was some whisky near by (showing a canteen), and if he would keep the ladder till he came back that he would divide the whisky with him. The offer was accepted, and the ladder was placed on the outside of the wall. The prisoner descended. The sentinel waited in vain for his return with the whisky. The prisoner was heard from in a few days. He was in Canada. He staid there.

On another occasion a prisoner, after having laid in a supply of cheese and crackers sufficient for a few days' journey, crawled over the "dead line" in the darkness, and quietly "scratched out," and succeeded in making his escape. The ground under the wall being of a loose, sandy nature, the prisoner scooped out a passway with his hands. In the morning the breach was discovered. The prisoner had left his bundle of cheese and crackers. The Federal officer expressed a hope that the prisoner would not be caught, and regretted that he did not succeed in getting his rations away also.

It was not only astonishing, but often amusing, to see with what alacrity and promptness a prisoner would obey the stern and rigid mandates of prison discipline. Men become humiliated and dejected as this state of affairs wears on their sensibilities beyond a certain limit. When it passes this limit they lose much of their manhood, and gradually droop and die.

As the situation became more desperate, the prisoners commenced enlisting in the United States armies for frontier service. The war soon ended, and the captive was set at liberty.

This sketch of Northern prison life has been given with no intention of reflecting in any manner upon the Federal authorities at the time the events occurred. At this period the vindictive feelings engendered by the sufferings and sacrifices of a four-years war were at their highest point. Peace soon came " with healing on her wings." " Man's inhumanity to man " was mutually forgiven, and as time moved onward it was comparatively forgotten.

ERRATA.

On page 325, Col. J. M. Hulin should be Colonel J. M. Hulm.

Page 333, Henderson should be Robertson.

Page 337, General Sugg should be Colonel Sugg.

Page 343, the last organization should contain the following officers: Of the consolidated regiment, O. A. Bradshaw, Colonel (formerly of Fourth Tennessee), G. W. Pease, Lieutenant-colonel (formerly of Fiftieth Tennessee), Dr. R. G. Rothroek, Surgeon (formerly Fiftieth Tennessee).

www.ingramcontent.com/pod-product-compliance
Lightning Source LLC
Chambersburg PA
CBHW020833020526
44114CB00040B/601